BROTHER
& *SISTER*

BROTHER
& *SISTER*

IVAN ROWE

Order this book online at www.trafford.com
or email orders@trafford.com

Most Trafford titles are also available at major online book retailers.

Printed in the United States of America.

ISBN: 978-1-4669-0081-3 (sc)
ISBN: 978-1-4669-0082-0 (hc)
ISBN: 978-1-4669-0083-7 (e)

Library of Congress Control Number: 2011918393

Trafford rev. 10/27/2011

www.trafford.com

North America & International
toll-free: 1 888 232 4444 (USA & Canada)
phone: 250 383 6864 • fax: 812 355 4082

CHAPTER #1

FALL WAS IN the air as the greyhound bus pulled into its terminal in Denver, Colorado. Slowly the large silver coach swung into the unloading area and stopped. Passengers were already standing, collecting their coats and small pieces of luggage as the bus came to a stop. They represented a cross section of middle and lower class America. Salesmen in suits wrinkled and worn, elderly tourists trying to have a good time in a world that just wanted their money, drifters going from one job to another and service men in their dress uniforms looking young and homesick.

Ed moved off the bus and shouldered the bag that held all of his worldly possessions (which amounted to some clothes, shaving gear, shoes and a coat). Heaving the hundred pound bag on his shoulder was done effortlessly. The powerful six foot four inch frame hid the youthful innocence it enclosed. With eagerness and a cat like grace he stepped off the bus and into the terminal lobby.

"Excuse me please." Ed said as he removed the bag from his shoulder to the floor.

The middle-aged woman looked up from behind the counter and smiled. "Can I help you?"

"Yes I just got off the bus and I need a hotel room. Do you know if there is one close by?"

"Sure, there's the Concord about three blocks down the street and the Embassy is about eight blocks straight out the door on Newberry."

"Which one is the cheapest?"

The woman smiled slowly as she gave Ed an understanding look. "The Embassy is cheaper than the Concord but it's not as nice and it's located in a bad part of town near Market Street."

"Thank you ma'am." Ed said as he shouldered his bag and walked to the door leading onto the street. Once outside he looked around and spotted the sign for Newberry Street and headed for the Embassy Hotel.

To a sixteen-year-old midwestern boy right off a Wisconsin Dairy Farm, Denver, Colorado, was one of the most exciting places he had ever read about. All the western magazines held tons of great stories and pictures identifying Denver and area as one of the truly great frontier towns in the old west. Of course, the articles had never described the fourteen-story petroleum club on Nineteenth and Broadway because they were written about an era before it existed. But, with a little imagination one could overlook such a thing.

Approaching the Embassy Hotel, Ed's thoughts turned from Denver of the late eighteen hundreds, to how long he was going to be able to afford to stay in this wonderful old hotel. Walking into the lobby was like a step back in time. Everything was made of wood and hand fitted, giving the interior an ageless appearance of elegance. Many years of traffic, cleaning and exposure to the elements dragged in on countless feet had put a distinctive weathered finish on the parts of the floor visible around the old thread bare Persian rugs laid on it. The occasional soft creak of the boards underfoot was pleasing to the ear. Walking past the ornately carved wooden pillars holding up the ceiling, Ed approached the lobby desk. Funny he thought, how similar it was to the desks described in some of the magazines he had read.

The medium sized man behind the counter walked up and said, "good afternoon, can I help you?"

"Yes sir, I'd like to rent a room for a week."

The clerk's eyes rose as he looked over the top of his glasses at the tall youth. "That'll be sixty five dollars", he said, making his remark half question and half statement. Ed winced as he reached in his pocket and pulled out the one hundred and ninety dollar bankroll. Peeling off the money he threw it down on the counter as the clerk wrote out the receipt.

"Please sign the registrar and fill in this card with your home address, phone, car make and license number.

"Ok, but I don't have a car, I came in on the bus."

"That's alright just leave that part blank."

Filling out the card took a bit more than you would expect. When you run away from home the last thing you want to so is put your home address down. Thinking back to his high school geography class last week Ed began recalling as many states and cities as he could. Coming up with a suitable imaginary address on the spot is not easy. Besides, he didn't want to stand there and appear to fumble. So he filled in the card as casually as he could and handed it to the clerk.

"Mr. Johnson from Billings, Montana. Are you here on business?"

"No, I just came to look for work," Ed said as he anxiously waited for his key. The last thing he wanted to do was get into a lengthy discussion. The clerk must have sensed something and handed over the key.

"Room 205, up the stairs to the right."

"Thank you" Ed said as he shouldered his bag and grabbed the key.

"Have a good night."

Nodding Ed turned and went to the large central staircase. "What a grand place, I'll bet some real colorful characters walked these stairs in its day," he thought as he started up the worn old staircase. Turning the corner into the hall he looked for his room number. About halfway down the hallway he found it, put the key in the lock and opened the door.

The room was clean and modestly furnished. The brass bed and wooden dressers spoke of a time when things were better. Sitting on a well-worn rug the furnishings still gave the feeling of a grandness that could only be imagined from years ago. "Well, it was clean paid for and home for a week." Ed thought as he sat back in the overstuffed chair and let out a sigh of relief. Sitting there in comfort for the first time in three days, his mind wandered back to when the journey had started.

Things had always seemed hard at home with only one older brother to talk to or fight with. The oldest brother had moved away before Ed could remember. Mom and Dad were in their early fifties and for a sixteen-year-old boy hard to talk to. It wasn't that they didn't care or didn't love him; it was an age barrier that caused the lack of communication. Somehow, the things that were interesting to talk about to Ed didn't seem important to his parents. That's why he used to stay in his room a lot, at least there he could create his own environment and be comfortable with the things that were important to him. It was not a hard decision to climb on a greyhound bus instead of a school bus and head West. The money to fund the trip had been easy to accumulate for a large strong high school boy. What really helped was the fact that he looked a couple of years older than he was. Ed remembered how nervous he had been as he sat in the house waiting for the cab to come and take him to the greyhound bus station.

Getting out of the overstuffed chair Ed walked to the window and leaned against the frame as he stared into the reflection in the glass. Standing there looking into the dirty glass his mind could see the house in Wisconsin he had left three days ago. "I wonder what Mom and Dad are doing now? I'll bet they called the police when I came up missing after school," he thought. Staring deeper into the reflection of the glass he remembered how his parents had left the house thinking he was waiting for the bus to take him to school. Mom had fixed his breakfast for him and his Dad just like any other morning. It had been hard to contain his nervousness until after they walked out the door.

Coming back to reality he moved away from the window then walked over to the bed and flopped down. "God, what have I done," he moaned as he lay there. The sudden realization that he was really alone for the first time in his life finally spread over him like a blanket. What a miserable feeling it was, especially with no one there to comfort him. Crying himself to sleep seemed to be the only consolation.

Waking was painful; the flood of tears had taken their toll by hardening and sticking his eyelids together. Rolling off the bed he stumbled out the door of the semi dark room into the dimly lit hallway to find the bathroom. Washing the tears and sleep out of his eyes with warm water felt good. It helped to take away some of the coldness he had experienced as he lay on the bed crying his heart, out.. The bathrooms in the Embassy were comm ood clad only in his jeans and socks, bare chested with a soaking, wet T-shirt in his hands. "What now?" He knew he couldn't stand out here forever, "maybe I can get into my room through a window", he thought as he moved to the window at the end of the hall. It opened unwillingly after a brief struggle and a few unkind words. "Naw, I don't think so," he mumbled as he looked at the ledge disappear around the corner of the building toward his room. Besides, it was too narrow and a long way from the ground. Closing the window he leaned against it while pondering his situation. Sneaking down the stairs, thorough the lobby and up to the desk bothered him, but it seemed to be the only was he was going to get back into his room. "What if someone sees me like this," he thought as he crept down the hallway to the head of the stairs that now looked as wide as a four-lane highway. It wouldn't be bad if he could just see the entire lobby, but with only a partial view of the area from the head of the stairs there was no way to tell how many people were waiting down there, ready to see him in this sorry condition. It wasn't that he had never been in public bare chested before. It was the fact that these people were total strangers and he was an adolescent sixteen year old looking like a fish out of water. Mustering all the courage possible he started down the stairs expecting the screams of laughter that would come when anybody saw him. I'll hurry," he thought as he increased his speed down the stairs. Reaching the bottom he could see the entire lobby and it was empty. Of course, at four o'clock in the morning most lobbies are. Moving toward the desk in the center of the large room the occasional loud squeak of those damn floorboards began to sound like something out of intersanctum. The clerk looked up from behind the desk just as Ed's toe caught on the upturned corner of the Old Persian rug. It's hard to graceful and composed when you're on your knees looking over the edge of a counter with both hands clamped firmly in place, holding a soggy T-shirt that just made the top of the counter, the paper work on it and the hotel clerk wet from hairline to belt buckle. Taking off his water-spattered glasses he leaned over the damp counter and with a great deal of composure smiled as he said; "are you alright?"

"I, ah, but, ah, door ah, locked, need, puff, puff, puff, key." Ed sounded like the end of a Porky Pig cartoon and felt like held just finished the Boston Marathon. Somewhat subdued Ed struggled to his feet as the clerk finished wiping off his glasses. "I'm sorry'," Ed said as he stood up and threw the drippy T-Shirt over his shoulder, trying not to wince as a cold trickle of water raced down the middle of his back past the belt line and into the dark recesses of his jeans.

"That's O'K follow me," the clerk said as he picked up a ring of keys and moved toward the staircase. Starting up the stairs he asked, "which room is yours?"

Ed told him and, they walked to the mahogany stained door with the brass number 205 on it. Unlocking it and pushing it open the clerk reached in, turned on the light, gave a quick glance around and said, "there you go, have a good night, I guess you could say morning by now."

"Ya, thanks," Ed said as the clerk turned and walked down the hall. It felt good to get into the room again. Now he could slip into some dry shorts. Hopefully that clerk would be off duty by the time he went out for breakfast and a day of job hunting.

After the sun was well established in the morning sky, Ed figured it would be safe to walk through the lobby without encountering the clerk he watered down last night. Passing through the lobby was a much better experience than it had been a few hours ago. He couldn't help but snicker at the water stains on the papers when he asked the day clerk where to find an inexpensive restaurant. Ed bought a paper from a corner newsstand and strolled into the recommended restaurant. He ate while looking through the help wanted ads and circled the ones that looked most promising. After he paid his bill, he set forth with all the optimism, anticipation and zeal that a sixteen year old can muster. . Most of the day was spent looking fruitlessly for a job. He was unconscious of the fact that without the inexperience and innocence of youth it would have been easier to quit and go home. As suppertime approached he finally called it a day and went back to his room, ready to resume the hunt the next day.

The next morning found him on the street again ready to walk endless, miles of concrete and talk to countless employers. It was about seven thirty as he-stood gazing at a display of western boots in Miller Stockman's show window when a car pulled up to the curb. A middle aged: man in a rumpled suit and overcoat rolled down the car window and said, "Hey you, kid, come here." Ed moved over to the car as the man pulled out a badge and held it so it could be seen.

"Have you got a job?" "Sure," Ed said lying through. his teeth. Looking down the street the Singer Sewing Machine Company sign was clearly visible "Right down there at Singer's."

"What do you do?"

"I'm a stock boy, I take care of the store room and sweep the floors."

"How come your not at work?"

"I don't have to be there until eight and I stopped to look at the boots in the window here." "O'K but I am going to check there later and you'd better not be lying to me." With that he rolled the car window and sped off into the morning traffic.

"Damn," Ed thought, "that was close. I don't need to get picked up for vagrancy. I better get off the street just in case that cop does check and came back looking for me."

Wandering in and out of stores all the way back to the hotel made him nervous as a cat. Going into a store he would stay fifteen or twenty minutes and then make a break to the next one spending as little time on the street as possible. By the time he did arrive at the hotel most of the morning was gone. Now, he was afraid to go out so he shut himself in the room for the rest of the day while he sulked and recuperated. Lying around all afternoon didn't produce anything good, in terms of attitude or a job. By supper time he was so worked up his stomach was growling and gurgling and he felt irritable and restless as a cat in heat. Pacing around the room was not the answer, so when night fell he decided to see what Denver had to offer in the way of entertainment. Standing in front of the hotel Ed could see the "Great White Way" beckoning up and down the street with a multitude of neon banners. After about a half an hour of wandering through winos, derelicts and ladies of the evening, Ed happened on a pool hall that looked inviting. The smoky interior and gentle click of the balls reminded him of the pool parlor he had hung out in as a high school student two weeks ago. It felt comfortable so he went in, rented a rack of balls, got a table and commenced to play by himself.

Shooting pool had always been relaxing to Ed. He liked the skill that the game demanded because it helped to make him a better than average player. The hall had about a dozen and a half full sized tables. Along with pool there was also billiards and snooker. By most standards this was a really large pool hall. Each table had enough room so players on opposite tables wouldn't lock sticks or have to wait for each other to shoot. Ed racked the pool balls to play another game. Two men who where playing pool on the next table moved over and one of them asked if he would care to "shoot a little nine ball" just for fun of course.

The two men were average looking; the taller of the two wore a brown medium brimmed hat with a wide satin band. He had a light complexion, light brown mustache and clear blue eyes. The used to be white shirt, was open at the neck, with a flowered tie hanging there ready to be tightened. A small pot gut bulged slightly above his belt. The brown tweed pants were in need of a good cleaning, as were the brown wing tipped shoes that they partially concealed. The other man was clean-shaven and his clothes didn't have that lived in look. He was shorter than the other man by about two inches, he wasn't fat but his torso was straight and didn't have a waist. His complexion was olive with black hair and dark eyes. His large Roman nose was the focal point of his face. He had on a yellow sweater with the collar of a tan shirt open at the neck over it. A dark green pair of slacks with a sharp crease casually led to a yellow pair of socks inserted into a brown pair of loafers.

Without any hesitation Ed heartily agreed to the invitation. Thinking about his self-acclaimed, superior, pool shooting skill and ability, acquired during his high school years, he felt nothing short of invincible. He was right too, the first three games he wiped up the table with those guys. Finally one of them said, "I'll tell you what, why don't we make this interesting and put a dollar on the nine ball." Thinking a minute Ed said, "sure, sounds good to me," he thought to himself, "alright, I'll make a couple of bucks here." Winning the next two games was easy, these guys were good but he was just a little better.

"Maybe we ought to raise it to two dollars," Ed said.

"I dunno the way you've been shooting I don't think we can beat you"

"Oh, I'm just hot right now, here's a chance for you to get your money back."

"Well maybe a couple of games, we can't afford much more."

They started playing once more and Ed backed off a little bit to keep the two men in the game. As they played Ed lost track of time until finally realizing that he had lightened up a bit too much in the wallet department. He knew if he was going to make his move it would have to be now. "Tell you what fellas it's getting late, I'm getting tired and I think we ought to shoot one more game for what I've got left in my pocket."

Ed threw two twenties, a ten and some ones on the table. Other than the twenty tucked away in his sock, that was all the money he had left. "That's alright" he thought, "I've been taking it easy on these turkey's. They're easy and I won't have any trouble winning my money back plus some." Oh by the way," he said aloud" "loser pays the tab on both of our tables also."

"I've got a bad feeling about this, but OK." The taller of the two men said.

Ed grinned to himself, "aha, I've got them now" and the game was on.

Confidence is one thing, ability is another thing, but when you don't get a chance to use either, that's a horse of a different color. Ed broke and that was the last shot he got. These guys made shots that would have made Minnesota Fats green with envy. It was all over in about ten minutes. Mouth open and watching through unbelieving eyes, Ed withered as he saw ball after ball drop in predetermined order. He stood there thinking what a stupid thing he had just done as the men picked up their winnings. The man in the yellow sweater looked up from gathering the money.

"Thanks partner, you shoot a mean game of pool."

Ed stood speechless. The two men put their coats on and the well dressed man threw five bucks on the table and said, "here you go, I don't want to leave you broke, you shoot a good game."

They left and Ed leaned back against the table trying to get his head screwed on right so he could walk up front and pay the bill.

"Well sport, how'd it go?"

Ed looked at the man that was talking and figuring the bill for both tables. His black whisker stubble was sticking out all over the top part of his neck and the bottom half of his face. Fleshy cheeks and a pair of brown eyes gave the illusion of two uncooked drumsticks with brown marbles sitting on top of them. The raunchy stub of an over chewed cigar butt stuck out of one side of his mouth partially exposing what was left of his yellow rotting teeth.

."Nineteen dollars and twenty-five cents."

"Ed groaned as he handed over the stashed twenty-dollar bill. "God," he thought, I've only got about six dollars to my name.

The rent had been paid for a week so Ed still had four days of hotel room left. What really concerned him, was the fact that his stomach was going to become extremely annoyed in the very near future if he didn't get a job or find a sugar mama to support his eating habits. He realized he was going to have to hit the bricks hard in the next three or four days if he was going to survive and stay independent. For the next two days he lived on potato chips and water, while he looked for a job. When nothing turned up except a noisy and painful stomach he knew he was in trouble. Sitting in his room thinking about the situation he realized if he didn't do something soon he would be at the mercy of every low life in town. Suddenly a thought crossed his mind, during his job hunting expeditions he had passed a Salvation Army soup kitchen that gave away meals and lodging to the homeless. The clientele was made up of bums, winos and derelicts, but he thought, "maybe I can eat there until my room rent runs out and I find a job." Knowing that he wasn't in a position to be picky he trotted his body down to the Market Street Rescue Mission about suppertime and got in line.

Swallowing his pride was not nearly as hard as trying to swallow the colored water they called soup. The beans weren't bad just hard and chewy, but they filled the gap between the stomach and the backbone. At least when he hit the street tomorrow job hunting it wouldn't be on an empty stomach. For three days Ed walked the streets and talked to employers about twelve hours a day. The job hunting was not going well at all and this was his last day in the hotel. Sitting in the old chair, staring at the wall, his situation enveloped him like a cold morning mist.

Sixteen years old, eighteen hundred miles away from a comfortable home and loving parents, flat broke and no place to go. What a lonely, scary, predicament to be in, especially when you've never been forced to do anything by circumstance except make it to the dinner table on time. For the first time in his life Ed was going to make decisions that would affect the very future of his existence. Thoughts like, "go home or hang in there and see if you can make it work," raced through his mind at the same time memories of a comfortable home, with loving family and friends, crowded in so hard he could barely stand it. All those good times came back, so vividly now. Reality came back with a loud knocking on the door.

"Mr. Johnson, I just wanted to find out if you'll be staying with us or leaving tomorrow? The hotel clerk said after Ed opened the door.

"I'll be leaving first thing in the morning." Closing the door Ed turned around, and walked over to the bed, flopped down on it scared to death and cried him self to sleep.

It only took a couple of minutes the next morning to pack his few belongings. It was just a matter of shoving everything into the old barracks bag that he brought his stuff in when he arrived seven days ago. It didn't matter to him anymore that he mixed the dirty clothes with the few clean ones that were left. Dragging the bag Ed shuffled down the stairs to the lobby, and turned in his key. The clerk thanked him as he retreated to an obscure corner full of easy chairs and sat down. Ed felt like a horse that had been rode hard and put up wet. Washing the dried tears and sleep from the previous night out of his red, swollen eyes suddenly was no longer very important. He sat there most of the day afraid to face the inevitable but, the time finally came to head for the rescue mission if he was going to get something to eat. The thought occurred to him to stay overnight at the mission, but when he got into the supper line and mingled with the human refuse that regularly showed up he couldn't bring himself to do it. After supper Ed started walking the streets getting a firsthand glimpse at a side of life held never seen or knew existed. His sheltered existence as a Midwestern farm boy hadn't prepared him for the things happening to him in this world. Knowing how to drive a tractor or a team of horses for a thrashing crew does not qualify you to deal with pimps, hustlers and the human trash that inhabits the side of town he entered.

Ed's up bringing had involved Church, family, things like respect, gentleness, responsibility and an open honesty that was non-existent here. His survival would depend on how quickly he left or adapted to the new way of life that was about to embrace him. Not knowing which way to go, he wandered in the cold, gathering darkness. When he got tired he threw his bag down and used it for a seat is he leaned against a wall or a light pole, knowing he was starting the trip that would make him like the bums that lived here.

Denver sits in the middle of the Rocky Mountains at an elevation of about fifty two hundred feet above sea level. When the sun goes down the temperature goes with it and even in the warm part of summer it will drop to forty degrees or less at night forcing you to sleep under a blanket or wear a jacket of some sort when you are out and about. The denim, Levi jacket Ed had on helped but it was nothing to sleep outside in. Since it was the fall of the year some nights were getting below freezing and a light frost was not uncommon before the sun rose and turned it to water. Looking for a place to sleep took all night and by morning he was feeling pretty rough. It was a good thing there were no mirrors handy, after three nights of surviving on the street his appearance was starting to make him fit into the neighborhood.

Lounging on Market Street in Denver is an experience that has to be lived to understand. In its heyday Market Street was one of the main streets in Denver. Now, it consists of flophouses and fleabag hotels that were nice pla at, but a matter of choosing how and whom you're going to hustle so you can eat. In the truest sense of the word, its "survival of the fittest," the fittest eat and the rest don't. Bums drag their cardboard box beds around, winos paw through trash cans looking for booze bottles with even a drop of moisture, pimps and prostitutes are on just about every corner plying their wares for those stupid enough to come to this part of town for that reason.

The recruitment rate on ladies of the evening is evidently very high on Market Street. Disease ridden and scarred, the burned out ones still walk the streets and sleep in alleys unable to change their existence even if they cared. Rats and garbage are everywhere. Some of the local connoisseur's find rat stew to be quite tasty, it's plentiful and easy to acquire, all you have to do is lay down in the garbage and they'll come to you.

Because of his appearance job hunting was no longer a possibility. Ed's clothes all needed washing and he smelled real bad. By now he had sunk into a state of depression that was making him a permanent resident here. The sad part was he didn't even realize it was happening.

One afternoon Ed walked into the lobby of a "more elegant flophouse" in that part of town. Ed threw himself into an old, musty smelling, stuffed chair, numbly sitting there he was unaware of the person sitting down in the chair next to him until he felt his arm being gently touched.

"Hey guy, you look like you're having a hard time of it, are you hungry?

"Ed turned his head slightly and looked at the clean white hand on his arm. Ed let his eyes follow the sweater-covered arm to the shoulder of its owner. Looking him over Ed guessed he was in his late twenties or early thirties. There were no visible scars on his clean-shaven face, but it seemed to have a hardness that had been acquired somewhere in the past. His button sweater was completely open in front exposing a white shirt, brown belt, and the tops of his blue slacks that hung over the black shined shoes. Shaking the hand off his arm Ed said, "yeah, I guess." And looked away.

"My name is Phillip Stoltz, the only reason I stopped is; you don't look like you belong here.

Let me buy you some dinner and we can talk about it."

Ed looked at the man again"What's your angle?" Ed said without looking at him.

"Nothing, you reminded me of myself at one time and I thought I could help you out a little, that's all."

"I really can't believe you want to do something for me with no strings attached."

"Suit yourself I was trying to help." Phillip said as he got up.

If the guy wanted to buy him some dinner, "why not?" Ed thought to himself. "OK, you got a deal."

Phillip walked up to the sleazy-desk clerk and told him to call a cab. He came back and sat down next to Ed.

"Where you from?" Phillip asked.

"Nowhere," was the response

"Oh, how long have you been in Denver?"

"Too long," Ed was starting to get irritated with all the personal questions this stranger was asking.

."Where do you plan to go from here?"

"Look I don't have a job or any money, so I don't know what's going to happen."

He was about to tell this guy to get lost when a man walked in and said; "who called the cab?"

Phillip stood up and said; "are you coming?"

Ed got to his feet, stood there a moment still unsure "Oh what the hell," and then followed Phillip out the door to the waiting cab.

The car felt comfortable as they sped down the street to a better part of town. Pulling up in front of the restaurant Ed and Phillip got out of the cab. Phillip paid the fare while Ed stood on the sidewalk salivating over the aroma leaking out of the restaurant onto the street.

"OK, let's go eat." Phillip said as he turned from paying the cabbie.

Sauntering through the door into the restaurant, savory odors of food being broiled, grilled, sautéed and prepared for human consumption can only be brought to an extreme level of appreciation by abstention. In Ed's case, he had been abstaining for the last three or four days so he was long on appreciation. He was so hungry he could have eaten the south end of a northbound skunk and never missed a step. Once seated things really began to get screwy, the aroma of the food and his body's realization that it would soon lay heir to something solid left him feeling light headed. The waitress came over and asked for their orders. Phillip ordered pork chops, mashed potatoes and gravy.

"I'll have the chicken dinner," Ed said.

"Why don't you go and wash up a little before we eat?" Phillip suggested after the waitress left.

"Yeah, I've got to go to the bathroom anyway." Once in the bathroom he had the chance to look in a mirror at his badly deteriorated condition. "God damn," he thought as he took a long look at his decaying condition. Greasy hair, dirt stained skin, clothes that looked and smelled slept in. It wasn't a pretty picture. Not having a simple thing like a mirror to look in may seem minor to some folks, but when you don't realize personal neglect because you don't have access to one it can be a real enlightening experience. By the time he used most of the soap and paper towels in the bathroom, his stomach reminded him about the chicken he ordered. The meal was already on the table when he arrived.

"What took you so long?" Phillip asked as he shoveled food into his mouth.

Ed didn't even answer; he just dived into the meal like a starved animal. He had lived on potato chips and water for four days, ate a bowl of soup and beans every day for the last three days. Now he was sitting in front of a real meal of chicken and all the trimmings. Ed had his whole meal finished before Phillip got to his second pork chop.

"Good grief, you must've really been hungry, want some more?"

"Yeah, it was pretty good."

Phillip waved the waitress over "give him another plate of chicken and what ever else he wants," waiving his fork in Ed's direction. After supper Phillip offered Ed a cigarette. Smoking wasn't new to him but it had been a while. The first couple of drags were a little rough but after that he inhaled deeper each time he sucked the smoke in.

"Where are you staying tonight Ed?"

Looking through the smoky cloud in front of him Ed replied, "I don't know."

"You don't look to prosperous, you sure you don't have any money?"

"I told you earlier I didn't," as Ed intensely studied the table and everything on it.

"I'm going to be in town for the night. I've got a room your welcome to bunk with me if you want. It'll give you a chance to take a bath and clean up."

"I don't know."

"Hey a shave and a good bath would probably feel real nice about now.

Thinking about it Ed imagined what it would feel like to be clean again.

"I guess your right it would feel good to be clean again."

Phillip and Ed walked out of the restaurant onto the street and headed for the hotel, its blinking neon could be seen about five blocks away. It was modest, clean, smelled good and even had a bath in each room. As soon as they got into the room Ed raced for the bath and filled the tub. Sliding into the hot, steamy water was pure ecstasy. Feeling the water move warmly over his feet, up his legs and into his crotch brought moans of great pleasure from his lips. Completing the slide into the tub was extremely sensuous as the water closed around his lean hips and over his hard flat stomach. "Oh God," Ed thought "sliding into something that soft and warm was like being in heaven." Moving slowly made the water caress and massage his body gently, it appeared to be reaching, begging him to sink deeper and deeper into its beckoning depths, eventually he succumbed and plunged chin deep. Once there he felt his whole body relax and give into the pleasure of the moment.

When he woke up he was cold and so was the water. Moving helped make the goose bumps recede, so before he got out he washed his hair and scrubbed hard. While he wiped dry Ed took a good look in the mirror and was surprised what a difference soap and water could make, his razor was in the duffel bag in the other room so he didn't bother to shave. Now it was time for a nice long nap in a real bed. Phillip was already under the covers of the double bed reading a book.

"Boy, did that feel good," Ed said as he peeled back the covers and slid underneath.

"I'll bet," was the reply.

"I can't believe how good this bed feels, Ed said as he snuggled a little deeper under the covers.

"It's been four days since I slept in a real bed." Ed said as he dozed off into his first sound sleep in days.

Sleeping with another male in the same bed was not foreign to Ed; he shared a bed with his older brother for years. It was common practice on midwestern farms for a number of reasons. Warmth during the winter because the big old two story farmhouses usually weren't insulated. Most of them only had wood stoves for heat and cooking. During the summer it was easier and more practical because everyone was outside working. A bedroom was a place to sleep, not to live in.

Ed woke up some time later in the night when he felt something touching him. He suddenly realized that a hand was slowly exploring his groin and genital area. Lying absolutely still and not breathing for a moment Ed didn't know what to do. Suddenly he gasped and yelled, "what the hell are you doing?"

Phillip replied, "I thought we'd have a little fun."

"What do you mean?"

"You know what I mean, I want you."

Ed couldn't believe what he was hearing. What Phillip was suggesting was totally disgusting and immoral. Ed had heard about people like this, but no one ever talked about them at home except in the most isolated and discrete situations. All of a sudden he was becoming very scared of this older man. Phillip kept grabbing Ed and threatening him as he tried to get away from his grasp. Making a hard lunge and rolling to get away Ed made it only as far as his stomach before Phillip was on top of him quick as a cat. Sitting on Ed's back Phillip started hitting him on the back and sides of the head. "Lay still you son of a bitch," Phillip screamed. By now Ed's head was ringing. He was too young and scared to fight the older man, so he lay still. Phillip moved off of Ed's back but kept an arm over the back of his neck while the hand on the other arm slid his shorts down and explored his rectum.

"Nice ass hole you got there kid. I got a feelin' it's going to be real tight. That's alright I got just the thing for that." Suddenly his finger plunged deep into Ed's rectum. Tensing at the unwanted entry, a cry of pain came along with the sobs and tears of helplessness that engulfed him. Eventually Phillip mounted him and performed his sordid act as Ed went into a state of shock. This was beyond anything his young mind could comprehend. Not only did he hurt, he felt so disgusting all he wanted to do is crawl away and die. Ed was afraid to move when Phillip finally did get off of his back. Phillip was trying to talk to him but it was indistinguishable through the crying.

"C'mon kid quit your crying and yelling, you ain't hurt. After we do it a couple more times you'll love it."

Pain racked and emotionally devastated Ed climbed out of bed, staggered into the bathroom and locked the door. Trying to get rid of the burning mess inside of him was impossible, no matter how hard he strained and grunted it wouldn't happen. Sitting on the stool pouring out his guts to the world it was loud enough to cause quite a commotion because the phone rang and Phillip answered.

"Hello; yes; no; we had a disagreement. Yes, we'll keep it down. No, no, that's OK I'll make sure the noise is kept down. Yes, I realize that. Please, we'll be quiet I promise. OK, thank you." Hanging up the phone Phillip walked over to the bathroom. The room was acting like an echo chamber because of its ceramic walls.

"Hey kid, you better shut up or they're going to kick us out of here. Quiet down and come out of there, I won't bother you anymore, OK?" All that did was cause louder and cries of despair.

"Damn it, if you don't shut up I'll kick this door down and slap the shit out of you." The barrage of wails and moans continued at an even louder rate.

"God damn it," Phillip said as he walked away from the bathroom door. He hadn't realized things would get out of hand like this, if he got picked up one more time he would go back to the State Penitentiary at Boulder, Colorado.

"Shit." He thought, "If this damn kid spills his guts to the wrong person I'm in trouble. If he don't shut up he'll have the hotel dick or the cops in here."

Moving quickly Phillip gathered his things into the suitcase he'd brought, got dressed and walked out the door. Ed heard the door slam but he didn't know Phillip had left. His crying reached its crescendo earlier and now was nothing more than low moans and sobs that kept racking his body at regular intervals. Ed had sat long enough on the toilet seat that his buttocks and thighs were numb. Standing up brought a burning sensation that ran all the way up his rectum to his kidneys. He couldn't control his legs real well and he felt like he would vomit at any moment. With his eyes swollen shut from crying, he stumbled around the bathroom until he found the tub. Turning on the water and crawling into the tub he knew it wouldn't feel the same as it did before, but he hoped it would relax and clean even though he would never lose the feelings he carried inside of him now.

Ed sat in the tub for a long time, knowing that sooner or later he was going to have to walk back into the other room and face Phillip. Trying to build the courage was tough, getting out of the tub and opening the bathroom door took everything he had in him. Looking around it was evident that Phillip was not there and his suitcase and clothes were gone, Ed raced to the door and locked it. Breathing a sigh of relief a great weight seemed to lift off his shoulders as he realized that he was the only one in the room. He was beyond thinking at this point, the events of the last two weeks and especially the last seven days were taking their toll. The optimistic outlook he brought with him to his western dream town was suffering badly. Realism was setting in and the boyish enthusiasm that always clouded his perspective was giving way to a more cynical attitude. The world didn't shine quite as bright as before and people weren't as interesting. He didn't know what would happen tomorrow, but for the rest of this night the room was paid for, the door was locked and he was the only one in it. It was time to take advantage of the situation even if it was a bad one. Ed didn't realize it as he crawled back into bed but he had just been enrolled into the school of hard knocks.

There would be many more lessons along the way. His education about life was just starting and time would tell what kind of metal he was made of as long as the lessons weren't overly cruel in the forging process.

CHAPTER #2

THE SUN SHINING in the window made him pull the covers over his head, the lights made it too easy too relive what happened last night. Throwing the covers off as he swung out of bed, Ed stood up and stretched.

"Ouch, that still hurts a bit," he mumbled as he rubbed the back of his head and his butt. Ed knew he was going to be back on the street in a couple of hours. While he was getting dressed he tried to figure out what to do next, understanding very well if he stayed in this part of town looking like he did it was a matter of time before the police picked him up for vagrancy. Even though he was shaved and bathed, his clothes were unwashed, wrinkled and smelled bad, this made employment impossible. Ed had sunk pretty low, but going to jail for any reason, even three squares and a flop, didn't appeal to him at all. He scrubbed his dirty clothes in the bath tub as best he could, put on his cleanest dirties, left the room about noon and headed for the rescue mission on Market Street.

The sun was out but the day seemed dull and dreary. Consciously walking back into that world of misery was hard. Ed knew the more time he spent there the harder it would be to escape. Walking with slumped shoulders and his head down, the sounds of the city pressed in on him. The weight that was pressing down on his shoulders felt like it was trying to meet the one in his guts working its way up. Every time he passed a bum or a wino cold shivers raced up and down his back so violently that by the time he reached the mission he was shaking and sobbing uncontrollably. Ed remained unseen around the corner of the building until he regained most of his composure. By the time he felt strong enough to face what lay ahead, the supper line started to form. Ed fell into line with his unwanted cohorts and he knew it was going to get easier and easier to beg. Masters of the art were all around him.

All he had to do was ask questions and watch the ones that were in the best shape.

After a hearty meal of nondescript stew, those who were going to stay the night formed a line to pick up a stained, worn out pillow and a course woolen blanket. Waiting in line for his bedding didn't leave him feeling as isolated as he thought it would, perhaps he was becoming comfortable with his surroundings or situation, anyway while he was standing in line the director of the mission came up to him.

"What's your name son?"

Before Ed replied he looked the man over. He was about forty-five years old, clean-shaven, white soft skin, soft-spoken and gentle mannered. The worn black shirt and trousers were a little small (especially around the stomach) but not bad. It was evident that physical work was not a constant companion, even though he transmitted an inner strength you could feel.

"My name is Ed."

"What brought you to Denver?"

"I'm looking for work," he said moving forward a step or two with the line as they talked.

"My office is right o ermon right now on how good God has been to me." As the thought passed through his mind he suddenly realized that his strong Missouri Synod Lutheran, every Sunday in Church, upbringing had suffered a major crack in its veneer. For some reason those wonderful, comfortable words and ceremonies that made him feel so good about himself at home, were distant and out of place here. Looking around Ed had a hard time believing that even God cared about anyone in this place. If he did, the words and pictures Ed had read in the Bible didn't describe what it was really like in this part of town.

"Hey you, ya want this stuff or not?" Startled; Ed looked up at the middle aged man behind the half door holding a blanket and pillow out for him.

"C'mon take it and move on or I'll give it to someone else."

Ed grabbed the folded, tattered and worn piece of wool with the stained pillow lying on top and moved toward the director's office.

Opening the door and walking into the office was like stepping into another world. The office contained nice furnishings, a large modern desk with a stuffed chair, and carpet so thick you could actually feel it give beneath your feet when you walked on it. The walls were painted and wall papered in very good taste with pictures and paintings that helped to accent the plush draperies covering the windows. Standing up and reaching over the desk with his open hand extended the director said, "welcome to the Market Street Rescue Mission, I'm John Kilpatrick."

John Kilpatrick was a major in the Salvation Army. He loved to wear the uniform, especially the jacket with the high red collar. His parents had migrated to America from Ireland when he was six years old. They lived in New York until John was ten years old. They moved to Denver after his father had secured a job with the Union Pacific Railroad as an engineer. John always wanted to help people. In his teens he joined the Salvation Army and worked his way up through the ranks until he arrived at the position he was in now.

Ed complied with the handshake as the director told him to sit in one of the two easy chairs facing the desk.

"So, You're staying the night with us?"

"I guess."

"Well, in that case there is some information that I must have for my records."

By now Ed was sitting on the edge of his seat, ready to drop the blanket and pillow he was clutching, so he could run. Evidently John sensed the nervousness in the young man and changed his approach.

"You look a little tense, how about a cup of coffee?"

"Sure."

"How do you take it?"

"Black'll be fine."

John got up from behind the desk and walked over to a table that supported a coffee pot and all the necessary accoutrements. Bringing two steaming cups of the black liquid over to his desk he sat his cup down. Walking around the large desk he handed Ed the other blue ceramic mug as he sat in the easy chair next to him. "Look I'm here to help you if you'll let me. If you don't want to tell me your name or where you're from that's OK; but at least talk to me so I know how to help you."

Ed stared at the balding man unable to find any words to say. Setting his coffee cup on the desk in front of him Ed started to get up. John reached out and touched Ed's arm just as he started to get up bringing a reaction that was totally unexpected. As soon as Ed felt his arm being touched instinct took control of his reactions. Dropping the bedding he stepped back and put up clenched fists much to the surprise of the director. "Touch me again and I'll drop you where you stand." The words came out completely by surprise. Two weeks ago his shy, polite nature would have made Ed incapable of such behavior.

"I'm sorry, I didn't mean to startle you. Please sit down I won't touch you again." John retreated to his side of the desk as Ed cautiously sat down in the chair once more. John studied the ragged youth as he thought to himself, "this youngster is as shy as a deer. He must have really been batted around to be so defensive." Leaning back in the swivel chair he studied the angry expression on the youths face trying to figure out a way to get him to open up and talk.

"You said you came here to find a job, what kind of work are you looking for?"

"Anything that pays money."

"That's pretty general, if I am going to help you I have to have more specific information. What can you do? How much experience do you have and is there something you would like to do in the future?"

"The future," Ed thought to himself. At this point in time it was about as foreign sounding as saying he was rich. In the last three weeks the thing that had been important was survival. The future had crashed in flames as far as Ed was concerned. Now, here it was again, resurrected by an unknown person and a few words.

"I just want something so I can get some money to live on."

Realizing he had struck a vital chord John pursued it even though he was still a little leery of the youth's hardness.

"I know a lot of the business owner's here in Denver, if I am going to help you get a job with one of them I have to know what you can do."

Ed grabbed the luke warm cup of coffee off the desk and sat back in the chair. He was beginning to feel a little more at ease with John, especially since the desk was between them. John was harmless and as straight arrow as they came, but after the recent experiences Ed had been through he was being as cautious as a long tailed cat in a crowd of people with this well intentioned do-gooder.

"I was born and raised on a farm. I'm good with animals, I can milk cows and drive any type of farm machinery." The memories of a small farm in Wisconsin started to come back as he sat there thinking about his recent past life.

"We don't have too many dairy farms out here, mostly ranches that run beef cattle. Are you from the East or the Midwest?"

Getting defensive at the pointed questioning Ed mumbled "the Midwest."

"What state?"

"Just the Midwest," Ed replied annoyingly.

Changing the subject John said, "let's see if we can get you a job!"

Interested Ed sat up in his seat and took a pull on the cold coffee. John opened a drawer in the desk and pulled out a piece of paper with the "Market Street Rescue Mission" letterhead on it. Scratching words onto the paper took only a few minutes. When he was done he leaned forward toward Ed holding the piece of paper so he could read it. Reaching out and holding the edge of the paper Ed read; "Mike, this boy needs a job on a farm or ranch. He is over eighteen, has a social security number and appears to be in good health. I would really appreciate it if you could do something for him he needs a break. Thank you. Sincerely, John Kilpatrick."

When John was sure that everything had been read he jerked the paper out of Ed's grasp and said, "Do you want a job or not?"

Ed looked down at the desk and dejectedly said, "yeah."

"Great because this letter will get it for you, but there are conditions."

Tensing at the statement Ed muttered; "what are they?"

"Your real name, where you're actually from and the letter is yours."

Ed sat back in his chair and closed his eyes as he thought to himself: "God, if I tell him and he notifies my folks they might call the cops, have me arrested and sent home. If I don't tell him there goes a good chance for a job."

Decisions are never easy, but this one was particularly hard, because it meant that everything he had gone through would be for nothing if he didn't give in to the director's request. Ed wished his recent experiences hadn't happened. If he was arrested now Ed didn't know how he could face anyone at home and explain the things that happened to him in the last three weeks. Realizing that this was a chance to get out of his pathetic situation, Ed understood that another chance might be a long time coming, if another one came at all.

"My real name is Ed Spitzer and I come from Hillsboro, Wisconsin."

"Good," John said as hurriedly wrote in a notebook lying open on his desk.

"Can I have the paper now?"

"How old are you Ed?"

"Eighteen," Ed lied.

"Are your folks still alive?"

"Wait a minute that wasn't part of the deal, you said my name and where I was from, are you changing things now?"

Remembering the previous confrontation John handed over the letter as he said; "no here you go."

Ed snatched the letter out of his hand as deftly as John had done to him earlier.

"Go down Market Street to fifteenth. You'll see the Acme Employment Agency on the leftside of the street in the middle of the block. Give the paper to Mike he runs the place; don't give it to anyone else. If things don't work out come back and see me, I'll find something else for you."

Ed picked up his blanket and pillow off the floor before he stood up.

"Be there as early as you can, he opens at eight, he gets rid of most all the jobs he has available by noon."

"OK, ah, thank you, Ed said as he turned and walked over to the barracks bag he had dropped by the door when he came in.

"You'd better leave that here until morning. It'll just get stolen out there."

Nodding, Ed sat the bag down and closed the door behind himself as he started down the hallway to the large auditorium where every body slept

Stepping into the open barracks housing that nights collection of human garbage, a sharp realization of his current status in life was brought back to him by the smell of vomited wine, stale urine and unwashed living bodies. All the bunks were stacked three high and about three feet apart. The room was large enough to hold five rows of fifteen triple bunks each. Wandering up and down the rows in the dimly lit room looking for an empty bunk was an experience in itself. He witnessed various types of depravity. Winos lying on bunks passed out in their own vomit, bums wracked with pain and shacking so hard from the DT's they could barely stay in bed, Some bunks held more than one occupant, modesty and embarrassment had become a luxury lost to the type of people that existed in this part of town. Sitting down on an empty bunk Ed checked the mattress over to see if it was wet or smelled bad. It wasn't wet but it did have a distinctively bad odor. Suppressing the urge to take his chances out on the street he swung his feet onto the poor excuse for a mattress and layed back.

"Hey Sonny," the voice came from the lower bunk next to him. Turning his head in the direction of the voice Ed leaned on one elbow and squinted in the dim light as he tried to see who was talking to him. "You got any cigarettes or booze?"

"No, I sure don't."

"This your first time here?"

"Yeah."

"Let me tell you a few things so you can wake up in the morning in one piece. Lay on your hand so you don't sleep to sound or to long, if you don't you might not like who you wake up next too, if you wake up at all. Are your shoes any good?"

"Yeah, real good."

"Well you'd better tie the laces together and sling them around your neck. Tie the laces long enough so you can put your shoes under your arms. If anyone wants a pair of shoes and they see them on the floor or on your feet they'll be gone for sure."

"OK, thanks." Ed removed his boots; after he had them off he tied the shoelaces together and swung them around his neck with the strings going across the throat and over the shoulders toward the back. Putting one shoe under each armpit he laid down, pulled the ragged blanket he'd been given completely over his body, and closed his eyes amidst the snores and obscene noises coming from around his bunk.

Sometime during the night Ed was awakened by low voices coming from the bunk of the man that befriended him earlier. Looking in that direction he could barely make out the forms of two or three people leaning over the bunk. It was so close between beds that he had to get out on the opposite side and walk around the end to see what was going on. The Denver police were shining their flashlights on the object of their attention, which was the bum who had given Ed such good advice. He was sporting two smiles because someone had cut the shoestrings and his throat from ear to ear to steal the shoes that he had so carefully tied there. A flashlight beam landed on Ed's face and a voice said, "hold it you, where did you get those shoes?"

'They're mine."

"Yeah, well let me see," as the cop stepped in front of him and looked at the shoestrings and shoes hung around his neck."No blood on the shoes or his hands and the laces are in one piece." He said to the other officers. "Empty your pockets on the bed here," the officer pointed to the empty rack that Ed had just got out of. Ed turned his pockets inside out to show he had nothing in them."Grab the top bunk and spread your legs." Ed flinched as the cop frisked him thoroughly."Nothing here, he's clean." One of the other two replied, "Let him go then.""OK bum, get out of here and don't let me catch you around here again." With that he gave Ed a vicious shove that sent him sprawling in the aisle. Ed picked him self up off the floor, stumbled outside and threw up. After he got over the heaves and the shakes, Ed put on his shoes and started walking into the dark night. After a couple hours of wandering Ed found himself standing in front of a doorway with a sign over it that said, "Acme Employment Agency." The cement steps lead up to a recessed doorway and it seemed to be the best spot to sit he had seen yet. Sitting down he wondered what went wrong with his life in the past three weeks. If he had been able to see into the future he never would have started on this journey. Sitting there thinking, some pretty terrible thoughts ran through his mind and at one point he thought to himself, "this is probably how a soldier feels after he has gone through a bloody battle, only to find himself alive and unhurt at its conclusion with the dead and dying lying all around him. Not a friend in the world, or anyone that would give a damn, could he turn to as he huddled in the alcove waiting for morning to arrive.

It was gray and dismal, the bitter chill of early morning moved over him as he sat perched half asleep in the cold stone doorway looking like a grounded bird too wet too fly. Sitting in the doorway with his head resting on his knees, Ed dozed in and out of consciousness waiting for the place to open. Sometime after daylight someone came to unlock the door. Ed didn't realize he was there until he felt the stab of pain in his ribs and elbows as he rolled down the hard concrete steps trying to get away from the vicious kicks the man was landing on his body

"Get the hell out of here you goddamn bum."

Ed picked himself up off the sidewalk as the man stalked in the door and slammed it shut. Rubbing his bruised ribs Ed limped up the stairs and through the unlocked door. The man turned and Ed could see he was used to dealing with the decaying humanity that inhabited the neighborhood. Even his features reflected the sleazy atmosphere of the Market Street side of town. Lazy eyelids, greasy black hair, pasty skin, the yellowed white shirt and threadbare trousers shouted his simple and mundane existence.

"I told you to get the hell out of here," as he walked toward Ed at the counter opening.

"But I have an interview with someone named Mike at eight o'clock," Ed said sheepishly as he handed over the letter the kind mission director had given him. Reaching over the counter Mike grunted as he grabbed the paper out of Ed's hand. Squinting and rubbing his chin Mike read it at least a half a dozen times.

"Wait here," he turned and walked into a back room through a curtain hung in the doorway.

Looking around the room Ed could see slips of paper thumb tacked to a corkboard with names, addresses and dollar amounts printed on them. While he stood and waited for Mike to return he could hear him talking in the back room and figured he had called John Kilpatrick at the Rescue mission. Pretty soon the curtain flew to one side and Mike walked into the room.

"OK kid, can you ride a horse?"

Ed's childhood days flashed back through his mind recalling all those times he had ridden everything from plow horses to the saw horses that inhabited his Wisconsin farm home. "Sure," he said with some degree of confidence.

"OK, I've got a job for you in Medicine Bow, Wyoming. They pay your bus ticket and hotel room. I get twenty five per cent of your first month's wages for finding you the job. They'll take that out and send it to me. It pays a hundred and twenty five a month and keep (meals and a place to sleep). Ed's jaw fell open as Mike handed him an envelope with the bus ticket, his employer's name and then told him to get out. Leaving the job office Ed felt like he was walking on air. What a beautiful day, the sun was out and the birds were singing, God it was good to be alive.

CHAPTER #3

AFTER AN UNEVENTFUL bus ride to Medicine Bow, Wyoming, Ed hopped down the steps of the musty smelling greyhound about six o'clock at night. Picking up his bag as the driver retrieved it from the side compartment of the bus he remembered how happy the director had been that he had followed through with the job appointment after the fracas at the mission. After his interview he had gone back to pick up his bag and thank the kind director for his help. Since the bus wouldn't leave until mid—afternoon John invited Ed to lunch and spent the rest of the morning just talking to him. It was a very pleasant experience and something Ed would remember for years to come.

Ed was impressed as he stood before the fairly modern four-story building called the Virginian Hotel. (It was named for a book that had been written about the area some years earlier.) Attached to it was collection of neat little stores selling everything from drugs to women's under garments.

Shouldering his bag he walked into the spacious lobby and looked around. A large dining room about three quarters full of people was located just beyond the hotel desk. A large staircase leading to the rooms upstairs hugged the wall opposite of the diners. The spacious sitting room had the usual compliment of stuffed chairs and end tables. It was the walls that caught your eye. Prints and original paintings by Remington and Russell adorned the walls. Landscapes, Indians and animals were depicted on canvas and paper as well as some original pencil sketches that appeared next to the finished product it inspired. Ed approached the desk and handed the clerk the paper the job agency had given him. He read it and looked over his glasses.

"Take the stairs all the way to the top. It's the room at the end of the hall. I'll call Mr. Schmidt. He'll pick you up in the morning.

The name brought a flash of memory from home since most of Ed's relatives were of German and Norwegian descent. It seemed kind of funny to hear a common name like that out here. Thinking about it a minute he tried to figure out what kind of a name would be synonymous with a western cowboy. Thinking back to all his readings there were a lot of first names like; Rex, Tex, Bart, Missouri, and so on, but he couldn't for the life of him remember any real western last names.

"Oh well," now that he was here in the heart of the real west it was, "a good bet he would find out," he mused as he walked toward the stairs. Just as Ed mounted the stairs he was bombarded with the aroma of food from the dining room, making his stomach remind him that it had been a while since anything had entered its domain. The tantalizing odor followed him up to the first floor. Since his room was on the fourth floor he was relieved when he walked away from it. Topping the last set of stairs he trudged to the end of the hall and unlocked the door to his room.

It wasn't much; there was only enough room for a bed and a chair. At one time it must have been a large closet where they stored extra blankets, mattresses and things like that. Bigger than a linen or broom closet but smaller than a regular room and it was up in a corner of the building where the roof angled so the ceiling inside was lower on one side than the other. The bed did have a box spring, mattress, and something Ed hadn't seen since he was a small kid, a feather tick. The room was unheated so it was a definite asset to a good nights sleep in this cold climate. Patting the linen covering Ed hurriedly stripped off his clothes in anticipation of a good nights sleep. The feather tick folded softly around him as he lay down in it and pulled the cover on top.

When Ed awoke in the morning he didn't want to move. Snuggled into that wonderfully soft, warm feather tick was the best thing his body had experienced in weeks. All the pain and misery he incurred in the recent past seemed far away, so he lounged and enjoyed as long as could. Once awake though, he was too young and active to just lay around, so he climbed out of bed into the morning's early chill. Making sure the door was unlocked he walked into the hallway, razor in hand, to find the bathroom. It was located down the hall a short distance from his room. Cleaning up wasn't hard because he didn't have a lot of things to clean up with. A small sliver of body soap that made the journey with him from Denver doubled as shaving cream and hair shampoo. Back in his room Ed sorted through his blue jeans to find the cleanest dirty pair and put them on.

Sitting in the lobby scanning a local paper he watched for someone who might look like an employer. After a couple of hours a bald man in his early fifties wearing a khaki shirt and bib overall's stopped at the lobby desk. The desk clerk talked to him for a few minutes and then pointed in Ed's direction. Ed could see the man was not fat but what you could call pudgy. He moved real easy, there didn't appear to be a clumsy bone in his body.

"I'm Emil Schmidt," Ed was glad he offered his hand so he could steady himself as he rose.

"I'm Ed Spitzer," as he took a good close up look at the stranger who was willing to give someone he had never seen before a job.

Emil Schmidt had been born and raised in the desert around Laramie and Medicine Bow, Wyoming. His brother Endel and two sisters still lived in the area. Emil's parents were German immigrants that came west in a wagon train and squatted on the land that the present day ranch now sits on. Emil was short and stocky; Endel was tall, lean and three years older. Both boys grew up on hard work and short rations, which was normal for the times. Material possessions weren't important because they were far and few between. Growing up in turn of the century Wyoming, Emil saw a lot of history being made. In nineteen thirteen the Lincoln Highway was being built a couple of thousand feet from the ranch house. This road (once known as the main street of America) is four hundred and fifty miles of Wyoming roadway that was later renamed U, S, Highway Thirty. The Schmidt's bonfire was one of thousands that lit the cement causeway all the way across the state on the night of the dedication celebration. As kids Emil and his siblings took the natural wonders of the area for granted. Playing in the petrified forest only miles from their house, (present day site is just out of Medicine Bow east of highway 487) they would bring home pieces of the subtropical stone trees that dated back 50 million years or more to line the walks or gardens with. The curious patterns and colors made these stones equally attractive to the local residents for building purposes. There are still some homes in the area that have their foundations made from the rocks acquired at this archeological site. The other playground was a place called Como Bluffs. It was discovered in 1877, and is a prehistoric bone yard. The children would ride horseback there and spend the day poking around looking for strange skulls or bones.

In 1924 the whole family went to Cheyenne to watch the inauguration of Nellie Tayloe Ross, one of the first women to be elected governor. She was the first women to serve in a high position in the national government, being appointed director of the mint in 1933 by Franklin Delano Roosevelt where she served for twenty years.

The wild Indians were gone by the time Emil was old enough to know who they were. The few that were left lived on the Wind River Reservation a hundred miles north of Medicine Bow and could only be seen this far south occasionally, begging or hunting for the meager existence they were allowed to have.

The land is not suited for farming. Even so people came and tried to scratch out a living planting crops in a climate that receives ten inches of rain a year on soil so alkaline that it will only support salt sage brush and a very hardy but sparse type of grass. The lakes and ponds that exist are man made or backwaters of the rivers that flow through the area. When the elder Schmidt's came to the area, the era of the cattle barons was in its early stages and they lived out of their wagon until a permanent structure could be built. Smart enough to see that farming was not only not profitable, and maybe even hazardous to the health, they worked at putting together their own herd of cattle. With nothing but coal oil lamps for light it was early to bed. Coal oil cost money and cash money was extremely short in the early years. Being very frugal, the older Schmidt's impressed their thrifty habits on their offspring with a vengeance. As the family grew from two to six so did their cattle herd and land holdings.

In those days cattle were not acquired according to how much land you had, it was the other way around. Land was plentiful, you used as much land as you needed and could control according to the size of your herd. A milk cow was considered a luxury not a necessity, beef cattle, mostly the Texas longhorn variety were the common bovine at that time. The buffalo were gone although once in a while a few would be spotted. Wild horses were a plentiful part of the landscape and they were hunted for everything from beasts of burden to meat. Once caught and broken to saddle or harness the wiry little beasts could be used as trading material for some of the more domestic things in life. This is how the milk cow was acquired when Emil was born.

Sparse vegetation and concentration of surface water forces the livestock to inhabit a corridor that follows either side of a river where the moister ground supports a more prosperous stand of grass. It takes ten acres to support one cow where there is no moisture, the closer you get to water the more abundantly the grass grows. This is one of the reasons Westerners of the late and early nineteen hundreds were so quick to shoot anything that competed with the cattle for grass. Cattle were a rate of exchange, money on the hoof, and they increased by themselves. You measured a man's wealth, by the number of cattle that he owned. Cash money was hard to come by and it was hard to use because only a few had it, but cattle could be sold, bartered, traded or exchanged for anything you needed. So, as the Schmidt family grew, so did their cattle herd and as the children got big enough to help work the cattle, the herd continued to grow. Then came the depression years. Nobody had any money to buy the meat or hides that supported the cattle industry. Many cattle were left to starve and some ranches went out of existence if they had any kind of debt load. Some simply left to keep from going into debt. Others were so disillusioned after working hard all their lives, they just walked off and left everything but the clothes on their back. The ones that stayed, ate their own product, hung on and waited for the market to come back, eventually prospered. The land they lived on was free and clear because it had been homesteaded by the older generation before the turn of the century. All that was required until things stabilized was living a Spartan life with plenty to eat and nothing to spend. The market did come back and it prospered during World War Two just as it had during World War One. By then the elder Schmidt's had passed away and left five thousand acres to the four children who were grown and had there own families.

The girls married and moved off to different locations with their new husbands. Joyce married a banker and they moved to Cheyenne. Rachael married the son of a wealthy rancher and moved to Rock Springs. Emil married a girl by the name of Marianne Bestoffe from

Rock River, Wyoming in nineteen thirty-one. Endel came close, but his bride to be came down with pneumonia and died two months before they were supposed to wed. He never dated after that and stayed single until the day he died.

Emil sired and raised two fine boys. One grew up to be a structural engineer and the other owns and operates his own ranch just outside of Wheatland, Wyoming. After his bride to died Endel decided to make his home there. Which meant the home ranch at Medicine Bow had to hire help to operate.

As Ed stood in the hotel lobby looking at Emil he saw a man about five foot ten inches tall, bald head, thick features, bushy eyebrows, blue eyes, straight nose, strong white teeth, firm square chin, all set on a short strong neck. When Emil Schmidt talked to you he looked straight at you and didn't blink or turn away. The bib overall's and brogan shoes made him look a lot like one of the farmer neighbors back in Wisconsin. The bibs were clean but worn around the edges. One of the pockets in front bulged with a billfold. It protruded enough see the rubber band that was wrapped around it and the partially visible wad of money it contained. The corner of a red print handkerchief stuck out of a lower front pocket, evidently for easy access.

"Had your breakfast yet?"

Ed mumbled a feeble," No."

"C'mon, lets eat before we go out to the ranch."

Ed wouldn't have believed eggs, pancakes, toast, ham, sausage, potatoes, coffee, juice and fruit dessert could taste so good until he had seconds on everything. His stomach had given into a monastic diet previously and was still sore from rubbing against his backbone. Even though now he looked about five months pregnant.

"You weren't a little hungry were you?"

"You might say that, it's been a couple of days since I ate last. Sorry if I ran the bill up."

Emil smiled and grunted remembering back to when he was a youngster and the times he missed meals because there wasn't anything to eat. Waddling out the door of the hotel behind Mr. Schmidt Ed got his first real look at his new surroundings.

Medicine Bow, Wyoming is located in southeastern Wyoming on old U.S. highway thirty about one hundred miles west of Laramie and hundred and fifty miles west of Cheyenne, the capital city of Wyoming. Medicine Bow sits on what is known as the North American high plains desert. The land is seemingly flat with low pointed hills and very few trees except along the rivers. Salt sage, bunch grass, (also know as buffalo grass) and small cactus cover the ground and line the arroyos and draws that make up the terrain. As they stood on the porch of the hotel, Ed looked at the cattle pens and railroad depot on the opposite side of U.S. Highway Thirty running past the front porch of the hotel.

"I'll bet that place could tell some stories," Ed thought as they moved down the steps and walked over to the old pickup truck that Emil drove. After a short drive west on highway thirty, they turned into a dusty lane leading to the ranch. Turning the truck into the yard they swung past a small white house with a neatly kept yard and white picket fence around it. About fifty yards away was a long solid building made of logs from who knows where.

"That's the bunkhouse." Emil said as the truck came to a stop. "Find a bed and I'll talk to you at dinner time, (noon).

Ed stood in the doorway and let his eyes become accustomed to the light, which was not very abundant. The place was deserted and dark with only one small window. It had electricity and

Ed flicked on the light switch. The inside looked and smelled like an army barracks, saloon and saddle shop. Clothes were scattered around the room in a purposely-disarranged fashion. Everything seemed to have a place wherever it was dropped, covering the sparse furnishings and sort of creeping on to the floor. A few whisky bottles with some liquor in each one could be found mixed in with the piles of clothes, sitting on the table or lying in arms reach under one of the bunks. The odd thing was how neat the riding equipment was kept. A couple of bridles were hung on nails by their respective owners bunks, spurs and ropes were hung off the protruding bed posts of the top bunk. The few tools needed to repair leather were on a shelf at one end of the room, along with a bottle of Dr. White's rubbing liniment, a tin of cloverine salve and an old soup can filled with assorted nails. Three sets of bunk beds stood against the walls. Ed walked over to one that appeared to be unclaimed and threw his duffel bag on it. It had been a long, tough road so far, but things were looking up, a new surge of energy crept into his soul as he went outside to look around.

There were only four buildings on the place so it didn't take long to inspect them. Ed walked over to the large corral behind the horse barn, propped a foot on the bottom rail and looked wistfully across the large enclosure at a herd of antelope grazing peacefully on the hillside. A voice behind him broke his concentration. As Ed turned around a man in his late forties stuck out his hand and said, "Hello I'm Jake." Ed always had a mental image of the tall, lean, brown skinned cowboy. (Especially when you're standing in a state as western as Wyoming where everyone is supposed to walk on high heeled boots with big fancy spurs attached, plus the rest of the envisioned gear all the way up to the big ten gallon hat).

"Ed," he said as he looked down at the man and pumped his chubby hand. Ed's gaze went from the steady amber eyes, down the once broken nose, to the smiling mouth with its pearly white teeth and one gold tooth. Sweeping his eyes over Jake's frame he felt a surge of disappointment. Jake wasn't wearing the right clothes! All he had on was a pair of farmer shoes, saggy jeans, a worn plaid shirt that was straining itself to the limit trying to contain the excess belly from spilling any farther over the half hidden belt buckle precariously holding everything together. Completing his outfit was a light vest, and a battered, sweat stained hat similar to one Ed's dad wore with his Sunday suit. "He was short, fat and he didn't dress right," Ed thought to himself.

"I'm the foreman, Emil said he'd took ya on."

"Yeah, I just got here today."

The man and the boy stood leaning against the corral boards talking about Ed and what he was capable of doing. Ed really thought he impressed Jake by relating to him the times he had driven the horse drawn cultivator and the bundle wagon for the threshing crews at home. But as Jake talked about a string of eight on a jerk line, wheelers, swings and leads pulling a dead sled, he began to realize he had a long way to go. They talked until the dinner bell rang. Jake said, "C'mon let's go eat," as he turned and walking toward the ranch house

The place where the men ate was a porch attached to the backside of the little white ranch house with the picket fence. Three steps up to a small landing with boot (mud) scrapers nailed to the sides by the entrance door. It had a small fuel oil stove in one corner for heat in the winter, a long picnic table sitting in the middle of the room and besides the entrance door, it had windows around all three sides that could be replaced with screens for summer. A doorway leads directly into the kitchen where Mrs. Schmidt fixed meals three times a day. While the three men sat and ate dinner (lunch) Jake and Emil talked about cattle, markets, weather and all the things that were to be done in the next week or so.

Mrs. Schmidt was middle aged, medium height, gray haired, slender but not skinny, with strong hands and an intense desire to persevere. After dinner she gave Ed his blankets, pillow and mattress cover that he needed for his bunk. "Put your wash in this bag," she said handing him a white canvas bag with a drawstring in it, "Bring it here and throw it in that corner," pointing to the wall opposite the oil stove. "I wash every Wednesday, bring it with you when you come to breakfast."

"Yes Ma'am."

The foreman walked over to the bunkhouse with Ed. While he put his bed together Jake filled him in on the upcoming events. "The boys should be in with the horses about suppertime. Tomorrow we'll spend the day cleaning 'em up and takin' the kinks out of 'em. By the way, you need a saddle don't you?" Ed nodded as he finished pulling the sack over his mattress. "Let me fill you in on how this works tomorrow. They'll be bringing in about thirty head this afternoon and everybody picks four. The rest we keep around for spares. First thing in the morning we bust 'em, trim 'em and try 'em in the order they're picked. It doesn't take long; usually most of the fun is over by, suppertime of the second day. As Ed was to find out later busting 'em meant roping the horse by the front feet with one lariat, then roping him by the hind feet with another lariat and pulling his feet out from under him. Once this was done, the ropes are wrapped on opposite posts and pulled. This made the horse fall its side with legs tied together stretched out unable to kick or move. Trimming 'em meant cutting the corns out of the bottom of the hoofs, (these are growths that occur when the horse runs on soft ground a lot). This also included roaching the mane, trimming the forelock, and tail. Trying 'em meant to put a saddle on his back, a bosal hackamore on his head and climb aboard much to the objection of the horse. This particular period of time is considered "fun time" by ranch hands to this day. It denotes the particular time of the year when the cattle must be worked before winter sets in.

Horses are still the only effective way to work cattle on the open range. Corrals are nice if one is available but the distance is usually to far to transport the cattle to a corral and it would take too large of a corral to work the number of cattle most ranches keep in one herd. Horses are needed to roundup the cattle and bring them into a central location, if your not using a corral you have to have horses and riders to guard the perimeters of the herd to preventing the critters from leaving. The herd must be held in one bunch while a horse and rider sort out the ones you keep for replacement from the ones that go to market. As each one is brought out of the main herd it must be taken a short distance away and held in a separate group by more horses and riders. The ones that have been cut out to for whatever reason will be moved back to the open range after the cutting session is over. Cutting is always done last. Otherwise you would have cattle trying to regain entry to the main herd while you were working with them. Anything that was not branded in the spring must be roped and branded now, the same holds true for medical treatment of pinkeye, water belly, or any other ailment that might be noticed.

Most of the horses used for this work are experienced cowponies. They're turned loose on the range to fend for themselves after the cattle have been worked in the late fall. A few saddle horses are kept around the ranch during the winter and summer to make getting around and rounding up the workhorses that are used to pull the feed sleds easier. In late summer the main herd is rounded up and brought in to work cattle once more. All this time on the range tends to leave them in a semi unbroken state, and when you climb aboard for the first time that year it's rodeo all the way. A good cow horse should fire (buck a few times when you first get on him for the day) on a daily basis. If he doesn't have enough energy to do that, he probably won't be worth much at the end of the day when you have to rope a thousand pound cow or hold a bunch of cattle. Once the horses get a few jumps out of their system they settle down and are all business. It's kind of like an athlete warming up before he participates in an event.

"Who picks first," Ed asked as he finished pulling the blanket in place on the bunk.

"I do," Jake said as he stared into Ed's eyes.

Dropping his eyes Ed mumbled, "oh."

"C'mon let's go down to the horse barn and I'll find you a saddle."

The man and the boy walked to the horse barn. Opening the squeaky old door the smell of hay, manure and sweat soaked leather enveloped them.

"Try that one over there."

Ed looked where Jake was pointing. It was a saddle, but a lot different than the shining brown, custom engraved, silver inlaid, sheepskin-lined pillion pictured in his mind. The rig the foreman pointed out was probably brown once upon a time. Age, oil, dirt, sweat and exposure had all left their mark, making it a nondescript dark brown or light black depending on how the light hit it. As Ed walked over to get a closer look at it he could see a few remnants of yellowish curly hair still clinging reluctantly to its underside. When he reached out and touched the leather it reminded him of the well-worn arm on Grandma's rocking chair.

"Get in it so we can set the stirrups."

Ed nodded and swung his leg over the exceptionally high back and slipped down into the deep hard seat.

"Once we get 'em set and laced it'll fit ya like a glove."

With the high wide front coming over the tops of his thighs and the four-inch cantle supporting the back part of him Ed understood what the foreman was talking about.

"There, that'll do," Jake tied the last knot in the leather string that held the stirrup leathers together as the sound of voices could be heard amidst the pounding of hooves. "Good the boys are back early." Jake said as he stood up.

Walking outside Ed had to cover his mouth and nose because of the dust the incoming horses were kicking up. What a glorious sight to see and hear, manes, tails and feet were flying everywhere in the large corral. It was color in motion. The paints, bays, sorrels, buckskins, roans, blacks and clay banks all running around in the enclosure like apparitions in a Halloween mist. One sleek black horse running in the dust caught Ed's eye. Watching him run Ed could picture the headless horseman chasing Icabod Crane through the woods on a foggy moonlit night. When they started to settle down he looked them over to figure which four he would like. The only thing he had to go on was color and looks so he mentally choose six of the prettiest ones and walked over with Jake to meet the three cowboys that drove the them in.

"Hi Jake, what'ch ya got taggin' along behind ya?" The hard lean Redhead said as he got down off his horse.

"We got us a brand new hand here, Ron. Boy's I'd like you to meet Ed. This here's Ron, that's Mike and that's Buck."

Shaking Ron's hand Ed could feel a gentle but definitely strong grip. Looking into his clear brown eyes made Ed feel like they could cut him in two. Mike had a grip like a vise. He was six feet tall and built like a lineman for the Green Bay Packers. What he lacked in eye contact he more than made up for in raw brute strength. Buck was a strange one; his dark skin, straight black hair and jet black eyes that never blinked under the big hat he wore made him look like a snake peeking out from under a rock. When Ed shook his hand it felt as emotionless as a dead cat.

"Well, now that you boy's know one another let's get busy and get somethin' done before supper."

The three men stripped the saddles from their horses and carried them into the barn. Ed was amazed at how those horses stood there with only the bridle reins hanging on the ground. The men came out of the barn coiled lariats in hand, walked to the horses, picked up the hanging reins and continuing to the corral gate, where they took the bridles off and turned them in with the other horses. "C'mon kid we'll put this gear away and have a drink," Mike said as they headed for the bunkhouse.

The bridles were hung on nails pounded in the wall near the foot of each ones bunk. Next came the chaps and jackets. Giving them a toss at the existing pile, their landing determined whether or not they made the upper or lower level of the creeping piles. Sitting on their bunks the three men took off their spurs and hung them and the lariats on the bedposts of their bunk.

Territory is very important to these men. Material possessions are not many, but what they do have is jealously kept in a certain manner as decided by the owner. They take great pride in what few possessions they own and the ones they are put in charge of. Each item has a place of importance and some places are more important than others. Why a nail left or right pounded into a log wall would have more significance than the one next to it, could only be decided by the possessor. When he moved on, the coveted place or item would fall heir to the highest-ranking individual and it would work its way on down the line. If for some reason the absentee's spot was not wanted then the acquisition would move down the line and its priority would lessen with each notch it fell in the pecking order. In the pecking order of the group each is subordinate only when an issue is to be decided among the group. Similar, but not the same as time invested in seniority at a union shop. The person who has been there the longest gets to pick first on everything. It would be bad manners to expedite your turn and more than likely would get you into a hell of a good fight. No one would dare sit on another man's bed or touch anything that didn't belong to him without asking first. Besides being fiercely independent most ranch hands are superstitious. Some more than others, and each superstition is different, but it is serious enough to the individual that one warning or an immediate fight is a certainty. These people are extremely physical and fiercely independent, probably because of the environment they are born into and live in.

A ranch hand has no future except winding up on skid row as a drunk. All the land is owned and handed down from family to family. Even the land and ranches that are put on the auction block or sold through realty agents are inaccessible to ninety nine per cent of the ranch hands that have the desire to own a ranch, because very few save any money. A hundred and fifty a month or less, is not enough wages to save for a down payment and the operating capital necessary to run a ranch long enough to make a profit. Ed didn't have any idea what he was getting into a hierarchy this delicately abstract, but he was about to find out.

"Damn this feels good," came the throaty groan as Ron lay back on his bunk.

"Want a drink?" Mike was holding a pint of whiskey up for anyone to accept.

"Sure, I'll take a pull of that," Jake and Ron said almost in unison.

"How about you kid," as Ron extended the half full bottle in Ed's direction.

"Sure," Ed said as he grabbed the bottle and took a small swig of the bitter sweet liquid. Ed had gone to some high school beer parties once or twice and he did drink a couple of mixed drinks on festive occasions around home but never anything straight. It burned a little going down, so he was glad that he hadn't taken a large drink. Ed made a face and gasped for a little air but all in all it wasn't bad. The one thing he did know was that he was being tested to see if he would fit in. The only one that didn't take a drink or two was Buck. He sat on his bunk expressionless, smoking a cigarette.

"OK boys, you got the dust out of your throats now let's go pick our string." The foreman said as he handed the bottle back to Mike. Everyone got up grabbed their lariat (except Ed, he didn't have one yet) and walked to the corral where the horses where waiting.

"Buck, would you rope my four?" Jake asked the Indian.

"Cost you ten bucks," Buck said flatly.

"No, I don't think so, unless you want to shovel shit until winter."

Realizing the futility of the situation Buck answered, "OK, boss, which ones do ya want."

Jake pointed out his four choices, two of them Ed had mentally picked earlier. Buck walked into the corral building a loop in his rope to catch the first horse. Ed was leaning against the corral boards watching with an extremely avid interest. He had read many times how cowboys roped their horses and now he was actually going to see it done. Buck walked slowly into the milling gang of horseflesh dragging the loop behind him in his right hand while he held the excess coiled in his left. Keeping his eyes on the one he wanted his body seemed to switch to automatic as he moved toward the animal. It was almost like he became part of the horse as he subtly countered each move it made. With a flick of his wrist the rope loop shot through the air, settled around the horse's neck and snapped shut as the wild eyed animal struggled to break through the mob that surrounded him. In the same motion Buck wrapped what was left of the coiled end of the rope around a post embedded in the ground. Buck pulled in the slack; the animal gave a halfhearted pull, shook his head from side to side a few times and stepped forward to make slack in the tightening rope. Any horse that has been caught with a rope learns quickly not to fight it. If he does resist he is allowed to choke himself almost into unconsciousness. One or two applications of this type of treatment and he learns not to fight the rope but to walk forward and make slack so he doesn't choke. If the harsh lesson is taught well the first time or two, it leaves a lasting impression on the animal for the rest of his life and every time a rope goes around his neck he knows to step forward in the direction of the pulling or he will choke. Moving toward the post as the slack is taken out the horse is snubbed down until he is close enough to have a braided rope halter placed over their head, then they're lead into a small-attached corral and tied to the board fence. This goes on until all the horses that the men present will use are caught and haltered. After Buck caught Jake's four, it was Ron's turn since he was the next after Jake in the pecking order.

The lean Redhead sprang lightly off the wooden fence with his rope and entered the pack of restless horses as easy as a breeze moves through the branches of a tree. Buck had a direct effortless style when he threw his rope, using only the amount of effort needed. Ron was just the opposite; his style was flamboyant and showy, although the results were the same. Ron carried the loop over his right shoulder until he threw. Then as it came off the shoulder it was flipped forward, down, back up, and over handed in an arc like, Los Angles Lakers Carem Abdul Jabahrs sky hook. The rope loop would pop in the air and come straight down over the head of the unsuspecting horse before he could blink an eye. As Ron caught his three, Mike haltered and led them out. One of Ed's hopeful's was in this bunch also.

Now it was Mike's turn. Lumbering into the corral among the crowd of equines that were moving around more freely because of their lesser numbers. Mike's stature gave anyone who didn't know him the impression that it would be easier for him to tackle the horses he wanted instead of trying to rope them. His style was typical of the head down and charge character he appeared to portray. He would get the intended horse moving to his right around the enclosure. Then Mike would cut across the arena to get a good shot at the head of the desired horse and throw. There was no finesse or poetry to it. Surprisingly he connected three times in a row. Ron returned the favor by haltering and tying Mike's four in the adjoining corral.

Next came Buck back to rope his three. Ed watched with keen interest because there were only about two-thirds as many horses, which meant there was more room for them to maneuver. Since all but a couple were rope broke they had a better chance to see the roper make his move and dodge the rope. The lesser numbers also helped the roper because all those heads weren't so close together. You see, the only rule is, you keep what you rope, if you missed and the rope found its way around the neck of something you didn't want, sorry, but he's yours until next year. The reason for this is the hands that have been on the ranch for more than a year are familiar with most of the horses and they know which ones handle or work cattle the best. The hands with the most seniority get to go first, this gives them the advantage for the best horses, unless they miss; of course, no one would ever admit to missing, whatever that rope caught is exactly what the roper would confess to throwing at. It's to bad the horses didn't understand this because every now and then one would run in front of the desired mount and be caught much to the self contained disgust of the roper.

Buck was carrying his rope a little different than he had earlier when he roped for Jake. He built a smaller loop and was holding it vertical to the ground next to his right leg. His wrist was bent outward slightly, and his hand hung down as the fingers curled gently around the rope. Buck picked out his quarry like a cat stalks prey and walked directly at the animal. This seemed to confuse or possibly mesmerize it until he was within eight yards or so, then it broke left and ran. The loop was on its way with a flick of the wrist before the horse made his second plunge. It snapped out in front of the horse's head in a vertical position and he simply ran into it. This underhand throw worked the same way on all three horses. It didn't matter if they broke right or left the first shot always counted. Buck was a legend in the area with a rope. He had forgotten more than most of the rest even knew about handling a rope. After Buck had his three, Mike walked over and handed Ed his rope.

"Here you go kid take you're four."

"Thanks," Ed said as he grabbed the braided sisal lariat from Mike's hand.

Even though he had just witnessed a roping seminar he was honest enough with him self to realize the only way he was going to catch anything by throwing a rope at it would be pure, dumb, blind luck. Looking over toward the four ranch hands waiting expectantly by the fence Ed knew he had to at least try. They reminded him of a bunch of vultures in a western movie waiting for the victim to expire. "I might just as well give it a try," he thought as he jumped down from the top rail where he had been perched for the last hour. Conscious of the eyes following him into the corral Ed tried to hold the rope like he saw Buck do it first. Buck had taken two of the ones Ed wanted, there was only one left out of the six he originally decided on. Looking the remaining fifteen head over he spotted the black mane and tailed buckskin he had spot picked when they were first run into the corral. She was in a group peeking at him from behind two other horses.

Remembering how Buck had kept his eye on the target Ed closed in nice and easy. It worked too, he got within eight yards or so before the two horses in front broke left and the buckskin broke right. Ed snapped the rope loop in a kind of a side arm motion but it turned side ways and fell short. Gathering the rope in Ed coiled it and shook out another loop slightly larger this time. "Maybe if I try it like Ron did it'll work," he thought to him self as he closed in on the group the buckskin was trying to hide in the middle of. Pitching the rope loop upward in the direction of the yellow horse it looked like it was going to come real close but fell over the head of a rawboned sorrel three feet to the right. The sorrel took off like a shot, (needless to say this was one of the few that was not rope broke) not knowing what to do with his end of the rope Ed stood there as the slack went out and it snapped out of his hand. "Get hold of the rope," everyone yelled. It must have been the funniest thing these guys had seen in a long time. They all laughed and hooted loudly, watching Ed run after the end of the rope as it bounced and slithered through the dirt. Getting hold of it was no small task. It wasn't until the horse stopped for a moment that Ed was able to reach down and get a good grip on it. Just about the time he felt he had the horse it took off again. This time Ed was determined to hang on and went face first in the dirt. He didn't really mind being laughed at but being dragged around the corral on his belly wasn't humorous as far as he was concerned.

"Hey kid, quit kicking up so much dust you're scaring the horses and making it hard to see," came the comment from the sidelines amidst screams of laughter.

"You gotta admit it saves on shoe leather," one of them yelled in a choking voice.

"Yeah, just think, if he took his Levis off he could keep 'em clean," more screams of laughter.

Ed couldn't hear anything being said as he surf boarded around the corral on his stomach but after about two laps he had enough and let go of the rope. It felt like someone had lit a fire on his front side when he rolled over on his back as he skidded to a stop. The excruciating pain only lasted for a few minutes, (as long as he didn't move) and then subsided to almost tolerable levels as the dust settled around his prostrate body reclining in the missionary position. Everyone came and stood over him, lying on his back, arms outstretched, knees up, eyes open and looking skyward.

Is he alive?"

"I dun no but his chest is moving. Besides if he was dead his eyes would be closed."

"Not really," Mike said leaning over the moaning teenager, "I saw a dead man once, his eyes were open but he smelled real bad," he leaned closer and sniffed, "maybe he is dead."

"No I'm not, help me up."

Everyone broke into loud peals of convulsive laughter as Mike and Jake each grabbed an arm and pulled Ed to his feet.

"We thought maybe you was trying to wear him down by letting him drag you around the corral," Jake said as everybody doubled up laughing again.

"C'mon boys let's give him a hand," Jake said, as he made a great show of trying to pound the dust off Ed's back who by now looked like a brown coal miner.

The four men left Ed standing with his arms and legs spread while they cornered the sorrel, haltered him and tied him in the next corral. Ed had some real bad feelings about that horse and he didn't know why. Taking the rope as Ron handed it to him, he looked for the buckskin again not realizing until he moved how the ground had sand papered the front of his legs and body. Ed knew he couldn't just quit in front of these guys, if he did they wouldn't accept him into the group. Gritting his teeth Ed went after the buckskin looking like a firewalker losing his confidence half way across a bed of hot coals. A half a dozen unsuccessful attempts later, Ed looked over at the group clustered around the corral fence.

"This could run into more than just one day, do we have the time?" Ed said. Everybody looked at Jake.

"Well, I'd like to be ready to go by the end of the week and we still got to trim 'em and bust 'em. "Oh." Ed mumbled as he looked at the ground." Swallowing his pride was not going to be easy," he thought as he turned tenderly back to the task at hand. Frustration set in as he stubbornly chased the horses around the corral. At one point he was ready to throw the rope down and start crying although he knew he never would. Not only would that be an insult to Mike who loaned him the rope, but if he cried in front of strangers it would show weakness. Biting his lip he thought, "Damn it, stop and start thinking about how you're going to do this." One thing he had noticed was the buckskin always hid behind another horse. When they broke and ran she always went the opposite direction of the one she used as a screen.

"Maybe if I watch the one in front I can get a throw in before she gets her momentum up." Holding the rope loop vertical to the ground like Buck had done Ed approached the crowd of horses one more time. There was a big, ugly, roman nosed, leopard appaloosa standing in front of the buckskin. Approaching the gang Ed's mental process started ticking as he watched the appaloosa's head.

"He'll run in the direction his head moves, so I'll throw the opposite way." For some reason they stood a little longer than usual and Ed was able to get within twenty feet before they broke. The appaloosa was looking intently at Ed as he closed in, his head started to swing left just a split second before his body moved. Ed started the rope in motion aiming at a spot ten feet behind his rump. The moment the appaloosa moved so did the buckskin. She ran exactly as Ed figured she would, running to the right as the rope slid neatly over her head and snapped shut.

"I'll be damned," Ron said as he got a surprised look on his face.

"Nice shot kid," Mike, yelled.

The buckskin had been roped many times before, as Ed flipped the rope behind his butt and leaned into it, the horse turned and walked toward him while the slack was being taken in. Jake brought a rope halter over and helped him put it on the now docile horse.

"Take her over and tie her with your other one, we'll finish after supper."

"Ok," Ed said as he coiled the rope and walked over to Mike leading the buckskin."Thanks for letting me use your rope it's a good one."

"Keep it until you get done tonight."

"Thanks," Ed said as Mike got out of the squatting position he had been watching the show from. Ed walked the horse into the other corral and tied her next to the sorrel. What a day this had been so far.

Supper was not fancy but it tasted good and there was plenty of it. Roast beef, mashed potatoes, gravy, steamed carrots, bread and butter, coffee, milk, and juice. There seemed to be an endless supply of food. Ed hadn't realized how hungry he was until he gingerly sat down on the bench at the supper table. The pain wasn't breath taking but it definitely hurt when his pants pressed against his legs as he sat down. He found out his face was beet red when he washed up for supper and his hands hurt (from the rope burns) as he used his knife and fork to eat. Fortunately youth can absorb a lot of physical abuse. The older you get the longer it takes the pain and stiffness to leave, as Ed would find out in years to come. The conversation around the table didn't get his attention until the third helping of everything had graced his plate. By then he slowed down to a normal eating pace and was able to look up between mouthfuls.

"My God Emil, don't tell me you're paying him and feeding him both?" Ron said.

Emil was about to speak as Mrs. Schmidt walked into the room.

"Well, I think it certainly is nice to see someone who enjoys eating for a change."

Ed looked up as he shoved another piece of beef into his mouth. No matter what anyone thought they would not argue or disagree with the owners wife openly. Besides, she was a women and even in these times you wanted to be damn careful how you talked to and treated another man's wife in the ranching community. Womanhood is almost canonized among these hard working, honest people.

Swallowing the half chewed mouthful Ed said, "I don't think I've ever tasted better."

This brought a smile to the elderly woman's face. "Would you gentlemen like some dried apple pie?"

Everybody agreed in unison as she cleared away the dirty plates. Returning from the kitchen she carried out a stack of small clean plates and the pie. Setting it in front of the owner she said, "Emil, you cut the pie while I get the cream."

The pie was larger than Ed had ever seen, it was in a round pan about fourteen inches across and three inches deep. Mrs. Schmidt set a large bowl of cream (not the watered down stuff, but real, thick, all butter fat, cream, skimmed off whole milk by a mechanical separator) on the table as Emil finished cutting the pie. Everybody got a large piece of pie and then the cream bowl was passed according to pecking order. The calories must have been almost uncountable as each man heaped on the cream. No one worried about cholesterol. No one had to; they were all lean and hard from the exposure and hard work. Most ranch hands have a sweet tooth the size of Texas and dessert of some kind is usually served at every meal including breakfast.

The typical working cowboy will put in a twelve to fifteen hour day, during calving he'll work round the clock and just catch bits and pieces of sleep and food when he can. Although it has its easy times by and large it is an extremely strenuous and Spartan way of life. This is why most of the "real working" cowboys are narrow waisted and flat bellied.

After supper the men walked outside and those that smoked lit up as everyone trudged back to the corral to watch the spectacle of Ed trying to catch his last two horses. It was just about dark by the time he finally caught the last one and they got to the log bunkhouse. Once again Ed looked around the dimly lit, cluttered interior of the log building, trying to absorb everything he could in his new home and become a part of it as quick as he could. It occurred to him as he sat there that he was living a childhood dream that most children think about but never realize. This was even better because in his wildest dreams he never could have invented the sights, sounds and smells that surrounded him now.

"Let me see your hands," Mike said as he walked over to where Ed was sitting at the worn table in the middle of the room. Opening the raw, blistered, rope burned hands hurt like crazy as Ed held them palm up for the big man to inspect.

"Boy you sure did a job on 'em I'll say that."

Turning away Mike walked to his bunk and pawed through a trunk pulled out from under his bed. Finding what he wanted he walked back over to Ed and said, "Let's see your hands again, this stuff will fix 'em right up," as he took the lid off a can of udder balm used to treat rashes and tender spots on milk cow udders. Gently rubbing the petroleum based salve on Ed's hands he said, "I've got a new pair of cotton gloves you can wear to bed tonight. Your hands will feel OK in the morning. This stuff'll take the soreness right out."

"Could I rub some on the front off my legs they're kind of tender too."

"Sure drop your pants and I'll do it." When Mike was done greasing the beet red legs Ed had exposed he put the lid on the container and walked back to his bunk. Putting the udder balm away he pulled out a pair of new cotton gloves and tossed them to Ed.

"Thanks Mike."

"Sure kid, return the favor someday."

"You got it. Say Mike, where are you from?"

Mike gave him a look that would have made a grizzly bear cower. His expression changed for the better as he said, "look kid, I don't know where you're from and I don't care. You better be real careful asking about things that are none of your business."

"I'm sorry, I didn't mean anything by it I was just trying to be friendly."

"Yeah I know, otherwise we would have went at it right here."

"It's bad manners to ask personal questions about someone," Ron interjected "Probably one of the quickest ways I know of to get in a good fight."

"How do you talk to anyone then," Ed asked.

"Just don't get personal, talk about the weather, work, horses, cattle, markets, yourself and so on. If the other guy wants you to know anything about himself he'll tell you on his own."

"Oh, ok." Ed didn't know what to say. Figuring silence would be "golden" he sat and listened to what the others talked about among themselves.

According to Mid-Western standards the men he was living with in that weather worn log shack would be considered vain. They only talk about themselves, what they have done or what is theirs, besides the chatter involving work and play. Material assets are not their long suits so there is not a great deal of time spent elaborating on them. Two things Ed figured out that night. The quickest way to get in a fight is to talk about somebody else or ask personal questions. Most of the night they talked about tomorrow, the individual horses, and how many times each of them would see the others dumped from the back of an unwilling horse. This is where Ed learned what was going to happen in the next couple of days.

"Who's going to cut corns and trim hooves?" Ron asked.

"I will," Mike said.

"I'll take care of the manes and tails," Buck said, breaking his usual silence.

"Good I'll bring 'em in and head 'em," Ron stated. "Jake 'll handle the hind end probably."

"How about the kid?" Mike asked.

"He can watch, maybe he'll learn something by next time," Ron said as he looked over at Ed and asked, "you ever been on a bronc before?"

Ed grinned and said, "No, but I rode a lot of horses at home. My folks used horses when I was younger to work the farm with and I always had a saddle horse to ride ever since I was old enough to get on one."

Everyone chuckled and shook their heads.

"Have you ever been bucked off before?" Ron kept at his line of questioning knowing he wouldn't offend the youngster.

"Yeah, a couple of times but I didn't get hurt."

"Let me give you some advice. When we finally get to your string you've got your work cut out for you cause you only got two good horses, the buckskin and the bay. The roan is slow and lazy; you have to make him do everything. He'll probably be a good one to start with. I doubt if you'll get more than half a dozen jumps out of him. The bay is a good thinker and if you let him he'll try to do it all by himself. He bucks straight away, he'll probably take you across the corral do a one eighty and take you back across the corral. When he gets to the other side his head'll come up and you got him. The buckskin is a real good horse. She's old but she really knows what she's doing. The only problem with her anymore is she runs out of gas real quick. But she'll give you one hell of a good ride the first time. She goes high and comes at the ground like a rocket. You had better have your feet well out in front of you when she hits the ground or she'll put you right over her ears. Then there's the sorrel. Now he's got some good habits and some bad habits." When the others heard this statement they squirmed and chuckled in anticipation as Ron continued, "he's a good cow horse, real quick but he's got a bad temper, and will blow up at the drop of a hat. You'll never know when it's coming. It could happen in the morning, afternoon, walking, running or standing still. The one thing you can count on is it will happen when you're not ready for it. You got a sample of his temper this afternoon, as many times as that horse has been roped he still fights it. His good side is, if he is actually working a critter he's as good as gold. As a cutting horse they don't come any better and he handles a rope real well too. You just can't trust him except, when he is actually doing something. He puts his whole heart into whatever he's doing, as you'll see the first time you climb aboard. There has been talk of making a rodeo horse out of him if he wasn't so damn good with cattle."

While Ron talked Ed got the impression that Ron really liked the horse except for his inconsistency. "When you try to take the kinks cut of him your in for the ride of your life. This horse stands on his head; sunfishes, sucks back and I've seen him do a half a turn in mid air. He's quick, he's strong and if he feels you get a little off balance he'll really turn it on."

"There isn't any way I could trade him for another is there?" Ed said pathetically.

Everyone laughed, as Mike said, "hey Ron, you're scarin' the boy, give him a break or he won't get on him at all."

Ed knew this was a polite challenge. If he was going to fit in here he was going to have to ride that sorrel. Any showing of cowardice or hesitation would alienate him from this group in a heartbeat.

"I'm not scared, maybe real nervous, but I'll try anything once, the good ones twice," Ed answered trying to make a joke to cover the tension he felt. Everyone looked at him and grinned like they knew something he didn't, and they were going to enjoy watching real soon.

"Ron," Ed asked, "how come when you throw your rope you flip it up in the air and when Buck throws his he kind of under hands it?"

'That's just the way I learned how. It don't matter how you do it as long as you wind up with something in the loop you throw."

"Do you ever miss?"

"No, but sometimes the critter on the other end doesn't cooperate." This brought snickers and grins from the others.

"Next to Buck here, I'm the best roper in these parts. My skill and ability are only exceeded by my intelligence and good looks."This brought good-natured moans and groans from the other two.

"Kid, you just opened a can of worms, now we won't get any sleep all night listening to him talk about himself."

Buck chimed in, "we could leave him here and sleep in the barn."

Mike looked over at Buck in disgust. "I ain't sleepin' in no barn and especially with a blanket ass."

Buck's eyes flashed and then went deadpan again as he looked at Mike.

"Be careful white man or I'll cut your heart out, and eat it; if you got one."

"You better make a quick trip to the reservation and get help cause that's the only way you red bastards are gonna get the job done."

Buck sat up on the edge of his bunk his white knuckled fingers gripping the edge of the bed. Mike continued on as Ed climbed onto the bunk he had claimed above him and sat with his legs crossed. "The only way a damn Injun ever whipped a white man is when the odds were twenty to one and the white man was out of ammo."

"Mike, be careful, you're making him edgy, you know he's got a knife," Ron said as he stood up and walked over to the corner of the room where his bunk was located.

"I don't give a damn if he's got a machete in each hand, he ain't got balls enough to use 'em.

With that statement Buck reached under his pillow and pulled out a hunting knife about ten inches long. Letting out one of the most hideous screams Ed had ever heard Buck knife in hand dived on top of Mike as he lay on his bunk underneath Ed. The bunk recoiled from the impact and Ed grabbed hold of the side rail as the bed banged against the wall.

Mike let out a scream, "Oh God, he stuck me, I'm killed, he's cutting my guts out, I'm dying, somebody help me."

This seemed to excite Buck even more, amidst the warwhoops and screams the bed shook and recoiled while the fighting and struggling went on out of sight below Ed.

Ron yelled, "Run kid before he gets you."

Ed bounded off the bed and hit the floor running hard and fast, expecting at any moment to feel a hot burning sensation in his back. Ed ran wildly out the door in his stocking feet, under shorts and T-shirt. When he finally came to his senses he was standing knee deep in sagebrush, in the dark, halfway to the highway. "What am I going to do," Ed thought shakily. "I've got to get help," he could still hear a lot of commotion going on in the bunkhouse. "Buck is probably attacking Ron." By now Ed's active imagination could picture Mike laying there with his stomach ripped open pumping red blood over the bunk onto the floor and Ron getting cut and stabbed while he was trying to fight Buck off. Ed looked around and saw a light coming from the windows in Emil's house. Running hard Ed flew up to the front door and beat on it as hard as he could.

"Help, Help, Mr. Schmidt, please help!"The outside lights came on and Emil opened the door as he finished sliding the strap to his bib overalls upon his shoulder.

"What's the matter Ed?" Emil said as he looked questioningly at the scantily clad youth.

"Please," Ed panted, still out of breath from his heated dash," Buck just killed Mike with a knife and I think he's killing Ron right now."

"Wait a minute," Emil disappeared and returned in a few minutes with a double-barreled shotgun which he loaded as they hurried toward the bunkhouse. Walking up to it he kicked the door open as Ed cowered in back of him shaking so hard he could barely walk.

"What the hell is going on in here?" Emil said as he leveled the shotgun at the three men convulsing so hard with laughter that tears were running down their cheeks. Trying to get hold of his emotions Ron croaked out.

"Everything is alright Emil, we were just hooraying the kid." This immediately sent all three hands into screaming, slobbering fits of choking laughter. They were totally out of control, holding their sides or hanging onto the bunks for support as the snorts and roar of laughter intensified allowing their emotions to feed off the noise each other was making.

"Jesus Christ, you know you guys just scared the shit out of Marianne, I'd suggest you apologize to her in the morning."

Emil turned around mumbling to himself as he walked toward the ranch house and waited for the Sheriff's car that was speeding up the lane with red lights and siren on. Ed walked in and looked things over, there was no blood and Mike was completely intact except for his composure, which turned to a cross between whimpering and short fits of laughter as he hung onto the bunk for support.

Ed thought, "no one could laugh that hard and be hurt."

Ron was sitting on the floor in the corner laughing so hard he had to cross his legs to keep from peeing his pants. Buck was sitting on the edge of his bed holding his sides; convulsing and snorting like an upset hog. Ed was shaking so hard his legs were refusing to hold him up so he disgustedly staggered outside and sat down against the wall of the bunkhouse. After about a half an hour the laughing settled down to an occasional small outburst by one of the three. Sitting outside in his socks and T-shirt was getting to be a cold proposition. Ed sat there shivering as long as he could while he thought about the initiation he'd just been subjected to. Although it had all been in good fun held never been so scared in his life. When Ed jumped off that bunk and ran he lost all sense of reason until he came to and found himself standing among the sagebrush in his stocking feet. Even as his faculties returned he was borderline, if anything had happened at that moment it would have triggered the emotions all over again and he probably would have run until he dropped.

He thought to himself, "I guess one of the differences between a coward and a hero is which way he runs."It finally got so cold he felt he was going to freeze to death. Reluctantly he got up and went inside to face the music with his three practical joking roommates.

"Hey kid, your face is red, is that windburn from high speed running or what?" The laughter from the three jokesters was down to a dull roar now.

"Very funny, you guys scared the shit out of me."This brought a good laugh from the fun loving trio.

"Well, we didn't think you'd wake up the old man and call the sheriff."

"I didn't he was up and Mrs. Schmidt called the police."

"Damn, I sure hope we don't get on her black list," Buck said shaking his head.

"Uhuh, the groceries could get-pretty skimpy around here if we do," Mike replied as he sat down by the small table. Ron got up from the corner and sat down at the table with Mike.

'Look kid, don't take it so hard, it was all in good fun. A good laugh is hard to find out here and as long as nobody was hurt, forget it."

Ed rolled over on his bunk and turned his back to them, knowing he would never forget what they did to him tonight. Realizing that sooner or later his turn would come to pay them back, he started to relax and snuggled into the blankets. Going to sleep was hard, Ed tried to push the nights events out of his mind while his thoughts drifted back eighteen hundred miles to a farm in Wisconsin, a young boy with a large imagination and a burning desire to see the other side of the mountain, not realizing the pitfalls and hardships that lurked in places so innocently and glamorously depicted in all his readings. The memories and feelings were still too real and fresh in his mind to forget the last month of his life and what it had taught him. How different things can look to the optimistic imagination of a naive sixteen year old starting a journey. Lying on his bunk in that indiscriminate spot on the map, Ed's past thoughts finally caught up with the present and he started to think of tomorrow as he slowly drifted into sleep.

CHAPTER #4

IT WAS STILL dark as the four ranch hands trudged toward the porch of the main house to eat breakfast. Those that had 'em hung their hats up as they walked in the door and sat down on a bench at the long table. It had a freshly washed red checkered table cloth underneath the worn blue china plates and bowls set at each man's place, with a coffee mug and silverware alongside. The big coffee urn was already in place at the end of the table making the air smell good as it bubbled and burped. Everyone passed their cups to the man on the end, which happened to be Ed. He filled the cups and passed them back. About that time Mrs. Schmidt came out of the house with a huge steaming platter of golden brown pancakes

."Good morning boys, I didn't know if I'd see you here this morning or not, what with the Indian uprising and all."

"Uh Mrs. Schmidt, I uh, we would kind of like to apologize for causing you any concern or anxious moments last night. We was just pullin' a joke on Ed. We didn't mean for it to bother you and Mr. Schmidt," Ron stumbled and stammered as he tried to work up an apology.

"That's ok, Ron, there was no harm done, in fact I even fixed your eggs a little bit special for you boys this morning."

"Well thank you Ma'am, the three culprits grinned and chirped with relief.

"Morning," Emil said as he walked in from the kitchen and sat in his chair at the end of the table opposite the coffee urn

"You boys ready to go this morning?"

Everybody nodded and mumbled a yup or yeah as Emil's coffee cup made its way down the table. Headlights flashed across the windows as Jake pulled in and parked. Hanging up his hat as he walked in Jake strode over to the table and sat down next to Ron.

"You boys don't look none the worse for wear. Your hair is still intact and all the parts seem to be hanging off your bodies in the right places. According to the gossip my wife heard last night it was a real massacre."

"Aw Jake, we was just havin' some fun," Mike said.

"I know, but if I was you I'd be real careful where I went in town for a while, the whole county thinks your scalps are hanging on Buck's coup stick. When you go drinking you three better stick close in case Buck needs help."

"Darn, this sure got out of hand," Buck said, over the steaming coffee cup he was holding under his mouth with both hands.

Ed noticed the switch in the language. Around the bunkhouse or outside it would have been "damn", here there was a woman within earshot and no one swore in the presence of; or around a woman, especially the boss's wife, for any reason. Mrs. Schmidt walked in from the kitchen, the platter with the eggs on it in one hand and the other hand held the platter with the sausage, ham and potatoes on it.

"Oh hi Jake," she said as she sat the platter with the meat and potatoes in front of Emil and put a couple of nicely done over easy eggs on his plate. She moved over and did the same for Jake and proceeded on to Ron. He looked up and grinned as she slid a couple of slightly heated raw, sunny side up, and snotty looking eggs onto his plate.

"Here are those special eggs I promised you boys, look good, don't they?" Making her way through Mike and Buck with the same dose of cackle berries. The three men looked at their eggs staring back at them like two eyes filled with pus from a bad cold. Jake looked over at Ron's plate, shuddered and grimaced as he looked away shaking his head.

"Something wrong boys?" Mrs. Schmidt asked as she slid two perfectly done over easy eggs onto Ed's plate.

"No ma'am," came the reluctant answer almost in unison.

"Good you better dig in, I worked awfully hard on those eggs. I wouldn't want to see 'em go to waste."

Ed laughed out loud and thought to himself, "I'll never make the mistake of getting her mad at me." The meat and potatoes were passed and the platter with the pancakes followed. It was the first time Ed ever saw any one chop up their eggs, pancakes, potatoes and meat together until you couldn't tell one from the other. Now, everything looked like it had a cold. Next, they drowned the whole pile in sorghum syrup. Now, it looked like a scummy Wisconsin swamp. Emil and Jake were trying hard not to look at the disgusting mess so they could finish eating their own breakfast. The three jokesters were still choking it down when Mrs. Schmidt came out and asked if anybody wanted seconds on anything.

"I could use a couple more of those delicious eggs. I don't think I've ever had any better," Ed commented as three sets of eyes glared at him while Emil and Jake choked back a laugh.

"Why thank you Ed, it's nice to have someone here who appreciates my cooking."

"Uh, ours was real good too," Mike, said as he forced the last mouthful in.

"Good, then you'll want a couple more, the same way right?"

All three spoke at once, "Oh no ma'am, we're stuffed, we couldn't eat another bite."

Mrs. Schmidt smiled knowingly, "Gee, that's too bad, I've got blueberries and cream for dessert.

But, since you're so full I'll just divide yours up between Emil, Jake and Ed."

The three men looked at each other like trapped rats. If there was one thing they liked it was dessert, especially blueberries and cream. But, since they had committed themselves there would be no changing their minds. They were destined to go without dessert this morning.

"Thanks men," Emil said, "I really love, blueberries and cream."

"Yeah, me too," Jake said.

Ed kept his mouth shut; he knew it would just cause him grief later on if he didn't. But, he couldn't resist making loud slurping noises and smacking his lips while spooning the berries and blue stained cream into his mouth.

"God Almighty, I've heard hogs eat quieter than that," Ron said.

"You forgot better looking too," Buck said as he got up to leave.

"You boys go down to the corral and get things started, I'll be there in a minute," Jake said as he handed Ed his cup for a refill. Ed filled the cup and handed it back

"When is Les and Don gonna get here?" Emil asked.

"Probably tomorrow, they said they'd be here on Friday, but I doubt if they're sober yet. It'll depend on when they ran out of money."

"Well, when they show up, kick their asses sober if you have to, I want those cattle ready to ship by the end of the month."

Jake nodded, "no problem, we'll get it done."

Ed finished his berries and got up to leave.

"Wait for me outside and I'll walk down to the corral with you," Jake said as he looked up.

Ed nodded and walked out the door. About five minutes later Jake walked out and Ed fell in beside him as he walked toward the corral.

"I hear-the boys hoorawed you last night."

"Yeah, they had quite a laugh all right."

Jake stopped and turned to look directly at Ed. "If they didn't like you it never would have happened. I don't know where you're from but this is a hard, lonely life and fun is when and where you make it. So, don't judge 'em too hard, they were just givin' you a welcome to the ranch."

Ed smiled and looked into Jake's eyes. "I'd hate to see what would happen if they didn't like me."

"You're right," Jake said as he turned and walked toward the corral again. Ed fell into step as Jake spoke again. "Make sure when you have to take the kinks out of your string that you don't give up no matter how tough it is. Otherwise you'll look bad to 'em.

"Ok, I'll give it a try."

"There is no try, if you want to be accepted by 'em you'll do, no matter what." Stopping again and looking at Ed he said, "you don't seem like the ordinary drunken bums we normally get around here. You strike me as a pretty decent kid, but you got a lot to learn. If you got as much pluck as I think you do, you'll get along fine."

Ed was a little embarrassed and looked at the ground during Jake's fatherly outburst. When it was completed Jake turned and started walking while Ed tagged along like a puppy following his mother. As they rounded the corner of the barn and came into view of the corral he got his first look at how ranch horses are handled.

All four of Jake's horses were in the big corral. Three of them were tied to the fence and the fourth was led in between the two posts planted in the middle of the enclosure. Two open loops were laying on the ground with a man on each as the third man maneuvered the horse so his feet stood in the loops. When this happened the ropes were snapped tight and dallied around the posts as the helpless animal had his feet pulled out from under him. With his front feet pulled North and his back feet pulled South, the man who led him into his predicament literally sits on the head to prevent the downed animal from flopping around and injuring himself. Once the horse was stretched so he couldn't kick or struggle the ropes were tied off. The man that ran the rope on the front feet would cut corns and trim hooves. The man that ran the rope on the back feet would thin the tail, roach the mane and trim the forelock with his jack-knife. All in all the whole operation from knock down to release took about fifteen minutes. This went on all day except for the dinner hour when everything ceased while they ate. By three o'clock in the afternoon all of the strings were done. Only the loose horses had to be done.

"Ed, you work with Mike and Buck. Sit on the head when they get 'em down."

"Sure," Ed said as he moved to the spot where the two hands were shaking out the loop in their ropes. Meanwhile Emil walked into the corral to work with Jake and Ron.

"I sure wish those other two yahoos were here, this would go a lot faster," Jake said as he picked up his rope.

The first horse that moved to the right was front footed and dropped in a cloud of dust by Ron as Jake ran up, dropped his rope around the back feet and Emil dived on the head. With the head held down and the feet forced together by the tightened rope loop the animal lay reasonably still long enough to tie the ropes to whatever posts were handy so the hacking and trimming necessary could be accomplished. Seeing how this was done Ed was eager when Buck dropped the horse they were after. Holding down a horse's head is easy. They have very little strength moving their head and neck sideways. The weight of one man is more than adequate to prevent the animal from lifting his head off the ground. By suppertime only three head remained untouched. The ones that were recently manicured were tied with rope halters around the corral fence.

"We'll finish these three after supper," Jake said as the bell sounded.

Everybody walked to the cement walled, ten by ten foot building next to the bunkhouse that housed a shower, a trough sink, a heater and a toilet. After cleaning up they trudged off to the porch to eat supper. Beefsteak, boiled potatoes, creamed corn, spiced apples, gravy, fresh biscuits, corn twists, (corn bread sticks) coffee, milk, lemonade and homemade German chocolate cake made up the supper. Everybody ate like they had at least one hollow leg. In Ed's case he ate like he was one big hollow leg. After supper Jake went home to his wife and the four hands went to the corral to finish catching and trimming the three horses that were still loose. When the last horse was let up Ron turned to Ed. "Take the halters off everything in this corral and hang them in the barn."

"Ok, what about our strings in the other one?"

"Leave 'em tied, we'll be tryin' 'em tomorrow." Ron stated as the three senior hands walked off toward the bunkhouse. Ron, Mike and Buck were all at the table playing poker when Ed walked in the door.

"Hey kid, you want sit in?"

"I don't have any money," Ed commented.

"That's ok, we'll take your I.O.U.," Mike eagerly replied.

"Yeah, I suppose. I'm not very good though."

"That's all right, sit down and take ten dollars worth of chips." Ron pushed a couple of piles of red, white and blue poker chips over as Ed sat down.

Poker is a card game that can be played at just about any level of intensity. It's an extremely flexible game. The dealer can make new rules with each new deal. Rules change according to the dealer and geography; every area has its own rules of how to play the game. Poker purists have no use for wild cards and are severely regimented in the official rules of the game. Needless to say the men that invited Ed to sit down and play were not even remotely close to being poker purists. But, they did have some new blood at the table and were circling for the kill like a bunch of hungry wolves. When the evening was over, Ed only lost a dollar and eighty cents of the ten that he had been staked to. When the game broke up Mike spoke up as he stretched and yawned, "I sure am going to enjoy seeing you yahoos get dumped on your ear tomorrow."

"I'll tell you what Mike," Ron countered, I'd be willing to bet money on how many times you bite the dust."

"I'll take a piece of that action," Buck laughed as he crawled between the covers.

"Hey! Give me a break," Mike moaned, "you guys are going to destroy all my self confidence."

"Mike, you can't destroy something that isn't there, goodnight," Ron said as he peeled off his Levis. Mike flashed a toothy smile and turned off the light before he turned in.

Morning came to the sound of an old battered wind up alarm clock, as the first streaks of light were barely visible on the horizon. It was a chilly walk to the bathhouse as the morning frost shimmered in the half-light of the newly born day. The four men used whatever part of the facility that suited their needs and went to eat breakfast. It was an absolutely beautiful Wyoming morning. The sun would soon break over the Eastern horizon. The light it gave off prior to its appearance made everything appear purple and violet, etched in pink and rose while giving off an aura of gold. Combined with the light scent of sage in the air it made the quiet coolness of the morning fill the senses to the limit. An artist's brush would not have been able to do justice to what everyone here took for granted on a daily basis.

The sun was just breaking the horizon when the men came out from breakfast and headed for the horses waiting in the corral. Tied to the corral fence for a day and a half was not considered cruel or harsh, because a horse normally sleeps standing. It also gave the feet time to lose whatever soreness removing the corns and trimming the hooves had caused. The men walked past the barn as Ron peeled off and went inside.Everyone else continued to the corral and ran the extra loose horses into the corral the picked horses were tied in.

"I think I'll try the paint first," Jake stated as he lead the beast into the now empty enclosure and tied him to one of the posts in the middle. At the same time Ron walked around the corner of the barn carrying a saddle and bridle, which he placed on the top rail of the corral.

The saddle was western style, with a deep-dished, high backed seat and round wooden stirrups. The protruding swells at the front of the seat helped keep the rider in when he squeezed his legs underneath them. They looked like a profile of a large breasted woman. The saddle horn had been removed and the finish was a nut-brown color over a basket weave design on the skirts and fenders. Judging by the nicks and scratches, Ed figured it had been through the upcoming ordeal many times.

The bridle had a leather headstall with the same basket weave design. Attached to it was a "bosal" hackamore, this device is similar in shape to a snowshoe. It's usually dried rawhide braided to about the size of a garden hose and has a large balance knot where the two ends come together so a set of reins can be tied on without being pulled over the bulky knot. It fits loosely around the horses nose and mouth putting pressure on the tender part of the nose and the bone that runs vertically up each side of the back of the jaw. When first applied the coarse weave of the stiff rawhide cuts, just enough to make the horse more sensitive each time he tries to resist. The rope reins used when riding rough stock are usually thicker for a better grip than the narrow ones used to work cattle with.

Jake walked over and grabbed the saddle and hackamore off the top rail. Walking back towad the uneasy horse, Jake looked at Mike and said, "help me with the bosal and then ear him down while I saddle him and climb aboard, will you Mike?"

"Sure Jake," Mike acknowledged as he walked over to the horses head.

The two men gently slid the apparatus over the horses nose and then put the headstall in place. While Jake picked up the saddle Mike grabbed the horses ear and bit down on it just hard enough to make the animal stand still as Jake gingerly slid the saddle onto its back and cinched it down. Done properly, biting the ear doesn't cause any damage and makes the animal concentrate on the discomfort to his ear rather than what's being done to his back. Easing the cinch tight, Jake tied off the strap and gently lowered the wooden stirrup into place. Reaching over and putting the rope reins around the horse's neck he placed his foot in the stirrup and swung easily into the saddle.

"Let him go Mike," Jake said, as Mike spat out the ear and stepped back. Jake didn't look like he belonged on the back of a bucking horse. His clothes were the same as the first day Ed had met him except for his footwear. The farmer shoes had been replaced by high heeled boots and spurs. His belly still protruded and hung over the large round belt buckle, like a wrinkle on a bloodhounds face. He could have been mistaken for a pregnant woman had he shaved and put on a dress. The minute Mike released the animal it put its head down, humped its back and made a long, hard leap forward. Jake had a good hold on both reins and his feet were stuck into the stirrups all the way to the heel. Jake moved his feet forward to the animals shoulders and turned his toes out as the horse's head went down, letting the dull round spur rowels make contact. The horse responded by making each jump harder and longer. Every time the animal made a jump he would push off with his back feet and land on his front feet. Jake would counter by spurring back towards the flanks as the horse pushed off and then forward to the shoulders as the horse descended. Once the horses' motion was established the rider could get in rhythm and stay aboard easily. Ed was shocked at how athletic Jake really was. Big belly or not the man could definitely ride. The rodeo went on for a minute or less then, the horse just stopped bucking, put its head up and the show was over. Jake climbed easily off the horse as it stood shaking and breathing hard trying to catch its breath.

"Good ride Jake." Mike said as he walked up to help strip the gear off the sweaty horse.

Pulling the saddle off Jake said, "let's try the roan next". He made perfect rides on his next three horses.

The whole process took about an hour. It was something to see because the books had not even come close to describing what it sounded, smelled and felt like. The books never described how the horse rolls his eyes and tenses when he is lead in the empty corral and tied to the post. Nor does it give much detail on how the animal and humans are interacting when the horse is subjected to being bitten on the ear hard enough to make him stand still. Each horse like each human has its own level of pain, so no two horses will respond to the same amount of pressure. Knowing how hard or how soft to bite is something you feel through the physical contact of your arm, hand or whatever part of your body that is touching the animal, sensing the muscle movements as the horse tries to withdraw, be submissive, nervous, angry, aggressive or whatever. Each minute, muscle movement transmits a message to the holder and he responds in turn with complimentary action. The idea is for the animal to become distracted without making him passive and unable to think for himself. The person putting the saddle on has to react to the actions of the horse and holder. If he reads both of them correctly the saddle will be placed on the reluctant horses' back and cinched down with no resistance.

There is always the sweet sour smelling aroma of horse sweat, human sweat, dust and leather present in the air. At times it depends on how much action is taking place but it goes from faint to pungent. It soaks into your clothes and mixes with your own body odor to produce a scent that lingers even after you take a bath. Everyone present is absorbed by it even those waiting their turn on the edge of the corral, cheering rider, horse or both enthusiastically on.

When these two athletes meet in contest and one weighs in at twelve hundred pounds and the other at one hundred and ninety pounds you think it an uneven match. Not so, the reins and the saddle are the equalizer. The spurs are not sharp but extremely dull, the rowels are usually round and roll quite freely. They are not used to hurt the horse but to make him buck with a rhythmic motion instead of an erratic motion so the rider has a chance of staying on. To watch this performed properly is the same as watching a gymnast go through his routine.

The sounds made by the animal and rider is from extreme physical exertion and the frustration of trying to out do each other. The horse squeals and bawls when starting each jump or while he is in the air. He grunts and farts as the air is expelled when he lands and starts another jump. There is the sound of the rider grunting and groaning from the force of the horses' jumps. Stirrup leathers pop and snap. Spur rowels are jingling as the rider rakes the sides of the animal in time with his movements. If the horse succeeds in loosening the rider from his seat; then there is the silence.

When a rider unintentionally parts company with his contrary partner there comes a split second of total quiet as he does various ungraceful maneuvers in the air on his way to a collision with Mother Earth. When the two meet it's usually the cowboy that fares the worst. Landing in a big cloud of dust with a thud and a loud grunt the man will try to roll over and get on his feet in one motion while looking for the indignant steed so he doesn't get accidentally stepped on. If a rider gets dumped, the men on the sidelines will make great sport out of it and even help catch the animal so the fallen hero can remount and try again. Usually the men around the edge of the corral are very vocal. Always making innocent comments, cheering and whooping just for the excitement and enjoyment of living life to its fullest. This is what they call an "introduction period" for the horse and rider.

This test by fire is necessary because no one has the time or the inclination for formal introductions. Work has to be done and the weather will not hold back just to accommodate the efforts of those who wasted too much time on formal introductions. The horses learn fast and after two or three years they are familiar with how to work cattle. By then, the individual personality of the horses is visible, they can think for themselves in a given situation, some can't and some won't. Each horse is rated on his ability to react to a situation with the least amount of guidance. If rider and horse don't get along you won't get the best out of either one. This is why each man gets to pick his own string. He will normally pick the horses he knows and is compatible with.

The day wore on as Ed watched with intense interest, trying to pick up any pointers that would help him when his turn came. Ron and the other two hands only had three head each to ride since one of their strings of four had been used to run the rest of the herd in. Ron rode with the same showy style that he roped with. Lots of yelling and extra curricular exercises that emphasized how athletic and strong he was. Most of the time it was an unconscious act on his part. Although whenever he had the chance to show off he used it.

Next came Mike, he rode his first horse out with no problem. The second horse was bucking extremely hard. Mike had a strong grip and see sawed the animals head back and forth with the rope reins as the animal jumped and pitched. Suddenly the horse lost his balance and went down in a cloud of dust taking Mike with him. Everybody on the sidelines jumped to their feet and ran toward the cloud of dust that was emitting horse sounds and human obscenities

"Get off me you son of a bitch," could be heard as the men approached the enveloping cloud. About the same time came a loud horse grunt and Mike came crawling out on his hands and knees.

"Get your rope quick Buck, looks like we got a real wild Cayuse here," Ron yelled.

Jake joined with; "I'll get the spare saddle and strap it on if someone wants to try him. Wait a minute; that's not a horse, that's Mike."

Buck chimed in, "You could have fooled me, he looks like an ugly old horse I used to have a few years ago. Only difference is he didn't wear clothes."

"What happened to him?" Ron asked.

Buck grinned as he answered, "he got emphysema from breathing too much dust and I had to shoot him."

"Don't stand there running off at the mouth like a couple of old women, help me up," Mike said choking and spitting like a five pack a day smoker.

"Good Lord, not only does it slither like a snake and walk like a dog but it talks like a man also," Jake added.

Mike hacked in reply, "if you don't help me up out of the damn dirt, I guarantee you'll get to see, how it feels when I get on my pins."

Ed moved over and held out his hand to help Mike up.

"Thanks kid, I'll sure remember who my friends are after today," as he gave the other three a menacing look. By this time the horse had gotten to his feet and was standing head down bruised but unhurt.

"Hold him for me will you kid?" Mike said as he limped over to remount.

"Sure," Ed walked over and grabbed the reins of the traumatized horse. Ron and Jake walked over and grabbed Mike under each arm as Ron said, "here let us help you up on your big wild horse before he runs away and you can't catch him."

Mike shrugged them off, "back off or I'll break both of your heads."

The two men laughed loudly and walked off. Ed held onto the horses' head while Mike climbed in the saddle and gathered the reins.

He said, "let him go kid, he doesn't have anything left, he'll be alright now." Mike turned the horse and made him walk over to the fence where he got down and stripped the saddle and hackamore off him. Everyone turned to look at the dust cloud coming down the lane from the highway. A blue pickup truck could be seen careening wildly in front of the expanding brown haze as it drew closer and finally slid to a halt next to the corral. "Hey," someone shouted, "Les and Don are back."

The horse breaking was temporarily forgotten as everyone in the corral crawled over the boards and ambled over to the pickup. The doors flew open and the two men inside got out.

Les was about six feet tall, brown hair, medium build, glasses and seemed to have a quiet nature. He was a great musician and could play just about any musical instrument well. He was especially good on wind instruments and wrote a lot of his own music. At twenty-three years old he looked like a college professor who had given up his calling and turned cowboy. His attire and manners were somewhere in between both worlds. Neither of them realized it at the time, but a storm cloud between Ed and Les was already brewing on the horizon.

Don was thin as a rail, had a hawk nose, brown eyes (which were still blood shot from the drunk they had been on) and a scar from his hairline down the right side of his face to the center of his long extended chin. The scar was a memento of building fence. He was helping to stretch an 80-rod (1/4 mile) strand of barbed wire it broke and came back at him, cutting the side of his face as he dove for cover. He was lucky, if he had got caught in the wire it would have wrapped around him and he would have bled to death before anyone could get help for him. The only other thing that stood out on him was the huge oval belt buckle he was wearing. It looked like solid gold. It had a bucking horse and rider above an engraved silver ribbon that said, "1942 RCA WORLD CHAMPION ALL AROUND." Don, was extremely proud of what it represented and wore it more as a badge of honor than a keeper of his pants.

"Hey Ya'll." Don yelled as he stood up and stepped around the open pickup door into the small group of eager comrades. Shaking hands and slapping backs he greeted each one personally while Les leaned on the roof of the drivers side with a big grin on his face.

"You guys look just as ugly and smell just as bad as you did last month." grinning sarcastically at the four sweat soaked, dust covered specimen's standing before him. A collection of moans, groans and obscene gestures acknowledged the statement.

"Who's the new guy?" Don asked as he looked in Ed's direction. Before anyone had time to answer Don walked over stuck out his hand

and said, "I'm Don, that's Les." Jerking his thumb in the direction of the dusty pickup truck. "Who are you?"

"I'm Ed."

"You a greenhorn?"

"Green as grass in June" Ed stated as he looked into the steel blue eyes.

"Well, whatever you do don't listen to these three yahoos (using his thumb on Ron, Buck and Mike) they'll lead you astray, teach you about wild women, booze and all kinds of bad habits. You'll never learn what you need to know about being a top-notch hand from these bums."

Amidst the booing and cat calling Ron could be heard to say, "Oh Lord, give me a break. That's like the cat teaching the mouse how to hunt"

Don continued undaunted by the derogatory remarks that were coming faster and louder as he spoke. "Stick with me and Les and you'll be a top hand in week, at least you'll know as much as these saddle bums. (Using the errant thumb on his three victims once more). Les smiled and the three objects of Don's sarcasm stood grinning like school boys meeting their first date.

Turning toward Jake Don asked, any broncs left?" as he switched his gaze to the horses in the corral.

"Yeah, after you two get yours, we'll have about half a dozen spares. You should' a been here earlier you got the bottom half to choose from."

Don shrugged and grunted "huh"

"Alright," Jake said in a booming voice, "social hour is over. Let's get back to work. Don you and Les get settled and come back for your strings." Then he turned and followed the men back to the horse corral.

Mike still had to top off his third horse. After two laps of bucking around the corral rail the horse quit. It was fun to watch because the horse was a straightaway bucker and Mike spurred him nose to tail as gracefully as a pro-rodeo saddle bronc rider. The horse bucked high and every time he hit the ground dust flew from Mike's clothes. Next came Buck.

His rides were fun to watch. He rode without spurs and no matter how the horse bucked he made it look extremely easy to stay on. It was almost like watching a ballet, he became one with the horse. Now, it was Ed's turn.

"Which two do you want first?" Jake asked.

Remembering Ron's candid advice in the bunkhouse two nights ago Ed said, "I'll take the roan and then the bay. Glancing in Ron's direction Ed saw him grin and knew he had been wise to take his advice.

Jake led the roan in and snubbed him to the post in the center of the corral. Meanwhile, Ed walked over and grabbed the bucking saddle off the corral fence. Walking up to the wild-eyed horse Jake stopped him and said, "If you want I'll show you a few things about the saddle and headstall," making it half comment and half question.

"Sure," Ed said with a nod and a grin. With that Jake gave Ed a short seminar on how to saddle, bridle and ride a western cowpony for the first time.

"Mike take care of his head will you?" Jake said as he looked at Mike and nodded in the direction of the nervous horse tied short to the snubbing post. Returning his attention to Ed he said; "first of all when you go to saddle 'em always put the blanket under the saddle skirts and hold it like this," as he slid the sweat stained wool under the rough leather underside of the worn saddle. Holding the blanket and saddle Jake placed his hands underneath at each end, 'Make sure you don't let the blanket touch the ground or it'll pick up burrs. If that happens you'll get a. good ride out of a dog. (Referring to horses that didn't buck hard on first contact.) Most working cowboys feel if a horse doesn't have the energy to "fire" or buck when mounted the first time each day, then the animal won't have what it takes when you need to rope and hold a thirteen hundred pound steer or cow after you've been on his back all day.

"Make sure you don't get the off stirrup tucked under the saddle as you slide it on him. They'll usually stand still if you go steady." Jake described each move as he made it. "Don't drop the saddle on his back, just kind of roll it up and on." Jake said as he slid the saddle onto the animals back in one easy motion. "Once you get it in place grab hold of the cinch strap where it hooks to the rigging with your left hand. Put your right hand on his side just underneath the saddle skirt and slid it low and steady under his belly. Make sure you keep contact with him all the while your going for the cinch. When you get hold of the cinch your right shoulder should be up against him like this;" as he deftly demonstrated. "Someday you'll run across one that'll take a swing at you. If you're in close and up against him he'll push you out of the way. If your not you'll get nailed every time."

Ed nodded appreciation and acknowledgement. Jake continued: "Bring the cinch toward you let it run through your hand as you slide your hand and arm back along his belly. Keep the cinch in contact with him at all times. What you're trying to do is replace the feel of your arm touching him with the cinch. They're a little goosey when they haven't been handled for a while, so remember go light and easy. Now, slide your left hand down the cinch latigo. Get hold of the end and put it through the ring attached to the saddle. Here's where it gets touchy. Run the cinch latigo through the ring and take up the slack but don't pull it tight. Now, run the end around the front of the strap and back through the underside of the ring and out the top," (as he demonstrated) "bring the end down through the strap like this. It's just like you'd knot a tie when you go to Church. Leave it loose until you pull up the slack in the cinch. Once you've put the latigo through the cinch ring you've put the saddle at risk so get the slack pulled and the knot tight in one motion. If you don't and he moves, the saddle could roll underneath him and he'll kick it to pieces."

Ed nodded again. The headstall had been put on when the horse was led in and tied to the post.

"Measure your reins like this" as the burly foreman slung them around the horses' neck and stretched them to the back of the saddle seat. "When he has his head up it usually gives you an idea where to grab 'em. Right where they hit the back of the saddle. It'll be real close; you can make a minor adjustment once he starts to pitch. If you get to close a rein he'll pull you over his head. If you get to much rein you go over the back of the saddle when he jumps." Looking hard at Ed he volunteered one last piece of information.

"Make sure you put your foot in the stirrup all the way to the heel."

Then Jake turned and walked toward the corral rail where everyone but Mike was lounging in assorted poses coolly anticipating the coming event.

Ed looked at Mike standing with his hand resting on the taunt rope holding the straining horses head within a foot of the worn, rope burned snubbing post.

"C'mon kid get aboard we're burning daylight," Mike said as he grabbed the horse's ear and clamped down on it with his teeth. This usually does no permanent damage, but it does focus the animal's attention on a specific spot. Kind of like getting rid of a backache by hitting your thumb with a hammer. It's a short diversion that allows the rider to get in the saddle and get set before the horse ever realizes what has happened. Since Mike was facing Ed, he knew the minute Ed was mounted. Spitting the dusty ear out of his mouth and pulling the knot loose that held the animal's head, he stepped back to watch the show.

It took the roan a few seconds to realize he was loose and someone was on his back. When he did Ed could feel his back rise under the saddle. The roan's legs tensed, his head went down, he lunged forward and up. Even though Ed was prepared the suddenness of the move threw him back into the saddle and snapped his head with such unexpected force that it almost put him backwards over the saddle. He definitely would have "bit the dust" on the first jump if he had not listened to Jake and got the proper hold on the thick cotton rope reins attached to the bosal hackamore encircling the horses nose and jaw. The horse completed the jump by landing on his front feet and immediately catapulting himself into the air again with his back feet. This was repeated over and over eight or ten times with a steady sustained fluid motion.

The concept of riding a bucking horse is to get a rhythm going that matches the movements of the horse. When he jumps up and forward your body should move forward and your feet should move back towards his flanks and the back part of the saddle. The fulcrum is where your butt meets the saddle. At the crest of the jump the rider should be sitting ninety degrees to the back of the horse with his heels in the horses flanks or touching the very back tips of the saddle skirts. (In rodeo this is known as cantle boarding). As the animal descends the riders feet come forward and his body leans back. When the horse hits the ground with his front feet the rider should be leaning back, have his legs straight and his feet should be in the animals' shoulders at a point where the neck joins. His body should form a straight line from head to toe when the horse hits the ground. Horse and rider should be almost parallel. Ranch cowboys are not rodeo cowboys and ranch horses are not rodeo horses. Every cowboy has his own distinctive style of riding rough stock and as long as it gets the job done that's all that matters. The horses will buck and some of them are pretty good at it. But these are cow horses that know what they have to do. Bucking a little bit for most of them is similar to an athlete getting the kinks out before he goes to work. But, it still takes a certain amount of athletic ability by the rider to spontaneously match each move the animal makes.

Ed's ride was over in about ten seconds although to him it seemed like an hour. With each jump he could feel his precarious perch slipping farther and farther away. The first thing to go was the right stirrup and then the left. Then one of the reins fell away as he grabbed the front of the saddle knowing he was going to be introduced to mother earth. Just as he was about to make his unintentional exit the horse stopped dead in his tracks and put his head up. Ed had lost all his senses. It was like a gray cloud had covered his eyes and he couldn't see, feel, hear or tell which way was up or down. As his senses came back he opened his eyes and righted himself in the saddle. His hearing returned to the cheers and catcalls from the peanut gallery by the corral fence. Once Ed's equilibrium recentered he couldn't tell which was pounding harder his head or his heart. Looking around he suddenly realized where he was and what had just happened.

"I did it!" he said aloud to himself. His tensed lips turned into a large grin. Touching the horse with his heels he walked it over to the rail where the tack was hung between rides.

"We thought you was a gone goose for a while," Jake said as he held the horse while Ed stripped the saddle off.

"At least you stuck with him," Ron chimed in.

"Aw hell, he didn't ride him. The horse wasn't much and he quit jumping before the kid fell off," Les piped in. The silence for the next few seconds was as thick as pea soup. Everyone there except Ed gave Les some real hard looks.

"It was a good ride kid," Mike said looking Les right in the eye as he said it. Les glanced away as Don said, "Just remember to keep your feet forward when he goes for the ground. Keep your body straight up and your toes out all the time. You'll be alright."

"Thanks," Ed said looking over his shoulder at the group as he picked the saddle off the rail of the corral fence and headed for the snubbing post as Jake led the bay into the corral. Walking up to Jake Ed held the saddle anxiously as the horse was tied to the post with a quick release knot. Once the animal was secured Jake looked at Ed and nodded. Walking to the left side of the horse Ed slid the saddle and blanket slowly onto the back of the animal like Jake had shown him earlier. After the saddle was cinched in place and the reins were hung over the neck of the horse, Jake bit down on the ear. Ed swung into the saddle, got his feet set in the stirrups, grabbed the right spot on the reins and nodded. Jake spit the ear out and pulled the knot loose. It all looked like one motion and took less than fifteen seconds from the time Jake chomped down on the horses' ear to the time he spit it out and pulled the knot loose.

The bay lunged to the right and forward. Ed went left and back, he hit the ground with a thud and a loud grunt as dusty terra firma kissed him hard. Youth and resiliency won out, he was back on his feet in a heartbeat.

"Hey kid, he went theta way," someone from the sidelines good-naturedly yelled.

"I don't think he liked you. Maybe he would be nice if you kissed him before you got on."

Everyone whooped and laughed at the candid comments directed toward Ed's futile attempts to ride the frisky bronc. Ed looked over at the group and grinned widely. He knew this was hazing in the rawest form, but it was given in a spirit of camaraderie. Malice and small mindedness are not part of the make up of most true Westerners. Mike and Jake held the horse while Ed remounted.

"C'mon kid don't take all day," Jake hissed through ear-clenched teeth. When Jake released the horse he jumped straight forward and began bucking in a straight line as hard and fast as he could. The take off was becoming very familiar to Ed. He was actually starting to get a feel for the balance and timing it took to keep his seat. He was finally holding his own as the horse bucked across the corral. Until the bay came to the corral fence did a one hundred and, eighty degree turn in mid stride depositing Ed in a heap on the outside of the fence.The fence sitters really turned it on.

"Was it a bird? Was it a plane? Naw, as hard as it hit it must have been a meteorite. Look at that big cloud of dust. Man, I've seen airplanes that didn't crash and burn that hard. Let's go see if his hat will cover his belt buckle when he stands up. I'll bet he's six inches shorter."

The group of well wishers walked to the fence and peered over the rail just as Ed was grabbing hold of the bottom rail to help himself up.

"You alright kid?" Mike asked.

"Yah, I think so," Ed said as he shakily used the corral rails to steady himself while he climbed to his feet. Wiping the dust and dirt off his face he came up with blood on his hand. Looking at it he asked, "where am I bleeding?"

"Oh, you just got a little cut on your cheek. Don't worry about it," Ron said.

"C'mon boys, let's catch his horse we're burning daylight," Jake said as he started across the corral toward the horse standing at the other end.

Feeling physically abused Ed slowly climbed the corral fence and reluctantly headed toward the group holding his unwilling mount. Climbing aboard amid the comments of; "you can do it, ride 'em kid," and a few painfully encouraging slaps on the back Ed found himself back in a self-induced vacuum that seemed to make everything move in slow motion. He concentrated on the head of the horse and the outside world disappeared. Each move the horse made Ed was able to anticipate and counter. After what seemed an eternity the horse stopped bucking and put his head up. Returning to conscious reality Ed relaxed his frozen grip on the reins as he got a more comfortable seat in the saddle. He laid the left rein against the horse's neck and touched him with his heels making him turn right and move out at a fast walk. All of a sudden Ed was aware of the cheering, yelling and shouts of approval from the sidelines.

"Good job kid, Ride 'em cowboy."

Ed's chest bulged with pride as he looked in the direction of the fence and flashed an ear-to-ear grin of appreciation. The pain of a few minutes ago was now replaced with a sense of pride and accomplishment. Pulling up next to the men that praised and complimented his performance Ed stepped off the bay with a lightness that even surprised him.

“Nice ride, Ed.” Jake said as he held the horse while Ed stripped the saddle off.

“Thanks, he really bucked hard. I didn’t think he would ever quit.”

Although this wasn’t true according to bucking horse standards, that’s what it felt like to Ed.

“What do you want next?” Jake asked as he led the horse off to the holding corral.

“I’ll take the buckskin.” Ed replied scooping a handful of water from the water tank onto his dusty, sweat stained face.

Ron walked over and said, “Mind if I give you a little advice?”

“Not at all, you’ve been right about the horse’s so far,” Ed, said, complimenting the red headed cowboy. Ron nodded acknowledgement.

“Get a good seat on this one and when she goes for the ground get your feet well out in front of you. Lay straight back and keep your knees bent a little or she’ll hurt you. If I was you I would shorten those stirrups by one notch. Ed returned the nod and turned to adjust the stirrup leathers. When he was done Ed grabbed the leather seat off the rail and sauntered toward the center of the corral where Mike was waiting with the buckskin. Once the saddle was in place, and the reins were measured, Ed swung aboard.

“Let’er go.” Mike pulled the rope and stepped back. The mare stumbled backwards and stopped dead still. Ed was braced and ready but the mare just stood there. Ed gave Mike a confused look.

“Pull one rein or the other,” Mike said.

Relaxing a little Ed pulled the right rein slightly and the mare exploded. Leaping horizontally in the air she snapped into a vertical position at the height of her ascent. Her front feet were reaching for the ground while her body and back legs formed a straight line pointing at the sky. She went vertical so hard and fast that the saddle’s cantle slammed into Ed’s back as he hit his head on the horse’s rump. Even though he was in the right position for the descent, the violent snap and the mare’s contact with the ground had the same effect as a pile driver. Ed stiffened his legs and felt himself being catapulted out of the saddle over the side of the mare’s head. A loud grunt came when his lungs expelled air as he slammed into the ground. Hardly able to breathe amidst the dust and sweat Ed lay on the ground convulsing and choking while Mike and Jake ambled over to help him up. They each grabbed an arm and pulled him to his feet while he gasped for air.

"Relax kid, you'll be alright. Get your wind back by trying to take quick small breathes," as Ed spasmodically choked and gagged from the lack of oxygen and the cloud of dust that lingered in the air. Ed's senses came back into focus as his lungs filled with air and the dust settled. He could hear his cheering section doing their job with all the wit and sympathy they could muster.

"Hey, he must be one hell'va swimmer. Anyone that can swan dive with that kind of form should go to the Olympics."

(Screams of laughter by all) "Ya, but it probably would be easier if he used water to practice in." (More screaming laughter) This egged the bystanders onto more satirical commentary metered with good-natured veracity.

"If you knew where he was going to land you could put a mattress down to break his fall."

"How about if we just tied one on him?"

"Ya, but which side do you tie it on? He ain't real choosey how he lands." (Now it's screaming and choking laughter.)

Ed coughed and groaned as he was finally able to stand straight and take in a few good gulps of fresh air. He was really feeling beat up, and couldn't ever remember having been in a fight or done anything that hurt him this bad. Mike and Jake released his arms as Ron led the buckskin up for Ed to remount.

"You had to short of a hold on the reins. Give her about another hand width. She pulled you right out of the saddle." Jake said as he helped Ed into the saddle.

"OK, I couldn't even see her head.

"You were laying a little farther back than I would have but that's not critical."

Ed nodded and swung aboard the stiff legged horse Mike was holding.

"Let'er go," and the two men stepped back. The mare exploded almost instantly. This time Ed felt more in control. He wasn't aware of anything except the sky and an occasional glimpse of the mare's ears between his booted feet in the stirrups. He managed to stay aboard as the mare made about ten or twelve good jumps and then quit. Once again it seemed like a long time but in reality was only a few seconds. The mare stood sweating with her sides heaving while she sucked in large gulps of air. Ed got his bearings back and rode the buckskin over to the fence just as the dinner bell rang. Ed took the saddle off and Don lead the horse away. Everyone crowded around Ed and gave him their best piece of advice, encouragement or both. Even Buck, who up until now had kept the stoic Indian image slapped him on the back and said, "You could make a pretty decent rider someday. Ed really valued that comment because he knew they weren't easily given. Don walked up to the group, hung the headstall on the corral post and said, "Let's get washed up I'm hungry."

Everyone turned and headed for the washhouse talking loudly with two or three conversations going on at the same time. Once everyone was seated Mrs. Schmidt started bringing the food in from the kitchen. There were steaming platters of antelope roast, (antelope are extremely plentiful in this area of Wyoming.) baked and sweet potatoes, corn on the cob, spinach, baked beans, gravy, fresh baked bread, two kinds of home made jam, honey, coffee, water, juice and milk. Slim and trim, as most ranch hands are they eat like there is no tomorrow.

Large plates of food disappeared as the conversation relived the days events.

"How far along are you?" Emil asked Jake as he filled his plate with food.

"Ed's got one left and Les and Don still have their four head to do."

Emil nodded as he shoved a fork full of roast antelope into his mouth. Everyone else buried themselves in their meal. It would have been bad manners to converse until the boss and the foreman were through discussing the work at hand.

"We should be ready to go by noon at the latest," Jake added. Finishing his sip of coffee Emil sat his cup down as he spoke.

"If you leave here right after dinner you should be able to have the horses at Rocky Butte by nightfall. We'll take the flat bed and have everything set up when you get there."

"OK, I'll try to get out of here as early as I can. Is the truck ready to go?"

"Yea, I took it in the first of the week and had George go through it. I picked it up yesterday and it runs like a top."

"OK, we'll meet you at Rocky Butte by dark," Jake said as he resumed eating.

"What time do you want to leave in the morning?" Ron asked Emil.

"We'll get out of here as soon as the truck is loaded. I want you boys up and at it by four in the morning," Emil stated as he looked down the table at his six ranch hands. Ed didn't quite understand everything that was going on but he knew if he kept his mouth shut and ears open he would find out. The rest of the meal consisted of small talk about the morning's events. Who was going to do what tomorrow and Ed's upcoming showdown with the sorrel. After dinner everyone including Emil, showed up at the corral. Ed thought this as kind of odd because Emil hadn't been there for any of the other rides. Mike led the sorrel into the corral and tied him to the post as Ed walked up with the saddle.

"Take a real deep seat on this one," Mike said as Ed was pulling the cinch tight. "Give him a second and pull the cinch tight again. There's enough daylight under the back of that saddle for a cat to stand up."

Ed looked. Sure enough, the sorrel had bloated himself with air and arched his back hard enough that there was a four inch gap between his spine and the back of the leather skirting that the saddle seat was fastened to. Ed tensed as a small knot started to form in his belly. (Otherwise know as a gut reaction.) But ignorance being bliss he nodded and pulled the cinch after a minute or so. The animal deflated with a grunt and the saddle sat flat on his back.

Throwing the reins over the sorrels' neck Ed noticed that he wasn't straining against the rope like the other three had done. He just stood there with his head hanging down leaving slack in the rope. Ed looked at Mike waiting for him to bite down on an ear.

"Go ahead kid, climb aboard he's OK but be ready."

Ed shrugged and anxiously climbed into the saddle. Something was not quite right here. He wasn't long in finding out either. Mike pulled the rope. The next thing Ed knew he was laying on the ground next to Mike looking up at him.

"Damn, you don't waste any time do you kid?" Ed looked up at him with a dazed expression.

"What happened?"

"You went one way and your horse went the other way."

Ed sat up and looked around. The sorrel stood about twenty feet away with his neck straight out from his body and one back legged cocked at he ankle in a relaxed position. The ends of the reins were on the ground and he was apparently unconcerned at what had just happened.

"Is he for real?" Ed asked Mike as he looked at the unsympathetic animal.

"Yea, I think he likes you though," Mike smirked, "Normally he doesn't relax like that."

"I'm impressed."

"Good, keep thinking that way. You're gonna need it."

Mike gave Ed his hand and helped him to his feet. They walked over to where the horse stood and Mike said with a grin.

"He ground ties real good. He'll stay wherever the reins hit the ground. It's just that sometimes he thinks a little different about how things should be done when you're on his back."

"Oh great, now I'm really impressed."

Mike gave a short laugh as he grabbed the reins and swung them around the sorrels' neck. Instead of biting down on an ear he simply stood there holding the reins next to the bosal knot under the horses jaw.

"Go ahead, climb aboard kid, he'll stand quite until I turn him loose."

Mike was right. Ed swung into the saddle got both feet set in the stirrups, took the right hold on the reins and lifted his arms to take up the slack as he nodded his head. The whole world seemed to go topsy-turvy with that nod. There was an extremely violent snapping motion. Something slammed into Ed's crotch and before he could scream in pain he felt a searing pain run from the side of his nose down the right side of his face just before his head and shoulder collided with the ground. Stiffening into the fetal position and puking up his dinner Ed lay convulsing in the dust of the corral. A couple of voices that sounded like they were talking in a whisper said, "you alright kid?" Ed opened his eyes and realized that someone was leaning over him as he lay there holding his crotch.

"Just lay still and get your bearings back you'll be alright."

Between the pain in his head and the pain in his crotch, Ed felt like his whole body had just been run over by a truck, a very large, fast moving truck. Eventually the pain subsided enough for him to speak in a shaky, tenor voice.

"Where am I? What happened? Oh God, I hurt.

Jake replied, "you just kinda went upside down in the saddle and ate a little bit of it on the way down."

Ed tried to sit up and fell back in a wave of pain.

"Will I ever walk again?" Ed agonized in a high baritone voice.

"Probably, you might talk with a little higher voice for a while though." Jake said as he poked Mike in the ribs with his elbow and grinned. "C'mon, let's get you up and walkin, that'll help take the kinks out."

The two men reached down grabbed the young man under the armpits and lifted him up still in the fetal position.

"Now c'mon Ed you got to put your feet on the ground were not going to carry you around like this."

"Do I have to?"

"Yup."

Gingerly Ed extended his legs toward the ground. Once the appendages touched terra firma the men relaxed their grip and allowed Ed to put some weight on his wobbly legs. Other than the pain in his crotch, back, sides, shoulders, nose, cheek and head he didn't feel to bad. The pain was a sharp sting in some places and a dull ache in others, Ed hoped as soon as it all equalized his body would start to work properly. The two men forced him to make a few stumbling steps forward as Ed whined;

"Oh God, I think I'm gonna puke again."

"Anywhere you want kid, just keep walking," Mike's consoling words came as he helped guide Ed around the dusty corral. After about two laps around the corral Ed moved easier. The waves of nausea and pain were subsiding and becoming more localized as his unwilling legs steadied and became controllable. Finally the three men walked over to where the sorrel was ground tied with his head down and relaxing.

"Hey look kid, you got him plum wore out," Jake said with a sarcastic grin.

"Yup, I don't know if we ought to let you try him again," Mike bantered as the horse blinked a fly off his half closed eyelid. Ed was mentally agreeing with Mike, but before he had a chance to vocalize his thoughts Jake said;" but Mike, now that Ed's got the upper hand, he should get on him and make one lap around the corral. He has to let the horse know who's the boss, besides, we wouldn't want him to lose his confidence, would we?"

"I agree, we definitely wouldn't want him to lose his confidence." Mike said as he slapped Ed on the back. Ed was still in favor of the earlier idea. While the two men stood on either side of him looking directly at him Ed's body was saying no, no, no, but his mouth said; "OK, help me up" and mentally all he could hear was DUMB, DUMB, DUMB; DUMB, to the tune of Beethoven's 5th. Jake reached over and grabbed the reins, swung them over the horses' neck as the sorrel opened his eyes and stood straight on all four legs. The mental picture of cocking a loaded revolver flashed through Ed's mind as he stuck his foot in the stirrup and climbed aboard. Grabbing the reins, he set his feet in the stirrups and weakly said "OK" never believing for a minute that the horse was through bucking. The sorrel took two steps forward, stopped and turned his head back as if to see whether or not his so called rider was still on his back. Then he straightened out his neck and went to bucking with a vengeance. Ed stayed aboard until the horse sucked back on the third jump and put him head first over the saddle onto the top of the pitching animals neck. Just as Ed's face came even with the sorrels ears the animals' head came up smashing into Ed's face. A loud crunching sound was all Ed could hear as his nose and mouth went numb. Instinctively he wrapped his arms and legs around the horses red neck as he slid underneath. There was a split second when Ed looked the animal right in the eye and felt his hot breath on his chest before he lost his hold and plowed into the ground on the back of his head and shoulders. Ed rolled over and got to his knees as he bent over choking and spitting out the dusty blood that was pouring into his mouth and running down his chin. Screams of laughter and encouraging words poured in from the sidelines as two sets of hands picked him up again and walked him to the water tank.

"Wash off his face and see what's broke," Jake said as Mike grabbed the wrecked youth by the back of his belt and the hair on his head. Moving close to the water trough Mike dunked Ed's head under water and pulled him back up after a short submersion. He gently felt Ed's jaw and cheekbones.

"He's pretty scratched up, his jaw and face is OK but his nose is broke and he's got some loose teeth in front."

Jake looked at the sorry sight in front of him. "Ed, you want to keep trying that horse or do you want to give him up?"

Ed had finally gotten to the point of being so beaten up that he was numb. Football players, rodeo riders, and other athletes that participate in physically demanding sports experience this feeling. The pain doesn't bother you until you stop doing whatever it is your doing and stiffen up. Then you have to start all over again and it hurts worse than before. Ed had never experienced pain at this level and nodded, misunderstanding the question because of his dazed condition.

Jake turned toward the group and said, "Anybody want the horse, Ed said he would give him up."

It was as if the world had come to an instant stop. Laughs and gestures died like you'd squash a bug as everyone turned and looked stone faced at Ed bleeding all over himself. No one moved or spoke, the silence was deafening. Finally Ed shoved Jake aside and walked toward the sorrel mumbling unintelligently through the blood running out of his nose and mouth. Walking up to the horse he threw the reins around its neck just as Mike walked up and grabbed the headstall.

"You got guts kid, good luck."

Ed didn't even respond as he climbed aboard. Four more times Ed was thrown from the back of the cantankerous horse. Finally the dinner bell rang, Ed pulled the saddle and hung it up for the night.

Washing up was just a matter of walking into the hot shower fully clothed. The hot water felt good, as it washed away the dried blood and dust. After everybody had gone to supper and the hot water ran out, Ed dragged his bruised and battered body to the bunkhouse removing soggy clothes as he went. By the time he walked through the door of the log shack all he had to do was remove his boots and pants. It took all the effort he had to undress and climb into his top bunk. He was so totally exhausted by the time he made the ascent that he rolled on his back and lay there naked arms and legs out spread, eyes wide open, too hurt to even sleep. Lying on the coarse woolen blanket Ed could hear the talk and occasional laughter mixed with the gentle clatter of the dishes coming from the screen porch through the open bunkhouse door.

"I'll tell you, that kid has got guts. He really took a beating out there today and wouldn't quit," Mike said as he shoved a wad of food in his mouth.

"I thought he was going to do alright after the ride he made on the buckskin. That sorrel sure knocked the stuffing out him. I don't know if he'll be able to make it up on his back, let alone stay with him." Ron said as Mrs. Schmidt walked into the room.

"Ron how is Ed? Is he going to come up for something to eat?

"No ma'am, I think he went to the bunkhouse, he's beat up pretty bad. I don't imagine he feels to much like food right now."

Giving Emil a concerned look the rancher's wife said, "Oh Emil, do you think we should call a doctor?"

"No, he's bruised pretty good but nothing major is broken. He'll need the same amount of time to heal whether the doc looks at him or not," Emil said as smiled faintly and gently waved her off. After she left the room Emil looked at the group seated at the table and said, "Make sure the boy doesn't get seriously hurt. I got about two hundred dollars invested in him that I want to get back before he quits."

Emil was not being cold hearted. Ranch hands move from job to job like the wind blows and this is what he was referring to.

"I'll tell you this he'll either ride the horse, or the horse 'll kill him. I've seen this before rodeoing. You got guys out there that are determined to make the ride but don't know what they're doing. They either figure out how to loosen up real quick or they get busted up real bad. I think this kid is one of them." Don said not letting go of his knife and fork as he put his hands on the table and looking up from his plate as he said his piece.

Les spoke up in a less serious voice "I thought I was going to get sick from laughing at the way he landed on sorrel's neck before he took that nasty hit in the face." Everyone chuckled. "Yea," Les went on, "I wish I would have had a camera. It would have made a great picture those two looking at each other eyeball to eyeball." Everyone chuckled again.

Mike chimed in, "I'll tell you something' though. If he does have enough pluck to ride this horse, I hope I never have to fight him." Mumbling their agreement everyone looked at Mike and nodded.

Ron said, "You know, I've never seen that horse turn on the way he did today. I don't know if it's because the kid is green or not but he sure was acting' funny."

"That horse always acts funny. If anyone can figure him out it would be a miracle." Emil said emphatically. "I think this is going to be his last year here. He's probably worth more as dog food for all the hospital bills I've paid on riders that thought they could handle him."

"Aw, he's a good horse he just needs someone 'that can keep up with him," Ron said as he picked up his coffee cup.

"Well, why don't you take him and save Ed the wear and tear?" Les said as the table talk went dead silent. Ron flashed a big toothy grin as he riveted an icy stare on Les.

"We may have to talk about that later, bucko."

After a moment of intense silence Ron continued; "I had him the second year I was here. Remember?" The red head said as he shifted his gaze to the rest of the men at the table. They all nodded their acquiescence. "I thought it was just the guy that picked him the year before. I still believe the right man would have that horse doing cartwheels, but it sure wasn't me."

Buck broke in with one of his rare comments. "This horse is (Indian word for crazy), he has a bad temper and doesn't know how to control it. He is like a young warrior in battle who loses control so badly that his own people must stop him from destroying himself and his comrades around him." Everyone looked at Buck with mouth agape.

"Good Lord Buck, I didn't think you knew more than half a dozen words. That's the most I've ever heard you say at one time." Emil said with a surprised look on his face.

"Oh he can talk plenty if he wants to. Especially when him and Jack Daniels goes out together."

Mike volunteered as everyone laughed.

"Well I don't know about you gents but I think I'm gonna get cleaned up and turn in tomorrow's gonna be an interesting day," Ron said as he swung his legs from under the table, over the bench seat and stood up. "Night all," Ron said as he moved toward the door. Everyone mumbled a return of some sort or another.

"Oh Ron;" Mrs. Schmidt called as she walked out of the kitchen and into the back porch mess hall. She was carrying a small cardboard box with a towel laid over the top to keep the heat in. "Please take this to the bunkhouse and try to get Ed to eat something. He must be very hungry. It will make him feel better if he eats something warm."

"Yes ma'am," Ron replied as he turned to receive the box of food. Mike spoke up as the kind woman walked past him at the table on her way to give Ron the box of food.

"If you don't mind Mrs. Schmidt, I'll take the food down to Ed while it's still hot. That way Ron can take his shower before he goes to the bunk house."

The three parties looked at each other a moment, then Ron nodded and said, "thanks Mike."

Mrs. Schmidt handed the warm cardboard box to the burly man and said, "sure Mike, I know he'll appreciate it more if it's warm. "

Mike got up box in hand and said his good nights as he walked toward the door. "Hey Don, give me a hand will you," he said as pushed the screen door open with his backside. Don looked up from his seat at the table and said "sure" getting the last gulp of coffee before he put his cup and napkin on the table. Once outside Mike turned to Don and said, "look, we gotta help this kid or he ain't gonna make it."

Don nodded, "what can we do?"

"According to that pie plate your wearing on your waist your one hellva bronc rider. There's gotta be something you can show that boy that'll help him to stay aboard that horse.

"Well, I don't know, I guess it depends on how bad he wants it and how good he listens."

"I don't care what it takes you make it happen."

"Is that a threat or are you asking?"

"I'm askin. Look, I like this kid, I think he's got guts. He reminds me a lot of when I was his age. I wish someone would've helped me when I really needed it. This kid is all heart, he'll do if it kills him. I just don't want to see him get hurt bad that's all."

"I'll do what I can Mike, you getting a little soft on the kid?"

"I just like his pluck that's all, and if you repeat any of this I'll wring your neck you hear?" as Mike stepped in front of Don and put his face close to the tall thin man's face.

"OK, OK, relax I ain't gonna say anything."

Mike nodded and they continued their walk to the bunkhouse.

The first thing they saw as they walked in the open door was the lump of wet jeans and soggy boots in a pile next to Mike's lower bunk. Ed was lying on the top bunk on his back. Naked and spread-eagled he stared at the ceiling moaning softly. Two black eyes offset by a swollen ugly looking two inch cut on right cheek highlighted the bruises plastered all over his face. The misshapen and discolored nose was still oozing occasional drops of blood onto the cut and swollen lips that were rapidly drying out and cracking.

From his hairline to his ankles he was black and blue.

"Man, he sure looks tough, don't he?" Don said as he surveyed the sad condition of Ed's face and body. "Is he gonna be able to ride tomorrow?"

"He will if we help him," Mike replied.

"Well, I'm game if you are," Don said with a shrug.

"Go get a bucket of really hot water from the wash house. We'll clean him up and soak some of the pain out if we can. I've got some drawing salve that's pretty good."

Don disappeared out the door and Mike opened his footlocker as Les walked in.

"Good God is he ever a miserable sight," Les said as he walked past the big man and the prostrate wretch moaning on the top bunk.

"Ya, Mike replied. "Hey, would you do me a favor and start a fire in the stove there?"

Les looked at Mike, "what for?"

"I want to heat a few rocks, wrap 'em in blankets and put 'em in bed with Ed to see if we can get him loosened up for tomorrow."

"My, aren't we getting motherly?"

For a man of his size Mike proved to be very quick as he stood up from his foot locker, spun around, covered the ten foot gap between them in one motion, grabbed Les by the front of his shirt and hit him in the face before he knew what was happening. Lying on the floor running the back of his hand across his bloody lip he looked up at Mike standing over him fists clenched, ready to do battle.

"Relax Mike, I was only kidding. I'll build the fire."

Mike lowered his clenched fists and turned back to his footlocker as he mumbled a sarcastic "thanks."

Les slowly got to his feet. All the while giving Mike dirty looks while his back was turned.

The bunkhouse door opened and Don walked in carrying a steaming hot bucket of water. He noticed the blood running down the man's chin as Les walked past him on his way out to get firewood. He looked at Mike pawing through his footlocker and thought better about saying anything. The way things were going this could get out of hand real easy. Don was not afraid of a fight but he knew he was no match for the big man. Mike stood up with some tins of Cloverine salve in his hands as Don set the steaming bucket on the floor next to Mike and Ed's set of bunk beds. Throwing the tins of unopened salve on the bottom bunk Mike said, "Hey kid, you feel like eating anything? Mrs. Schmidt sent over some hot soup."

Ed emitted a loud unintelligible groan.

Well, it sounded like a yes to me," Mike said as he pulled the towel off the top of the cardboard box. Inside were six more towels folded and neatly packed around the container of soup.

"What a woman, Emil sure is a lucky man," Mike said as he dunked a couple of the towels in the hot water of the bucket. Ringing the excess water out of the towels he gently laid them over Ed's bruised and battered body.

"We'll put these on and replace 'em as they cool," Mike said talking over his shoulder to Don. "Wet another towel and start dobbing his face with it. Get his lips warm and moist so I can feed him some soup. I'll replace these towels and then start feeding him."

Once the towel swap had been made Mike grabbed the soup container and started spooning the warm broth into his bruised mouth. Les walked into the room with an armload of split firewood and a clean Ron followed him through the door. Ron walked to his own bunk, laid his shaving gear down walked over to Ed's bed and said to Mike.

"You keep feeding him and I'll change the towels."

Mike nodded, "Don can you find a half dozen rocks? Something that won't crumble or blow up in the stove."

Don nodded, "about soup bowl size?"

"Yeah."

Les got the fire burning nicely as Don started carrying the rocks in. "Well, that's the last of the soup," Mike said as he scrped the last spoonful from the bottom of the bowl. Ed painfully moved his eyeballs toward the men attending him.

"Thank you," he whispered hoarsely."

"Hey, don't thank us kid, if we don't get you going then we gotta do your share of the work. We're just thinking about ourselves," Mike said lying through his teeth.

Buck walked in and sat on his bunk, his black eyes taking in the proceedings. The room started to get warm, very warm. Warm enough that the men stripped down to their long johns or shorts. Except for Buck who was naked once he took off his shirt and jeans. After about two hours of hot towels Mike said, "someone get the rocks out of the stove and wrap three to a blanket so we can lay them alongside him. Meanwhile the cloverine salve was liberally administered. Once this was done the rolled blankets with the hot rocks in side were laid vertically on each side of him. Next a blanket was laid over Ed's body covering him to his chin. Even though it caused him to sweat some he could feel the heat relaxing his stiff and sore muscles. As Mike and Don put the last rock filled blanket in place and covered everything with another blanket Mike said, "How do you feel now?"

Ed looked at the big man and replied in a shaky voice, "better, at least some of the pain is going away."

"Good we'll keep you warm all night. In the morning put on a lot of clothes so you don't lose any body heat. You can shed 'em as you need to. Make sure you eat a good breakfast even if you don't feel like it. If we can keep you from stiffening up while you get your rest you'll be OK." Mike looked at Don and with a nod toward the motionless patient "your turn."

Nodding, Don stood by Ed's bunk and started to talk. "Look, this horse is strong and quick. The problem is he knows what he's doing and you don't. Those other three you got in your string put together couldn't buck on their best day as good as he can buck on his worst day.

What you learned from them isn't much but it's all you got and it will help you some. Couple of things I noticed when I saw you ride. You're too tense. This slows you down and limits your reaction time. Not only that but you don't open your eyes all the way. You've got to watch his head if you're gonna stay in time with him and you can't do that if you squint or close your eyes. You gotta concentrate when you get on him. Get loose, keep your eyes wide open and don't be afraid to get bucked off. In the morning I'll get you in the saddle, set it for you and show you how to spur. I think you can ride this horse if you can learn how to get in time with him." Don patted Ed's arm gently and walked toward his bunk at the far end of the room.

About the same time Buck got up off his bunk, walked over and stood by Ed's bedside.

"My father was a very brave man. He gave me this when I came back from my first medicine dream. He said it was very powerful medicine and if I wore it into battle it would protect me and make me stronger than my enemies. My father did not lie to me. It has protected me at the battle of Casino and the landing at Normandy on "D" Day. Wear this tomorrow and you will be strong." With that he took a small leather pouch tied to a piece of rawhide lacing from under his shirt. It was about the size of a large silver dollar, containing objects that made the leather bulge slightly. He untied the thong from around his neck, slipped it under Ed's neck and tied it. Completed he simply turned around, walked back to his bunk and sat down.

Lying on his bunk racked with pain Ed was totally dumbfounded by the tough gentleness found here. These men would beat each other senseless at the slightest breach of self-determined etiquette. Yet would put their life on the line to save an animal or human in distress. Happy go lucky and relishing a good fight whether it was man or beast, they were as honest and dependable as the earth itself. Footloose and fancy free yet as proud as a new father and as open as a little child. The contrasts were hard to fathom. Remorsefully, Ed realized this was a dying breed. All night Ed drifted in and out of sleep while the men took turns keeping the fire going and the warm rocks replaced in Ed's bed. Even though it was extremely uncomfortable the door was never opened and no one complained. Morning came with a quiet darkness familiar to people who get up early. The lights came on and

Ron shouted "C'mon let's get cleaned up and start loading the truck." Everyone but Ed got out of bed and dressed enough to make the trip to the washhouse. As they filed out the bunkhouse door Mike walked over to Ed's bed.

"C'mon kid, get up and get dressed. We'll see you at breakfast. Remember, put on lots of clothes. Don't lose that body heat or you'll stiffen up." He smiled and walked out the door closing it behind him.

Ed lay still afraid of the consequences of moving. There didn't seem to be any pain just a bit of stiffness. Since he had been pinned to his bed by the restrictive blankets and warm rocks, he didn't know what to expect. "Well, let's try something simple, thinking out loud to himself. Wiggle your toes and fingers. HMMMM, that worked pretty good," he thought after the exercise was completed. "Now, let's try more." It wasn't until both knees were about a foot off the bed that the pain hit. His feet stopped sliding on the sheets as the shock hit him like a whiplash. He screamed through clenched teeth loud enough to wake the dead as the tears spurted from his eyes and the sweat soaked him instantly. After what seemed an eternity, the convulsing pain reached a tolerable level and Ed was able to relax enough to try again. While he lay trying to build enough courage to make his next move, his thoughts were on his roommates' group departure from the bunkhouse.

There wasn't room enough for everyone to use the washhouse at the same time. Two of them would have to wait outside in the cold gray dawn. Usually they drifted over one or two at a time and then finished getting dressed in the bunkhouse before they went to breakfast. He thought Mike was going to stay and help him but he had left also. Lying in his own misery the light finally flashed. The men weren't being thoughtless or uncaring. They knew what pain Ed would be going through and they allowed him the dignity and privacy to cry, yell or react to it without an audience.

Gritting his teeth Ed tensed as he started the upward movement of his knees again. The pain made him sweat and catch his breath but it was nowhere near as severe as it was initially. "Now all I have to do is let my feet and legs slid off the edge of the bed as I sit up," he thought. It took all of the sweat soaked, breath-holding effort he could muster. Stifling a pain filled scream through clenched teeth he finally made it to a sitting position with his legs dangling over the edge of the top bunk. Normally he would simply push off and leap to the floor in a single bound. Those five feet may as well have been five miles. It just wasn't going to happen this time. He had to figure a way to reach the floor without any hard or sudden moves that the excruciating pain would make uncontrollable. A bad landing from the top bunk on the wooden floor could compound his problems. He lay on his back and rolled onto his stomach, so from the waist down he was vertical to the floor. Searching with his feet he found the bunk below his. Getting a grip on the far side of the bunk he was laying on, he eased himself toward the floor as gently as he could until his feet were firmly planted on the bunk below. The pain was nauseating but becoming bearable. Ed lay still until the nausea subsided and he felt like he could move again. The next step required bending one leg while the other one slowly reached for the floor. Hanging on with sweaty, white knuckled hands to the round pipe headboard, Ed got one foot on the floor and then the other. Teeth clenched, and sweating, Ed held his breath and muffled the screams that accompanied each move. Finally he was standing flat footed on the floor of the bunkhouse with a death grip on the bunk above. He was weak and shaky but at least, he was upright and on his feet. Ed let his head lay on the top bunk until be regained his composure. Turning slowly from the bunk he moved like a Frankenstein monster as he clumped to the nail holding his shirt and jeans that someone hung up to dry overnight. Luckily, he found some underclothes close to the top in his duffel bag leaning against the wall. Getting dressed with one hand holding onto the rail of the top bunk was a slow, deliberate, careful maneuver. But, it got the job done, and didn't require sitting down. It was a long walk to the porch where breakfast was being served. By the time Ed got to the house he was able to put his arms down and make the rest of his body act with some resemblance of normalcy. He hadn't cleaned up or combed his hair. He knew he looked bad, but he was resigned to mask as much as he could any external signs of pain in front of those that he would be eating breakfast with. The half dozen stairs up were hard, but the handrail helped a lot. Ed walked stiffly into the room as everyone greeted him without bringing attention to his lameness. Ed thought, "the men must have really taken their time cleaning up this morning." Otherwise by now the meal would have been down to the blueberries and cream stage. Ed sat down slowly on the end of the board seat and gingerly swung his legs underneath.

Ron was talking to Emil; "we've got about an hour to go before the truck is loaded.

Emil looked up from his plate, "OK, Marianne and I'll start filling the grub box.

Everyone avoided looking directly at Ed as he ate his breakfast. His bruised and battered face made every mouthful of his breakfast painful and difficult to eat. Even though he had arrived late and ate slowly, everybody else seemed to finish at the same time so desert could be served to all. No one seemed to pay any attention to how slowly and shakily Ed refilled the passed coffee cups.

In some circles making Ed continue his expected breakfast duties in his condition would seem insensitive and uncaring. Not so, these people are fiercely independent. They have a keen sense of pride in not asking for help but in giving it even at their own expense. They keep their word no matter what the circumstance and they are willing to stand by their beliefs. Respect for another person's privacy is paramount. You are taken only as you prove yourself to be. If you are honest and upright that's how you'll be treated. If you're lazy or a complainer no one will make fun of you, they will look you in the eye and tell you what they think of you. Liars and cheats are not tolerated and don't last long on the roster. When it comes to your responsibilities you do it as best you can and don't complain. Just because you hurt doesn't exempt you from life.

After breakfast everyone headed out the door except Ed. He looked at Emil and said, "I'm sorry I didn't get my string topped off. I know I was supposed to help load the truck."

"That's alright, get your last horse rode out and come up with Jake," Emil said as he stood up from the table.

"Thanks," Ed said as he hobbled out the door. By the time he got to the corral he was sore but the stiffness was almost gone. Moving around seemed to loosen him up. Opening the gate he entered the corral as Don walked over with the bucking saddle.

"Here, climb into this and I'll set it for you." Don said as he put the saddle on a blanket he had already placed on the ground. Getting down on the saddle hurt but it wasn't impossible.

"Put your feet into the stirrups." Ed stretched his legs straightforward and gave a low moan as he reached to put the stirrups over each foot. "Now, grab the front of the saddle and pull it off the ground as you lean back." "Slid your knees under the swells and keep "em there while I adjust the stirrups.' Don said as he moved the buckles to the proper positions. "The idea is to be able to flex your leg at the knee while keeping yourself locked in the saddle with the upper part of your leg squeezed under the swells. If you can get the lower part of your leg moving in time with the up and down motion of the horse you'll sit tight in the saddle. When his front feet hit the ground your leg should be straight with your spurs in his shoulders and your toes pointed out. As his front feet leave the ground for the next jump your feet should be starting to move back toward his rump. Your upper leg shouldn't move from under the swells at anytime. Your lower leg will do a kind of a Pendulum motion. That also helps you to keep your knees in tight. Remember, always sit up straight hold the rein hand out in front of you and look at his head. That'll give you balance and tell you which way he's going." Don grabbed Ed's foot and moved it a couple of times forward and back in the proper spurring motion. "That's why the stirrups on a bucking saddle are usually shorter than a working saddle." He said as he worked Ed's leg.

Ed nodded as he looked up. "Yah, it sure wouldn't be very comfortable to ride like that."

Don nodded, "your right, but each kind of riding requires its own style. O.K., you understand what I'm trying to tell you?"

"Yah. I didn't realize you had to lock yourself in so hard.

"It's the only way you can stay on and keep a rhythm going. Now, let's see you spur a couple of times. Move the right leg from the forward position all the way to the cantle then back out in front of you again. Now do the same thing with your left leg. Remember to bend only at the knees. Keep your knees under the swells as much as you can. Now try it with both legs at the same time. Lean back and pull up on the front of the saddle as your legs come back and let the front of the saddle go down as your legs come forward. It's kind of like a rocking motion. This is what I mean when I say you gotta get in time with the horse. It's the same motion only faster and more exaggerated. Ed made the moves as Don talked to him. He began to feel and understand what Don was trying to show him. After about five minutes of going through the motions Don finally nodded stood up, "good now let's see if you learned anything." Ed got out of the saddle and stood just as Jake led the sorrel up.

"You two wanna kiss and make up? Jake grinned sarcastically and nodded at the placid looking animal.

"God, it probably wouldn't hurt." Ed bantered back as he walked over and planted a big juicy kiss on the animals' soft nose. "Look me in the eye horse, just because they're black doesn't mean I'm a raccoon. I'm the guy who's going to ride you today." The horse reacted to the sudden close movement by pulling back and snorting.

"Ha, you got him spooked kid, now go get him." Jake said with a grin.

Ed picked up the saddle and was actually anticipating the ride. Confident that he could hold his own after the lessons he had just learned. The sorrel stood dead still while Jake held his head as Ed saddled and mounted him. The saddle felt good to Ed With his feet in the shorter stirrups and his legs locked snugly under the swells of the saddle. Picking up the halter rein Ed got the right distance on it and nodded.

The horse sucked back and spun left in one motion. Ed had his eyes wide open for the first time he could see the sorrel's head. Each time the horse jumped Ed could tell which way he was going by how he swung his head. Concentrating on keeping his knees in tight to the saddle he could feel the muscles in his thighs straining to the point of breaking. He could feel the saddle try to spread his legs apart as the force of the horses bucking drove him forward into the swells. Then slammed him backward into the cantle. Then from one side to the other as the horse tried to spin out from under him. Ed began to feel the rhythm that Don mentioned as the horse bucked. It is very similar to a dance, once the beat is established it very seldom changes. With a bucking horse the beat or rhythm is usually established in the first few jumps and normally doesn't change until the horse gives up or the rider is bucked off. In a dance if you get out of time with the music you and your partner can stop momentarily and start over again. Here is where the similarity ends with a horse. One; he doesn't know how to dance. Two; he's an unwilling twelve hundred pound partner that doesn't want to stop. All he knows is that if he can dislodge you from his back the dance is over until you climb aboard again.

The sorrel went high in the air and sun fished, forcing Ed to loose his seat, which meant the leg hold was gone also. Half a second after the sorrel's front feet hit the ground so did Ed. Groaning Ed rolled over onto his knees as Jake walked up and grabbed the dangling halter rein. Jake looked at Ed as he stumbled to his feet.

"You better get something else before you get hurt." He turned and started to lead the horse away. "Besides we've got to get out of here before noon or we'll never make Rocky Butte by dark."

"I will like hell, that's my horse and I'm going to ride him Ed screamed."

Jake and the horse stopped dead in their tracks. Jake half turned showing a toothy grin. "Well, my little buckaroo let's see you do it," he said mockingly.

Ed grabbed the rein and stepped aboard. The adrenalin was flowing and pain was no longer an issue as he slammed himself into position and said "TURN HIM LOOSE" the horse lunged forward two jumps, spun left, sucked back, spun right, and did a quick sunfish. At the height of his jump he straightened out and went for the ground like a Stuka dive-bomber. Ed's eyes were wide open and he was matching the animal move for move with a vengeance. The horse did a series of straight away bucks as fast and hard as he could only to slam on the brakes, suck back, go into the air horizontally, do a 180-degree turn, sunfish and dive for the ground. He would buck left and right and then do it all over again. The harder the horse bucked the madder Ed got and the harder he raked him with the spurs Don had let him use, this ride turned into a war. Normally a ride will last fifteen to twenty seconds and the horse will concede if the rider can stay aboard that long. This went on for a full two minutes. The horse was soaking wet and covered with lather so bad that his color was indistinguishable. Every time he would jump he would throw lather and sweat fifteen feet in all directions.

Ed was in the same condition. There wasn't a dry piece of clothing on his body and the sweat was running down his legs so hard that his socks were getting wet. Exhaustion was setting in to both horse and rider. All of a sudden the horses legs buckled and he went down on his belly with his head sticking straight out in front of him in the muddy dust. He lay there in the dirt gasping for air and groaning while Ed straddled him still in the saddle, feet in the stirrups standing on the ground gasping for air as hard as the downed horse. The sweat burned as it poured off Ed's forehead and ran into his eyes. He was completely awash in his own sweat and shaking like a bullfighter with a broken leg. Jake, Don and Les were suddenly there pounding him on the back and yelling all kinds of praises and compliments that Ed only caught bits and pieces of. "What a ride" "I've never seen anything like that" "I'd never believed it if I hadn't seen it with my own eyes". Ed didn't know who was saying what, he was just glad that it was over. Swinging his shaky leg over the still downed, heaving horse he looked up and saw the flatbed truck sitting at the edge of the corral with everyone including Mrs. Schmidt, shouting, clapping, jumping up and down and just generally letting it all hang out in appreciation for the spectacle they had just witnessed.

"OK boys, the holiday is over now let's get to work. Good ride kid," Emil said as he climbed into the cab and prepared to drive off. The truck lurched forward as everyone standing on the back waved and yelled. Mrs. Schmidt leaned on the top rail of the corral and said, "Ed, are you alright?"

"Yes ma'am."

"That was quite a ride thank you for the show." She said as she turned and walked toward the ranch house.

Jake's voice broke the silence. "Let's get him up boys," nodding toward the sorrel. The four men walked over to the soaked, panting horse.

Don said, "I'll take his head you guys get his butt." Don reached down and picked the muddy reins out of the dust and pulled as everyone else swatted the downed animal with their hats and yelled. The horse leaped to his feet and stood exhausted with his head down and muscles convulsing so bad that he started to teeter

"Walk him around before he falls over." Jake said to Ed as he adjusted his hat. "After he gets his pins back under him get on him and walk him around the corral a couple of laps before you pull the saddle." Turning he looked at Don and Les. "In the mean time you two figure out which ones your gonna use and get 'em caught and rode out."

Both men nodded and went into the adjoining corral to get their four head. Since there was only a little over a dozen horses left and the corral was smaller, they had their strings caught and tied in the big corral by the time Ed was pulling the saddle off the sorrel.

What a glorious moment it was for Ed to ride the sorrel around the corral. All the pain was temporarily forgotten as the animal walked placidly around the corral to the spot Ed picked out to unsaddle him. By the time Ed got the sorrel unsaddled and walked out Don and Les were riding out the horses they had picked for their string. Les was climbing off his last horse as Jake was backing the truck into the loading chute. Don and Les were tying the last of their string to the corral rail as Jake got out of the truck and walked into the corral to indicate which ones were to be loaded for the other hands. It wasn't necessary to take all the horses. Each person would only need three head. They only intended to be out for a week to ten days."You better pick out your three and get 'em loaded" Jake mentioned to Ed as he led four horses past on his way to the truck. "We want to get moving as soon as possible."

Ed nodded and thought a minute. With his newfound prowess and inflated courage there was no doubt in his mind that the sorrel was going to go. He pondered over the other three and finally came up with the bay and the buckskin. After he led them over to the loading chute he tied the lead rope to their halters. Jake had said not to tie them in the truck because it would be impossible for them to get up if they fell down. Don loaded two more head, dropped the tailgate and the truck except for the human occupants was ready to roll.

CHAPTER #5

THE RIDE TO the cow camp was long, dusty and rough. They arrived just as the sun was starting to set on the western horizon. Emil was in the process of cooking supper. It was simple but plentiful and good. Beefsteaks wrapped with bacon, pieces of onion, garlic, and vegetables rolled inside, and skewered on a six foot steel rod like a giant shiskabob. Baked beans in a huge cast iron pot with a lid, hung from a tripod by a chain, over a hole filled with hot coals from the main cooking fire. Soft, fluffy biscuits baked in a Dutch oven next to the beans. All the fixing's were on the tail board of a cook box mounted to the back end of the flat bed truck that Emil and crew drove up earlier in the day. There were three kinds condiments; jam, honey and all the butter you could eat. The men ate in the shadow of the large rock outcrop called rocky butte as the pink sky etched the tops of the sagebrush with a golden hue. The purple mountains in the distance framed the panorama as a kaleidoscope of colors gave way to the black of night. When supper was over the eater scraped his plate (if there was anything left on it) into a metal bucket and then scrubbed it out with the coarse, sandy soil that made up the terrain in this part of the country, before he stacked it on the tailboard of the cook box. The coffee pot had been rebrewed so everyone could get a cup or two before bed.

Sleeping on the ground in the vast open plains of Wyoming, looking at an incredible canopy of stars, is one of the truly great experiences in life. On the Wyoming plains (where pollution is non-existent) you get a total new sense of being. Lying on his back inside a nice cozy, warm, sleeping bag looking at the vastness, the motion, the orderliness and the complexity of the night sky gave Ed a whole new feeling about a creator and his inconsequential place in the scheme of things. The night sky looked like an enormous piece of black velvet jeweled with millions of diamonds. Some were a pale red or blue or yellow and did everything from blink to streak across the sky, all in all it was a great way to drift off to sleep

Dawn came amid the banging of pans and Emil's shout to roll out. The horizon was dimly lit with a touch of gold, pink and purple. The smell of sage and wood smoke mingled with that of food cooking drifted through the air as Ed stiffly crawled out of his sleeping bag, shivering in the cold morning air while he checked his boots for critters and foreign objects before pulling them on his feet. Standing up he put on his hat and coat and headed for the warmth of the campfire blazing brightly near the chuck wagon.

"Morning' Emil said as he leaned over a huge frying pan containing a dozen eggs and a pound of half-inch beef slices cooking in butter. Next to that was a flat piece of five eight's inch steel plate about four feet by two feet on steel legs sitting directly over the fire with pancakes and cut potatoes cooking on it.

"Coffee's made,' Emil nodded toward the large boiling pot hanging from its chain over a bed of glowing coals. Ed walked over to the cook box grabbed a metal cup from the rack, poured the steaming liquid into his cup, and wrapped his cold hands around the warmth while he stood watching Emil cook the morning meal. Between the hot coffee, the cold morning air and the aroma of the cooking food Ed began to realize just how hungry he was as the rest of the crew straggled up to the cooking fire.

"You should have a bigger pan Emil," Ed said over his steaming mug of coffee. "If these other guys are as hungry as I am, I'd hate to see them have to wait while I eat in front of 'em."

"Hey. Watch your mouth," came the unison response as the group hovered around the coffee pot filling their cups.

"Never mind them just get your plate and get over here, it's first come first serve out here."

Ed grabbed a twelve-inch metal pie plate and held it out while Emil piled the beef, eggs, potatoes and pancakes on his plate.

"Say when."

"When," Ed said as he put his cup under the heavy ladened plate to support it.

Ron held out his plate for Emil as he looked at the mountain of food Ed was holding. "Damn. I'm glad I'm not your horse today."

Ed smiled and turned to walk away as Emil said, "There's a can of peaches and fixing's on the cook box."

Ed and Ron walked over to the three-pound can and each took a cereal bowl full of the canned fruit, before sitting cross-legged on the ground to eat. The rest of the hands sat down and Ed noticed how easily they assumed the cross-legged position while balancing cup, plate and bowl.

The sky had gone from a deep indigo blue with rose-colored edges and golden overtones to a variety of pastels covering the whole color spectrum. It was breathtaking. Everyone scrubbed and stacked their own dishes as they finished eating. It was light enough to see by now, so the men rolled their bedrolls, put them on the truck, grabbed their saddles and headed for the rope enclosure containing the horses. The haltered horses nickered and snorted as the men moved amongst them getting their particular mount saddled and ready to go. Ed saddled the sorrel, he could feel the animal tense as he pulled the cinch.

"Put your knee in his gut, that'll take some of the kink out of his back while you get ready." Jake said as he saddled his horse next to Ed.

"OK" Ed jammed his knee in hard next to the cinch, and he felt the horse exhale as he pulled the slack. Once the saddles were on the men retired to the supply truck and dug out their spurs, chaps, bridles and whatever else they needed for the day. While they were putting their riding gear on Jake began to give the orders for the day.

"Ron you and Buck work to the east of the butte. Mike and Ed you two work south of the butte and Les and Don you work the west side. Make sure you go all the way to the line fence before you start the drive back. We're gonna hold 'em on that flat that faces the camp."

Everyone nodded, grabbed their bridles and headed for the corral. Although the orders were simply given each man knew what was expected. The object was to spread out and cover half the rectangle, starting at the perimeter and work back to the center where the holding area was located. The size of the area determined how long it took to do a proper search. Once the area was swept a couple of times and the cattle were herded to the holding ground and dealt with, the other half of the rectangle would receive the same treatment. This particular "pasture" as the local vernacular would describe it, was about ten sections of land bounded by one (line) fence.

A section is one square mile or six hundred and forty acres or one of thirty-six subdivisions of a township. This half of the area the men were working amounted to almost ten square miles or sixty four hundred acres of land. Considering that the area is full of draws, arroyos, canyons and hills covered with vegetation ranging from sagebrush to pinion trees, trying to find cattle and their increase makes the job iffy at best. Strays were always a problem and a final ride through the area is always done before breaking camp. This was the most colorful part of the whole operation.

The strays were crafty and spooky enough to avoid the first and second drives they were as wild as anything that Mother Nature raised out here. The only way to check them over, vaccinate and brand them was to rope 'em, build a fire and do it on the spot. Normally, with a herd of six or seven hundred head you'll get a rate of three to six percent of strays depending on all the factors involved.

The holding area would be a natural barrier, like a three-sided canyon, a sharp bend in a river or something that was bounded on two or three sides by a physical barrier, either natural or man-made. The major requirement was grass and water. If these didn't exist the cattle would become edgy and impossible to hold after a couple of days. It should be an area that a couple of men could easily hold the cattle in as they were brought off the range. The holding area in this instance was built like a step on a spiral staircase. Narrow at one end and widening all the way to a half a mile at the other end.

On one side was a vertical, sheer lava rock wall about 50 to 75 ft. high with a flat grassy plain in front of it that dropped off about the same height at a 60 degree slope of loose shale. The only access down was a small game trail along the face of the rock wall at the narrow end of the escarpment. The other opening was at the head of the game trial in the sheer rock wall about one hundred yards wide that lead to the other side of rocky butte and the range beyond. At the wide end of the escarpment was a small waterfall coming out of the rock wall that closed off the back end of the holding area. A tank made of rocks and dirt had been built to hold the water on its way down the sheer face of the drop off. The escarpment was flat and covered in knee-high grass.

The men headed for the corral to mount their horses and start the sweep. Each horse would give a few halfhearted jumps after it was mounted and then settle down as if it knew it was time to go to work. With one exception; Ed barely got his seat as the sorrel fired and bucked as hard as he ever had dumping Ed in the dirt after three or four good jumps. Instead of stopping as he usually did he kept on bucking and bawling loudly like he was trying to get rid of the saddle. Ron rode along side and scooped up the dangling reins and dallied them around his saddle horn as he brought the unruly animals head up.

"Someone check the blanket" he said as he brought the cantankerous: animal still kicking over to the group of onlookers. Buck jumped down off his horse and ran his hand underneath the saddle blanket.

"UGHHH" he grunted as he pulled his hand from underneath the blanket with a large sand burr stuck to it.

"Kid, you gotta learn to check the blanket before you put it on." Ron said harshly.

"But I did and it was clean." Ed replied.

"Well you must of missed something then. Be careful where you lay it, this ground is full of burrs.

"My blanket was on the truck with the rest of them. I carried it and my saddle right to the horse.

"All I know is what I see. Somehow you picked up a couple of sand burrs and you didn't get 'em off your blanket before you put it on your horse. Now pull that saddle, check that blanket and the horses back. We gotta get going"

About that time Emil and Jake walked over. "What the hell is the holdup?" Emil asked as he watched Ed taking the saddle off his horse.

"You yahoos gonna screw around here and waste daylight?"

"No sir," Ron said "Ed missed a burr in his blanket and we wanted to make sure he got going ok".

Jake opened up. "Mike can wait for the kid, the rest of you get going."

Everyone nodded and started off in their assigned directions. In the meantime Ed finished checking the blanket and his horses back. Satisfied that both were clean he resaddled and tightened the cinch as Jake walked over.

"You better be more careful next time we don't have the extras to replace a horse with a sore back."

Ed looked Jake straight in the eyes. 'That blanket was clean when I put it on my horse. I don't know how those burrs got there."

Jake's icy blues returned the stare. "They're small and hard to see. If you don't know what you're looking for they're easy to miss." With that he turned and walked away talking to Emil in low tones. "The kid is new and probably didn't know enough to check his blanket. He'll be alright." Jake told the owner after they were out of earshot.

"I hope so. We don't have time to nurse maid a green horn. The weather could go sour anytime on us now.

"Mike'll show him the ropes." Jake said as Emil shrugged and walked away.

"Mike that blanket was clean." Ed said as he mounted the sorrel. "This time the animal made a couple of half-hearted jumps and then walked off.

"I believe you kid, we walked to the corral together and I never saw you let your blanket touch the ground.

"How could they have gotten there?"

"I don't know kid, I don't know." Mike said thoughtfully as they rode out of camp.

Riding five miles on horseback across open range may not seem like much to someone used to riding groomed, flat trails. Riding in brushy, broken rangeland is a totally different story. It takes agility, endurance and common sense horseman ship to be able to last the fifteen to twenty hours or more a day when your gathering cattle. This is the reason the cowboys won't even bother riding a horse that doesn't have enough fire to buck a little when he's first mounted.

By the time Mike and Ed reached the line fence the sun was already high in the sky.

"Damn, we shouldn't have gotten such a late start" Mike muttered as they rode up to the line fence.

"That was my fault," Ed said flatly.

"Maybe, but now we gotta start moving. It's gonna be a full moon tonight or we probably would have to dry camp. Do you think you can move any cattle by yourself?"

Ed remembered how on his father's dairy farm in Wisconsin he used to ride his horse bareback down the fenced lane to the pasture and bring in the milk cows.

"Sure, I grew up on a farm and used to drive them to the barn for my dad."

Mike rolled his eyes and groaned. "Now look.You see that ridge with the three notches there to the north?"

Ed nodded his agreement.

"We're gonna be about a mile apart maybe more. Zigzag your way as best you can toward the left hand notch. I'll work toward the right hand notch. We'll use the center notch as the dividing line between us. We should get a glimpse of each other now and then. Go through that notch with the cattle it's a lot bigger than it looks from here. You should be able to see Rocky Butte from there. Drive the cattle to the base of the butte and then to the right along the bottom of it. Jake and Emil will be there to help you get 'em in to the holding ground. OK?"

Ed nodded his acknowledgement.

"Well let's go then," Mike said as he wheeled his horse and trotted away.

Ed watched him go for a minute and then turned the sorrel in the opposite direction. Heading for a sagebrush filled draw about five hundred yards away that looked like it might be promising. Riding the rim of the draw he spotted eight head of cattle feeding on the sparse grass that grew in the bottom. The wind and sun didn't suck the moisture out of the ground down there like it did on top. In this treeless landscape these draws provided cover and shelter from constant wind. Vegetation grew better at the bottom because any moisture from rain or flood survived longer there. The cattle stopped feeding and raised their heads the moment Ed rode into view.

Range cattle are not the docile bovines that barnyard cousins are. Although they are not vicious, they will attack anything they perceive as a threat to them or there young. They can be quite easily driven or herded on horseback but they show no fear or respect for a man on foot. Ed learned this at a later date when he roped a calf he was going to doctor and the mother cow knocked his horse out from under him. Once off the horse, the cow focused her attention on Ed. If he had not mounted as the horse was getting to its feet she would have run him down easily. Another future incident I will relate here to help those readers who are not familiar with range cattle understand how serious it is to be afoot around them. One sunny day during the calving season.

(February to the end of April) Ed was at the home ranch building and noticed a coyote slip over the top of a knoll on the hillside over looking the ranch. From his position Ed could see the whole hillside as the drama unraveled. The coyote was trying to sneak up on a baby calf that had been placed under a clump of brush on the hillside by its mother. She and the other cows grazed peacefully within sight but no closer than a hundred yards or so from the baby calf. They appeared to be scattered in a haphazard fashion along the face of the hill. The coyote would crawl on his belly toward the calf as long as the cows had their heads down and grazing. The minute a head would come up the coyote would freeze and lay motionless. This went on for about a half an hour as the coyote slowly worked his way toward the baby calf. The cows slowly moved as they grazed, apparently unaware of the impending tragedy. When Mr. coyote was about ten yards away from the baby calf he suddenly stood up and looked around. Ed could see why from his vantage point. The cows that had appeared to be unaware of Mr. coyote's presence had casually moved themselves into a large circle around the calf and the coyote as they grazed. Too late the Coyote realized that he was now the hunted instead of his intended victim. The heads of the cows all came up as one the minute he stood up. They tightened the circle as the coyote tried to escape. The smaller the circle became the faster the coyote ran and the more frantic he became. Every time he tried to run between the cows they would charge at him with heads lowered and strike at him with their front feet. All the while they were constantly closing the circle until they were literally standing shoulder to shoulder, in a tight circle around the coyote and the baby calf. The coyote made a desperate attempt to escape between two cows, one of them connected. A sharp yelp and a maddening bawl followed by a lot of milling around by the cows, and the coyote became a soggy but permanent part of the landscape. Ed knew at that moment what everyone had told him about not being on foot around range cattle was true. "Don't get off your horse around the cattle, especially when you're alone." The other men constantly told him.

Ed moved his horse down into the ravine and the cattle started to move ahead of him. The only problem was they didn't all move in the same direction. Each time a cow would start up the side of the ravine Ed would try to head it off. The problem was he couldn't get above them quick enough. The cattle would reach the top of the steep bank before he could turn them and when he left the main bunch they would start to scatter in the other directions. This was like trying to push wet noodles with a stick. It was like trying to play marbles on uneven ground.

Then there is distance; when a stranger walks up to you, how close can they get before you tense up or start to move away? This is called aura, every living thing has it, and every ones aura or space is different. It's the same with cattle singly or collectively. This is where experience makes the difference in how to get the animals from point "A" to point "B". The experienced cowboy understands the group aura (maybe not consciously) in relation to himself and the single aura amongst the cattle themselves. Call it instinct, experience or whatever but he knows how close and at what angle to approach the animals so they will do what he wants them to. Ed's problem was he didn't have that experience yet, and when an animal left the group he would lose control of one or all. Throw in broken terrain and you can imagine what a frustrating situation it must have been for him trying to "push" cattle for the first time.

After an hour of running his horse up and down the sides of the ravine. The animal was working up a serious lather and breathing extremely hard. Although Ed was mad, frustrated and on the edge of being out of control he realized that if he didn't rest his horse they would never make it back today. He rode up out of the ravine to catch the ever-present breeze on the open range. Sitting on his jaded mount he pondered the fact that he hadn't been able to move the cattle more than four or five hundred yards in the past hour. This would have to change in a hurry because Ed did not want to spend the night alone out here. Once his horse was breathing normally again he walked him into the ravine toward the cattle. He got them moving ahead of him and up a little draw that led out of the ravine. At least on top if they did try to scatter he had room to work. Ed he found that if he kept them walking at a steady pace they stayed together and after a while even started to walk single file. Ed wasn't sure if this was good or not but it seemed to work. The hard part was leaving them to pick up others along the way. Ed knew he was only going to be able to pick up the ones that were easy and obvious, otherwise he would lose the whole bunch. Ed stayed with the shallow draws and flat ground until he collected about thirty head of cattle. By the time he drove them through the notch that had looked so high and narrow (in reality it was wide and easy to pass through) it was mid to late after noon. The land had risen gently to this point and now fell away sharply, into a bunch of draws and arroyos that spread out like fingers eventually fading into an old dry lakebed that swept around the base of rocky butte. Although a little over five miles away rocky butte gave off a purple hue that made it look farther than it actually was. Ed gulped because he knew that he would run out of light somewhere down in those arroyos. "Well, I better get going" he mumbled to himself.

He started the cattle toward a specific draw that looked like it had steep sides and no outlets until it receded into the grassy incline leading up to base of rocky butte. The sun disappeared behind the far corner of rocky butte as Ed and the cattle reached the head of the draw that lead into the long chute like arroyo, it was still light enough to see it and still looked like a good way to go. Ed figured if he pushed the cattle hard once they were in the narrow channel they would make good time until the light ran out. Then he would have to get them walking steady again. He knew they wouldn't try to turn back because of how narrow and high the sidewalls were, and from where he had entered the draw it should be only a couple of hours or more until he got to the rendezvous with Emil and Jake at the base of rocky butte.

About an hour into the arroyo it got real dark because the moon hadn't come up yet. Ed relaxed on the reins and allowed the horse to put his head down and pick his way. All Ed could do was sit there smelling the cattle, hearing the shuffle of their feet in the soft alkali soil, the dislodging of a rock or the swishing sound as they brushed against a bush. Their almost invisible profiles blended them together to form an undulating, oscillating shadow that crept on into the darkness. All of a sudden there was the sound of feet pounding and bodies bumping. Ed's horse backed up and wheeled around almost dumping him on the ground. He fought to keep his seat and get the frightened animal under control. Ed finally got the horse turned around and headed back in the right direction, as the sound of the running cattle faded into the night. Moving his horse as fast as he could back to the spot where he thought he lost them, he stopped to listen, but the cattle could no longer be heard.

"They've got to be at the end of the arroyo where it empties onto the old lake bed. It's the only way they could go." Ed thought to himself started the horse down the black chute. "By the time I get out of here the moon should be up and I'll be able to see them." He thought out load as the horse carefully picked his way along.

The western moon is a great source of light. When the moon is out its radiance is so intense that a man on can hold his hand out and count the fingers from the sharply defined shadow on the ground. In pioneer days this was the preferred time to travel to escape the heat of the day and also avoid Indians. By the same token the shadows created by the moon from brush, rock piles, ledges, etc. could be quite dangerous because they are extremely black, and deep.

Ed broke out of the draw onto the dry lakebed just as the moon made its appearance over the top of rocky butte a mile away. There was only one problem: Not a cow was to be seen or heard anywhere. It was as if the earth had swallowed them and Ed was in a real dilemma. He had worked all day just to lose the cattle he collected near the end of his drive. Ed sat on his horse pondering the situation. "Should he ride into camp? He could be there in an hour or should he ride back into the draw and see if there was some other route the cattle had taken? But, what had spooked them? Was it a wolf or a mountain lion? What if he got in there and something jumped on him from the shadows or the top of the banks? He had no weapon to defend himself and if he did he probably wouldn't be able to use it before it was too late anyhow". Ed's imagination was working overtime, but knew he was going to have to try and find those cattle, showing up in camp could mean anything from being the butt of every joke for who knows how long, to being fired. Ed was not in the mood for any of it. Shaking his head and shivering from the cold he knew he had to start moving, all he had on was a light Levi jacket and the night air was getting colder.

Cautiously moving his horse back into the draw Ed's heart pounded like a big bass drum. Expecting to be jumped on and eaten alive at any moment he was glued to the saddle and his eyes were trying to look in every direction at the same time. The moon was up and it was light enough to see (except in the shadows) as Ed's horse picked his way through the draw at a good pace. At the deepest part of the draw Ed saw what happened. The draw split and the cattle had taken the left fork while he had taken the right fork. Following their tracks in the soft sand was easy, because of the steep sidewalls that made the draw he knew they would stay together until they reached the dry lakebed to the West. The moonlight wouldn't fade for another three or four hours yet so he thought he might be able to catch up with them before they got too far. Putting his horse into a slow lope Ed started down the side draw following the fresh tracks. An hour later he broke out onto the bed of the dry lake, he figured if he rode the lakebed around to where he had come out of the arroyo on the North end it would take about forty-five minutes to an hour longer once he caught up to the errant cattle. Following the tracks of the thirty head of cattle he had collected, onto the lakebed, he was surprised when they joined with the tracks of a whole bunch of cattle. Ed couldn't tell how many there were but from the swath they left he knew it a really big bunch. Since they were headed for Rocky Butte Ed figured he would follow them. As he rode along the bottom of the Butte toward the rendezvous point he could see a light. It was yellowish and high above the ground. He understood its purpose, there were people out gathering cattle yet and the light would be where Emil and Jake would meet the incoming cattle. From there they would help move them to the holding ground on the other side of the Butte. Riding toward the light Ed could see a man on horseback waiting beneath it. The lantern had been hoisted high above the trail with a rope that was thrown over a protruding rock.

"Hi Jake," Ed said as he rode up to the man on horseback. The foreman gave him a hard look and said where are your cattle"

"I lost them." Ed said looking at the ground.

"How so?"

"I don't know, they spooked on me just after dark in one of those arroyos." Ed said pointing across the lakebed. "I thought it went straight but it forked. I couldn't see because the moon wasn't up yet.They went one way and I went the other. I followed them after the moon came up and they joined with a big bunch out on the lakebed so I followed them all the way up here." Ed said proudly.

"They must've mixed with that bunch Les brought in an hour ago, at least we didn't lose 'em. While Jake and Ed were talking a rider appeared from the cut through Rocky Butte. "Here comes Emil back from helping Les," Jake nodded as they sat and watched as the rider slowly approached.

"Where's your cattle Ed?" Emil asked as he rode alongside Ed's horse and looked him in the eye.

"Uhh, they spooked in the dark and got away. But I followed them after the moon came up and they joined up with Les's bunch so at least we didn't lose them." Ed rattled on as he gasped for air while the blood pounded in his head.

"How many did you have?"

"About thirty head."

"Damn," Emil said sharply. "Jake, You take Ed's place tomorrow, otherwise we'll be out here 'til thanksgiving. Emil looked into Ed's fallen face. "You stay in camp with me and help drive 'em to the holding ground tomorrow."

"Yes sir." Ed said dejectedly.

"Look. It's nothing personal but we only got so much time to get this done. You just need some time to learn what to do that's all."

Ed nodded as he looked down at the saddle horn.

"From the looks of your horse you've had a long day, head in and get some sleep." Emil said as the sound of hooves could be heard. Turning in his saddle he looked at Jake. "That's got to be Don. Let's help him in and then hit the hay, it's been a long day."

The three riders moved off the trail and sat motionless as Don drove close to eighty-five head of cattle toward them. Emil took the point as the cattle approached. Jake sat and waited until half the cattle were past him then he fell in along side and walked with them. Ed sat and waited as the cattle shuffled past. He was tired, dejected and felt like a total failure. Don was riding off to the side, about half way between the middle and the end of the strung out cattle. He smiled but lost it when Ed put his head down and didn't look at him. The tail end of the cattle came by Ed moved into the enveloping cloud of dust they created. It felt good, at least it gave him a place to sulk and hide for a while.

The trail wound through a maze of large rocks that had fallen from the sheer cliff of the butte over the century and then past the camp onto the holding ground on the escarpment. Once past the camp the line of cattle disintegrated into the cattle already being held there. The four men dismounted and walked over to the campfire where the other four men were surrounding the coffee pot that was hanging on its chain above a fire.

"Jake, you take first watch. Ed you take second watch. I want everybody out of here before daylight." Emil stated as he poured himself a cup of coffee. Jake mounted his horse and turned toward the cattle. Emil, Don and Ed stripped the gear off their horses and turned them into the rope corral. It was already close to one thirty in the morning and each watch was about two hours long. The open end of the escarpment by the camp, had to be patrolled by a man on horseback to make sure cattle didn't sneak away during the night. It was boring but two hours was doable even if you were tired. Everyone finished their coffee and spread their bedrolls for the short nights sleep.

"C'mon kid, get up and get your horse saddled it's your turn." Jake said as he shook Ed out of a deep sleep. "C'mon get up I gotta get everyone else going too." as he turned and started moving amongst the prone bodies, saying a word here and kicking a foot there. Ed got up and pulled his jacket on while he wandered over to the already burning campfire to pour a cup of coffee. "You ain't got time for that, besides it ain't ready, now get your horse and get out there." Jake snapped.

Ed veered from the fire and walked over to the truck to get his saddle and blanket. Grabbing them off the truck bed he turned, walked into the rope corral and threw them on the back of the bay. Once the saddle was cinched Ed walked the horse away from camp to loosen him up, out of sight from the camp he retightened the cinch and mounted. He was glad he had walked away from camp to get on. Even though he cheeked the bay and spun him in a tight circle as he swung into the saddle the horse still put his head down and bucked a half a dozen times after Ed gave him his head. He didn't buck hard, so Ed stayed with him easily. Once the horse had flexed his muscles he was ready to go to work and walked off. Ed approached the cattle as those that were lying down got to their feet and looked at him suspiciously. "I guess I'd better back off." Ed thought to himself moving the horse away from the nervous cattle.

Looking back toward camp Ed could see activity as the men moved around getting ready for the day. The aroma of coffee and bacon was in the air making Eds mouth water. He wanted to go in and eat breakfast but he knew he was supposed to stay with the cattle. Sitting on his horse in the dark he thought to himself; "Maybe I wouldn't get breakfast this morning. Maybe it was Emil's way of punishing him for yesterday. He sure hadn't scored any brownie points with Emil or Jake that's for sure. Oh well, no supper, no breakfast he'd just have to get by. No wonder these men were so slim and trim j twenty hours in the saddle and only one meal."

It was just starting to break day as the men rode out of camp. Ed sat on his horse in the dark feeling sorry for himself as the sound of their horses hooves faded into the glowing horizon.

"You hungry for breakfast?" Emil said as he rode along side Ed bringing him back to the real world.

"Oh, yeah" Ed said with a start.

"Go on in I got a plate in the hot box for you. Bread and peaches are in the pantry."

"OK, thanks" Ed replied as he turned his horse toward camp.

By the time Ed had finished breakfast, wiped and stacked his dishes it was full daylight. The sun above the horizon was a bright yellow against a turquoise blue sky.

Emil sat his horse overlooking the grassy rampart that led to the open ranges below as Ed rode in next to him.

"Pretty isn't it?" Emil said as he gazed wistfully over the broken landscape pockmarked with shadows from the early morning sun.

"Yeah, it sure is. I didn't realize how big it is out here." Ed said looking from horizon to horizon.

"It's a lot smaller than when I grew up," Emil said as his memories drifted through his mind.

The two of them sat on their horses gazing out over the ageless landscape and talked about the land, what it was like in years past, and the people that had lived and died here.

"Yeah I saw some wild Indians when I was a little kid, by that time they were pretty much reduced to beggars and drunks. The Indians that my father and the old timers talked about were all gone by the middle eighteen hundreds. They were a proud self-sufficient people, but they couldn't cope with change and that's what eventually brought 'em down. The same as it's done to the cattlemen or anyone else who don't keep up with the times. It seems things are always changing and if we don't change with 'em we'll get left behind too." Emil paused and shifted in his saddle. "Just about the time you get comfortable with something it changes. If you don't follow the trail you get lost, even these hills change. A lot slower than we do but they are constantly changing." Emil fell silent and stared off into the memory of his younger years. After a few moments he shook his head and said "C'mon lets go in and have a cup of coffee we can watch the cattle from camp now that it's daylight. The two men rode slowly back to camp.

"Get down but keep him close." Emil said as he swung down out of the saddle and dropped the reins on the ground. "I'll brew us a fresh pot."

The rest of the day was spent drinking coffee, talking and occasionally riding back and forth across the grassy rampart. The sun was a huge, orange red fireball, sitting on the horizon when Emil turned to Ed and said.

"You better head out to where you met us last night. I'll stay here with the cattle. When one of the others gets in we can both go out and help bring 'em in."

Ed nodded and started for his horse.

"Make sure you got matches and light the lantern before dark. There's a can of oil below the rock it hangs from."

Ed waved his arm as he rode away to show acknowledgement.

Riding to the spot where the lantern was hanging, it was still light enough for Ed to make out a couple of dust clouds in the distance. By the time he had filled the lantern, lighted it and hung it he could hear cattle. Mike showed up first and right behind him was Jake. Between them they had close to one hundred and seventy five head of cattle.

"Hi, Mike." Ed shouted as the man came into view. The lead cattle stopped and looked at Ed and his horse with wild eyes. Slowly Ed turned his horse and headed back on the trail to camp in front of them. The spooky leaders started to follow as the ones behind crowded into them and forced them to move. "OOOPS", Ed thought, "I almost screwed up there." Ed looked over his shoulder as Mike smiled and gave him thumbs up as the bunched leaders moved back onto the trail. By now Jake's group came up behind Mike's group and turned it into one big line as the leaders of the second bunch caught up with the drags. After the cattle were deposited on the holding ground Emil said to Jake and Mike. "You two watch 'em. Ed and I will go back for the others."

"Ed." Jake said as he rode over to the young man. "Why did you get off your horse at the split the other night? I thought you said your horse spooked and when you got him going again you took the wrong fork?"

Ed looked him right in the eye as he leaned forward in the saddle. "That's exactly what happened. I never got off my horse."

"I believe you. Would you do me a favor?"

"Sure."

"Step down into that soft dirt and let me see your foot print."

Ed nodded as he stepped off the horse into the spot indicated. "How's that?" Ed said as he remounted his horse. The foreman rode over and looked at the footprint in the fading light.

"Uhuh thanks. Why don't you help Mike here Emil and I will bring in the next bunch. The look Jake gave Ed made this a question you couldn't say no to.

"OK." Ed said with a wondering look.

"Emil, Somebody's messing with the kid." Jake said after the two men had ridden out of earshot.

"How so."

"On my way out this morning I stopped and looked at the spot where he lost the cattle. It bothered me that some didn't go each way. I thought maybe a critter had spooked 'em and I was right. But this critter walked on two legs and wore boots. Evidently someone was waiting there for him. When the cattle spooked it was real dark in there 'cause the moon hadn't come up yet. The cattle were intentionally spooked and spooked Ed's horse. While Ed was trying to get him under control our critter got on his horse and chased the cattle down the west draw to the old lakebed, mixed 'em in with his and drove 'em in. Once Ed got his horse going again, the horse took the most obvious fork in the dark, which was the one straight ahead.

"Les?" Emil questioned.

"I'd be willing to bet my wages on it since he was making the sweep next to Ed, but I'll know for sure once I see his tracks. The final proof will be that gray gelding he rode yesterday. If he single foots like I think he does then he's our boy."

"Why?" Emil said sternly.

"I don't know, they hardly know each other."

"Finish checking it out, if this works out like you say I don't want a word said to any of 'em. We'll give the son of a bitch enough rope to hang himself. I need him until we get these cattle shipped." Emil got real quiet. Jake knew the man well enough to leave him alone, knowing he was already making his plans for retribution on the anarchist.

The operation went smoothly for the next couple of days. All the cattle that could be found on the half of the range the men were working were rounded up and brought in to the holding area. Emil had shown Ed a lot during those two days about how to handle cattle, horses and himself on the open range. A kinship was starting to develop between the two that neither one was consciously aware of.

The fifth day of the roundup dawned on a new set of activities. Everyone got to sleep until the crack of dawn. By the time breakfast was over and the horses were saddled it was broad daylight. Ed pulled the last watch so he met the men riding out of camp as he rode in. Jake stopped next to him as the group rode by and said; "Go get something to eat and a little sleep if you want. When you get up look me up and I'll fill you in on what's going on." Ed nodded and continued into camp. Once there he washed down a couple of small warm steaks, some beans and biscuits with a couple of cups of hot coffee, spread his bedroll in the shade of the truck bed and went to sleep.

The Sun was high in the sky when Ed finally opened his eyes, the smell of burning hair was chorused by the bawling of cows and calves separated from each other during the ordeal of being vaccinated, castrated and branded. Getting up from the bedroll, Ed shaded his eyes so he could better see the men as they moved back and forth between the propane gas stove that kept the branding irons hot, the table with the vacillation supplies and the castrating knives, and the animals they were working on. One man on horseback roped a calf by his hind feet and dragged him to a spot close to the branding stove where two men were waiting. One man would grab the reluctant calf and throw it to the ground on its side. The other man would remove the rope, grab the leg that was off the ground, and tuck the shin under his armpit as he sat on the ground. He held the leg in place under his arm by pulling on the knee with both hands as he planted a foot in the animal's crotch and pushed. The man on the head put one knee on the downed animal's neck where it meets the shoulder, grabbed the front leg at the hock and bent it back so the animal couldn't struggle, while placing his hand just below the animal's ear and pushing to keep the head down. Then three men would come over; one branded, one would vaccinate, and the other would notch an ear, put a tag on the other ear and remove the testicles if it were a bull calf. (Some outfits preferred to use an emasculator and rubber bands to remove them. With either process infection was always possible and had to be monitored by a man or men on horseback for the next couple of days.) The removed testicles were thrown into a water bucket to be cleaned and cooked at a later date. Although many would find their way onto the branding stove to be cooked and eaten like a bratwurst. Once the animal was then released, it would get up and head back into the herd to find Mama and the process would start all over again. Usually there were two sets of holders so no one would have to stand around. The scene was always extremely busy with a lot going on from start to finish. It only lasted one day for each bunch because this was a clean up procedure to get what had been missed in the spring branding or any strays that had been missed at the fall roundup the year before.

Ed figured he better not stand around watching too long, so, he climbed on his horse, rode out to the group and stopped alongside Jake who was running the branding irons.

"Park your horse over there," he said pointing to a spot about twenty feet away from the smoking iron. Ed did what he was told and walked back to the gas stove where the foreman was adjusting the hot branding irons.

"Take Les's place holding calves," Jake said as he pointed in the direction of the calf holders. Ed nodded and walked over to where Les was releasing a calf and getting up off the ground.

"Well, Sleeping Beauty finally arrived from her morning nap. Sure glad you could join us poor working folks. Les said with a sneering grin as he glanced at Ed.

"Jake told me to take your place." Ed said feeling irritated as he surveyed the ground in front of his boots.

"You'll never be man enough to take my place," Les said as he walked off.

Ed gave him a questioning look and shrugged as he turned his attention to the calf being dragged in for him and Mike to hold. Mike leaned over the struggling animal and since it was already down as it was being dragged in he merely grabbed the front leg, put his knee in the shoulder and pushed the head down.

"Make sure you grab him by the thigh just above the knee. Tuck his foot under your arm, keep your elbow down and pull hard as you push your foot into the back of his other leg. If you keep the leg under your arm straight and keep some pressure on the other leg, you'll take away all his power. Otherwise he'll jerk that leg loose and kick your teeth out." Mike said with a sadistic snicker.

Ed nodded and did what he was told. The work stopped at sunset and every one returned to camp dirty and tired. Tomorrow the larger cattle that were too big for the holders would be roped and vaccinated. In Ed's case he was dirty, tired, and sore, he used muscles he didn't even know he had.

Emil went to camp an hour earlier to heat water and start supper. The men took turns washing in the little tin basin because there would be no showers until they returned to the ranch. The men cleaned up and picked up their plates, cups and eating utensils from the food box. Supper was beef stew and sour dough biscuits with butter and honey. Blueberry cobbler with a big scoop of cream finished the meal. After he finished eating Ed rolled out his sleeping bag and sat down on it to take his boots off. When he pulled the first boot off his sleeping bag moved underneath him. Jumping up and flipping the bag back revealed two snakes coiled up and hissing ominously at him as he stood in the dirt one boot on, one in his hand.

"Snakes," he shouted as he jumped back away from the bag.

Les was sitting on his bedroll about thirty feet away. "You better look out kid, you made 'em mad when you sat on 'em. Now, they'll get you." About that time the two reptiles slithered out of the bedroll in Ed's direction. Ed was scared to death of snakes and running was an automatic response. He ran to the truck and jumped up on the flat bed, one boot still held in his hand. Les was laughing so hard he could barely sit up.

"Hey boys, look! The snakes treed the kid." No one else seemed to appreciate the humor as much while Ed stood perched on the truck bed scared to death.

"Les, did you put those bull snakes in Ed's bedroll?" Emil shouted from the cook fire.

"No sir, I don't have the faintest idea how they got there. They probably crawled in there to get warm." Les replied with a straight face.

"If I find out you did I'll fire you on the spot, after I kick your ass."

"Nope, don't know anything about it," Les mumbled as he lay back on his bedroll and turned his back to the ranch owner.

Emil set his jaw and walked over to where Ed was standing on the truck bed. "It's ok, they're just bull snakes. They look and act like rattlesnakes, but they're harmless. Go ahead and go to bed."

Shakily Ed got down, walked over to his bedroll and shook it until he was satisfied that nothing was left inside. Needless to say sleep was out of the question. Every little sound brought him to a sitting position to look around and make sure his slimy slithering bedfellows weren't sneaking up on him. From that time on Ed tried to give Les as much room as possible, he didn't know why the man didn't like him. But it didn't matter what the reason, he would steer clear of him if as much as he could.

Morning came with the incoming night watch rider waking everyone up to start the new day. Ed had not fallen into a sound sleep all night. Rolling out into the cold morning air was like experiencing a bad hangover. Everyone was crowded around the cook fire getting their food as Les walked up and laughingly said: "Hey kid, see any more snakes?"

Ed looked at him and said "no."

"Well, you better watch where you sit. I saw 'em crawling around your bedroll again this morning."

Mike turned and glared at the grinning prankster. "Why don't you leave him alone?" Les shrugged and looked at his plate as he held it out for Emil to fill.

While the men ate breakfast Jake passed out the orders for the day. "Buck you and Ron do the roping until we finish. Emil and I will take care of the groundwork. I figure we should get done about noon. After dinner we'll start cutting out the replacements. Ron you do the cutting. Mike,Don, Les and Ed hold the herd. Emil, Buck and I will hold the replacements." Everyone acknowledged the orders with some kind of audible gesture as they finished eating their breakfast.

Holding cattle in one spot on the open range while a man on horseback moves slowly amongst them requires a horse that is calm but quick. For this reason Ed decided to use the buckskin. She was a veteran at this type of work. She winded quick because of her age but there was nothing strenuous or enduring about holding cattle in one spot. Even though she was old she was smart and quick and Ed needed all the help he could get.

The rider doing the cutting works the selected animal beyond the outside perimeter of the herd. The riders holding the replacement stock that is being cut out of the main herd meet the rider and animal and escort it away from its companions to the replacement herd. Which is held far enough away that it won't return to the main herd of its own volition. The problem is when an animal is being removed from the main herd another animal may try to follow. The outriders have to be on their toes to intercept and turn it back into the herd before it can break through the perimeter and the rest of the herd follows.

It was mid afternoon and Ron was working a particularly obnoxious cow out of the herd. Ed was fascinated with how Ron and his horse seemed as one with each other as they worked a single cow out of the mass without disturbing the rest of the cattle. When he finally worked the cow beyond the perimeter of the herd Emil and Jake took over and headed for the opening through rocky butte. Ed caught some motion out of the corner of his right eye. A cow was making a break from the edge of the herd. Wheeling the buckskin he gave the mare her head as the cow broke into a hard run to join her companions being ushered to the open range. Ed was thrown hard into the back of the saddle as the mare took off in pursuit. Clinging to the saddle horn they raced off at a dead run to head the critter off. The horse was much faster than the cow and no thanks to Ed's ability came up alongside her and started turning her back toward the herd. As cow, horse and rider made the sweeping turn they inadvertently wound up running along a shale slide on the finger of land that protruding from the lower escarpment to the range below. The cow was trapped between the shale slide and the horse as they raced toward the rock wall where the game trail started down. Suddenly realizing her predicament she slid to a stop and swapped ends. The buckskin being an excellent cowpony anticipated this move and did the same, facing the cow all the time. Staying on a horse executing a one hundred and eighty degree turn at full speed (about thirty miles an hour) takes a lot of experience and horsemanship, both of which Ed was sorely lacking. The long and the short of the whole maneuver was the horse went north and the rider went south. All Ed could remember when he woke up a week later in the hospital was the falling sensation.

CHAPTER #6

THE WATER RIPPLED each time the flat stone touched it and skipped. The next flat stone sank immediately with a loud "kerplunk" when it hit the water. Les wrinkled his nose and sighed. He didn't understand why his Mom and Dad did some of the things they did. They were the adults but they didn't make being seven years old any easier. When he felt like this he just wanted to be alone. He could hunt and fish or just roam through the Pennsylvania woods that engulfed his rural home. Since there were no siblings for him to play with he learned to entertain himself. His curious mind was always working, whether he was trying to figure out animal tracks or why rocks look like they do. The great outdoors allowed him a mental and physical release when things troubled him. Les turned and started walking. He was frustrated and walking helped sometimes. He moved easily through the trees trying to imitate the birdcalls around him. Tiring of this he flopped down on a grassy knoll that over looked a small pond hoping to see a deer or coyote stop for a drink. After a half an hour of seeing nothing except a few turtles he laid back and started cloud watching. His vivid imagination made the clouds come to life with all sorts of animals and objects. He became so totally engrossed that he lost all track of time until the evening shadows brought him back to reality. Getting to his feet he yawned, stretched and started to walk home. Approaching the house Les noticed his parents company was gone. "Good," he thought to himself, "I won't have to say, hello or goodbye and watch them leave." Opening the door on the back porch of the large two-story farmhouse Les took off his shoes and snuck quietly up the stairs to his room.

"Les, is that you?" His Mother called from the bottom of the stairs.

"Ya Ma, I just came in."

"I have some supper in the warmer over the top of the stove, come down and get it."

"OK, in a minute."

"Don't be long now," his mother said before walking back into the living room where she and her husband were doing their evening reading.

"Robert I swear that boy is always out in the woods. What if a wild animal attacked him or he fell and broke a leg?"

"Now Julia, the boy is seven years old. He's been running around in these woods since he was old enough to walk. He knows every nook and cranny for a couple of miles around. He doesn't go into the deep woods he just plays around the pastures and woodlots."

"Just the same I'd feel a whole lot better if he wasn't gone so much. He could do a lot more around here instead of cruising the timber with you so much. Robert closed the book he had been reading and laid it in his lap as he reflected back.

Robert and Juliet met in college the year before Robert received his bachelor's degree in agronomy and agriculture in 1914. After he graduated from college Robert joined the U.S. Army to help fight the Kaiser's army in Europe. He came back in one piece, renewed his relationship with Juliet and married her in June of 1918. They settled in Pittsburgh, Pennsylvania. Robert got a job in a steel mill and Juliet worked in a restaurant at the bottom of squirrel hill. In the fall of 1919 they bought a farm Southeast of Pittsburgh near a little town called Latrobe, Pennsylvania. It was 300 acres of woods and farmland surrounding a two-story house, large dairy barn and outbuildings. This was what Robert had trained for in college. They used all their savings and the mustering out pay Robert received from the military for a down payment and to stock the place. The first four years were hard and lean, but by the time Les was born in 1925, Robert and Juliet paid back a quarter of the money they had borrowed against the farm. The next four years were good, the family prospered and paid back half the money left on the mortgage against the farm. Then came 1929!!! The stock market crashed and so did the markets that bought the commodities that agriculture produced. No markets, no income. The family couldn't sell the crops, the milk or the livestock. Everyone else was in the same shape. Payments couldn't be made because there was no income or cash flow. The banks had no choice but to call in the notes as they came due.

The Corbett's still owed a little less than half of the mortgage money, plus the money borrowed for machinery, seed, etc. When the bank foreclosed they lost everything they had except the clothes on their backs. All they had to live on was whatever came out of the garden, milk from a cow that had mysteriously disappeared into the woods just before the trucks had come to take the others away. A sow pig that would farrow (have babies) in a month and a bunch of chickens, ducks and geese that was not worth taking. Also, the woods was full of wild game, fish in the streams and ponds, wild berries and nuts were everywhere. The haymow in the barn was full of baled hay. The cribs and grain bins were full of corn and wheat. The machinery that was worth anything was taken. "Oh well," Robert said to try and comfort his frantic wife as they watched the trucks roll out of there driveway in a cloud of dust. "There wasn't any money to buy gas anyhow."

The house had a large wood-burning cook stove in the kitchen. There was a parlor stove that burned wood in the dining room, a fireplace and a silver trimmed potbellied wood burner in the living room. The bank allowed the Corbett's to live on the place just so it wouldn't be vandalized or deteriorate until the economy improved and/or a buyer could be found. The basic needs of food, heat and shelter were satisfied and plentiful, survival was ensured.

In 1930 an elderly couple from Lily hammer, Switzerland bought twenty five hundred acres of hardwood forestland from the bank for pennies on the dollar. This included the land and buildings the Corbett's had previously owned. The Swiss couple owned a number of fine furniture stores and wood crafting shops that created furniture exclusively for them. The fine first growth timber in Europe was becoming expensive and hard to get. Thanks to the American depression they were able to buy large chunks of land in the Midwest, East and South for little or nothing. The land they purchased in Pennsylvania was heavily forested with mature oak, beech wood, butternut, black cherry, walnut and other assorted hardwoods used for fine furniture.

Shortly after their land purchase was finalized, the Krueger's showed up on the Corbett's doorstep and introduced themselves. They were a fine old couple and liked the Corbett's (especially Robert) the minute they met them.

"The reason we came to see you was to introduce ourselves and let you know what our intentions are and find out what yours are. My name is Johan and this is my wife Hilda. We bought twenty-five hundred acres of land in this area. According to what Mr. Harrison at the bank told us you originally owned some land and these buildings here."

"That's true." Robert replied "We owned three hundred acres until the economy collapsed and then we lost it all. The bank has been letting us live here rent-free until they could sell it or we could afford to start paying rent."

"It looks like you're faring pretty well." Johan replied.

"Oh, we have plenty to eat, we just don't have any money to spend that's all. We thought about going back to Pittsburgh to find jobs but our friends and relation seem to be worse off than we are, it seems there is no work to be had."

"Work is very hard to find. However, your economy will come back eventually. That's why we came over here and bought so much land. Not only for the timber but it will be a good investment for the future."

"The future." Robert said a little bitterly. "When I got my degrees from college I thought my future was pretty well set and if I worked hard I would become wealthy and provide a good life for my family. The best I can say right now is we're alive."

Johan looked up with interest. "You have degrees from a university? In what fields?"

"I have a bachelors degree in agriculture and agronomy."

"Do you know anything about forestry?"

"Some, why?"

"I am looking for some one to manage the property that I just bought here. Do you know anything about logging and reforestation?"

"Look Mr. Krueger I won't waste your time or mine. The fields I trained in go hand in hand with what your looking for but they're not specifically along those lines. If you're offering me a job I'll tell you what I'll do. There's a small college at Latrobe and another one at Jeannette, if you hire me I will take whatever classes I need to be able to do the job."

The elder Krueger sat quietly in thought for a moment. "Deal." He said as he stuck out his hand. "You work out a class schedule. I need to plan the operation and figure out what to pay you."

Robert grabbed the extended hand and pumped vigorously. "Thank you sir. You won't be sorry, I promise you."

"I wouldn't have made the offer if I thought I would be. Now, it is getting late and Hilda and I must be going. The first Sunday of next month you and your family come to our house for dinner and we will finalize our plans. We are staying in the old Richards place two miles west of here."

"I know the place. We will be there at three o'clock sharp."

"Good. Thank you very much." The old Swiss said as Juliet handed the couple their coats.

"Thank you sir, you don't know how much your visit tonight has meant to us. You have literally turned our life around. Once again thank you," Juliet said as she genuflected.

After the Krueger's left, Robert and Juliet grabbed each other and hugged tightly. "Things are going to be all right now baby," Robert said as he kissed her on the forehead. "Tomorrow I will check out the colleges and then we'll sit down and figure out how to finance my education." Returning from his thoughts Robert looked over at his wife and wondered how much longer it would be until the baby arrived. He smiled as he opened the book in his lap and started to read.

Things went well for the Corbett's during the years they worked for the Krueger's. The Swiss couple put Robert in charge of the management, logging and reforestation of the whole parcel. He did a good job and made the old couple a lot of money. Robert and Juliet decided on a plan to put Robert through school two weeks after the conversation with the Krueger's. He managed to get his Master's degree in forestry while working for the elderly couple. The eventual goal was a Doctorate degree and University tenure.

In 1939 Johan Krueger died. His wife continued to run the operation until 1940. Then she sold everything and went back to her native Switzerland. Before she left she gave all of the managers 100 shares of stock and a large cash settlement. When Johan died Robert was far-sighted enough to see the handwriting on the wall and applied at a number of universities in the East and Midwest for a teaching position with eventual tenure while working for his PHD. Two months after Hilda went back to Switzerland, Pennsylvania State University at State College, Pennsylvania accepted Robert for a teaching position in their science department with possible tenure.

CHAPTER #7

THE EXCITEMENT WAS almost unbearable for Les as his parents finished their breakfast. This was his first day of High School in State College. He was starting his sophomore year and he didn't know what to expect. The High School at Latrobe paled in comparison to the size and sheer numbers of students here. Les was not physically intimidated. At fifteen years old he was 6' 4" tall and weighed 185 lbs, he was lean, strong and good-looking. He had square jawed Clark Kent look about him. He didn't know how his one-room schoolhouse education would compare to the sophisticated big city education and mentally he was intimidated.

"Dad are you ready to go. I don't want to be late on my first day."

"In a minute son." Robert said as he finished a last swig of coffee "OK, grab your stuff and let's go."

Les beat his dad to the door and the car. Robert smiled at his son's eagerness knowing he would excel in the intellectual and physical challenges that lay ahead of him. When they arrived in front of the School Les climbed out of the car and stared as his father sped away. The building was huge. It was a three story red brick with lots of windows and four sets of doors in the front. A boy dismounted from a car that had pulled up just behind Les. The boy walked alongside, stuck out his hand as he said, "Hi, I'am Grant Bishop.

"Les Corbett," grabbing the hand and giving it a couple of pumps.

"Your dad teaches at Penn State, right?"

"Ya, how did you know?"

"My Mom works in the office. She does a lot of secretarial work for his research."

"Great." Les commented as they walked the cement sidewalk leading to the large brick building.

"Is this your first year?" Grant asked with a smile.

"No, I'm a sophomore."

"Me too. How long have you lived here?"

"We just moved here in June. We lived out side of a little town called Latrobe, Southeast of Pittsburgh. My dad started at Penn State last fall. My parents didn't want to take me out of school there so my dad commuted and house hunted until school was out. Have you lived here very long?"

"All my life." Grant said proudly.

"Then you know most of the kids here, right?"

"Sure why wouldn't I? Grant looked at Les, "Oh, I got it, new kid on the block, I'll tell you what if you want to hang with me, I'll show you around."

"Sure, what's your first class?"

"Biology, what's yours?"

"English."

Grant thought a minute, "I have math 3rd hour and study hall the 4th."

Les replied, "I have study hall 4th hour too."

"Good I'll see you then," Grant replied as they went opposite directions down the hallway.

Les was elated after his first day. He found out he wasn't different from anyone else. Actually, he had the edge over most of the boys because of his large athletic body and good looks. All those formative years he had been running around the woods had given him a long lean body and an extraordinary amount of ability and coordination. His shy, soft-spoken, backwoods manner added to his demeanor and the girls flocked around him.

Grant was to be one of his best friends. They competed in sports and hung out together out of school. The first year saw the two of them letter in football. They were both excellent scholars carrying a four-point grade average with honors. In their junior year Grant played basketball and lettered in track, Les lettered in football again and also in swimming and became captain of the defensive football squad. Both continued to carry a four point academic average with honors.

After the junior prom everyone went to a pre-determined spot in the country and drank until daylight. This was the first time Les ever got drunk and needless to say there were all lot of unhappy parents when their bedraggled, smelly dirty little darlings staggered into the house. Robert and Juliet were no exception.

"Where in the hell have you been all night?" Robert roared at Les who was on his knees noisily puking into the toilet. "Do you realize you were responsible for the safety and return of the girl you picked up and took there? What the hell were you thinking about, anyway?"

"Everybody went." Augggh puke!!!!!!!!!

"I don't give a damn who went or who's idea it was, you are old enough to be responsible for your actions. If your going to act like a child we'll treat you like one. You just forfeited your allowance and any car privileges for the next month. I know a few of your teachers and after I have a talk with them I am sure you won't have a lot of free time for a while."

Les laid his neck on the edge of the toilet bowl, his nose hanging inches from the colored water, moaning softly as his Dad reached over and pushed the flush handle. The spray from the yellow chunky water misted his face as his parents stormed out of the bathroom. Eventually life at home and in town returned to normal. Les finished the year with his usual four-point grade average.

During his senior year Les applied to half a dozen Universities for entrance. He received two acceptance replies. One from the University of Maryland and one from Penn State where his dad was a professor. Les and his parents spent the rest of his high school year discussing options for his future. Since his father was now a tenured academic at Penn State, Les valued his opinion about what fields were going to be the most lucrative in the future. The two of them had many long talks together and Les was leaning toward pursuing a degree in law. His father helped him secure scholarships to Penn State in football and academics based on the grades and honors he achieved in High School.

It was 1944 and Les was a strapping 6'6" 200 pound good-looking college freshman. Grant joined the Marine corps and was sent to Europe after his boot camp training. Les excelled in everything he did and by the end of his first year he was captain of the rowing team and was on his way to becoming a candidate for the Heisman trophy and the all American football award. His academic average was 4.0 and he was on the Dean's list.

When Les graduated High School his father started making extended field trips to the western states doing research for his doctorate degree. Returning home in March of 1945 after an eight-month field trip, Robert Corbett talked excitedly over breakfast to Juliet and Les about how close he was to completing his thesis and securing his PHD. Elaborating on his plans to his captive audience he looked at Les and asked: "How would you like to work on a real cattle ranch for the summer?" Les looked at his dad curiously as Robert continued talking without waiting for an answer. "I met an engineer at one of the potash plants outside of Rock Springs, Wyoming. His father owns a pretty good-sized spread near Medicine Bow, Wyoming. He said he might be looking for help for the summer. He gave me his name, phone number and told me to call him. I gave him a call about a week later. He said he always hired extra hands during the summer to build fence. I told him I would talk to you when I got home and then give him a call if you were interested. So, what do you think?"

Les looked into his father's enthusiastic eyes. "Sure, it sounds like fun," he said almost as a matter of fact.

Juliet broke into the conversation with, "that's a long way to go for a job."

Robert gave her a hard look. "It's good honest work. He'll be able to see a different side of life and meet some real interesting people."

Juliet replied, "I don't know if I want him to be that far away."

Irritated Robert replied, "My God Julia, he's twenty years old, for Christ's sake cut the cord."

Juliet Corbett gave her husband an icy stare, threw her napkin on the table and stormed out of the room.

Robert felt Les's concern, "She'll be alright. She's just being a mother now, should we make that call?"

Les gave a worried look at the doorway his mother had disappeared through and then looked back at his dad. "Ya, I guess so."

Robert almost knocked the chair he was sitting in over a he leapt for the phone hanging on the kitchen wall. He turned the crank twice and anxiously taped his foot on the floor while he waited for the operator to answer. "Yes operator, I would like 786-2955 in Medicine Bow, Wyoming. A mister Emil Schmidt. Yes, that's OK." (More foot taping) "Hello Mr. Schmidt. This is Robert Corbett I' am calling from State College, Pennsylvania. We talked three weeks ago about my son working for you over the summer. (Pause) That's right, I met him over by Rock Springs. No, I am a professor at Pennsylvania State College. My research took me out to the plant and your Son and I met there." (Pause) "Oh, he did talk to you then. (Pause) "Well, thank you, I was equally impressed by him. He helped to forward my research efforts a lot. (Pause) "Yes, we talked and he said he was interested." (Pause) "He's twenty years old, 6'6" tall and weighs about two hundred pounds." (Pause) "No, he'll be starting his second year here at Penn State this fall." (Pause) "No, he's just looking for a summer job. The only thing around here for the summer is grocery clerk or mowing lawn." (Pause) "I understand." (Pause) "No, I wouldn't expect you to, I'll pay his ticket out and back." It's not so much the money as it is the experience. He leads a pretty sheltered life here and I would like to see him experience a little bit of life before he graduates." (Pause) "Sure, I realize there is no guarantee, I really appreciate this. Thank you, I'll let you talk to him. His name is Lester, but we all call him Les." Robert held out the earpiece and motioned for Les to come to the phone. "His name is Emil Schmidt and he wants to talk to you," Robert said in a low voice as Les grabbed the phone and put it to his ear.

"Hello Mr. Schmidt, my name is Les Corbett."

The voice over the crackling phone was strong and masculine. "Hello son, have you ever worked on a ranch before?"

"No sir, but I did grow up on a dairy farm back here."

"You now how to build fence then?"

"Yes sir, we had a lot of barbed wire fence on the farm where we lived."

"Have you ever worked with horses?"

"We had a couple of teams of work horses that we worked the fields with."

"You know if you come out here to work I won't give you any guarantees. The work is hard and the hours long. The pay is $100.00 a month and keep. You probably can make more money back there after you figure your expenses coming out here and back. If you can't do the work I won't keep you. Is that clear?"

"Yes sir, I can do the work. My dad said it would be a good experience and he would pay for the train tickets."

"Well, understand it's hard physical work. All you'll be doing is building fence."

"I understand, that's fine with me I like hard work."

"When can you be out here?"

"My final exams are in May. I know I could be there by the middle of June."

"When would you have to leave?"

"My classes start right after labor day. I should be back by the first of September."

"OK, here's the deal. You be here by the fifteenth of June and stay until a week before Labor Day. I'll give you $100.00 a month, room and board and more work than you can handle. Is it a deal?"

"Yes sir."

"Good, when you get off the train in Medicine Bow walk across the highway to the Virginian Hotel. Tell the clerk to call me and I'll pick you up there."

"Yes sir, Thank you. I'll see you in June."

"OK, until then. Bye."

"Goodbye."

Robert slapped his son on the back. "You'll love it out there it's like nothing you've ever seen before. The sheer size of it will boggle your mind."

"It's really that good?" Les said giving his dad a questioning look.

"You bet. The sunrises and the sunsets are indescribable. Every color of the spectrum and the aroma from the sage and pinion will take your breath away."

Robert's enthusiasm was beginning to infect Les. "Alright, this ought to be a fun summer."

"You should be able to bring home a couple of hundred dollars to go to school. I'll spring for the train tickets to and from, otherwise you won't have much left when you return."

"Thanks dad."

Robert smiled and returned to his breakfast. He didn't tell Les his ulterior motive was the scenario of the ranch and the people he would encounter. Robert knew Les would learn values and experience life, as he never would be able to in the psuedo urban setting of a place like State College, Pennsylvania.

CHAPTER #8

The journey to Medicine Bow, Wyoming took five days. There was a six-hour layover in Chicago, Illinois and an eight-hour layover in Omaha, Nebraska plus a bunch of stops along the way. Les watched the landscape and the people change as the train made its way west. In the East and Midwest most of the fields grew corn or some kind of a cash crop. The people wore low-heeled shoes and walked or rode in a motorized vehicle to get around. The scenery started to change about central Nebraska. The fields got larger and grew mostly hay and grass. The cattle changed from dairy to beef. Large herds of cattle and horses were becoming a common sight. Most of the people wore high-heeled riding boots and their mode of conveyance was pick-up truck, horse and wagon or horseback.

When Les stepped off the train at Medicine Bow, the strong acid smell of manure from the stock pens greeted him. Cattle were being driven into the holding pens adjacent to the tracks. Men on horseback were swinging ropes, shouting and whistling at the cattle as they moved them into the pens. Les recognized the sicky sweet smell of sweat amidst the clouds of dust and the confusion of noise. Otherwise this was a new experience for him, even though he had been raised on a farm he'd never seen cattle handled like this. He was fascinated and walked across the highway to get a better view from the porch of the hotel. Sitting on one of the available chairs he leaned back against the wall and absorbed him self in the action across the road. He wanted to get a feel for the place before he called Mr. Schmidt. It was about two o'clock in the after noon when Les got out of the chair and went inside to have the clerk call, Emil Schmidt showed up an hour later. In the meantime Les gave his surroundings the once over.

The hotel was four stories. It had a porch the full length of the front with a shingled roof to keep the elements off anyone sitting in the assorted chairs furnished by the hotel. There were two entrances, one for the hotel and one for the bar. Next to the main structure was a neat row of little shops. Les walked inside through the hotel entrance and looked around. The main dining room was to the left. The staircase to the upstairs was straight ahead through the lobby and the desk was to the right. Behind the desk was a large sitting room and the entrances to the adjoining bar and a large dance/ banquet hall complete with a kitchen. The dining room was formal and decorated elegantly with red velvet curtains and drapes. The walls were decorated with original Russell and Remington paintings. Some were accompanied by the pencil sketch that inspired them. The huge claw legged tables were covered with fine linen tablecloths and napkins. English bone china, crystal glassware and the finest silver settings were in place for the anticipated daily dinner quests. The lobby was small and consisted of a large Persian rug on a hardwood floor and the hotel desk. The desk was a tall wooden piece very ornately carved. The adjoining staircase was carpeted and had an ornately carved banister. The sitting room behind the clerk's desk was as luxurious as the dining room. The walls were also covered with Russell and Remington paintings. Large leather covered easy chairs, leather covered divans, solid wood end and coffee tables enveloped the room. The kitchen was attached to the dance hall/banquet room. It had a wide hallway that led under the stairs to the dining room. The bar was the most frequented and the most conservative room in the whole building. The bar it self was "L" shaped and solid wood with a brass foot rail its full length. The floor was tongue and grooved oak. Three large wooden columns held up the ceiling. In back of the bar was a plate glass mirror with the normal array of liquor bottles and glasses sitting on the cabinet counter top underneath it. The walls were made of four-inch pine boards put together in a herringbone design. Animal heads, antlers, branding irons, cowboy garb, horse gear and just about anything else that was small enough to hang, depicted the way of live that existed here. Burned into a small wall next to the short side of the bar were the brands that represented all the ranches in the area. This was the gathering place for all the locals. This is where all the news and gossip was hashed over, either at the card tables or leaning on the bar with a foot resting on the brass rail.

Les had finished his tour of the establishment and was sitting in one of the plush leather covered chairs reading the paper when Emil Schmidt walked up.

"You must be Les Corbett?" he asked as Les looked up.

Putting down the paper and standing up Les stuck out his hand and said, "yes sir."

Les looked down at the stocky man in the bib overalls and khaki hat. Emil wasn't quite what Les had mentally pictured him to be. He wasn't as tall or slim as Les thought his voice over the phone had portrayed him to be. He dressed like the farmer neighbors the Corbett's had in Latrobe. Les had pictured him in cowboy clothes with a big wide brimmed hat and maybe a gun on his hip.

"I'm Emil Schmidt," The man said as he shook Les's hand with an iron grip. "If your ready grab your bags and let's go, Marianne has supper cooking."

"My bag is over at the train station." Les said as he motioned in the direction of the building across the road.

"Well, let's go get it then," Emil said starting for the door. The two men climbed into Emil's pickup truck and drove across the road. While Les retrieved his luggage Emil walked over to the men on horseback. They had finished pushing the cattle into the holding pens and were sitting on their horses in a group conversing. "Hi Emil, you taken on a new hand?" the dusty cowboy said as Emil walked up.

"Ya, I needed someone to build fence this summer. Is Jim shipping early this year?" (Referring to the man's boss and the cattle in the pens.)

"Naw, these are just some barrens (cows that didn't produce calves and would take grass away from the ones that did) that we culled. We were about to head over to the hotel and have a drink care to join us?"

"Not today, Marianne has supper waiting and I need to get the new hand settled in."

The rider nodded and said, "Well, maybe next time."

Emil nodded, "sounds good to me. You boys be careful and don't raise to much hell." The men smiled, nodded and turned their horses for the hotel. Emil walked to the pickup truck where Les was leaning against a fender. They got in and headed for the ranch.

The ranch was located about four miles west of Medicine Bow. Approaching the house down the dusty lane Emil called a driveway Les was surprised at how neat and well kept the house was in comparison to the other buildings. The house was freshly painted white with neatly kept flowerbeds, a manicured lawn and a white picket fence surrounding it. Emil stopped the pickup truck in front of a weathered log building.

"This is the bunkhouse, that cement building over there is the wash house. Get settled, cleaned up and then come up to the porch on the backside of the house. That's where we eat, just walk in and we'll talk about what I want you to do over supper."

Les nodded and got out of the truck. "Thank you," he said as Emil drove the truck away.

Walking into the bunkhouse was like nothing he had experienced before. The first thing he encountered was the smell. It was a cross between a saddle shop, a saloon, and a veterinarian office. The odor wasn't overpowering but it definitely was there. Clothes were piled here and there and various pieces of riding gear were hanging neatly from the wall and bedposts. A few whisky bottles were sitting on the table or under a couple of the double bunk beds in the room. Since there was only one small window the single overhead light had to be on to illuminate the room. Les threw his bags on an empty bunk and grabbed his towel before he went to the washhouse. After he cleaned up and changed clothes he headed for the main house to eat. On the way he had a chance to look around at his surroundings. The only other building other than the bunkhouse and washhouse was the barn. Like the other two buildings, the barn was structurally sound but unpainted and weathered. Next to it were two wood pole corrals, a large oval about two hundred feet long by a hundred feet wide and a smaller round one about fifty feet in diameter. They were attached so you could go from one to the other through a gate. The larger corral had a large scarred and worn wooden post in the middle, sticking about five feet out of the ground. A large wooden water trough sitting on a couple of logs was accessible from either corral. A low-decked wagon was sitting along side the big corral with loose hay on it, obviously for the horses inside the corral. As Les approached the porch he could hear voices. The voices stopped as he mounted the steps and walked through the door. The room consisted of oil stove in the corner, screened widows on all three walls and a long table with benches and a large silver coffee urn sitting at one end. The table was set with plates and silverware. Emil and five other men were at the table drinking coffee.

"C'mon in and sit down." Emil said as he pointed to an empty seat by the silver coffee urn. "Boy's, I want you to meet Les. He'll be building fence for us this summer." Everyone nodded. Emil continued with the introductions, "this is Jake," he said nodding toward the pot bellied, balding man next to him. "He's the foreman here. You take all your orders from him and whatever he says goes. The redheaded galoot next to him is Ron, (Ron flashed a big toothy grin) the big ugly one next to him is Mike, (Mike knew Emil was teasing him and didn't take offence) the quiet and shy one on my left here is Buck. He doesn't say much but he's a good hand. (Buck gave a little grunt and looked at Les) the long skinny drink of water next to him is Don, our newest addition, until you that is." About the time the introductions were over a tall, good-looking, middle-aged woman walked in with two huge platters of food and set them on the table. "Les, this is Mrs. Schmidt," Emil said as she straitened up from setting the platters on the table.

Les stood up as he greeted the woman. "Pleased to meet you Mrs. Schmidt," as he bowed slightly.

"It's nice to meet you Les, before you leave see me. I'll fill you in on how we do the laundry, and give you your bedding."

"Yes ma'am." Les said as he sat down. The talk at the table resumed as the men ate. After supper Emil, Jake and Les sat at the table discussing what Les would be doing during his employment at the ranch.

"We start our day around here at five am. Clean up and come eat breakfast. Then get to work. If you are close to the ranch you get to eat dinner. If not, then supper's the next meal. If you get drunk other than your day off you're fired. I don't care if you come to work with a hang over, just don't let it interfere with your work. Jake will work with you tomorrow and show you the ropes. After that you're on your own. Don't be afraid to ask questions, if you don't understand or know something. I'd rather have you ask than screw something up." Les nodded as Emil continued. "You said over the phone that you worked with horses on your farm?" Les nodded and said, "that's right we used them to work the farm." "Good, cause that's what we use to pull with around here. You'll have a team to use for the summer on the fencing wagon. Any questions?"

Les shook his head, "No, not right now."

"Good, I'll leave you with Jake and I'll send Marianne out." With that he got up and walked through the open doorway into the house.

Jake asked, "Emil said you grew up on a farm in Pennsylvania?"

"That's right, we had a sixty five head of dairy cows and three teams of workhorses. We farmed about one hundred and fifty acres and a hundred and fifty acres was pasture and woods."

"Sounds like it was a pretty good sized operation. What kind of horses did you work?"

"We had a team of Percherons, the rest where mongrels."

Mrs. Schmidt walked into the room and both men started to get up. "Oh, sit tight you two. Les here is your bedding, washday is Wednesday, put your dirties in this sack and when you come to breakfast throw it on the floor by that wall," she said pointing to the wall across from the heater.

"Yes ma'am."

"You two have a good night, I'll see you in the morning." Both men stood as she turned and left the room.

"Well, I've got to get home," Jake said, "I'll see you in the morning also." With that he walked to the hat rack by the porch door put his hat on and left. Les followed him out and walked to the bunkhouse.

The hands were playing cards as Les walked into the bunkhouse and threw his bedding on the bunk he'd picked.

Don spoke up and said, "You want to join us?"

Les replied, "No thanks, I'm going to make my bed and then I'll watch."

"If you need money I'll stake you," Don stated.

"No, I've got money I just don't feel like playing right now."

The men returned to their game as Les made his bed. After it was made he hopped on it and watched as the men played their game of poker. Les purposely had not mentioned that he didn't know how to play poker. He knew the game and had occasionally seen others play it but it had never interested him so he didn't bother learning how to play it. He was smart enough to realize that in this setting he probably should learn for future entertainment. So, he watched as the men played and by the end of the night felt he could play with reasonable skill.

Morning came with the splendid beauty that most western sunrises have. Les was on his way to the washhouse when he stopped and watched in wonder as the morning kaleidoscope unfolded before him. Don stopped on his way back to the bunkhouse, "Pretty isn't it."

Les nodded, "It sure is, I've never seen anything quite like it."

"This is what it's like almost every morning out here. We see it so much I guess we just take it for granted. You better hurry up or you be late for breakfast," Don said as he headed for the bunkhouse.

"Ok, see you there."

Breakfast reminded Les of the meals his mother used to serve when they were on the farm. It consisted of eggs, ham, sausage, steak, potatoes, pancakes, toast, jam, syrup butter, coffee, milk, water, fresh strawberries and a large bowl of pure cream, separated and refrigerated after the cow had been milked the night before. Les thought he ate a lot, but compared to these men he was not a big eater. His appetite would improve once he started building fence but for right now he was not physical enough. When breakfast was finished and the men were filing out of the room Jake said, "Les, wait for me outside."

Les nodded and walked out with the others. Presently Jake came out and barked, "let's go," as he walked toward the barn. Once in the barn Jake pointed to a saddle and bridle. "Grab those and a blanket and bring 'em out to the corral."

There were three horses loose in the large corral. Jake ran them into the smaller corral so he could rope a couple for him and Les to ride. While they were saddling their mounts Jake explained to Les what was going to happen. "We'll round up the work horses and run 'em in the corral. Once we figure out which ones we want we'll turn the rest loose. We don't keep our hay in the barn like they do back East. It's all kept outside in loose stacks, we don't bale anything. When you deal with the numbers we do it's easier to handle that way. The barn is just for storing harness, riding gear and a couple of saddle horses during the winter. All the stock except a few saddle horses are turned out to feed on the grass until we need them." The two men rode out of the corral and headed for the Little Medicine Bow River, which ran about two hundred yards behind the barn. "They usually hang around the river bottoms where the grass is thicker and sweeter." After about a half an hour of riding Jake spotted a small herd of the cumbersome looking beasts. "They're not pretty to look at but they sure can work." Jake said as the two men started driving the bulky, ungroomed animals toward the ranch. Once the horses were secured in the corral Jake and Les rode alongside the fence that needed repairing. Jake talked as they walked their horses appraising what needed to be done." We don't have individual pastures. The only fence that exists is a "line fence" it keeps our cattle from mixing with the neighbor's cattle most of the time. Everyone has a rider out patching the fence all the time. We have over a hundred miles of fence. It's always in need of repair at some point. About every five years you have to go through and replace it. That's what you're going to be doing. You'll leave right after breakfast. First thing you'll do before you come to breakfast is harness your team and grain 'em. After you eat you'll hitch 'em to the wagon and take off. When you get in at night feed and brush your team down. Make sure they're dry before you grain 'em. Then load your wagon with any supplies (wire, posts, staples or tools) you need for the next day. Then get cleaned up and come to supper. Mrs. Schmidt will have supper ready for you at nine o'clock. If you miss it, all your going to get is a sandwich from the leftovers and a cup of coffee. Now as far as the fence goes we hang five strands of barbed wire on hedge posts. (Osage wood) It comes from Oklahoma, absolutely will not rot in the ground, hard as a rock and that's the only problem. It's so hard you can't drive a staple into it, you have to wire the barbed wire to the post with wire. Every eighty rods (quarter of a mile) we put in brace posts with creosoted railroad ties. It takes three six-foot ties and two four-foot pieces for bracing. We hold it together with number nine galvanized smooth wire. Here's one right here." The two men rode over to the three posts buried in an upright position. They were notched to accommodate the spacer beams and the number nine wire was strung from top to top and then twisted to prevent separation. "We tie the barbed wire to the center post and stretch it a quarter mile at a time. The rest is pretty much common sense."

Les looked at Jake and nodded. "Fence building out here ought to be pretty easy, you don't have a lot of trees."

"Huh," Jake expelled, "We don't have many trees but I'll guarantee your gonna hit a lot of rocks. The only saving grace is most of the rocks out here are flat and about pie plate size. You can move most of them out real easy with a pry bar. The soil is dry and sandy. A posthole digger won't do you much good. A shovel and a pry bar are about all you need to dig a hole. I guarantee by the end of the summer you'll be in really great shape."

"It sounds like it, maybe I'll build a few muscles."

Jake laughed, "You'll build muscles all right. When you go back in the fall you're definitely going to be stronger than you are right now. It's a lot of hard work and there's no shade. Make sure you have a good hat and a good pair of leather gloves. Your gonna be a long ways from home, always carry a canteen of water with you and a bedroll cause the farther you get from the ranch the more you'll spend the night sleeping under the stars."

Les thought about that statement for a while. He wondered what it would be like to sleep out on the wide-open prairie. He had spent nights in the woods back in Pennsylvania, but there were always tree branches to build a lean to or a canvas for shelter, something to crawl under. Out here the only thing to crawl under would be the wagon or large sagebrush and you probably wouldn't want to do that because of the reptiles you might have to share the ground with.

"Well, let's get back and get those horses in harness so you can go to work."

"Getting those horses in harness" turned out to be a little more involved than it first appeared. "We'll use four head to take out a couple of loads of posts and railroad ties that way you'll have a spare team in case one of 'em goes lame or something. I've had the boys loading the big wagon and the flat bed truck with posts and ties. They're going to take the truck to the base of Elk, (Mountain) and we'll take the wagon about ten miles out. That should give you a pretty good pile of posts fairly close to draw from. To start with load the fence wagon from the post pile here, as you get farther out use those piles. We have a corral and a cabin at the base of Elk. I'll have the boys take hay and grain for the horses and food and water for you up there before the end of the week."

Les had seen four head driven before. The frisky workhorses didn't take long to settle down pulling the big heavy wagon once they were under way. Jake knew how to drive four in hand. He kept them into their collars all the way out. By the time Jake and Les got the wagon unloaded and back to the ranch it was dark. They took care of the horses and Jake said, "we'll load your fence wagon tomorrow when we can see what we're doing.

"That's fine by me," Les said "It's nine o'clock I'm going to supper.

"Me too," Jake replied as the two men headed for the washhouse.

After supper Les walked over to the bunkhouse where the rest of the men could be heard playing the ongoing poker game and this time Les participated. A casual conversation continued throughout the game. Les was never a real big talker, which was fine with these westerners. It was the way Les answered their questions and talked that bothered them. Les didn't like small talk, he would answer their questions but he never did really get into the conversation with them. Although Les was not trying to be a snob or act like he was better than the men he was living with. His Alpha Beta fraternity was showing and he didn't even know it. He didn't fit in because of his eastern image and didn't get a chance to interact with the men and change it because of his solitary job building fence. He didn't have a chance to work with them during the day, so for the first year they were cold to him.

Les and Mike never did get along real well. They were civil to each other but there was no attempt at friendliness. Les wasn't afraid of a fight, the ones that he'd been in proved he could hold his own if he had to. He was a good-sized boy and his football experience had exposed him to physical contact, so he wasn't afraid of rough and tumble. Les was just shy and kind of with drawn from his solitary days in the woods as a youngster. He didn't mix real well especially with the men in the bunkhouse; they appeared self centered, boisterous and alcoholic. A totally different breed than he was used to.

Don was different for some unknown reason him and Les hit it off right from the start. Maybe because Don had only been there a very short time before Les came or they just liked each other at first glance.

It was a cold but beautiful morning as Les finished feeding his team of horses and headed for the breakfast table himself.

"Morning," everyone said as Les walked in and sat down.

"Morning," Les said as he sat down and poured himself a cup of coffee.

Emil passed his cup down the line for Les to refill. "Are you already to go?"

"Yup," just have to load a few fence posts and I'm out of here."

"Good, Don't push it the first day. Get a handle on what your doing and then you'll be able to move right along."

After breakfast Jake helped Les hitch the team and load what posts he needed. Les climbed on the wagon and "Jake said you go ahead and get started. I'll catch up with you later and see how you're doing."

Les nodded as he shook the lines and clucked to the horses. Jake had shown him where to ford the river yesterday; he made the crossing with no problems and headed for the line fence three miles away. He was at the fence and starting to work by eight o'clock. The back of the wagon was set up so you could unroll five spools of barbed wire at the same time. All you did was tie them to the brace post at five different heights about twelve inches apart and slowly drive off. If everything went all right you could unroll the full eighty rods (quarter mile or 1320 ft.) stop, stretch it and tie it to the brace post. Then you drove the wagon back to the beginning and started putting in posts and hanging wire until you arrived at the end where you started the procedure all over again. This is what Les did day after day six days a week. At first all Les did on his Sunday off was lay around the bunkhouse or go for rides on horseback. After a few of these came and went he got bored and longed to go into town with the rest of the men on Saturday night. He talked to Jake about it and Jake told him to ask Emil at the next meal. Emil agreed to let Les come in at four o'clock on Saturdays if he would work one Sunday a month. Les agreed and started going out on the town with Don on Saturday nights.

Les drank beer; the rest of the men drank whiskey. Drinking whiskey is kind of a western thing in as much as during the eighteen hundreds there was no way to keep any thing cold out on the range. Since whiskey doesn't need to be cooled it was the drink of choice and most of the time necessity. Besides, the alcohol in it helped disinfect any cuts or open wounds that were always being encountered. Infection is a big killer when your living in the open and don't have access to hygiene and medical facilities. Since whiskey was more available than beer, most westerners to this day prefer it because they have developed a taste for it. Les would take an occasional drink of whiskey in the bunkhouse because that's all that was there. He couldn't hold his liquor like the other men did. It always amazed him how they could drink all night Saturday and all day Sunday and still be able to function and be sober by Monday morning. Everyone understood that it meant their job if they showed up intoxicated or didn't show up at the breakfast table because they were drunk on Monday morning.

That's how Les spent his summer. Even though the hours were long and the work hard Les enjoyed his summer at the ranch. He put in about twenty-five miles of new fence. He was in the best shape he had ever been in, he was an inch taller and twenty pounds of muscle heavier. He was lean, hard, had broad shoulders, small waist and moved with more athletic grace than when he first came to the ranch. Les was pleased when Emil asked him to come back for the next couple of years and finish the job. He agreed and became a regular fixture each summer. On August twentieth Les boarded a train back to State College, Pennsylvania and returned to the world he was comfortable in.

The summer of nineteen forty-six looked like it was going to be a boring repeat of the previous summer. It was the end of July and Les had just laid out the eighty rods of barbed wire. One strand came up short when he was about ten feet from the brace posts so he knew there must be a snag somewhere down the line. Les stood on the wagon and shaded his eyes as he looked back trying to see where the snag was.

"See anything?" The voice behind him said.

Les turned with a start. "Jesus, you scared the shit out of me." Looking at Don sitting on his horse close behind him, smiling like the cat that got the mouse. "Where in the hell did you come from?"

"That dry wash just ahead of you. I been riding line fence all morning and couldn't resist sneaking up on you."

"Thanks. Hey, I've got a snag somewhere down the line. Would you ride down and see if you can untangle it?"

"Sure, it's the least I can do for making you brown your shorts." He said as he rode around the wagon and started down the line of wire. Les watched him go and then disappear over the top of a little knoll. In the mean time Les unhooked the first strand of barbed wire from the spool and hooked it to the brace post. The second strand was the one that had come up short. Once Les saw it move he knew Don had found the problem and was freeing it. Les took it off the spool and now the wire gave enough to reach the brace post. Les put the stretcher on it and pulled it tight. One last pull and the wire went slack. Les looked in the direction Don had went and saw the wire coming. It was rolling in big loops and coming right for Les and the wagon. Les grabbed the wire cutters out of his back pocket and cut the wire. It took off in the direction of the wire coming at him, collided and stopped in a tangled mess fifteen yards from where he was standing. Les was visibly shaken. After a few moments he collected himself and called out for Don. There was no answer and no Don. Quickly he unhooked the remaining three strands of wire from the wagon and wrapped them around the brace post. Jumping into the wagon he grabbed the lines and laid them hard over the rumps of the workhorses. They leapt forward so hard they threw Les over the back of the seat. By the time he recovered and got the lines back they were in the dry wash running all out. Les let them run and pulled hard on the right line. The horses hit the sloping bank at a dead run. The wagon came off the ground as they cleared the top and fencing supplies went everywhere. The wagon stayed upright and Les whipped them on with the line ends as hard as he could. They flew past the spot he had just been when the wire broke and went flying over the knoll where he had last seen Don. Braking over the knoll he could see Don's horse spook about five hundred yards away. Drawing closer he could see Don sitting on the ground leaning forward with his head between his spread legs. Pulling the team in hard Les finally got them stopped and tied the lines hard to the line stay before he jumped off the wagon. "Don, are you OK?" Don was moaning and bobbing back and forth in his leaned over in the sitting position holding his head in his hands. Les kneeled down and grabbed the hair on his head and pulled his head back as he said, "Let me see. OH God," Les murmured as the side of Don's face was exposed. The right side of Don's face was cut from the hairline above his ear down the side of his cheek to a spot under the left side of his jaw. Les could see Don's teeth and both jawbones through the bleeding cut.

"Shit." Les screamed as he ripped his shirt off and tried to slow the bleeding. "Don, Listen to me." Les screamed as he held his bloody shirt to Don's face. "I'm going to load you on the wagon. I'm going to set you on the floor behind the seat. I'm going to tie you to the seat. I need you to help me or we ain't gonna make it. I'll tie your head between your knees so we can keep pressure on the wound and slow the bleeding. Les was talking as he was carrying Don to the wagon. He threw a couple of rolls of wire out and tied Don in. Les new that time was everything. Don would bleed to death if he didn't get him help in a hurry. He would have to drive hard over rough terrain and couldn't hold on to Don and control the horses too. Once he had Don tied in he whipped up the horses. "Now don't you go passing out on me. You hear? If you do I'm gonna kick your ass. It was almost an hour and a half before the ranch came into sight Les had realized shortly after they took off that if he didn't slow down the horses would never make it all the way to the ranch. The blood had slowed but Don was sitting a good-sized puddle of it. Les couldn't tell whether he was alive or dead by the time they crossed the river behind the barn. Once on the other side he whipped the jaded horses into a full staggering run. Jake was on the hay wagon throwing hay to the horses inside the corral when he saw Les charge through the river with the wagon. He knew instantly something was wrong and slid down the hay to the ground as Les jerked the team to a halt. "Don's been hurt bad. he needs a doctor get something to take him in, hurry." Jake didn't even try to look at Don he broke into a dead run for Emil's pickup truck sitting by the side of the house. The keys were in it as usual and Jake bailed in, started it and drove over to the wagon as Les was cutting the ropes that held Don in place. The two men sat him in the metal truck bed against the cab. "You get back there and hold him." Jake said as he jumped in the cab and roared through the yard. Mrs. Schmidt had heard the commotion and was coming across the yard. She took one look at the back of the pickup and ran back in the house to let the doctor in Medicine Bow know they were coming. Jake came to a sliding halt in just as the doctor and a nurse came running out the door. The doctor took one look at the blood soaked duo and told Jake, "Get him in here now." Les handed Don to Jake from the bed of the pickup; he was chalky white, pasty and limp as a wet dishrag. Jake laid him on a table covered with a white sheet and the doctor bent over him with a stethoscope.

"Is he alive Doc.?" Jake asked anxiously.

"Barely, now you get out of here so I can work."

"We'll be right outside." Jake said as he walked out to the waiting room. In the waiting room Les related everything that happened. "Sit tight." He told Les "I'm gonna call the ranch and let them know what's going on. I'll have the boys take care of the horses and pick up the stuff that's scattered. About a half an hour later Emil and Mrs. Schmidt walked into the waiting room.

"Any word?" Emil said as they walked up to Jake and Les.

"Nothing yet." Jake replied. The little group waited about forty-five minutes before the doctor walked into the waiting room. The doctor walked up to Emil. "Your man is alive, just barely but I've got him stabilized and an ambulance is coming from Laramie to pick him up. I've done all I can do for him here. He needs the hospital where they can replace the blood he's lost. The man is lucky to be alive. Another fifteen minutes and I don't think he would have made it."

'Thanks Doc, I appreciate what you did."

"Don't thank me. Thank whoever got him here when they did. Whatever they did for him saved his life."

Everyone waited until the ambulance showed up and loaded Don in. It was about six o'clock in the evening and Emil said to Jake. "You take my pickup home. We'll take Les back to the ranch with us.

"OK," Jake turned to Les. "Good job Les. You used your head out there, Don's alive thanks to you." Les nodded and looked at the floor. He was dirty, blood soaked, tired and the adrenalin that had kept him in high gear was wearing off. The Schmidt's had him relate what happened as they drove back to the ranch. He was still shaken as he told the men in the bunkhouse what happened after he showered. When Les did hit the hay he slept like a log.

Don recovered after a long stay in the hospital. He would always wear the scar from his brush with death but other than that he eventually came back to his old self.

In June of nineteen hundred forty-eight, Les Corbett, graduated with a bachelor's degree in business and music, cum laudi, from Pennsylvania State University. Now he would start his master's degree and law school. That fall he planned to take a few months off his scholastic schedule so he could participate in the fall roundup at the ranch. June fifteenth found Les at the ranch. His position was now accepted by the others because he had proven he was dependable and a hard worker. Les had completed the fence building last summer and was going to spend this summer riding line fence and fixing any breaks that he came across. His time became more flexible and he didn't have to put in the long hours that he did before. Don was back at the ranch and he recovered nicely except for the scar down the side of his face and under his jaw. It had been two years and it was just now starting to lose its color. Don had developed an infectious blood problem from the accident and was taking treatments in Laramie at the hospital. He had one series left that would last a week. The Doctors claimed the swelling would disappear and he wouldn't have trouble swallowing anymore. Les hoped so; he really liked the young man. Don and him had become close friends over the last few years. Because of his trips back and forth to Laramie Don bought a pickup truck. Occasionally he would have Les drive him if he was going for an extended stay and then Les would bring the truck back to the ranch until Don needed to be picked up. Emil said he didn't care as long as it didn't interfere with the work that needed to be done. So, Les spent the hour and a half it took to drive the sixty miles to Laramie after he was done with his days work. One rainy weekday in early July Les was trapped in the bunkhouse because it was too wet to do anything outside. Being bored and restless he figured he would run into Laramie and see Don who wasn't coming home until the weekend. When he arrived at the sleeping room Don kept, it was empty. Les figured he would check the hospital and see if his friend was there. Walking into the lobby he stopped at the nurse's station. He had been there so many times with Don that they knew him by sight and name. "Hi Laura," Les said to the older redhead.

"Hi sweetie, if your looking for your friend he's on the third floor. He'll be busy for about an hour. Go have a cup of coffee or something to eat. I'll call you when he gets free."

"OK, thanks," and Les headed for the cafeteria. Walking through the door he could see the place was crowded. There were only a few tables that weren't completely taken and they had one or two people sitting at them. Les ordered his food. After it was served and he paid for it he looked the tables over. There were two tables that had one person sitting at each. Les mentally rejected the table the guy was sitting at for the table with the cute brunette.

"Hi." Les said as he stood by the table holding his food tray. "Do you mind if I sit down?"

The girl looked up from the paper she was writing on and said "No, help yourself." Nodding toward the empty chair across the table from her.

Les sat down and took the food off his tray. The girl was pondering over the form she was trying to fill out.

"You look like your having trouble filling that out. Can I help?"

The girl looked up at Les. She was brunette, had hazel colored eyes, small well-formed mouth and nose, white even teeth were visible through the easy smile that was framed by her lightly tanned complexion. "I'm applying for a job here and I'm having a tough time answering some of the questions because I don't have a lot of experience."

"You mean in filling out applications or job experience."

"Both, I graduated high school a month ago and I want to be a nurse. I worked as a volunteer candy striper at the hospital in Cheyenne while I was going to high school but that's the only practical experience I've got."

"Why don't you go to nursing school?"

"I will, but I want to get a job at a hospital that has a program I can attend while I work."

"If you enter nursing school at an accredited University, they all have hospital programs included."

"True, it may come down to that but I would really like to do it on my own. My father offered to put me through but he is always footing the bill and I want to see if I can do it myself, my way."

"It seems like your going at it the hard way. Let me help you fill out the application. I just graduated college and that's all I've been doing for the last four years is composing papers and filling out forms."

"Ok, if you don't mind answering questions while your eating."

"No problem, I do some of my best work with a fork in my hand." Les said with a grin. "By the way, my name is Les Corbett. What's yours?"

"Alice Bernard. Pleased to meet you." She said as she reached across the table to shake his hand. "Are you from around here?"

"No, I live in State College, Pennsylvania. I work on a ranch out here during the summer. How about you?"

"I live with my parents in Cheyenne."

"What brought you over here? Doesn't Cheyenne have a hospital?"

"Sure it does. But Laramie has the Wyoming University School of Nursing. I've applied at the hospital in Cheyenne, the one in Denver and now here in Laramie. I want to stay reasonably close so I can go home on my days off. The bigger hospitals in the state are affiliated with the University of Wyoming. Those are the only ones I'll apply at except Denver and that would be my last choice since I'd have to give up my Wyoming residency."

Les finished eating and moved around the table to a chair next to Alice. "Let's see if we can get this application filled out properly."

The two of them spent the next hour working on the application. When they were finished Alice said, "Thank you for your help. I think I really messed up the other applications I filled out. I'll get those letters of recommendation from my principal and the rest of the people you suggested. Do you think I should mail them or hand deliver them?"

Les replied. "I would hand deliver them and try to get an interview at the same time. Remember you have to be persistent. Find out who actually does the hiring and show up on their doorstep or call them every day. Bug the hell out of 'em. Most employers are looking for aggressive self-starters. If you don't have enough gumption doing whatever you need to get their attention your application will end up on the bottom of the pile."

"Great, I sure want to thank you for your help. I learned a lot."

"My pleasure. Would it be possible to see you again and maybe go to a movie or something?"

Alice thought about the idea a minute. "Sure that would be fun. The next time I come to Laramie to check on my application would be good."

"When will that be?"

"I don't know, probably before next weekend. Why don't you call me at home on Wednesday night about eight o'clock, I should know by then."

"Ok, it's a deal. I've got your address and phone number from your application." Les said as they both stood up and Alice gathered her papers to go.

"You're pretty quick aren't you," Alice said with a grin.

"You do what you gotta do." Les said with a grin.

"Call me." Alice said as she walked away.

"I intend to." Les said looking at her pretty, little, animated backside as she sauntered out of the cafeteria. Picking up his coffee cup he started back to the food line to get a refill. The intercom told him to come to the main desk, as he was about to fill his cup. Don was talking to Laura as Les walked up. Turning Don said "Hi, sorry to keep you waiting."

"Oh that's Ok, I went to the cafeteria and got something to eat."

Don looked up at the tall man, "So, what do you want to do?"

"Let's go get a drink."

"I can't drink alcohol for twenty four hours after my treatment, I'll have a soda. Hey Laura, why don't you come with us?" Don said as he winked at the red headed nurse, "You'd have more fun than a cat in a herd of mice." Don smiled a big toothy grin and batted his eyes at her.

"I know what your up to." Laura said going along with the teasing. "You two would take me out, get me drunk and then take advantage of me. Even though I'm old enough to be your mother, I'd probably have twins. Then my husband would have to hunt you down and shoot you. After he tortured you and forced you to hand over all that big money you guys make working on a ranch." The two men laughed, walked out the door and went to a bar five blocks down the street.

Alice and Les went to supper and a show a couple of days later. They had a good time and agreed to see each other whenever they could. Les spent the rest of the summer between the ranch, Laramie and Cheyenne. Les made a couple of trips to Laramie during the summer so he could meet Alice while she was being interviewed at the hospital.

In August they attended Les's first rodeo, the "Cheyenne Frontier Days" celebration. Les was fascinated by the impressive athletic ability of the cowboys showing off their skills in the competition. Les really wanted to get serious with Alice but she was of another mind. They kissed some and held hands but that was as far as Alice would let it go. Claiming she was too young and wanted to get her career started before she got serious over anyone. It frustrated the hell out of Les. Alice got a job at the Laramie hospital right after Labor Day, in the therapy department. It wasn't a prestigious job, but it was a job. She wasn't enrolled in Nurse's School and all she was allowed to do was assist the technician's and do their grunt work for them. She rented a small apartment near the hospital and went to work with the idea of saving her money to enter college next year.

Don finished his therapy in the middle of September and was declared healed by the doctors who attended him. Les got permission from Emil to take a couple days off to celebrate with Don over the end of his ordeal. The celebration went a little longer than the few days they had been allotted. Les and Don stayed drunk for a week. When the two errant drunks ran out of money they headed for the ranch. The two of them knew they would probably get their butts chewed for taking the extra time to party but they also knew they wouldn't lose their jobs because this late in the year there were no hands available. The cattle had to be worked and shipped if the ranch was to receive an income.

Driving down the dusty lane the two men could see activity in the corrals by the small barn. Stopping in a cloud of dust Les and Don got out of the pickup. Les leaned on the roof of the truck while Don greeted the ragged bunch of dusty men that stopped work to welcome him back.

Les looked the new man over. "A kid actually," thinking to himself. "Big and well built but he looks eighteen and acts fifteen." After the greetings were over Les and Don headed for the bunkhouse to stow Don's gear. "Dang," Don uttered, "looks like the new guy has got my old bunk."

"Above Buck is the only one open." Les commented.

"Well, beggars can't be choosey," Don said as he set his duffel bag against the wall at the end of the bunk beds. "Let's get back out there and watch the fun."

The two men walked to the corrals and fell in with the bunch that was being loud and obnoxious. Les didn't know why but he knew in his gut that he didn't like the new guy, Ed. Especially after the way he was treated by the others (particularly Mike) when he made a comment on Ed's ride. Les and the big man still weren't doing anymore than tolerating each other. After that Les wouldn't go out of his way to harass Ed, but any chance that came up he did. The snakes and the cattle incident were (so he thought, two of his best). He really did feel bad when Ed fell off his horse at the cow camp and tumbled down the shale slide. He looked more dead than alive when Emil and Mike put him in the stock truck and took off for the ranch; his body was pretty chewed up. Ed's Levi Jacket was ragged when Les first saw him, but now it was nothing more than bloody rags. Ed borrowed an old pair of chaps that were hanging in the barn. They had some pretty bad gouges and were ripped in a few places but they definitely saved Ed's legs and hips. The two men returned after a couple of days and said Ed was in the hospital at Laramie. They described the frantic trip to the ranch. How they met the ambulance Mrs. Schmidt called, before they left the yard, on highway thirty east of Rock River and made the transfer. Emil and Mike followed it to the hospital to wait for the prognosis. The doctor assured them he would do all that he could. Ed was unconscious with severe lacerations over eighty percent of his upper body and head. He was unconscious and the doctor didn't know when or if he would wake up so they could check for internal injuries. They put him in traction because of the possibility of spinal injuries. The only thing the doctor could say for sure was if Ed did wake up he would be there for at least a month.

CHAPTER #9

ED'S EYES FLUTTERED open. All he saw was white fading to gray then nothing. He drifted in and out of consciousness. The angel in white next to him turned out to be a nurse trying to say something to him. "Well, look who returned to the land of the living. Welcome back," the middle aged woman chirped.

"Where am I?" Ed hoarsely whispered.

"Your in Mercy General Hospital, Laramie, Wyoming.

"Oh." Ed sighed as he looked between his elevated feet and slipped back into unconsciousness. When he woke again he was able to comprehend more of his surroundings. Time seemed to stand still in the dimly lit room. He didn't know how long he lay there before he tried to move. The bed straps held him firmly in place. When Ed woke again the sun was shining between the slats of the Venetian blinds that covered the windows. He could see his legs were elevated and he was very warm. His bandaged hands made it impossible to push the covers off his sweaty body besides; it was far too painful to move his arms. Ed was trying to survey his situation when a nurse walked to his bedside accompanied by an older man in a white coat.

"Hi sugar, this is Dr. Kowalski. He's here to check you out."

Ed blinked and gave a soft moan in acknowledgement.

"Looks like you took a pretty nasty fall young man." The Doctor said as he pulled the covers back and gazed at Ed's bandaged body. "You have some broken ribs and severe lacerations to the head, back and arms. Those are the external things we can see." He said as he bent over to look into Ed's eyes "We will leave you in traction to keep you from moving until we can determine whether or not you have any cranial, spinal or internal damage. When you can stay awake for more that two hours at a time well start taking x-rays. Once we determine what needs attention and what doesn't we will be able to give you an accurate picture of what your facing. In the meantime try to remain as motionless as possible. I realize that will be difficult, but it's for your own good."

Ed blinked acknowledgement as the Doctor straitened up.

"We will start as soon as you're able." The doctor said before he turned and walked away.

Ed drifted in and out of consciousness. Over the next two days the longevity of his consciousness improved steadily. By the end of the second day he was able to stay awake for almost four hours at a time. During his wakeful periods on the second day he talked with the nurse who was there whenever he woke up. She would talk to Ed until he drifted back into never, never land. Her nametag said she was Joyce Weston. Late in the afternoon the Doctor came during one of the chat sessions. After checking Ed over he informed him that he would go to x-ray the next morning.

The morning clatter of dishes in the ward had barely subsided when the nurse and two attendants came to take Ed downstairs. They wheeled him bed, counterweights and all to the x-ray room. He was filmed in the bed and the taken back to the ward. About two hours later Dr. Kowalski walked up to his bed with a manila envelope tucked under his arm.

"Well son, I've got good news for you. You don't appear to have anything more than a severe concussion, seven broken ribs and lots of cuts and bruises. We stitched all of the large lacerations when you were first admitted. There will probably be some scaring. After we get you out of traction we will need to do more specific x-rays. The ones we did here were to determine if you had any major injuries to your skeletal system before we let you move around. We will take you out of traction gradually over the next two or three days. It would be too traumatic to release the weight all at once. You have to release the tension slowly if you've had it applied a week or more."

"A week or more?" Ed spoke hoarsely through tensed lips.

"Oh yes. You have been unconscious for four and a half days and in a semi conscious state for three. You are going to have some real killer headaches for a while, but eventually they will subside. In the meantime we will keep you on pain medication so you can function."

Ed blinked. The Doctor smiled, turned and left the room.

Over the course of the next two days, a middle-aged man wearing glasses, and a white t-shirt stretched over a growing potbelly, from the therapy department, showed up twice a day with a good looking brunette girl named Alice. The man with the potbelly was obviously in charge and enjoyed giving orders to the girl who did most of the work. At the end of the second day Rick (the potbelly) informed Ed that tomorrow they would start the process of removing the weights. The weights were lessened each time until they could be completely removed. He did a ghoulish impersonation and said with a sadistic laugh, "tomorrow we remove you from the rack, let me know how you like your newly elongated stature, my Lord."

"Ed smiled as Alice winked at him and said, "you'll be running through the clover in no time."

"And leaping anthills and sagebrush in a single bound," Ed said as he looked at the girl.

She laughed and looked at Rick. "Boris I don't think our victim was under enough pressure. Can we hook him up again? A few good screams would take that smirk off his face."

Rick responded with a hunchback impersonation and a bad Hungarian accent. "The master said he was to be removed from the rack gently. He needs a new scarecrow for his garden and wants him to be able to stand."

Alice joined in the fun with her own bad impersonation. "You mean he won't be given a spear handle enema to stand him in the garden?"

Rick kept it going. "No, my pet, the master wants this one alive. When he outgrows the garden, the master plans on using him to herd his cattle."

By now Ed was laughing so hard it hurt.

Joyce walked in to give Ed his medicine. "What are you two up to now?" She said as she surveyed the scene of Ed laughing with tears of pain running down his cheeks, Rick and Alice were looking ridicules as they stood over him bent and drooling. "We were just finishing our torture session, my lady." Rick mumbled, "He's yours to do with as you please, for now."

Joyce laughed and said, "Oh get out of here."

Rick laughed and said to Ed in his worst accent yet, as they were leaving. "We will be back!"

The nurse laughed and shook her head, "I think sometimes the people in the therapy department stand to close to the oxygen." Ed explained to the nurse what Rick and Alice said they going to do over the next couple of days as he took his medicine.

"That's great, sounds like you'll be up and at 'em in no time."

"How long do you think it'll be before I can leave here?" Ed asked Joyce.

"I have no idea, sugar. After you get unstraped from the bed, the doctor wants to look you over real good. Depending on what he finds will determine how long your stay with us will be."

"Oh. When will he start testing?"

"I don't know for sure, normally it's a couple of days after the traction is removed. Well, I have to go for now." She picked up the tray she brought with her and said, "don't let the bedbugs bite."

"Very funny." Ed said as she left.

Moving was not an option. So, Ed stared at the ceiling trying to recall what happened. He kept coming up with a blank beyond the free fall from the horse. Over the next two days the weights and the bed straps were removed. At least he was conscious of the present, he thought to himself, as he watched a candy striper moving amongst the patients in the ward. She was doing her normal duties picking up bedpans, fluffing pillows and giving what words of cheer she could. Since the bed straps had been removed Ed felt more in control of his senses. This feeling changed the first time he tried to move as painful memories of his bouts with the sorrel returned when he worked up the courage to try and roll over. Fortunately they were short lived as the pain from the movement put him into a semi conscious state. Coming back to consciousness some time later Ed opened his eyes. He definitely felt stronger and found himself in a fetal position on his right side. "At least the view is different," he thought staring at the candy striper putting fresh sheets on the empty bed next to him.

The Schmidt's, Jake and all the ranch hands visited Ed a couple of days later. Even Les showed up with the group, but his motives were different from the rest. It gave him the time off to come to Laramie and see Alice. Everyone filled him in on what happened at the cow camp.

"We thought you was a goner." Mike said, "You sure were beat up. You were gray as Les's gelding and limp as a wet dishrag. I held you all the way to where the ambulance took you, all you did was bleed and moan"

"Thanks Mike. I owe you a lot."

Mike blushed and got uncomfortable. Jake stepped in and explained how they finished up working the cattle plus a few other things that were going on. It meant a lot to Ed to know that the men he worked with cared enough to come a hundred miles on their time off to see him. Les only showed up the first time with the group. But he was using Ed as an excuse for time off to see Alice.

Dr. Kowalski started the x-rays and tests two days after the bed straps were removed. The only thing he found that he didn't already know about was the bruised kidneys and lower spinal trauma. It wasn't anything permanent but it would need therapy to help it heal. He ordered whirlpool baths and limited exercise for the first week, to be increased slowly over the next three weeks.

She moved with the easy athletic grace of youth. Alice was good looking and well built but not what you would call outstanding. Auburn hair, cut shoulder length page boy style, hazel eyes, nice complexion, white teeth and an infectious grin. Her body was nicely proportioned with long legs and piano players hands. She was five feet six inches tall and tipped the scales at one hundred and ten pounds. Walking around the end of the bed the young girl noticed Ed was awake and watching her.

"Well, well, are we starting to come back to the real world? I'm here to take you down to therapy. Do you feel up to it?" She said as she rolled the wheelchair next to the bed and set the brakes.

Ed looked at her and laughed. He knew it was one of those questions you couldn't say no to. "What if I told you I didn't want to go?"

"Then I'd say you don't have a choice."

"Then why did you ask?"

"Because I'm so damn pukey polite. Now get in the chair."

"Oh, your hard, but I love you anyway. Marry me and I'll follow you anywhere." Ed said with a grimace as Alice helped him into the wheelchair.

Alice laughed at the good-natured reply. "You ranch hands are all alike, you wear hats on your head but your brains are in your pants."

"You found me out. Now I'll probably be so traumatized that I won't be able to eat and I'll waste away to nothing and die."

"Not only are you guys oversexed, but you're the biggest bunch of bull shitters I've ever met in my life."

"Alice, you're breaking my heart. You wouldn't want to see me go downhill and die would you?"

'The only thing you're going to die from is talking too much. Do ranch hands get their gift of gab and sex drive from hanging around animals, boredom or a combination of both?"

"Ok, you win. I'll keep my hands in my pockets and my mouth shut."

Alice laughed out loud as she wheeled Ed through the door into the therapy department. "You don't have pockets and I'll believe you'll keep your mouth shut when I see it. Ok Romeo, your bath is waiting . . . Let the fun begin."

Alice and another attendant helped Ed out of the wheelchair and into the chair connected to the hoist that lifted him into the whirlpool tub. After his treatments were over Alice wheeled him back to the ward and helped him back into bed. "See you tomorrow." She said as she pushed the empty chair out of the room.

Joyce the nurse had propped Ed up a half an hour before Alice came so he could look around a little easier.

"Hi!" Alice said as she walked to Ed's bed pushing the wheelchair. "It's time to go again."

Ed nodded and let her help him into the chair. "Alice, do you live in Laramie?" Ed asked as she pushed him down the hallway.

"Yeah, I've got a small apartment on Front Street."

"Lived here long?"

"No, I moved here around the end of August. I started here right after Labor Day." Wheeling Ed into the therapy department she stopped the chair by the whirlpool. "It's time to go to work."

Each day on their way to and from the therapy department the conversation increased. At the end of the first week Ed was no longer pushed in the wheelchair. He was required to use a walker to get back and forth to therapy. Alice had to accompany him in case he had trouble. It took him longer to get there at first but Ed didn't mind, he loved the extra conversation time. Each day they talked and learned about each other's background. Ed found out that Alice was only a year and a half older than he was and her parents lived in Cheyenne. By the end of the second week, the doctor ordered Ed to walk on his own with a walker as often as he could. Alice no longer came to accompany him to therapy. She would be there when he arrived and monitor his progress on the different machines as he used them. One day while he was waiting his turn on a particular machine, he stood talking to Alice.

"Alice. I was looking out the window yesterday and noticed a park across the street. I would like to go there but they won't let me leave the hospital by myself. Is there anyway I could get you to go with me?"

"I can't unless it's part of the therapy. Talk to the Doctor and see if you can get him to authorize it."

"Do you think he would?"

"You never know until you ask, do you?"

"Your right, I see him tomorrow, I'll ask then."

Ed talked to Dr. Kowalski excitedly about going across the street to the park. He brought the Doctor to the window and pointed it out to him even though Dr. Kowalski was completely aware of its existence. The Doctor was not receptive at first. The longer he listened to Ed's excited appeal the more he began to relent and finally agree The Doctor started Ed with a half an hour a day only if the sun was shining and he must be accompanied by someone from the therapy department. Writing out the instructions on the bed chart he told Ed he would prescribe the exercise for a week and then make a decision whether to rescind the treatment or expand on it. Since Alice was the therapy department "gopher" she was giving the job of accompanying Ed to the park and back. Ed felt like Alice was the only one he could talk to that understood him. Walking around the hospital he carried on conversations about the weather, politics and whatever with other patients, but he didn't feel a bond with them like he did Alice. He couldn't talk to them about things that mattered or concerned him like he could Alice because each time they went to the park they found out more about each other.

"Ed, how long have you been working at the ranch?"

"I started in August. I'm originally from Wisconsin. I screwed up and ran away from home a couple of months ago."

"Why?"

"I don't know, things seemed hard, my parents were hard to talk to, I wasn't doing well in school . . . things weren't going well for me, or so I thought. I was wrong, but I didn't realize it until I got out here."

Looking at her watch Alice announced that it was time to go back to the hospital. "By the way do you like to read?" she asked as they crossed the street.

"Sure," Ed replied.

"What do you like?"

"I like anything from the poems of Robert Service, to Ivanhoe, to a good Zane Grey novel."

"Wow, you sure have a wide range of interest, don't you?"

"My Mother was an avid reader. When I was young, she used to read to me a lot, everything from the Bible and the classics to riders of the purple sage and the dictionary."

"The dictionary?

"Yes. Before I could read she read it to me. In the third grade she had me start reading it to her one page a day."

"Maybe I can get something you'll like at the library. You don't look like you'll be up to reading for a while, so maybe I'll do it for you."

"I would really appreciate that. I've tried reading some of the magazines in the hospital but after about five minutes my head starts to hurt so bad my eyes go blurry."

"Your brain is probably still swollen from the concussion. You might want to mention that to the doctor."

"I will. It just gets so boring lying around. There's not a lot to do except make small talk, tease nurses and aides." Ed said as he looked at Alice out of the corner of his eye and grinned.

Alice smiled but wouldn't rise to the bait. "I'll bet." They had returned from the park and were in the hallway by Ed's ward. "I'm going to leave you here. I've got things to do I'll see you tomorrow."

"Ok, I'm counting on that." Ed said as she walked away.

The next day came but Alice did not. When Joyce the nurse came in to give him his medications Ed asked her if Alice was working that day. "No, but she left a message for you. She called and switched today with her regular day off. She'll be in Saturday. She said she would see you then.'

"Oh . . . Ok . . . thanks." Ed said dejectedly.

"Are you falling for her?" Joyce said as she fluffed Ed's pillow.

"No, I hardly know her except for the therapy she's been helping me with. She was going to read to me and I was looking forward to it that's all."

"Well, don't be too disappointed honey, she'll be back tomorrow. In the meantime I need you to sit up on the edge of the bed so I can check that I.V. needle in your arm. It looks like it might need to be taken out and cleaned."

Joyce pulled the blankets back as Ed swung his legs out of the bed. The hospital gown was pulled up exposing Ed's maleness. He was still too sore to move quickly enough to cover himself before she got a good look at him. Struggling to sit up and cover himself he blushed as he looked at the nurse helping him.

"I suppose you've seen a lot of men, working here, haven't you, ma'am?" Ed said showing his embarrassment.

"My name is Joyce and I have seen and handled men's private parts both personally and professionally since I was fourteen years old. Don't get embarrassed on my account. I'm old enough to be your mother and I've got three kids. Trust me, your built just like any other man. Maybe not as big as some; but defiantly bigger than others. Now hold still while I take this needle out it may smart a little." She was right it created a sharp pain where the needle had been. Joyce placed a piece of gauze and tape over the wound. "There now we'll put a clean one in the other side." She said as she cleaned the spot with alcohol.

"Joyce?"

"What?" She said momentarily annoyed at the break in her concentration.

"Am I bigger or smaller than your husband?" Ed was shocked at his own boldness; the question had come out before he realized it.

Joyce stifled a laugh. "I'd say about the same. But I don't have a husband anymore. I've been officially separated pending a divorce for six months now. Now hold still while I put this IV in."

Ed winced as the needle penetrated the skin on his arm. "How old are you?"

"Thirty two. How old are you?"

"Seventeen."

"Pretty good sized boy for your age."

"Thank you."

"There we got you all plumbed again now, let's hook up the water works." Joyce said as she completed the task of hooking the saline solution and getting the drip going. "You want to stay up or lay down?"

"The needle burns, and why is it bulging?"

"Oh I probably missed the vein and the saline is going under the skin."

"Can you fix it? Will it be alright?"

"Relax and don't be a baby, all I have to do is move it to another spot. The swelling will go away as the solution is absorbed into your arm."

"Here I was going to ask you to marry me and you treat me like this. What'll you do if I die? OH God it's getting dark. I think I'm passing into the next world. Help me Auuuuugh!!!!!"

"Get real and sit still while I change this or you really will think your passing into another world . . . of pain." Ed sat quietly while she redid the IV.

"There, how does that feel?" She said when she completed the operation.

"Great. It doesn't burn now."

"Good, I'll see you tomorrow."

"I'll be waiting with open arms. Remember my offer, your kids need a father." Ed said in his most serious voice while in side he was screaming with laughter.

"Ya right, three kids are enough. I don't need a fourth to raise." Joyce said bantering back good-naturedly.

"I'm hurt Joyce. I thought you really loved me. I'm going to lay here and pine. I'll probably pass on during the night from heartbreak."

Joyce laughed and waved him off as she left the ward.

Ed smiled and fell into a relaxed sleep. It was dark when he woke up. He could hear the clatter of food trays and talking coming from the hallway outside the ward so he knew it was close to morning.

"Good morning everyone," the aide said as she switched the lights on in the ward. "First we clean up then we eat." The way she said it was like this was everybody's first day. The other aide's moved among the patients and got them ready for the day. Those that could do for themselves grabbed their toiletries and headed down the hall. The rest were attended to in their own little curtained off compartments.

Ed was leaving the bathroom when all of a sudden his feet slipped on some water someone had leaked or spilled on the waxed tile floor. Ed went down hard but only wounded his pride. Looking up from his prone position he saw Joyce standing over him looking down. "Are you alright?" she asked with a concerned look on her face.

Ed couldn't resist the opportunity. "I don't know, I hurt really bad, could you help me to my bed." He said in his most pathetic voice. Joyce helped him up and put her arm around his waist. "Put your hand on my shoulder and I'll walk you to bed."

Putting his hand on Joyce's shoulder Ed couldn't resist teasing her. "Joyce your one hell'va woman. How many kids are we going to have once I get out of here?"

"You're sick and I don't mean your obvious aliment. If you keep having this delirium I'll have to sedate you."

"I know, you just want my virgin body and you're afraid I'll resist."

"God, I'm beginning to wonder if you're kidding or not."

Ed grinned and really turned it on. "Joyce I want you. Just let me hold you, fondle you," Ed said as he brought his free hand up toward her chest.

"Touch me and I'll show you how to give yourself an enema with your own hand. Quit your damn fooling around it's not funny anymore."

"Ok, I'm sorry. I was just trying to have some fun with you. I wasn't serious."

"I hope so, you were beginning to scare me."

"I'll behave myself and do whatever you say. Honest I was just kidding."

"Ok, let's walk then."

"Joyce?"

"Now what?"

"If we trip and I fall on top of you, you won't get the wrong idea will you?" Ed said as he gave her a sidelong grin.

"I give up you're hopeless. You can walk the rest of the way on your own." They both laughed as Ed walked over to his bed and sat on it." I've had it. I think I'll lay down for a while."

Joyce turned and started to leave as Ed spoke. "Joyce?" she stopped and turned. "I want you to know I appreciate the care and your help. I hope you weren't offended by my kidding around."

"Don't worry about it, you had me going there for awhile though."

"I've never talked to a woman like that before I don't know what came over me."

"It's all part of growing up some people call it hormones. Remember though, if you dish it out you better be able to take it when it comes back at you."

"Is that a threat or a promise?"

"Relax, you're healing faster than you think." With that she turned and walked out of the ward.

Ed thought to himself as he watched her leave the ward. "God, I wish I was fifteen years older or she was fifteen years younger."

Later in the day Dr. Kowalski came to see Ed. "I want you to use your walker for another week. Then we will look you over and decide whether or not you are strong enough to walk with a cane. The x-rays show the swelling to your spine and brain are receding. I want you walking as much as you possibly can. When you get tired or start hurting stop and rest until you feel better. I don't want you overdoing it or falling and injuring yourself. I am going to have the physical therapy department walk you twice a day for an hour each time and progressively increase the time. By the way, how are your walks in the park coming?"

"Great, I walk until I'm tired and then sit down on one of the benches. The cement walkway through the park makes it easy to move my feet."

"Does anyone accompany you?" The doctor asked seriously.

"Oh yes, therapy always sends someone with me."

"Good, the fresh air seems to be helping. I will tell them to walk you there as much as the weather will permit."

"Thank you, I really look forward to those walks."

"I can imagine, I would assume it gets very tedious sitting in here looking out all the time."

"Any idea when I'll get out of here?"

"I would say your looking at another couple of weeks. You should see quite a bit of improvement in your mobility between now and then. You are healing fine but we need to make sure there aren't any blood clots or edemas after the swelling recedes to a level where you can function and not have to rely too heavily on pain medicine. Addiction could turn into a nasty side affect, before we release you we will make sure you can tolerate the level of pain you are experiencing."

"Thanks Doc."

"Sounds like supper is about to be served." The doctor said as the sound of dishes clattering, echoed through the hallway outside the ward. "I will see you in a couple of days." The good Doctor said as he patted Ed's blanket covered leg before he rose and left the room.

"See you Doc." Ed said to Doctor Kowalski's backside as he walked through the ward doors.

Ed laid in his bed staring at the ceiling as the sunlight coming through the windows faded and gave way to the fluorescent lighting inside the building.

Ed woke for breakfast and completed his ritual hygiene before he ate. His full stomach made him drowsy and he crawled on top of the covers of his newly made bed and drifted off into a deep sleep.

A voice and a hand gently shaking his arm woke Ed out of his deep sleep. Alice was standing next to Ed's bed with a book in one hand and shaking his arm with the other hand.

"Hi! I brought a book of poems by Robert Service. If you want to sleep I'll come back later."

"No, I'm awake now, please don't leave!"

Alice smiled and sat on a chair next to Ed's bed while she read to him. During a pause in the reading Ed asked her why she didn't show up on Friday.

"Oh, I am sorry, but a friend of mine got some tickets to a rodeo in Cheyenne at the auditorium for Friday evening. Saturday is my day off; I switched it with Friday so I could go to the rodeo with him. I left a message with your nurse Joyce, didn't you get it?"

"I did, I was really looking forward to you reading to me and I was a little disappointed I guess."

"I'm sorry, I didn't realize it meant that much to you. I didn't know Les was going to get tickets or I would have had him get them for Saturday."

"Did you say Les?"

"Yes, Les Corbett. He works for the same ranch you do. Why?"

Ed looked away, "Oh nothing. I didn't know you knew him." Ed mumbled dejectedly.

"He said he knew you and that he was there when you had your accident."

"Never mind. I'm tired. I think I'll take a nap before my walk." Ed said and rolled over.

Alice gave him a kind of quizzical look and closed the book. "Ok," she said as she got out of the chair. "I'll see you then."

"Ok great." Ed said in a tired voice.

Alice came back about an hour later. Ed was sitting on the edge of his bed.

"Are you ready for your walk?"

"Sure, let's go." Ed said as he grabbed his walker and headed for the door. Once in the park Alice asked Ed if something was wrong because he was acting so melancholy.

"No, I guess I'm getting tired of being in the hospital. It sure is boring."

"It probably won't be much longer before the doctor releases you."

"I asked him about it and he seemed to think it would happen in a couple of weeks."

"I hope so for your sake."

"Thanks. Alice have you ever been out of Wyoming?" Ed said trying to change the subject and keep the conversation alive.

"Sure, I'm not a native you know."

"Oh really, where are you from?"

"Originally, from Cincinnati, Ohio."

"What brought you out here?"

"I was born in Cincinnati and lived there until I was six years old. My dad is an aeronautical engineer. The company he works for has contracts with the military. They moved us out here lock stock and barrel so he could work on some project at the Army Aircorp base in Cheyenne. We've been out here since 1936."

"So, how old are you?"

"I'll be nineteen next June. How old are you?" She asked.

"I'll be seventeen next April."

Alice looked at her watch. "Grab your walking companion there. Its time to shuffle back to the dungeon."

After lunch Joyce came into the ward. "Well, how's our in house stud today?" loud enough so the rest of the patients in the ward could hear every word being said.

Ed blushed, "I guess I had that coming?"

"You sure did Let's get your vitals. Any new aches or pains?" She shook her finger at Ed before he could say anything. "Don't get cute or I'll have to give you that enema I told you about the other day."

"No ma'am," Ed said mockingly "nothing that I haven't already experienced over the last couple of weeks.

"That's what I was afraid of." She said as she took his temperature. "I hear Dr. Kowalski upped your walking time to two hours a day?"

"That's right I have to walk twice a day and I need a chaperone." Ed said as he over exaggeratedly batted his eyes at Joyce.

"Joyce returned the animated expression with a fake smile. "I'd love to honey, but my schedule won't allow it. We leave stuff like that up to the aides in therapy."

"Yeah, that's what the Doctor said."

Joyce rolled her eyes and mumbled to herself "Oh Lord, Why me?" Finishing her blood pressure test she told Ed to stand up and walk to the wall and back. Ed grabbed the walker and made the lap successfully. "You really know how to use that thing don't you?" She said trying to pay Ed a compliment.

"You are talking about the walker, aren't you?' Ed said giving Joyce a sly grin.

"Get your mind out of the gutter, you're getting more out of control every day."

"Hey, who said something about giving and taking?"

Joyce bowed her head and wagged it from side to side. "Lord give me strength. I'm not a murderer, but it's becoming appealing."

"I'm kidding Joyce, you gotta lighten up. I'll try not to make lewd remarks anymore."

"I'll believe that when I hear it?" Joyce said sarcastically.

"What can I say?" Ed said holding his hands out pleadingly.

"The less the better. Don't try to walk too fast or the walker will trip you. Make each move planned and deliberate. You're making good progress. Don't let it go to your head and fall doing something stupid. I'll be by everyday to monitor your vitals, but you gotta take the initiative and help your self heal. The harder you work at it the sooner you'll get out of here."

"Thanks Joyce. I understand what you're saying and I want you to know you could monitor my vitals anytime."

Joyce rolled her eyes "You never quit do you?"

"It's a bad habit I've got."

"Yeah right." She turned to leave and said "I'll catch you later."

"Later." Ed said as he stared at her shapely bottom making her dress roll and twist as she walked away.

About two hours later Rick the male aide from the therapy department found Ed in the sitting room reading a magazine.

"How are you Ed? Ed looked up from his reading and nodded. "Let's go for your walk."

Ed smiled and said in a feminine voice; "but I really don't know you, will you be gentle?"

"Joyce warned me about you. She said if you get mouthy or uncooperative to give you an enema." Rick whipped out a rubber glove and put it on as he held the gloved hand upright. "Your choice." He said smiling down at Ed.

"I'll walk, I'll walk!! God people get serious around here." Ed said as Rick helped him out of his chair. "Lead the way and I'll follow, any place but the bathroom that is." Ed said as they started down the hallway toward the elevators.

Rick laughed, "You learn real quick don't you?"

Ed mumbled under his breath as they moved slowly down the corridor. As the elevator opened Alice walked out. "Hi Ed, looks like your doing well, you'll be out of here in no time."

"Hi Alice. I hope so the help is getting meaner and uglier all the time," he said as he nodded his head toward Rick and winked. "You are going to take me for my walk this afternoon aren't you?"

"Of course, unless Rick here has taken a liking to you and really insists on doing it himself." Alice smiled at Jim and with wide sparkling eyes.

"Well I have grown fond of him in the last three minutes." Rick said joining in the fun with his bad Hungarian accent.

"Oh God, you gotta help me Alice," Ed said with a large amount of theatrical emotion. "Did you see the rubber glove Boris has? He threatened to do bad things to my body if I didn't walk with him. I'm a captive. He's gonna take me into the park and do who knows what to me." By now Rick and Alice were laughing openly.

"Man, I wish all our patients were this fun to be around." Rick said to Alice.

"I agree." Laughing as she continued down the hall.

The routine was pretty well set by now. Dr. Kowalski came in after breakfast twice a week. An aide came about nine a.m. to walk with Ed. Joyce came right after lunch to check his vitals. Alice would go with him on his afternoon walk and read to him for an hour after they got back into the hospital. It was during these afternoon walks that Ed and Alice got to know each other and became good friends.

Sitting on a bench in the park Ed and Alice were engaged in conversation about each other. "As I said before we moved here from Cincinnati in 1936. I graduated from Cheyenne high school last May. I want to go into nursing, that's why I'm working here. I work full time in the therapy department during the day and part-time three nights a week in the laundry. I should have enough money saved for tuition to attend the university here by next fall.

'Wow!! You must really want to be a nurse."

"I've wanted to be a registered nurse ever since fifth grade."

"How did you get such an intense desire to become a nurse?"

"My Mom and I were visiting my Dad at the air base one day. A plane crashed on the runway and caught fire just before it slammed into a hanger. There were a lot of people burned and badly hurt. I witnessed the whole thing. It made a big impression on me and from that day on I knew I wanted to be a nurse. Well, so much for me. What about you? Where are you from?"

"I grew up in southwestern Wisconsin on a dairy farm. I don't know what I want to be, at least not yet."

"How did you end up out here?"

"I ran away from home and went to Denver. Things didn't work out there so I went through one of those employment agencies that you pay for finding a job and got hired at the ranch in Medicine Bow."

"Why did you run away? Were your parents mean to you?"

"No, not at all. I love my parents and I know they love me. It's just that, it seemed hard to talk to them. They didn't seem to understand how I felt or what I was interested in. I wanted to go places and see things. But, we never could because of the farm. The cows had to be milked twice a day, seven days a week. We milked almost fifty head; that, plus the rest of the livestock that needed daily care. I had to get up at three every morning to help with chores before I went to school and I had to come home right after school to help with chores and the evening milking. I couldn't go out for spots or any activities after school because of my chores. During the summer when there wasn't any school we had field work, so we couldn't do anything more than visit neighbors or have a picnic for a couple of hours on Sunday afternoons."

"That's too bad. Do you think you'll ever go back?"

"I don't know; maybe." Ed said wistfully.

Looking at her watch Alice announced it was time to head back to the hospital. They chatted all the way back to Ed's bedside. "I've got a new book to start on." Alice held it up for Ed to see. "Sherlock Holmes mysteries" she announced with excited anticipation.

"Good." Ed acknowledged. "I like Sir Arthur's writings. He weaves a good mystery."

Alice read to Ed for almost an hour, and then he was left to fend for himself for the rest of the day.

The following morning after breakfast Doctor Kowalski came to give Ed his routine check-up. After looking him over completely the doctor announced that Ed was ready to be discharged. "I am going to discharge you Friday at noon young man," was his statement after the examination was completed. "I don't want you doing anything more than light work. Rest when you get tired and don't push yourself for the first couple of weeks. Then you should only do what you can tolerate. Your energy and stamina will improve with time. I would guess you will be back to normal in a couple of months."

Ed gulped, he didn't even know if he had a place to go to when he got out. This was Tuesday so he only had three days to make arrangements of some kind concerning his immediate future. He thanked the Doctor before the physician left the ward and then pondered his bewildering position. After going through all of his possibilities Ed decided that his only recourse was to call the ranch and see if Emil could help him. When Mrs. Schmidt answered the phone Ed told her what his problem was. She assured him Emil would pick him up from the hospital Friday afternoon. "I know your going to need money for your hospital bill and a place to stay for a while. I'll have Emil call you tonight so you two can work something out."

"Thank you Mrs. Schmidt I can't tell you how much I appreciate your help."

"You relax and I'll have Emil call you tonight."

"Thank you Ma'am, bye."

"Goodbye."

A sigh of relief came as Ed hung up the phone. The rest of his day dragged as he looked forward to his walk with Alice. She was the one person he had to talk to and confide in. He knew she would be interested in his news about being discharged.

That afternoon when Alice showed up Ed told her about the Doctors visit as they walked across the street to the park. Ed and Alice walked slowly on the grass as they talked. Ed was saying; "I know how old you are and where you're from but that's all I know about you."

"Why do you want to know more?" Alice asked looking at her feet shuffle through the short grass.

"Your about the only friend I've got that I can talk to. When I leave Friday I won't have that."

"Where are you going from here?"

"Back to the ranch at Medicine Bow. I work for the Schmidt's at the lazy "S".

"That's right you told me once. I guess I mentioned my friend Les works there also. How come you two don't get along? You're both nice guys."

"I don't know. I'd never met him until I came to the ranch and I don't think I've said more than two dozen words to him all the while I've been there. He's always making me the butt of his jokes, and he's made it quite obvious to the rest of the hands that he doesn't like me. Why I don't know."

"That's interesting. The next time I see him I'll ask him about it."

"Be my guest, I'd like to know why myself. I was going to ask you if I could get your address and phone number so I could write you a letter or call you now and then. But I guess if he's your boyfriend then that's out of the question?"

"I'd like to get letters from you. Les and I are friends just like you and I are. We go to supper, a movie or some other activity together when he's in town, nothing more. I would hope you would come to Laramie now and then so we could do the same.

Ed's heart soared, "that would be great."

Alice continued; "I'm alone here in Laramie. I have a small apartment down on Front Street. My parents and friends all live in Cheyenne and I can't afford to run home all the time. The only time I see any of my relation is when we go back to Cincinnati on vacations."

"So you don't have a steady boyfriend?"

"No way. I don't intend to be tied down right now, besides all a steady wants is sex. When I go to bed with someone it's going to be Mr. Right."

A cold wind had started blowing, "Alice, I'm getting chilly let's go back, I want to hear you read some more Sherlock Holmes." They walked back to the hospital and Alice spent the next hour reading to Ed. After she left Ed waited for Mr. Schmidt to call. About eight o'clock that night a nurse came to take him to the phone.

"Hello Mr. Schmidt."

"Hello Ed, how do you feel?"

"I'm fine, but I'm in kind of a pickle here."

"Yeah, That's what Marianne said, here's the deal. I'll pay your hospital bill and you can stay in the bunkhouse until you're well enough to move on if you want to. We need to talk more about this but we can do that on the way to the ranch."

"Fair enough. I appreciate the help. The doctor said I could leave Friday afternoon."

"Ok, Marianne and I will be there sometime between three and four."

"Great, I'll see you then." Ed said as he hung up the phone.

The following day Alice came as usual to walk with Ed in the park. They were completely comfortable around each other, and the questions they asked were more in depth and personal.

"What was Cincinnati like before you left?" Ed asked Alice as they strolled along in the brisk fall air.

"I remember the neighborhood we lived in and the people that lived close around us. It was near the Ohio River where Kentucky, Indiana and Ohio come together. We lived off Glenway Ave in Covedale. It sure has changed over the years. It's different every time we go back to visit the relatives. We lived in a big two-story house with a large front porch. I can remember sitting in the porch swing and rocking for hours. The swing was big enough that it would hold four of us kids. We would get it going so hard that it would bang against the side of the house. My mother would come out and chase us off it. There were a lot of big old trees that lined the streets. I had a friend fall out of one once and break her arm. What about you? What did you do when you were a kid?"

Ed thought a minute. "My real dad was killed in a farm accident when I was two years old. The only reason I know is my mother told me about him years ago. Evidently he got his pant leg caught in a drive shaft. It sucked him into the machine and tore him up pretty bad. She said he was out in a field by himself about a mile away from the house. No one knew he was in trouble until he didn't come in for supper. When they found him he was dead. He either died from shock or bleed to death, probably both."

"I'm sorry," Alice said placing her hand on Ed's arm.

"It's ok. I barely remember anything about him. About a year after my real dad's death my mother remarried. My step dad is the only father I have ever known. He's a good man and always treated me like

I was his own. I love him like he was my real father. He even adopted me right after he married my Mom."

"It just blows my mind that you would leave everything to see what's on the other side of the mountain."

"If I had it to do all over again, I don't know if I would leave. The grass always looks greener on the other side of the fence, I guess.

"Did you ever contact your parents after you left?"

"No, but the Salvation Army did." Ed told her everything about Denver except being raped. "So what are your plans for the future?" Ed asked Alice after completing his uncomfortable dissertation.

"I want to be an RN and have a family."

"That's pretty straightforward and simple." Ed commented.

"Right, that's the way I like to keep my life. How about you? Do you intend to cowboy all your life?"

"No, I want to settle down and have a family someday, but not now. I still have an itch that needs to be scratched."

"Don't you have any plans or dreams about your future other than living from day to day?"

"Not right now, there are some things I want to do later on. Like electronics or one of the trades."

"Well, at least your honest. C'mon let's walk back."

The Schmidt's arrived at the hospital about two thirty in the afternoon. Marianne helped Ed get dressed while Emil went to pay the bill and talk to Dr. Kowalski. Once they were in the car and headed for the ranch Emil filled Ed in on what the doctor recommended. It was basically the same thing the Doctor told Ed earlier.

"Like I said when I talked to you on the phone; you can stay in the bunkhouse until you're healed. I paid your hospital bill and it was a pretty large chunk. Marianne and I talked it over and since you got hurt working for us on our livestock I guess that makes us responsible. Here's the deal if you'll take it; stick with us until the hands come back at the beginning of April and live on fifty dollars a month. You can leave anytime after that you want."

Ed sat quietly thinking over his options for a long time. "What would I have to do?

"We'll keep you on this winter to do chores and help feed cattle."

"That's great, thank you, I really appreciate your helping me." Ed said knowing that it wasn't going to be a vacation, but also knowing that Emil didn't have to keep him at all. Once the fall work was done it only took one person to keep things going until spring and Jake was permanent. Keeping Ed around on the payroll even at a reduced rate was not necessary. It was merely a sense of responsibility and the natural instinct to do the right thing on Emil's part. There was no insurance; just a self-inflicted obligation of the Schmidt's to another human being who needed help.

Each day since his release from the hospital Ed felt a little stronger. He puttered around the ranch doing light chores; milking the cow, doing small repairs to harness and tack and generally doing tasks his mobility would allow him to do. Ed's first week and a half out of the hospital amounted to nothing more than doing a few chores, sitting around the bunkhouse or corrals and showing up for meals. It was a good chance for him to write to Alice, let her know how he was and what was going on. He spent most of his sitting around time writing her and managed to get a letter a day off for the first two weeks he was back at the ranch. One day Les stormed into the bunkhouse and started screaming obscenities and threats at Ed.

"You son-of-a-bitch what are you doing writing to my girl?"

"I didn't know she was your girl." Ed stated flatly.

"She sure as hell is and if I find one more letter of yours in her hands, recovering or not I'll kick your ass. Do you understand me?"

"I didn't mean anything by it Les. Alice and I are just friends. She told me I could write to her after I got out of the hospital."

"I don't give a shit what she said. You write her any more letters and you and I will tangle. Is that clear?"

Ed looked at the big man's frantic eyes and knew he wasn't joking. "Ok, I won't write her anymore." Ed knew Les would be leaving soon so he said what the man wanted to hear to appease him.

It took until the end of November to wrap up the ranch business. The work was done and it was time for the ranch hands to leave. Ron, Mike and Buck had a ranch in New Mexico that they worked for during the winter months. Don went to a ranch in Southern Texas, and Les went home to State College, Pennsylvania to work on his law degree. Before they left on their respective journeys Emil walked into the bunkhouse with everybody's paychecks in his hand. "Here you go boys I gave each of you an extra hundred for the great job you did this year." Emil handed out the checks and said." Les I want to talk to you for a minute, c'mon over to the corral."

"Sure," Les said looking up from his paycheck and he followed Emil as they walked out of the bunkhouse toward the corrals. When they reached the poled enclosures Emil turned and faced Les. "I've got a few things to ask you and I want straight answers, you understand me?" Les looked intently at the older man and nodded as he mumbled, "yes sir."

"You've done a good job for me over the last four years. But, some things happened this year that could've cost me time and money, not to speak of disruption and hard feelings amongst the men. Did you stampede the cattle Ed was driving into camp during the roundup and mix 'em with your own?"

Les looked at the ground while he made circles in the dirt with the toe of his boot and thought hard about the answer to Emil's question. "Looking up at the ranch owner he looked him in the eye and said; "yes I did."

"Why?"

"I honestly don't know other than I don't like him."

"Do you realize the delay to the roundup and possible injury to Ed that you could have caused?"

"I do and I apologize for it."

"You know I had you figured wrong. I thought when I put you on the spot that you'd lie to me. Then I would have kicked your ass and fired you. Now I'm gonna ask you if you want to come back next year?"

Les drew more circles with the toe of his boot as he thought about the question. "Sure, I want to come back for the summer"

"Do you think you can get along with Ed if he's still here?"

More circles. "Yeah, I do."

"Understand if you come back here next year to work, that's what I pay you for, to work, not screwing around. If you two can't get along both of you will be history. Do you understand?"

"Yes sir."

"Ok. Then I guess we'll see you next year." Emil said as he held out his hand for Les to shake.

Les grabbed the extended hand and shook it vigorously as he nodded and said; "see you next year."

The ranch hands all said their farewells to Ed before they left, promising to see him in the spring. Les said goodbye to everyone but Ed and left. Ed was not sad to see him go.

CHAPTER #10

WINTER IN WYOMING is cruel. The wind howls across the sagebrush covered hills and mountains with a deadly vengeance. Even though the mean temperature will hover in the twenties and low thirties during most of the winter, it can and does plummet at times to thirty and forty below zero. There are days during the winter when it gets so cold, the sap in the cottonwood trees by the Little Medicine Bow river freezes and makes the trees crack loudly, like gunshots. It's extremely dangerous going out into those conditions to feed cattle even though they were brought in close to the ranch after the roundup so they would be more accessible to the hay that was stacked for them during the summer. Hay is put up loose in ten to fifteen ton stacks. A thirty-foot square wooden crib ten feet high is built and the loose hay dumped inside of it. The hay extends about ten or fifteen feet above the top of the crib. The crib is not intended to contain the hay, but to keep the cattle from tearing the haystack apart until it can be fed out. When a haystack is to be fed out the crib must be torn apart in order to get the "sled" next to it so the hay can be cabled onto the sled deck.

The sled is a low-decked wagon on truck tires that measures fifteen feet wide by thirty feet long. A half inch steel cable seventy-five feet long hooks to the front corner of the sled after it is positioned next to the stack. The cable is then dragged around the stack and across the back end of the sled. The horses are hitched to a rubber-tired chariot with a fixed clevis that allows quick and easy attachment to the tongue of the sled. The horse drawn chariot is unhooked from the sled and rehooked to the cable now wrapped around the haystack. The top half of the haystack is then pulled slowly onto the deck of the sled. If it is pulled to far it goes on the ground and has to be pitch forked onto the sled by hand. If all goes well and the horses are stopped at just the right moment half the haystack (approximately five tons of it) is sitting intact on the sled ready to transport to the feeding grounds, which is usually the immediate area. If you aren't lined up perfectly straight with the cable the chariot will dig one wheel or the other in and roll, throwing the operator off or worse. The hay is pulled off by hand as the horses walk along pulling the sled. Once the sled has been stripped of its load the remainder of the stack is cabled onto the sled and either fed out or taken outside the feeding grounds to be fed the next day. If the sled sits overnight with five ton of hay on it boards are placed under the tires so they won't freeze to the snow.

Every second day a new stack is opened up and cabled onto the sled. Every other day the loaded sled is pulled to the feeding ground unloaded and the crib boards from the previous days stack loaded onto it and taken back to the ranch. It normally takes four to five hours from the time you pull up to the stack until the last forkful of hay is taken off the sled. If things don't go right you could be loading the second half of the stack as it's getting dark. In order to take advantage of the most daylight you have to be at the stack at the crack of dawn. Some of the stacks are two and three miles away from the ranch. Which means your day starts at about three am and goes until you're done. This is in addition to the daily harnessing and hitching of horses, milking the cow, and making any repairs to equipment that needs to be done.

Workhorses are the only dependable source of pulling power in winter conditions. If the snow is deep you hitched six or eight head two abreast. Giddy up, gee, haw, whoa and a jerk line is used to maneuver and stop them. The leads break the trail and guide the rest of the team through the turns. In deep snow the leads are switched with the first set of swings at noon in order to keep them going. If the snow is not a factor they are hitched four abreast behind two in front. Only the two in front and the inside two in back are actually driven.

Since Jake and Ed were both working this particular winter they split the work. Ed would feed the cattle in the far pasture one day and the next day he would stay around the ranch to feed the pregnant cows; do chores and repairs while Jake fed the cattle in the far pasture. They switched off like this all winter. Winter is not a sit by the fire, feed a few barn animals. It is a brutal time of the year to work outside. The hours are long, and usually you're working by yourself, long distances from any kind of help, during the dead of winter in a remote area with no roads or civilization.

Calving season on the open range is usually from the last half of February through March to the first half of April. It can vary from ranch to ranch but it will be in this approximate time frame. Some of the worst winter storms occur during this time of year. In order to get a calf crop at this particular time of the year the bulls must be turned in with the cows about nine months prior, because the accepted gestation period for cattle is two hundred and eighty four days. The cows are allowed to birth on the open range at that time of the year for a number of reasons; there are no facilities large enough to hold upwards of five hundred head plus the increase, the cold helps to keep disease and infection minimal, and the whole herd can be moved to a clean pasture where there is no blood or afterbirth to contaminate the ground. A three percent loss of the calf crop is expected. The weather no matter how cold is usually not a factor to the newborn calves. After the calf is on the ground and its mother licks it dry, the stimulation from her rough tongue is enough to get the calf up and sucking. Once the calf gets mothers milk in its belly it can withstand weather that would cause the mother to freeze to death standing up. The only effective way to check all the expectant mothers on a section of land is to move among them on horseback. If you find one that's having trouble then you stay with her until the situation is resolved. If a calf is backwards it must be turned by hand and pulled. If a leg isn't straight, you have to reach in and straighten it. When it's zero or colder and a twenty mile an hour wind is blowing (which is usually the case in Wyoming during the winter) frostbite is a distinct possibility unless you get your wet arm and hand covered immediately. The way to do that is; take your arm out of the coat sleeve but leave the coat on and buttoned at the throat so it doesn't fall off your shoulder. Insert your hand and arm into the cow, do what you have to do and when you extract your arm put it back into the sleeve immediately and put your hand in a pocket or a glove. This way you won't expose any wet, bare flesh to the elements. It is extremely important to your survival in harsh weather when your miles from home to make sure you don't get frostbite or hurt.

A certain amount of tools and veterinarian supplies are always carried in the saddle bags such as; calf pulling chains, (they resemble a dogs choke chain collar about two feet long with solid rings on each end) syringes and needles, procaine penicillin, iodine, curved sewing needles, catgut or some kind of dissolvable suture, a couple of surgical clamps, razor blades, a few rags, a sharp knife and a pistol.

The problems incurred by the rider with the cattle and/or the weather will determine how much time he might have to spend outside. When the calving started Emil took over all the chores around the ranch. Jake and Ed switched on and off taking care of the cattle. One would check the pregnant cows and feed them since they were kept within a mile of the ranch. The other one would ride horseback ten miles to the feeding ground where the yearlings and the increase were kept and feed them. By changing off it gave you a chance to warm up, eat some hot food and sleep in a warm bed almost every day. This is what Ed's winter consisted of: Going to bed sometime after nine p.m. and up at three a.m. every day seven days a week. Jake and Ed would meet at the same time each morning to get the horses harnessed and hitched to the sled. After a warm breakfast everyone went their own way to do their jobs.

Jake and Ed got to know each other extremely well, the Schmidt's became like a second family to Ed and he found contentment in those harsh surroundings that he was to find at no other time in his life. Many long conversations took place over the supper table between the four of them. Ever since the ranch hands had left Mrs. Schmidt had been eating with Emil, Jake and Ed. Jake usually ate supper at the ranch even though he lived in town with his wife. Occasionally he would come down to the bunkhouse after supper and keep Ed company for an hour or so. Talk and cards were all it amounted to but it meant a lot to Ed and a genuine friendship developed between the two men.

One night after a couple of decks of blackjack, Jake got up to leave and said; "be careful out there tomorrow. There's a big storm coming in. Don't take any chances. The cattle can go without food for a day or two if they have to. If it hits don't get caught in the open, we can replace cattle."

Ed looked at the older man standing in the doorway, framed by the black night and the dimly lit room.

"Ok, I'll keep an eye on the weather and head for home if it starts to turn."

"Listen, it's ten miles from here to the feeding ground where you're going. The tallest thing out there is probably a bunch of grass that's been knocked flat by the wind or the snow. If we get a real blow, which I think we will in the next twenty-four hours, don't get caught in the open or you're a dead man. If it starts to snow even a little bit, get home or hole up in a haystack, which ever is closer."

Ed grinned and nodded as the potbellied form in Levis and farmers' shoes disappeared out of the doorway into the night.

At three am the alarm clock brought Ed out of a sound sleep. Getting out of bed he shut the noisemaker off and got dressed. The dull moan of the wind serenaded him as he moved around in side the dimly lit room. Dressing was a hurry up exercise in the chilly room. The fire in the wood-burning stove had gone out a long time ago. Pulling on his heavy coat, hat and rubber overshoes before he headed for the heated washhouse. Once he was washed and his hygiene needs met he headed for the horse barn. Jake drove in and parked as Ed entered the barn and turned on the lights. Jake entered the barn saying, "Man it's cold out there. When I left the house the thermometer said it was fifteen below."

Ed grabbed a set of harness and started out the door. Hanging the harness on the corral He looked over at Jake doing the same thing. "Not a cloud in the sky, I think your storm went around us." Ed said as he looked up at the dark star studded sky.

"Maybe, but my bones sure ached yesterday and the way the horses were running around I still think we're gonna get hit."

All the harness needed was dragged out and hung on the corral. Then the horses were caught and harnessed. Each one was led over and tied to a long wooden grain trough along with Ed's saddle horse. A mixture of oats and corn was then dumped into the trough for the horses to eat while the men went to the ranch house and put on the feedbag. After breakfast Mrs. Schmidt gave Ed the usual fare for the person riding to the far feeding ground. A sheet of newspaper folded around two sandwiches and secured with a string. He stuck the package in his coat pocket and headed for the corral. Jake was there putting the bridles on the workhorses. Ed helped him finish and then they hitched the team to the sled. Jake waved as he drove off into the cold dark morning. Ed walked into the corral and bridled his bay horse and led him out of the corral. Ed closed the gate, mounted and rode off into the crisp morning air after a couple of good jumps by the horse.

Ed looked at the lead colored sky as he rode away from the ranch. "Looks like it could storm." He talked out loud to the animal steadily plodding along beneath him. "Guess we better move right along," he said, putting the bay into a slow ground-covering shuffle.

They made it through the gate in the home fence located a hundred yards behind the ranch house, and then it was ten miles as the crow flies to the gate that lead into the south feeding grounds. It took Ed the better part of three hours to arrive and start rounding up the workhorses that were released into the pasture after the feeding is done each day. Ed ran the six equines into a small pole corral built just for the purpose of harnessing horses during the winter or holding a cow or two for whatever reason. A small outhouse looking building was attached to the rail of the corral. A door had been provided so there was access from inside the corral and to keep unwanted critters out. Horse harness, hayforks, shovels, post hole diggers, a spare hay cable and some tools to repair things made up the contents of the shack. The corral contained two gates opposite of each other large enough to drive the team and sled completely through after the horses were hitched to it. The bridle was removed from the saddle horse but the saddle was left on and the animal was placed inside the corral and fed hay.

Workhorses have their own personal set of harness. It's adjusted through a series of buckles to specifically fit the horse that wears it and takes about fifteen minutes to put on. After all the horses are harnessed they are the hitched together to the wagon and the trek to the haystack begins.

Ed hitched the six head to the chariot, drove them outside the corral and hooked to the sled. The exertion of getting everything ready to go had kept Ed warm. Driving the rig toward the haystack he was going to use, Ed could feel that it was colder and that the wind had picked up in the last or hour so. Shivering a little Ed was glad the haystack was only about a quarter mile away. Pulling up to the stack he took the crib apart and spent the next four hours pitch forking the hay that he pulled over the sled onto the ground back onto the sled, so he could feed it out. By the time Ed got the second load cabled onto the sled, drove it inside the corral, hung up the horse harness and mounted his saddle horse to head for the ranch, a few snow flakes were drifting lazily out of the slate gray sky. He looked at his pocket watch and it was five minutes to three o'clock in the afternoon and the daylight was failing fast. Going home always went a little faster because the horse knew a warm barn and hay were waiting. Ed figured they should arrive shortly after dark about six o'clock.

Riding to the gate in the pasture fence he opened it, went through it and closed it without getting off the horses back. This was an accomplishment Ed recognized with pride. He was actually becoming a good enough horseman to do this maneuver that seemed so simple to everyone else out here. It was definitely getting colder and the wind was starting to blow hard enough that he pulled his knitted ski mask out of his coat pocket and put it on his head after the gate was secure. Half an hour later the storm hit in full force!!!

In Wyoming during the winter it's not a question of does the wind blow; it's a question of how hard. The wind had been blowing lightly all day, but suddenly it turned into a gale. Previously only a few random snowflakes were lazily falling out of the sky. Now, it was snowing and blowing so hard Ed couldn't see more than ten feet in any direction, if that. The cold that he felt run through him was not caused by the elements. It was caused by the realization that he couldn't see where to go and had no idea which way was which. Stopping the horse Ed tried to get his thoughts and emotions together. He knew he was in bad trouble, if he didn't come up with a plan real quick he would die. There were no landmarks because of the blinding snow and it was getting worse. He was only a twenty-minute ride from the gate he had just come through and two hundred yards from there stood the sled with five ton of hay that he could burrow into and survive the storm. The problem was orientation; he had no idea which way to go, all he could see was white. No matter what he did it better be right the first time or he was a dead man. Ed was too scared and too cold to cry. His past experiences had hardened him a little and he was able to control his emotions better in tight situations and think. Ed knew if he allowed his emotions to rule he would lose control, do something stupid and die. Making a decision had to be done and quick!!!

Ed decided to continue on, thinking that the horse would head for the barn. This may be true when you're close to the barn, but it doesn't apply when you're nine miles away in the middle of a howling snowstorm. The horse will turn his butt to the wind and drift with it as long as he can because it's strictly a survival thing. His butt is the biggest part of his body and has the most mass, so it does a better job of blocking the wind. Ed didn't know this but he did notice that the horse kept turning away from the wind. When the storm started, the wind was hitting the side of his face at about a forty-five degree angle from the right front. He figured from the mental pictures he created of the home fence and his direction of travel toward it that he must keep the wind blowing in his face from that direction. Otherwise they would go in circles in a pasture that measured ten square miles with no cover. If the wind didn't change Ed figured he should be able to hold a straight enough line to make it to the home fence. By now the whiteness was turning to a very dull gray as twilight settled on the snow swept plains. It was too cold riding the bay for any length of time, so Ed rode a while and walked on the downwind side of the horse for a while. Walking was good exertion and the animal's body heat helped keep his circulation going, besides blocking the relentless wind. It was a fight to keep the animal walking sideways to the wind but Ed knew he must keep moving. He might have appreciated the fact that he had dressed for the weather he was trapped in if he hadn't been concentrating on surviving so hard. The weather changed during the last hour, it got worse. The wind was blowing so hard that the snow appeared to be going straight sideways. Snow was beginning to turn into ice on his clothes and facemask. He was getting tired and it was dark. The only thing he could see through the frozen slits in the ski mask was his horse. Everything else around him was a dark gray, blowing mist. He had been out in the storm almost three hours and couldn't distinguish anything that was more than three or four feet away. Ed still had some go in him but he was fading fast. Stopping his horse he got off and tied the reins hard and fast to his wrist. He thought to himself as he secured the reins to his wrist. "If I fall down and lose the horse it'll be curtains for sure." Ed had no idea where he was. His only hope was to keep going until he hit a fence and then try to figure out where the ranch was from there. He had been trying to walk with the wind on the right side of his face but he had no way of knowing if the wind changed or if he had been drifting too far left or right. Ed couldn't ever remember being so cold. For someone from a cold state like Wisconsin that's saying a lot. Fear and panic was not a factor now. He was so tired and cold that he was becoming dangerously complacent. All he could do was shuffle along and use the direction of the merciless wind for his bearings. Moving was becoming more and more difficult. One foot in front of the other was starting to require a lot of concentration. "At least it's starting to warm up." Ed thought to himself as the horse stumbled, bumping into him, breaking his dazed concentration and momentarily bringing him back to reality. "Oh God," he thought, "feeling warm is one of the first signs of freezing to death." He had no idea where or how far away the ranch was. "I have to keep moving," Ed thought aloud to himself. "Think about the bunk house, talk to your horse, anything, but don't let your mind wander or think about the fix your in." Ed was really getting tired all he wanted to do was lie down and go to sleep. He knew if that happened he would never get up again. The horse was stumbling a lot now and constantly wanted to stop. "Freezing to death probably wouldn't be a bad death." Ed mumbled through the ice that encrusted the breathing hole on his facemask. A dilemma was engulfing Ed and he didn't even realize it because of the cold and exhaustion he was experiencing. The common custom for most ranch hands during the winter is to let their beards grow. It helps protect their face and neck from the harsh weather. The frost from Ed's breath and the blowing snow had caused ice to form imbedding itself in the cloth fiber of the mask and the hair of his beard. The ice had been building for the last three and a half hours; it was now a couple of inches thick and encrusted everything from his nose down to the second button on his coat. The eyeholes were just icy slits and a small opening in the nose hole was the only thing that was left to breathe through. "Maybe I could lay down and get a little sleep." Ed hallucinated to him self. Suddenly he returned to reality as he tripped and went head first into the snow on the ground. Some snow had gone down the collar of his coat and hit warm skin. It brought him around enough that he saw the tree branch on the ground when he struggled to his feet. A small surge of energy went through him. The wind and snow were howling so bad that he didn't see the tree until he literally walked into it, but he knew exactly what it represented. Years ago, after the ranch had been built, a row of Lombardy poplar trees were planted in a five hundred yard row, at a forty-five degree angle from the fence on the pasture side as a windbreak for buildings and cattle.

These trees were now fully matured and stood eighty to a hundred feet tall. Between Ed's condition and the severity of the storm he couldn't see them until he ran into them. But, he knew if he went to his right along the line of trees he would come to the fence and if he went to the right along the fence he would find the gate into the home pasture. He opened the gate and let it drop. Then he stood in its opening. "I have to walk straight ahead for about a hundred yards and I will find the picket fence around Emil's yard." Ed thought as he tried hard to concentrate on the final lap of his ordeal. The last hundred yards was flat and filled with sagebrush. The storm hadn't let up in the least as he stumbled on into the howling, dark gray swirling emptiness around him. After what seemed like an eternity Ed banged into the white picket fence. There was only one gate so all he had to do was stay with the fence until he found the gate. With his hands guiding and supporting him he came to a corner and followed the fence. Now he could see a faint glow, it had to be the lights from the ranch house. All of a sudden the fence moved under his left hand. He found the gate and could hear the sound of a bell ringing in the distance. Ed pushed the gate open, staggered through and tripped, only to fall flat on his face. He started to struggle to his feet but a sudden gust of wind knocked him down, he tried to get up but couldn't do it and collapsed. "God don't tell me I'm going to die twenty feet from the house?" The bell stopped ringing and Ed heard voices.

"Jake, Jake, get out here and give me a hand, he's home and needs help." Emil shouted into the open door of the house as he walked back from ringing the big dinner bell. Jake came out of the house on a run as Emil was cutting the reins loose from Ed's wrist with his pocketknife. Mrs. Schmidt had followed Jake outside. "Marianne," start a hot bath. Jake, you get his horse in the barn and tend to it." Jake nodded and guided the wobbly animal to the barn. Marianne turned and ran into the house as Emil dragged Ed by his coat collar through the door. Marianne was shocked at Ed's pitiful condition as Emil dragged him into the bathroom like a dead animal. "Good grief, is he alive? She said as Emil turned him around parallel with the tub. "Barely, grab his feet and help me get him into the tub after I get his boots off. We'll have to leave everything else on until we get the ice on his head and neck thawed. Then we can take his coat and stuff off as he thaws out." The couple gently laid Ed in the tub "He wouldn't have lasted ten more minutes out there." Emil said as they scooped warm water over Ed for the next half hour. "If he hadn't been tied to his horse I would never have seen him laying there. All I could see when I got done ringing the bell and started back toward the house was a big dark shape by the gate. I didn't see him until I darned near tripped over him."

"Thank God you found him. If he doesn't wind up with double phenomena he'll be lucky."

"I'm worried about frostbite. We won't know anything about that until we get these clothes thawed out and off him."

Finally the ice was melted enough they were able to remove everything but the ski mask and knotted bandanna he used to hold his hat on. It was still caked with an inch of ice and snow. The only thing left open when Emil brought him in was a slit in the left eyehole and a hole about the size of a drinking straw in the breathing area of his nose. Every half hour for the next three hours Emil and Marianne came in to reheat the water and check on him. Ed's skin color went from bluish white to beet red as his body heat slowly returned. A couple of hours into the prolonged sauna Emil asked Ed, "Do any parts of your body hurt or tingle?"

Ed thought a minute, "I guess my whole body does. Do you think I froze anything?'

"It doesn't appear that way. We'll know in the next twelve hours or so. If anything starts hurting real bad or starts to turn black we'll need to get you to Doc Larsen in Medicine Bow. Let me know when you want to get out of the tub, you'll probably need me to help you stand up. Marianne fixed a bed for Jake because it was too nasty for him to drive home. You can bunk in with him until this storm is over with.

"Thanks Emil, seems like you're always saving my bacon, I'll owe you so much you'll have free labor for the next ten years."

"We'll talk about that when it happens. You just take it easy, you'll hurt and be stiff for the next three or four days but I don't think any real damage was done."

"Thanks, I've never come that close to dying in my life. It's sure gonna make me look at things differently from now on."

"Well, you had a couple of things going for you out there tonight. Your young, strong and God was definitely with you. If I was you, I'd be on my knees first chance I got and him and me would have a long talk."

"Don't worry about that. If I ever believed in my maker, this night brought it home for sure. I don't think I'll ever look at the world quite the same anymore."

"Good." Emil said with a satisfied look on his face. "A man ought to know humility." With that he turned and left the room. After a short period of time Emil and Marianne returned. Mrs. Schmidt had an old terry cloth robe and some large towels. "How about it; feel like getting out of the tub?" Emil asked as he grabbed Ed's hand. Mrs. Schmidt took his other hand, helped pull him out of the water and handed him the towel and the robe. Ed was not embarrassed about being naked in front of Mrs. Schmidt because none of them thought anything about the situation other than what had to be done to keep Ed from getting frostbite. When Ed dried off and put the robe on that Mrs. Schmidt had left, he came out of the bathroom at the same time she came out of the living room. Pointing down the hall, she said; "second door on the right, have a good nights sleep, Ed."

"Goodnight and thank you Ma'am." Ed turned and went to his temporary room.

The room was about twelve feet square and modestly furnished. It contained a darkly stained wooden double bed carrying a feather tick and a large, heavy cotton comforter, a brown wooden dresser with a mirror and porcelain drawer pulls, a matching tall chest of drawers, a brown wooden footlocker, its finish worn thin by time, positioned at the foot of the bed. A brass floor lamp with a sea green colored glass shade was standing in the corner next to the bed, on a rust and gold colored Persian rug that was a little smaller than the room. The warm polished glow of the hard wood floor showed around its white-fringed edges. The only window in the room was alongside the bed hidden behind a set of green floral curtains. Ed could hear the same howling wind that had almost killed him, moaning its soft deadly lullaby out side the curtained window as he drifted off to sleep.

Morning came; the storm had lost its intensity but was still very much alive. It was just barely daylight and when Jake got out of bed his stirring woke Ed, who was peeking out the window between the drapes when Jake returned from the bathroom fully dressed.

"Good morning" the foreman said as he entered the room. "Sorry if I woke you. I figured you'd sleep in after your ordeal yesterday."

Ed dropped the curtain and turned. "I feel ok, a little warm and stiff is all."

"You're lucky. You came real close to dying out there."

"I know. Emil and I talked about that last night."

"You'll lose the red glow and the stiffness after a couple of days. In the meantime I'll feed the far pasture and you can take care of the home stock. If you need help Emil said he'd give you a hand."

"Great, I'll do what I can."

Jake nodded and left the room. He normally would have been up at three a.m. to head for the far feeding ground. The blizzard outside made that a momentary impossibility. If it let up by noon he would he would ride out with a sleeping bag tied behind his saddle and plan on spending the night burrowed into a haystack. The cattle must be checked and fed as soon as the storm subsided enough to move around in safety. Standing in freezing temperatures for a couple of days or more without hay, could prove fatal to the weaker animals.

Emil stopped by the room shortly after Jake got up and informed Ed he would feed and do chores that day. "You rest for a day, tomorrow will be soon enough for you to go back to work. C'mon to the kitchen Marianne has breakfast ready" He said as he retreated from the doorway. Ed pulled on his clothes over the long johns he wore to bed and headed down the hall to the kitchen.

"Good morning!" Mrs. Schmidt exclaimed as he walked into the room. "How are you feeling this morning?"

"A little stiff is all ma'am." Ed said as he pulled the chair under him and slid up to the table.

"Your sure you don't have any burning sensations anywhere or anything that looks like a bruise?"

"No ma'am. I feel a little warm, but Jake said that would pass in a day or two."

"You're certainly flushed, you're almost as red as that sorrel we got rid of." This was the only reference to the fate of the sorrel horse that caused Ed so much pain when he first arrived at the ranch. "But, Jake is right it'll pass in a day or two."

Emil spoke up as Mrs. Schmidt put breakfast on the table. "Jake don't leave until you're real sure this storm is over with. If we lose a few head, so be it, we can stand the loss of a few cattle."

Jake nodded "don't worry I've been through a couple of storms before."

"I know, but I've seen these storms double back when you least expect it. Just make sure before you go is all I'm saying."

"Thanks Emil, I'll be careful."

"Ed, you relax in the bunkhouse today. I'll take care of the stock and the chores. Plan on feeding the first thing tomorrow morning though. If you want help let me know at breakfast."

Ed looked at the ranch owner as he turned to his plate. "Ok, and thanks."

Emil acted as if he hadn't heard but Ed knew he had and choose to ignore the compliment. Everyone sat around the table drinking coffee and talking. The storm broke about eleven a.m. in the morning and Emil left to feed the home stock. Ed walked to the bunkhouse and built a fire. Jake bundled up and Ed watched him ride off into the gray and white world that had almost killed him twenty-four hours earlier.

CHAPTER #11

LYING AROUND THE bunkhouse was fine for about the first hour. The few books that were stacked on the wall shelf Ed had read at least two or three times. So, he decided to write Alice a letter. He had written her two letters a month since Les's departure. Since he had all this time on his hands he figured he would compose a nice long letter and tell her about his recent brush with death. It turned into a three-page hand written description of the last forty-eight hours. When the dinner bell rang Ed walked to the house letter in hand. Mrs. Schmidt had homemade chicken noodle soup and hard crust bread ready and waiting.

"This should warm you up." She said as she ladled the golden mixture into his bowl.

"Yes ma'am. It sure smells good.' Ed said as he inhaled the steam rising from the bowl.

"You look like you've lost some of your color, you're sure nothing hurts?"

"No ma'am I'm fine. I have a letter to mail. Would it be ok if I took the pickup out to the road and put it in the box before the mailman comes?

"I don't see why not, another one for that girl in Laramie?"

"Yes ma'am."

"You two sweet on each other?"

"No, we're just good friends is all. She helped me get my pins under me when I was in the hospital. She used to read Ivanhoe, Jules Verne and Robert Service to me and we talked a lot when she helped me walk."

"It's good you have some one your own age to talk to."

"Yeah, it sure is. Jake and I talk sometimes in the bunkhouse. I really like him, but he reminds me of my dad. He doesn't say it but I can tell by the look on his face he doesn't understand my thinking on some of the things we talk about."

"Jake is from the old school. He's got a heart of gold but he came up through hard times and it's difficult for him to see anything other than reality."

"I suppose. In the last six months I got a glimpse of that side of life. I'm sure he's seen a lot more of it than I have."

"Oh yes, anyone that came through the depression definitely saw hard times. It was a learning experience for some and a tragedy for others, his parents died because of it."

"I didn't know."

"He doesn't talk about it, but for a long time it ate on him bad. I think he's come to gripes with it over the last five or six years, and getting married helped him a lot."

"Did you and Emil go through the depression?"

"Not as a married couple. We were married in thirty-one, times were still tough though. We ate good but there was no cash money to buy anything with. It didn't get better until thirty-eight when Hitler decided to go to war. Then the demand for beef increased and we were able to sell enough cattle to show a profit."

"I lived on a dairy farm in Wisconsin and my parents told me the same thing."

"Those were tough years for Emil and I but they were good ones too. We were able to raise our family when others couldn't make ends meet."

Ed finished his second bowl of soup and stood up. "Thank you for the soup it was excellent. If I'm going to mail this letter I better be going."

"Ok, watch out for snowdrifts."

"I will, the pickup has chains and about five hundred pounds of cotton cake in back so I should be able to bust through any drifts I come across."

"See you at suppertime" Mrs. Schmidt said as Ed donned his hat and coat.

"Yes ma'am" Ed returned as he went out the door toward the pickup truck. Ed made it to the road just as the mail truck pulled up. They traded mail; Ed drove back to the house, and retired to the bunkhouse to read a letter from Alice he had extracted from the postal delivery.

On Saturday evening of the following weekend everyone was sitting around the kitchen table making small talk and drinking coffee as a car drove into the ranch yard. A door slammed, footsteps could be heard and then came a knock on the door. Emil got up to answer the front door. A familiar voice asked, "is Ed Spitzer here?"

Emil replied, "Yes he is. Come on in, he's in the kitchen."

Alice walked into the room as Ed and Jake got to their feet.

"Hi Alice, What are you doing here?"

"I got your letter and wanted to see if you were alright."

Emil pulled out a spare chair as he asked, "Miss, do you want a cup of coffee?"

"I would love one, thank you."

Mrs. Schmidt sat a cup of the steaming black liquid in front of her. "cream and sugar are right there on the table."

"Thank you."

Mrs. Schmidt looked across the table at Ed, "Are you going to introduce us or do we have to do it ourselves?"

Ed blushed, "I'm sorry, everyone, this is Alice Bernard. She was one of the therapists that helped me get back on my feet at the hospital. Alice, this is Emil, my boss and Mrs. Schmidt his wife. This is Jake he's the foreman."

"Glad to meet all of you," Everyone nodded as Alice continued.

"The reason I'm here is because I got a letter from Ed yesterday saying that he almost froze to death. He said he was ok, but I was worried and decided to drive out and see for myself."

Mrs. Schmidt spoke up. "Ed's fine. He had a close call, but he's just fine."

The five of them spent the next two hours talking. Finally Alice stood up and announced she had to leave and get back to Laramie.

"You'll do nothing of the sort young lady." Mrs. Schmidt stated. "It's late and dark out there. You can drive back tomorrow when it's daylight. We have a spare bedroom and would love to have you stay the night."

Emil gave his wife a surprised look but knew better than to say anything at the moment.

"That's very kind of you Mrs. Schmidt. Are you sure it won't be an inconvenience?"

"Positive, and the name is Marianne. C'mon we'll get you one of my night gowns and I'll show you your room."

Alice got up and looked at Ed. "Have a good night, I'll see you in the morning."

Ed stood up and mumbled, "Yeah, ah, ok, goodnight."

After the two women left the room Emil looked at Ed and said," you sly devil you. All the while I thought you were too shy and bashful to have a girl. She's a real cutie."

"But I,,,we,,, we're just friends. She helped me get around in the hospital and we talked. That's all!!!

Jake piped in with a big smile and a laugh, "You try and tell her that. She's got you in her sights bucko."

Ed started for the door. "I'm going to bed. Goodnight!!!"

"Goodniiigghhtt," came the sarcastic reply in unison.

After a restless night, morning came with the noisy alarm clock shattering the quiet stillness. Ed crawled out of bed still confused and wondering what was going on. His thoughts were in turmoil and he didn't know quite why. He cleaned up and headed for the barn as Jake drove into the yard. After the normal greetings the two men harnessed and fed the horses in total silence.

Walking into the warm kitchen Jake and Ed were greeted by Mrs. Schmidt, Emil and Alice. Alice had an apron tied around her waist and was helping Mrs. Schmidt cook breakfast.

Everyone exchanged greetings as Jake and Ed sat down. The women served breakfast and sat down also. The conversation was comfortable, but Ed couldn't wait for the meal to end. He liked the company he was in, but Alice made him nervous. He really appreciated her concern for his near death experience but he was not particularly pleased that she showed up on his employer's doorstep. Ed felt it implied more than was actually there. Everyone, especially Mrs. Schmidt was acting like Alice was Ed's girlfriend.

Ed finished his meal, stood up and announced, "I'm going to get started. It looks like it might snow and I want to get done before it does." Everyone looked in mild surprise between him and Alice. Emil and Jake finally gave him an understanding look, nodded and went back to eating.

"Alice, why don't you walk Ed to the corral and then come back and finish your breakfast?" Mrs. Schmidt said as she gave Ed a hard stare. Ed knew this was not a request.

"Sure," Alice said as she got up to get her coat.

Once outside they walked quietly to the corral where the horses were tied. They stopped at the gate. Ed was having a hard time finding the words he wanted.

"Alice I want to thank you for coming out to see if I was alright."

"I was worried about you. It hasn't been that long since you got out of the hospital."

"I appreciate that." Ed shuffled nervously. "Look, I don't have a lot of time to talk, but I hope you don't think we're anything more than pen pals." Alice inhaled and looked at the ground.

Ed continued. "I really like you but I'm just not ready for romance right now. Alice gave a little sob and turned away. "Damn." Ed felt like a rat. "Please don't cry. I'm just trying to be honest with you." Alice stood unmoving with her back to Ed, now he felt like a shitty rat. "Please talk to me I feel bad that I made you cry."

Alice slowly turned with her head down. When she looked up at Ed he could see the tears running down her cheeks. "After I read your letter I thought you wanted to get something started. I really like you and thought you'd be happy to see me."

Ed was starting to get very uncomfortable. "I said I was glad to see you. I was just surprised when you showed up is all."

"You sure didn't act like it you never looked at me more than twice last night. This morning you never said more than three words to me."

Now Ed was starting to get irritated at being pinned down. "Look, I've got to go to work. Please let me keep writing to you. I won't promise you anything, but you never know what time will bring."

Alice took a step back, looked Ed in the eye furiously and said, "Go to hell!!!"

Ed stood with his mouth hanging open as he watched her run toward the lighted ranch house.

"Shit," he thought to himself. "You really screwed that one up." Turning he walked into the corral and started putting the bridles on the workhorses. He was buckling on the last one as Jake walked up.

"Didn't go well did it?"

"No," Ed said irritated.

"It's none of my business, but if you want someone to talk to let me know."

"Thanks."

The two men hitched the team in silence. When it was done Ed climbed onto the feed sled and drove off. The whole day was a disaster. When he was taking the crib apart, a nail in one of the boards stuck in his coat and made long bad tear in the right sleeve. The horses seemed to pick up on his bad attitude and he fought with them all day. They pulled both loads of hay past the feed sled and Ed had to pitchfork the loose hay back on. It was dark and late by the time Ed got back to the ranch. After he put the horses and equipment away he washed up and went directly to the bunkhouse. He was discouraged, tired and not in the least bit hungry. Sleep was a welcome escape from the day's events.

The alarm clock made its irritating announcement of the new day. Ed got dressed and headed for the washhouse. Jake pulled in while he was cleaning up. The talk between the two men was functional as they harnessed the horses and walked to breakfast. The talk around the breakfast table was always easy and comfortable, but today it was strained. Mrs. Schmidt normally was very bubbly and talkative. This morning she said very little and left the table the moment she was done eating. This went on for a week or so until one warm sunny winter day when Ed got the feeding done early and was hanging around the bunkhouse waiting for supper, a knock on the door announced someone's presence. Opening the door he was surprised to see Mrs. Schmidt standing there. "Hi." Ed said with an uncertain look on his face.

"Hello Ed, I'm sorry to bother you but Emil's went to town and I need your help."

"Yes ma'am, what can I do for you?"

"I'm changing the living room around and I need help moving some of the furniture."

"Be glad to. I'll get my coat." Ed grabbed his coat and put it on as he walked out the door.

"I'd wait until Emil got home and have him help me but I think he's going to be late."

Ed nodded in silence as they walked to the house. Once inside the house Ed shed his coat and followed Mrs. Schmidt into the living room. After she explained how she wanted the furniture arranged they started to move things around. Half an hour later the job was done and Ed turned to leave.

"Sit in the kitchen with me and have a cup of coffee. You might as well wait here it's only about an hour until supper."

Ed was curious but cautious. "Thank you but I think I'll go back to the bunkhouse and do a little reading."

Mrs. Schmidt rolled her eyes. "I want to talk to you. Let's do it over a cup of coffee."

"Yes ma'am." Ed knew this was an offer he couldn't refuse. After the coffee was poured Mrs. Schmidt sat down and looked Ed in the eye. "I won't beat around the bush. Do you like that little girl, Alice?"

Ed was shocked by her bold directness. "Ah,,, I guess. I don't really know." He stammered.

"She really likes you, you know."

"I know. I like her too, but not the same way. I guess I'm just not interested in romance right now."

"Please excuse my bluntness, but you're a fool." Ed blushed and stared at his coffee cup. "If I say something you don't agree with speak up. I won't be offended. We need to clear the air this is affecting everyone here. Emil told me not to say anything to you but I don't like the tenseness when we all sit down to eat."

Ed moved uneasily on his chair. "I'm sorry I didn't mean to cause any trouble between you and Emil."

"You didn't. Emil and I have been married for almost nineteen years now. We've faced some real challenges together. We like you and are trying to help. I might be sticking my nose in where it don't belong but, be that as it may I think this little gal is the best thing that'll ever happen to you. If you don't show any interest you're gonna lose her."

"But I'm not sure I really want to get involved."

"Ed, look around. What do you think your future as a ranch hand is?"

"I never gave it much thought."

"You should. You're young, intelligent and you have your whole life before you. I'm sure you don't want end up on skid row living out of a bottle like ninety nine percent of the hands do after they're too old to work.' Ed shuddered at the memories this brought back.

"No ma'am."

"Then you need to look to your future. Alice and I had a long talk the day she was here. She thinks a lot of you and would like to see you now and then. You don't have to try to fall in or out of love, but you ought to at least get to know each other. If you two hit it off, fine, if you don't that's fine too. At least you won't look back in later years and wonder if it would have worked."

Ed was totally confused. "I suppose"

"God, men are hard headed." Mrs. Schmidt exclaimed shaking her head.

Ed was shocked at her outburst and sat staring at his coffee cup not knowing what to say.

Raising her head the matchmaker asked. "Ed, tell me, have you ever had a girlfriend?"

Ed looked up from his coffee cup. "Yes, I took a couple of girls to movies when my parents could drive us." Thinking a minute he added; "and I took them to some school dances too."

The middle-aged ranch wife sighed and rolled her eyes. "You really led a sheltered life didn't you? I thought you said you were raised on a farm? Don't you know anything about the birds and the bees?"

Ed blushed and said, "Yes ma'am."

Mrs. Schmidt sighed, "We're getting nowhere here."

"I'm sorry, I don't mean to frustrate you, but I don't know what you want me to do."

"Ed, it's not about what I want you to do. You've got a cute, hard working, intelligent girl that would like to get to know you and you don't have a clue about how to have a relationship with a women."

"No ma'am, I don't think I do."

"You men are all alike, sometimes I think it comes from being around animals too much."

"Alice told me the same thing when I was in the hospital." Mrs. Schmidt and Ed both laughed at the same time.

"Maybe there's a message there that you ought to be listening to."

Ed looked at the concerned woman and said seriously; "What do you think I should do? I don't even know how I feel except that I'm confused. I want to know her but yet I don't want to. What's wrong with me Mrs. Schmidt? Did the fall scramble my brains or what?"

"No Ed, your normal. Men don't seem to understand their emotions real good unless they're simple and straightforward. I think it comes from having to deal with the real world all the time. Women on the other hand tend to deal with abstract things better. The things you're feeling are normal. Your world has just been threatened by change and from what I've seen of men that's very unsettling. It'll pass, but if you don't want to at least investigate the change, then you'll fall back into your old habits and never have a life. It all boils down to what you want out of life."

"I want a home and family eventually, but not right now."

"There's nothing wrong with that. But, you need to check out all of your possibilities as they appear. You're only going to run across one, maybe two women that you'll want to live and die for in your lifetime. If you don't check out everyone you meet you'll never know which ones they are."

A look of understanding came across Ed's face.

Mrs. Schmidt continued; "You don't have to commit to anything just enjoy being together and let the relationship go which ever way it wants to."

"How would I get started?"

"The same way you did before. Dig out your pencil and paper and start writing."

Ed felt much better and quietly decided he would sit down after supper and write a letter to Alice. Realizing that their talk was over Ed started to get out of his chair as Emil parked in the yard outside of the house. "You might as well sit, I'll be putting supper on the table shortly." Mrs. Schmidt said as she refilled Ed's coffee cup. Emil walked in the door, looked at Ed and then gave his wife a questioning look. Mrs. Schmidt announced; "I know you didn't want me to say anything, but I really felt I had to talk to Ed about that little girl, Alice, that showed up here the other day." With a small smile Emil shrugged and walked out of the room to wash up for supper.

Once in the bunkhouse Ed sat and composed his letter to Alice. It took a lot of rewriting and changing to get it to say what he wanted, but after a couple of hours he finally sealed the envelope. The next morning at breakfast Ed handed the letter to Mrs. Schmidt and said "Thank you."

She smiled knowingly and set it on the counter, "I'll make sure it goes out today."

A week later Ed found a letter from Alice laying on his bunk when he walked into the log bunkhouse after supper. It read:

Dear Ed:

Thanks for the letter. Yes I would like to get to know you better. I think it would be fun to do something together. I will give you my home and work phone number so you can contact me when you are available . . . .

Sincerely,
Alice

The letter consisted of three pages and was pretty generic. Alice talked about what she had been doing and apologized for her behavior the day she visited the ranch. She ended the letter with her apartment and work phone numbers. Ed and Alice became weekly pen pals. Occasionally Alice would come to the ranch on her days off. Mrs. Schmidt would insist she spend the night and put her up in the spare bedroom. Ed couldn't leave the ranch because feeding the cattle was a seven-day a week job. Over the course of the winter-feeding season Alice showed up three times. Each time she went with Ed to help him feed and check for calves. The weather was getting warmer as the equinox pushed its way towards spring. With the coming of April, the calving season was drawing to a close and feeding took a lot less effort. By the end of the month all the calves were born. The weather had warmed up considerably and the snow was completely gone. Every weekend Alice had come to the ranch to help with the cattle and see Ed.

Ed was completely healed from the slide down the rocky embankment and his close encounter in the blizzard. Physically he had matured. He stood six foot four in his stocking feet, weighed one hundred eighty pounds, his chest measured thirty-six inches and his waist measured thirty-two. He was exceptionally strong. (Able to lift his own weight plus, completely over his head with ease and hold it.) He had become an excellent horseman and worked hard at performing various feats of agility from horseback for Alice's benefit.

The last weekend in April had been designated as the time when the calves would start to be weaned from their mothers. Alice showed up at suppertime on Friday night and Emil announced what would take place over the next two days.

"We'll all be mounted and move a hundred head of cattle with the oldest calves into the large corral. We don't care if they are paired off or not. Then we'll separate the cows from the calves and move 'em through the adjoining corral over to the pasture south of the house. After we get the cows through the gate we'll move the calves into the adjoining corral and hold them there. We'll go get another bunch and gate cut the cows from the calves using the squeeze chute. We've got about six hundred head of cows with calves out there. We'll do about two hundred every two weeks and be done by the end of May. The grass'll be good enough by then to take the cows to the summer pasture."

Ed had always wondered why the fence line he tried so hard to find during the blizzard was built of woven wire when all the rest of the fences were built of barbed wire, now he understood. "How do you get the cows to give up on the calves?" Ed asked.

"Food. Actually it's a natural process. The cows stomp or eat the grass close to the fence and each day they have to move farther and farther away from the fence to eat. The calves are kept in the corral and feed cotton cake pellets and hay for a week and a half. (Cotton cake is a mixture of cottonseed, nutrients, vitamins and molasses pressed into pellets and cubes) Then we brand, vaccinate and castrate before we move 'em with the cattle truck to a close clean pasture and start the process all over again. We feed each bunch cotton cake cubes for about a month after we turn 'em out. That way we're sure they're doing good and can survive on just grass."

Ed was still curious. "Are we going to have enough people to do this?"

Emil smiled, "Yeah, we'll all help drive the bunch in. Once we get 'em in the corral Jake and I will run the gate, Marianne, you Ed and Alice will push 'em to us on horseback. I want to warn you right now," Emil said sitting up in his chair and looking directly at Ed and Alice. "Do not get off your horse in the corral with the cattle. They'll get you in a heartbeat. If you go down stay down and one of us will get to you. Understood?" Ed and Alice nodded in unison as Emil continued. "I talked to the other hands yesterday on the phone. Ron, Mike and Buck said they would be here about the twentieth of May. Don is coming right after Memorial Day and Les will be here about the fifth of June."

Ed's body tensed, he looked at Alice but she was staring at the floor.

Emil pushed his chair back and stood up. "I don't know about you folks, but I'm going to bed. I want everyone mounted and ready to go by first light."

Mrs. Schmidt stood up and said; "Breakfast will be an hour earlier we'll eat at four O'clock instead of five. Everyone else got up and went their respective ways except Alice. She turned to Ed, as he was getting ready to leave and said, "I'll walk you to the bunkhouse." Ed was glad; he wanted to talk to her also. Once outside they walked slowly in the cool comfortable night air.

"This should be fun tomorrow." Ed said trying to get the conversation started.

"I feel sorry for the baby calves. They're going to be orphan's." Ed gave a small laugh.

"You laugh, it'll probably be very traumatic for them."

"Yeah, it probably will. But they'll get over it and grow up to be big cows that'll have calves or be sold to the slaughterhouses for food." Approaching the corral Ed looked at Alice and asked "What about Les?"

They stopped and Alice looked at Ed. "What about Les?" she replied.

Ed was getting uncomfortable. "Are you going to see him?"

"I don't know, that's up to you."

Ed walked the few feet to the corral fence. "Shit," he mumbled under his breath.

"I'm sorry, did you say something?" Alice said as she walked up beside him.

"No, I was just thinking out loud." He said as Alice stood quietly and waited for him to continue. "What about us?"

"What about us?"

"Damn it, every time I ask you a question you answer me with the same question, why?"

"Because I would like to hear how you feel about us."

"I don't know how I feel. Why do I have to make a commitment?"

"You don't. But I really would like to hear it from your lips if you're interested in me."

Ed walked back and forth mumbling to himself. Finally he stood still and said in an irritated voice. "I am interested in you but you're so damn pushy."

Alice smiled, "Thank you that's good enough for now." Turning she headed for the ranch house as she said "Goodnight."

Ed didn't even reply. He turned and stomped to the bunkhouse mumbling to himself as he went.

Morning came with a cool breeze blowing the sounds of night birds and coyotes through the small window Ed had left open. The night sky still held the panorama of bright stars captive as Ed walked to the washhouse. He cleaned up and headed for the barn to get the horses grained and saddled. Jake was already there tying them to the feed trough.

"Morning Jake." Ed greeted the foreman as he walked through the barn door.

"Morning Ed. Looks like it's going to be a great day. The sky is clear as a bell."

Ed measured the grain in an old coffee can and dumped each horses portion into the trough in front of them.

Two weeks ago the two men had gone to the far feeding grounds and collected the animals they were going to use today. Since Jake knew the horses, he picked for the ranch owner and the two women. They brought back a couple of spares just in case. Both men had the two saddle horses that they kept at the ranch for the winter-feeding routine so they only brought five head. Jake picked out a well put up dun for Mrs.Scmidt and a blood colored sorrel for Emil. Evidently these animals were the owners preferred mounts. For Alice he grabbed a red and white paint and a black Appaloosa with a real pretty blanket design covering his butt. The last one was the roan that Ed had picked when he first came to the ranch. Ed was impressed with the new colts in the horse herd. There were about ten of them, which brought the head count of the herd to almost forty-five. Once the new horses were back at the ranch Jake and Ed rode them constantly so they would be ready to work when the time came. Ed rode the two that were meant for Alice and Jake rode the dun and the sorrel. The roan was turned out with the ranch horses. The other four were kept in the corral when not in use. Ed had talked to Alice on the phone a week before Jake and him collected the horses. They discussed her riding experience. She was no stranger to a horse, but she was not a cowboy either. (Cowgirl?) Ed spent as much time as he could riding the two horses trying to determine which would be the best one for Alice. The previous weekend when Alice accompanied him to feed the cattle they took both horses. She had a chance to try each one and settled on the Appaloosa. Ed kept the paint in the corral and rode it occasionally just to keep the kinks out. The weather was nice now and the cattle were getting a little bit of green grass. They weren't eating as much hay, so the feeding schedule had been reduced to every other day.

The two men finished saddling and feeding the horses and headed for the ranch house.

Breakfast was plentiful because there probably wouldn't be any lunch. Daylight was barely showing on the horizon as the group walked toward the barn. It appeared from the growing pink and purple glow spreading its golden hue across the tops of the sagebrush, that it was going to be a clear, sunny day. Ed loved the sweet smell of the new sage; intensified by the damp, spring morning air. The women's horses were led inside the corral and held while they mounted. Ed had told Alice her horse might buck a little when she first got on. He had ridden the horse long and hard for the past week so he didn't think it would amount to more than a couple of jumps. Alice could feel the horse tense as she swung into the saddle. Ed was holding the horse by the bridle with his free hand against the animal's neck. "When I let go pull his head to one side or the other and spin him in a circle until you feel the kink go out of his back." Alice nodded and said, "Ok, let him go."

Ed released the bridle and stepped back as Alice pulled the horse's head hard to the left before he had time to put it down between his front legs and start bucking. She spun the animal in a fast tight circle about half a dozen times and then gave him his head. The horse stopped immediately and stiff leggedly waited a few seconds for the dizziness to go away. "Gig him with your spurs and make him walk out before he has time to think about it." Ed said totally impressed with Alice's performance. She did what Ed told her and the horse stepped out with no problem. "He still might stick his head in the dirt, but if he does it won't amount to much." Alice smiled and rode out of the corral. Mrs. Schmidt was a horsewoman. Emil held the mare while she got on and got her seat. When he released his hold on the mare she put her head down and made three good jumps straightforward. Mrs. Schmidt was with her all the way, and pulled the mare's head up with no problem. Jake had done a good job breaking the horse in. The three men had tied their horses on the outside of the corral now mounted took the kinks out of their mounts, then everyone headed for the pasture containing the cow herd.

The five riders cut into the spread out herd of feeding cattle and took what looked to be approximately one hundred head of cows. Pushing the bunch ahead of them Jake moved up one side and Emil moved up the other side. Jake kept moving to the front and Ed took his place on the side as the two women pushed from the rear. The trick was to keep them moving through the gate in the barbed wire fence and into the corral before they had time to think about what was going on. If a calf got left behind when they were moving the selected cows away from the rest of the herd it might cause a problem. If the calf decided to follow and catch up with mom everything would be all right, if it stood back and bawled its head off, momma would probably try to go to her baby. If she did, she might take a bunch with her and the whole gathering procedure would have to be done over again. Jake and Emil and his wife had the experience so they led the cut and everyone fell into position the minute the bunch was moving in the right direction. It was about two miles from where the cattle were gathered to the corral. The five riders moved the herd into the enclosure with no problem. Now the sorting process started.

Emil tied his horse outside of the corral and walked into the empty small corral. Jake, Ed and the two women stayed on their horses in the large corral with the cattle. Emil ran the squeeze chute. The squeeze chute is a device primarily used for catching and holding large animals as they pass through its narrow opening. It has a split gate that is manually operated and can be opened and closed behind the animal once in the chute. If a calf tries to follow its mother through, the entrance gate is closed to deny it access.

The front gate is designed to allow the head of the animal to come through, but not the body. It has a lever-operated bar that comes down on top of the neck to stop the animal. Then the sides of the chute are squeezed to keep the animal from struggling and hurting itself. When a cow enters the chute it can be closed to trap her or opened to let her pass through. Some squeeze chutes are permanent, and some are on removable wheels. The one Emil and company were using had the wheels temporarily removed. It was tied with wire to the fence, and the end of the opened gate, inside the small adjoining corral. This formed an opening that narrowed down to the entrance of the loading chute like a funnel. Jake would force a cow into the wide part of the funnel area. When she saw the narrow opening she would dive through it, thinking about her calf only after she was on the other side. Jake would run the calf out of the funnel and everyone else would push more cows in his direction. This went on most of the morning. By noon the cows were separated from the calves and driven into the South pasture a hundred yards from the corral. Lining up on the far side of the fence they stood shoulder to shoulder bawling loudly for their babies. The baby calves were driven into a temporary woven wire enclosure that was attached to the corral. It was used to hold the orphan calves while the next batch of cattle were worked.

Emil told Ed and Alice about the noise and the dust before they started, and suggested they stuff their ears with cotton and wear a bandana over their nose and mouth. He was right. The noise level was deafening and the choking dust covered everything like a brown gritty blanket. By the time they were through with the first bunch of cattle and headed out for the second bunch all of them looked like brown miners in baseball caps.

Riding up alongside Emil, Ed asked; "When do we castrate and vaccinate?"

"We'll leave 'em get used to being without their mothers for three or four days. If you do it to soon, some of 'em will die from the stress. If you wait too long, you take the chance of putting them out on pasture before you're sure they're all healing good. Plus they usually go off their feed for a day or two. I like to get 'em trained to the truck horn when I feed 'em. It makes counting a lot easier, because they come to the truck"

"How do you do that?"

"You blow the truck horn before you feed 'em. Pretty soon they get the idea and come running when they hear it."

Ed could see the benefits to the idea immediately. The second bunch of cows and calves were gathered and taken to the corral. In the afternoon with only fifteen head of cows to go Mrs. Schmidt and Alice retired to the house to clean up and prepare supper. After the calves were turned back into the two corrals and fed, the three men unsaddled the horses and fed them before they turned all but two of them loose. Jake and Ed headed for the washhouse and Emil went to the ranch house.

Supper was basic, hot and plentiful; meat, potatoes gravy and vegetable, with a buffalo berry cobbler and fresh cream for dessert. The noisy din created by cows and calves could easily be heard inside the house while everyone ate.

Alice asked in a concerned voice; "How long before they give up?"

Jake looked at her and said, "It'll taper off after a day or so. Ed probably won't get a whole lot of sleep tonight, but he'll get over it." The foreman looked over at Ed and grinned.

"Maybe I'll go for a nice long ride."

Alice piped in, "That would be fun. Can I go to?"

Ed wished he'd never said anything. "I was just kidding it's dark out there."

Mrs. Schmidt spoke up. "The moon will be up in another hour. Since it's full you'll be able to see quite well."

Ed had that trapped rat sensation run through him. "Yes ma'am, your right." Ed said with resignation.

"Oh, could we go Ed? I bet it would be so beautiful to see what it looks like at night."

"Jake, can I borrow your horse? I'll let her ride mine he isn't as spooky."

Jake gave Ed a compassionate look and nodded. "Go ahead."

"Thanks," Ed got up from the table. "I guess I'll go get 'em ready."

"I'll be out as soon as I'm done helping Marianne clean up the dishes."

Ed took mental note of the fact that Alice had called Mrs. Schmidt by her name and not her title. It didn't take him long to get the horses saddled and ready to go. Sitting on a truck tire that leaned against a post inside the barn, he contemplated his situation while he waited for Alice to show up. Knowing sooner or later he was going to have to decide one way or the other on his relationship with her. He liked being around Alice, but was uncertain of whether or not he wanted to make any serious commitments. Ed was sitting on the tire with his back against the post and staring at the floor when Alice walked into the barn.

Stopping in front of him she asked, "Are you ok?"

Ed stood up, "Yeah, I was just thinking."

"Oh, what about."

"Us, I guess."

Alice put her hands on her hips. "Well, let's hear it."

"Could we talk while we're riding? I feel trapped in here."

"Sure, that's what we intended to do isn't it?"

"Yeah." Ed said as he walked around her. He untied the saddle horses and led them outside. "I call him bowzer. He reminds me of a dog I had back in Wisconsin." Ed nodded toward the horse Alice was going to ride. "He'll make a couple of easy jumps straight ahead. Do you think you can stay with him?"

"Of course. If I can't we don't ride. Right?" Looking Ed directly in the eye.

Ed looked away uncomfortably "I suppose."

Alice smiled and expelled a soft "humph" as she stuck her foot in the stirrup and mounted the waiting horse. Ed was right, when he released the animal, the horse made a couple of halfhearted jumps forward before it allowed Alice to pull its head up. Once the animal stood quietly Alice looked at Ed. "I'm ready."

Ed nodded, mounted his horse and spun him in tight fast circle until he wobbled and then hit him with the spurs to make him step out before the dizziness wore off. The horse stumbled forward and they rode off quietly into the growing silver glow of the moonlight. They rode to the top of a high bluff that overlooked the little Medicine Bow River. Sitting quietly on their horses Ed and Alice listened to the muffled din the cattle below them were making, along with the eerie howling and yapping of a pack of coyotes in the distance somewhere behind them. The view was spectacular.

The low hills in front of them reflected the moon's silvery light. The river looked like a bright silver ribbon winding its way in and out of the darkly shadowed gullies and draws that covered the landscape. They could see the lights from the town of Medicine Bow five miles away and a couple of dim lights from the ranch house below them.

Alice spoke first. "Sure is peaceful."

Ed got off his horse "It sure is. I love it up here. Everything looks so different. Up here everything seems to make sense. The stars and moon are where they should be, nothing seems to change."

"Sounds like you're afraid of change?"

"No, not really. Some changes I don't understand. Especially if I don't instigate 'em."

"Do you think being with me would change you?"

"Of course it would. I'm not sure exactly how, but things just wouldn't be the same. Hell, I had a whole speech worked up, before we came up here and now it won't come out. Look, I really like you and I want to see you; a lot. But, I don't know how to say it or what to do."

"Seems to me you just did that. Where do we go from here?"

"I don't know." Ed mounted his horse and started back to the ranch.

After the horses were put away and Ed was in the bunkhouse, he cussed himself. "Damn dummy, here was your chance to tell her how you felt and you couldn't even do it. What's wrong with you? Evidently she scares the shit out of you. She's only a girl and your acting like she's the baddest thing around. You better make up your mind whether or not you want to get serious about her. If you do then don't be such a damn wimp and go after her. If not at least have balls enough to tell her your not interested." Ed felt better after chastising himself. He knew immediately which way he wanted to go. After breakfast Ed asked Alice if she would walk him to the barn. Once inside Ed turned to her; "Alice I'm sorry I acted like such a fool last night." Alice started to speak, but Ed raised his hand to stop her and continued. "If you interrupt me I'm not gonna be able to say this. I want to see you and hope we can become more than friends." The light in Alice's eyes glowed brightly. Ed held up his hand again. "To be down right honest with you I don't know the first thing about women. I guess that's why they scare me when they get close. I would like to come to town and take you out when I get a chance. Beyond that I don't know what to do."

"It's easy." Alice replied. "Just do what feels right and figure out how to work as a team. Just like a pair of workhorses do when they're pulling. If they don't pull together one does all the work. When they pull together they can move more weight with half the effort."

Ed could relate to the analogy. He shook his head and said "Yeah I see what you mean."

"I promise I won't hurt you. You'll know if we are right for each other."

"OK, I guess I better get to work." With that he grabbed her by the shoulders and planted a clumsy kiss half on her lips and half on her cheek.

Pushing his arms away, Alice said, "we can do better than that. Let me show you." Ed stood there with his arms hanging at his side as Alice slid her hands behind his neck and gently pulled his face down to hers. Slightly opening her mouth she slowly placed her lips on his and moved them in a slow puckering motion. At the same time moving her body against his. Arching her back slightly she moved her groin slowly against his. Then just as gently she released her hold and stepped back. "See it doesn't hurt." Ed stood dumbfounded with beads of sweat running down his forehead and an uncontrollable bulge in his pants as she left and closed the barn door behind her. He was still standing in the same condition when Jake walked in. The foreman took one look and laughed. "Oh Lord, our resident ranch hand has fallen in love. Come on bucko, it'll go away once you start moving around."

CHAPTER #12

RON, MIKE AND Buck arrived just as they had said on the twentieth of May. Ed was feeding the calves their daily ration of cotton cake in a pasture two miles away from the ranch, so he didn't see them until he came in for the noon meal. When he walked into the bunkhouse they were seated at the table playing cards. The three of them rose as one and slowly walked around Ed in a close circle.

"Well, would you look at this? I think I recognize him but he doesn't smell the same." Ron said with a serious look on his face.

Mike loudly sniffed the air. "He doesn't smell green anymore."

Ed stood still and grinned waiting for the pranksters to finish. Buck was his usual self and joined the circle but didn't say anything. Ed finally spoke and said, "maybe my scent has changed, but you guys sure haven't changed yours. Do you mind standing downwind?"

The three pranksters stopped their shuffle. Mike spoke up first. "Hear how he talks. After all we done for him."

"Done to me is a better way of putting it. How in the hell are you guys? It's good to see you again." Ed replied with a big wide grin as he grabbed each one of the men by the hand and pumped vigorously.

"It's good to see you again." Ron said. "You've grown and put on some muscle."

"Yeah, and I can actually ride a horse across the corral with out falling off!!"

Everyone laughed as Mike spoke up, "Do you mean we don't have to line the corral with mattresses anymore?" Everyone laughed including Ed. The four men talked and laughed all the way to the back porch chuck house after the dinner bell rang. Now that the ranch hands were back Ed lost his kitchen privileges and Mrs. Schmidt no longer ate with the group. Don arrived on the second of June. He still had the same old beat up, green pickup truck that he left in last fall.

He hadn't changed in size or attitude. The only thing different was the dinner plate belt buckle; it was new. It said "1949 All AROUND CHAMPION" and had a gold raised relief of a man on a saddle bronc. Three days later on the fifth of June Les arrived. He walked into the bunkhouse an hour after supper was over. Everybody greeted him and shook his hand. Everyone except Ed. He sat up on his bunk and quietly watched. Finally Les broke away from the group, walked over to Ed, stuck out his hand and said: "How are you Ed?" Ed looked warily at the man and mumbled, "Ok, I guess."

Les looked right at Ed, "Look I know you and I got off to a bad start, but I really want to get along. How about it?"

Ed jumped down off his bunk, shook Les's hand and said; "fine with me."

Ed and Les were almost identical physically. Both had matured into tall, well-muscled, good-looking young men. As they stood toe to toe looking at each other the tension made your hair want to stand on end.

Ron spoke up; "seems to me we've got enough people here for a hell've a good poker game. Besides, no one's been to town yet, so we all have money in our pockets. Right?"

Everyone acknowledged and sat down at the table.

Jake, Ron, Buck, Don and Ed finished working the cattle, while Mike and Les got the hay machinery ready to use. The hay was cut with four teams and mowers. After it dried for a few days it was windrowed with horse drawn dump rakes, allowed to dry for a couple more days and then collected by four head hooked to a tailboard sweep. A tailboard sweep is a strange looking device that extends in front and behind the horses hooked to it. A set of wooden tines six to eight feet long slide on the ground in front of the workhorses. The horses are hooked to the apparatus with eveners in back and single trees in front. The driver stands over a set of wheels on a board about six feet long and twelve inches wide. A wooden rack is mounted vertically ahead of the tailboard. It is there for the operator to hang onto as he moves left and right on the tailboard. The tailboard is on a levered pivot connected to gears driven by the wheels. Depending which way the driver moves from the pivot point determines whether the wooden tines in front of the horses move up or down.

The purpose of the machine is to sweep as much hay as the horses can move to the stacker where it can be pushed onto a similar set of tines and lifted into a wire cage to build the hay stack.

The stacker has only one purpose. Dump loose hay into the cage as the man inside walks around compressing it with his body weight as best he can. There are two basic types of stackers: The slide or the overshot. The slide has two long wooden beams forty-five degrees to the stack that the tines holding the hay slide up. It is pulled by a team of workhorses hooked to a steel cable that runs through a series of pulleys for maximum leverage. When the head gets to the top it hits a stop and the tines full of hay are forced into a vertical position that allows the hay to fall off into the wire cage. The head is then allowed to slide back to the ground to receive more hay.

The overshot stacker has the tines mounted solid at the end of two wooden beams that are slightly taller than the cage of the stacker. The other end of the wooden beams are mounted with large steel bolts to the frame of the stacker so they act like hinges and allow the beams to pivot as the head is raised by workhorses, pulleys and cables in the same manner as the slide stacker. When the head and beams hit the vertical stop, the hay is deposited in the cage and the tines are lowered to receive more hay. The overshot stacker is mounted on wheels and is the most popular because of its mobility. The wire cage is framed with iron pipe and split in back. A wheel is mounted on each side of the split so the cage can be opened and pulled away from the stack. Once pulled away from the stack the cage is closed and the stacker is pulled to a spot closer to where the hay is being gathered. This is what Ed and the rest of the hands would spend most of their waking hours doing. The amount of hay put up was based on the number of cattle and increase that would be held over the winter. This hay season would be longer than usual since Emil had announced his purchase of the neighboring ranch. (About five thousand acres) Figuring ten acres to support one cow meant putting up enough hay for five hundred more head.

Emil knew there wouldn't be a lot of time off once the haying started. He told the men at Friday night supper to take Saturday and Sunday off. Elated, Ed figured he would call Alice after his chores Saturday morning and they could go to a movie or something. By ten o'clock in the morning Ed had his work done. Everyone else was gone already, so Ed asked the Schmidt's if he could use their telephone to call Alice. Mrs. Schmidt agreed before Emil could say a word. 'You go right ahead Ed," she said, "and say hi to her for us, will you?"

"Yes ma'am," Ed smiled at her and winked. Ed called her apartment and got no answer, so he called the hospital and left a message with the therapy department. As he walked through the kitchen Mrs. Schmidt said; "After you get cleaned up come back and try again."

"Thank you Mrs. Schmidt I will."

Ed returned about an hour later, but had the same results. Alice evidently wasn't home and the hospital didn't know where she was at since Saturday and Sunday were her days off.

When Mrs. Schmidt questioned him Ed replied; "She might have gone to Cheyenne to visit her folks or she just might be out doing something, it is a pretty day out there. I think I'll hitch hike to Laramie and see if I can find her. If I can't, I'll find something to do. Maybe go to a movie."

"Whatever, have fun."

"Thanks, I will." With that Ed Walked out of the house and down the lane to the highway. He got a ride with the first vehicle that came along. It was a neighboring rancher that he knew. Ed climbed into the pickup and greeted the man who said he was only going as far as Rock River. Ed caught a ride to Laramie from the general store with a rancher who knew the man Ed was riding with. Once in Laramie Ed went straight to Alice's apartment on Front Street. She lived on the second floor, and he was getting ready to leave when an elderly man with a small sack of groceries came up the stairs and started to open the door of the adjoining apartment.

"She probably won't be back until late."

"Why's that?" Ed turned and took half dozen steps to the elderly man.

"Her boyfriend picked her up about an hour ago."

"Her boyfriend?" Ed said in a concerned voice.

"Yeah, a guy about your size and build. Good looking with glasses. I walked out right behind them on my way to the grocery store. I think I heard her call him Les as they left." Ed stood mortified.

The man looked at Ed. "Sorry, I gave you bad news. If your sweet on her at least you ought to know there's someone else."

Ed turned and numbly started for the stairs, "Yeah, thanks." Out on the street Ed was devastated. For the first time since he came to Wyoming tears swelled in his eyes. Quickly he wiped them away and headed for the nearest bar.

Inside the bar Ed found the darkest corner as he drank and brooded. How could she do this to him after the things she said and the way she kissed him? Downing his third beer Ed got up and went to the bathroom. Finishing his nature call Ed walked to the bar to get another beer. He stood leaning on the bar waiting to be served when a familiar voice caused him to turn and look.

"Give me another beer George. Looking down the bar she looked at Ed who was leaning on the bar looking at her.

"Joyce, how are you?"

Ed's former nurse looked at him. "I thought you looked familiar. Ahh, Ed wasn't it?"

"Yeah, you were my nurse in the hospital. I was the one that went down the rock slide on my head."

"Sure, I remember now. You were always giving me a hard time. Probably the biggest tease I've ever run into. You've sure changed your looks though. You look like you've put on ten pounds and muscled up some."

Ed blushed; "Thanks, what're you doing in here?"

"Drinking, what does it look like? I'm celebrating one year of freedom from my asshole ex husband. Why are you here?"

Ed looked in the direction of the noisy jukebox that someone had just plugged. He looked back at Joyce and said loudly; "Bring your beer over to my table I really need someone to talk to."

Joyce looked at Ed for a moment, shrugged and said; "Oh, what the hell. Lead on McDuff." Joyce followed Ed to the dark corner and sat down. "So, what's on your mind."

"Do you remember the little girl in the therapy department, that took me for walks in the park? Her name is Alice Bernard."

"Sure I see her all the time at work."

"We were getting kind of serious toward each other and tonight I found out she dumped me for the guy she was seeing before me."

"Let me tell you, you win some and you lose some. It hurts like hell at first, but you'll live to find another woman no matter how many times it doesn't work."

Ed got up from the table, "Sit tight, I'll get us a couple more beers." Joyce nodded.

Ed returned and sat a beer in front of Joyce. They sat talking until the bar closed. Both of them were in no shape to go very far by themselves. Ed was probably the soberest of either of them. Ed figured he would get a hotel room, sleep off the liquor and go back to the ranch Sunday after he woke up.

"I have to call a cab." He told Joyce as they finished the last swallows of their beers.

"Nonsense, I have my car I'll take you. Where do you want to go?"

"I've got to get a room I'll never make it back to the ranch tonight feeling like this."

"C'mon," Joyce got up and headed for the door: Night George." she said as she walked past the bar tender washing glasses.

"Night Joyce," he said looking up momentarily.

Staggering to her car Joyce pointed to the other door, "get in."

Twenty minutes later Joyce pulled the car into the driveway of a neatly kept, two story house. "I can't go any farther, you're welcome to the couch." Getting out of the car she staggered toward the house and Ed followed. The inside was as neat and well kept as the outside. Joyce had made it as far as the couch and flopped. She was snoring loudly by the time Ed got to her and he was only ten or fifteen feet behind her.

"Damn," He said realizing he was going to have to sleep somewhere else. Walking farther into the house he found the bathroom and what appeared to be Joyce's bedroom. Looking around he spotted a spare blanket lying on a hope chest at the foot of the bed. Picking it up, Ed walked to the sofa and covered Joyce with it. Turning he walked into the bedroom, undressed and crawled under the covers. He was asleep as soon as his head hit the pillow. Sometime during the night Joyce came into the room and crawled into bed. It was dark so it startled both of them.

"What are you doing here?" Joyce asked in an irate voice.

"You fell on the couch and passed out, so I figured you wouldn't mind me using your bed." Ed started to get up. "I'm sorry."

"No, don't get up it's four o'clock in the morning. I haven't snuggled with anybody in about six months. Besides the liquor has got me feeling a little horny. When was the last time you got layed?" Joyce moved close to Ed and gently put her hand on his inner thigh while she layed her head next to his and softly blew in his ear. Ed tensed. "Relax honey, you're going to enjoy this." Moving her hand toward his stiffening penis, she used the tip of her fingernails to slowly and gently caress his testicals, working her way up the swelling shaft to the throbbing purple head of his enlarging penis. "Oh baby, you are ready aren't you? Have you ever been with a woman before?"

Ed was breathing like a wind broke horse; his penis was so hard it felt like the skin at its head was ready to split. He managed to get out a weak "no."

"That's what I figured. Well I've never had a cherry before, so this will be a first for both of us. You lay back; we'll get you initiated and then get down to some serious sex. I am gonna teach you some moves tonight that will make every girl you fuck from now on roll her eyes back in her head and scream for more." Sitting up Joyce swung her leg over Ed's body grabbing his large throbbing cock and guiding the head into the clit of her warm, soft, moist, pussy. Ed gasped as he felt the head of his rock hard shaft engulfed by the warm, wetness. Leaning over his face Joyce hung her large nippled, size thirty-six "C' breasts above his face and whispered "Suck on my tits." Ed responded. Slowly at first, then as Joyce drove him deeper and deeper into her willing body Ed reached up with both hands grabbed her breasts and fiercely sucked on one nipple and then the other. Joyce groaned as their pubic hairs met. She spread her knees as far as she could to get every bit of Ed's eight-inch, iron hard organ inside of her that she could. Slowly undulating her pelvis she tightened her vaginal muscles every time she pushed Ed into the depths of her body. After a few minutes Ed experienced a feeling he'd never felt before. This was close to masturbating but much, much more intense. He felt like he wanted to shove his exploding penis clear to Joyce's eyebrows. Grabbing her hips he pulled her down onto him as hard as he could, at the same time arching his back to give her everything he had. Joyce closed her eyes as she threw her head back and moaned loudly. Joyce sat on him undulating, tightening, pushing and pulling with her well-lubricated pussy, moving back and forth over his throbbing, spitting rod until Ed stopped coming and she felt him soften.

"I'm going to climb off now. If you feel a flood cover your crotch it's only what you deposited inside of me. God, I don't think I've ever had anyone come that hard or that long. You must have shot at least a gallon of sperm up me." Both of them were sweating profusely. "I'm going to rinse out. You wanna take a shower with me so we can do this again?"

"Sure," Ed said as Joyce got up and turned the light on.

Ed climbed out of bed still semi hard, with a slick clear film covering the hair of his crotch. Ed had mixed emotions of surprise, embarrassment, curiousness and delight as he stood in the shower. Joyce was a looker. She stood five foot six in her bare feet. Blond hair, nice smooth creamy skin and a great smile that showed a set of straight white teeth beneath a pair of pouty lips. Her neck was straight as were her shoulders. A small mole was visible at the top of one of her well-formed breasts that hung gracefully from her chest like firm malleable pears with large, brown, erect, nipples pointing proudly up at a forty-five degree angle. Her stomach was flat as a pancake and the bellybutton was small and petite. It sat above her pelvic bush like the moon above the earth. Her legs were long and well proportioned. They had the same creamy look as the rest of her body. Her hips had a little width to them but not enough to take away from the rest of the package that framed a thick bunch of curly yellow hair hiding the pleasure palace Ed had just entered. After a long touchy feely shower and a cup of coffee, Joyce and Ed headed back to bed.

"Now, I'm going to show you how to please a woman and turn her on."(Ed was already hard) "Just remember a woman likes to be romanced. Small tender kisses turn into long passionate ones, which leads to touching and stroking, which leads to the glory hole. So let's start with some tender nuzzling. Then we'll do some long kisses and some French kisses. I'll guide your head and hands from there. Ready?"

"You bet." Ed said with eager anticipation.

They started by touching noses and giving little kisses on the lips. "Work your way around to my ear. Gently nibble the edges. Then trace the inside with the tip of your tongue. Oh yes!!! Now gently and slowly suck on the lobe a couple times. Work your way slowly straight down the side of her neck, kissing and nibbling with your lips. If she isn't making any noise or pushing her tits at you don't go any further, she's not ready for you. Work your way back up her neck along the front. Play under her chin with your lips and come around her chin to her mouth. Do the little kisses and a long tender one. Then go for the ear again. If you can't make it down onto the nipples of her tits you won't make it any further. Keep going back to the mouth and start from there until she lets you suck on her nipples. Spend some time on her tits. Suck the nipples, run your tongue in small circles over the whole breast. Take the nipples in your teeth. Gently close down and tug gently, at the same time massage the nipple with the tip of your tongue. If she isn't excited and her nipples aren't hard don't use your teeth, it'll hurt her and your fun night is probably over. Be careful even if the nipples are hard and standing tall, grab them as close to the breast with your teeth as you can. Remember the word here is slow and extremely gentle." Joyce talked Ed through each and every move by the time they got this far they were both hotter than two smoking guns. "I think it's time to relieve a little pressure." Joyce said as she rolled over on her back. "It's your turn on top. Get between my legs. Don't lie on me; hold yourself up with your hands. Now, put the head of your cock against my pussy just far enough that you can feel the wetness with the very tip of it. Move your ass forward and back, as hard as you are that'll make the head of your dick massage my clit from one end to the other and help to moisten and open it. When things feel really wet and warm move in a little further. Don't get anymore than the head in. Now move back and forth, exaggerate it. At the same time do just a little bit of in and out; be careful not to go any deeper than the head of your cock. When she is ready for more of you she'll be matching you stroke for stroke, but only go in a little bit at a time. If you go to deep too fast she'll feel like she's getting fucked, not having sex."

By the time Ed was completely inside of Joyce she was pulling on his hips and pounding his back and bottom with her heels screaming "fuck me, fuck me, fuck me harder, AUGHHHHHHHH" Just as Ed came Joyce went into convulsions, she whimpered and wined like a little puppy. Ed slowly kept pumping. Joyce stopped and lay quietly. Looking up at Ed slowing sliding his organ in and out of her she whispered, "You can quit now, I need a little nap." Ed smiled and pulled his wet, moderately hard member out of her. "Lay down next to me and hold my tits. We'll nap, clean up and go at it again." Ed smiled; this was one great day.

The next sex session started where the previous one left off. "I'm going to show you how to eat a woman out. Suck on my tits a little to get things going." Ed eagerly did what he was told. "Use your tongue and nibble your way down to the belly button. Run the tip of your tongue around the belly button a couple of times. Don't spend a lot of time there. By now you'll have her so hot she can't wait for you to bury your head in her bush. Nibble your way down to the top of the hairline and spend some time there nibbling, kissing and tracing with your tongue. If she isn't moaning and pushing her pussy in your face go back to her tits and start over. If you make it past the hair line she should be so wet you'll be covered with juice from your nose to your chin." Ed moved his face into Joyce's bush and found what she said to be true. She was extremely moist and willing. Her opening had a nutty taste and smell to it. Ed found it pleasant and exciting. "Joyce was talking in a very high excited voice by now. "First run your nose back and forth the full length of the slit and then do the same thing with your tongue." Now bury your nose and tongue in me as deep as you can. Let me fuck your face until I come." Ed complied, Joyce started undulating, slowly moving her wet, warm pussy back and forth, the lips of her hole closing and sucking at Ed's face. Finally she let out a scream and wrapped her legs around the back of Ed's head, almost suffocating him as she pulled his face deeper into the wet quivering gash between her legs. "Fuck," she cried as her body convulsed leaving her whimpering and whining. They laid around for about an hour before either of them moved Finally Joyce rolled over and started kissing Ed's bare belly. His organ responded to the call and came to attention. Joyce ran the tips of her fingernails along the bottom of Ed's testicals as she nibbled and kissed her way to the base of Ed's hard, pulsating cock. Slowly she worked her way to the top of the dripping dark red head and then started kissing and nibbling her way down to Ed's testicals. She was still massaging them with the tips of her fingernails when she maneuvered them into her mouth to gently tug and pull on them with her teeth. When they were soft and pliable she released them and worked her way nibbling and kissing up the hardened shaft to the head of Ed's penis. Slowly she wrapped her lips around the throbbing, dripping head and held it softly in the warm, moist confines of her mouth. Then ever so slowly she released it. Then she went back down on the bulging member taking part of the hardened shaft in her sweet mouth. Joyce repeated this maneuver until she had completely inhaled all of Ed's cock down to the hairline. Now she sucked as she slowly withdrew to the very tip of the head of Ed's incredibly hard organ. Slowly she took him in again. She swallowed him so completely she had to kneel over him with her knees on each side of his head above his shoulders. Ed could feel her swallowing deep in her throat against the head of his penis. Since she had her pussy hanging above his face he reached up with his hands and stroked it, running his fingers to the top of her clit and massaging the vulva. Ed knew he couldn't hold his come much longer, increasing the speed of motion on Joyce's vulva he tried to hold his climax until he felt her come. It didn't work. Ed came really hard, he wanted to grab Joyce's head and pull it down on himself even further, but he knew she was at the bottom and he might hurt her. Even after he shot his last wad down her throat, he kept massaging her vulva. Finally she moaned and sat on his face convulsing and crying. Exhausted Joyce fell back on the bed.

"We're going to screw one more time and then you're out of here. But first I gotta call my girlfriend she's watching my kids and I want to tell her I'm gonna be a little late."

"When can I see you again."

"Never. This has been fun. Most of the guys that I go to bed with are duds. Those that can get it up and have something to get up just want a piece of ass. That's not my idea of sex. You were as pure as the driven snow. You made love to me, today has been as much fun for me as it has for you. I really needed someone like you just to realize there are caring men out there yet. All I gotta do is look until I find one. I'll be good for four or five months now. It gives me time to shop."

"Maybe we can get together again in four or five months."

"No way,"

"Why not?"

"For one I'm fourteen years older than you are and I have three kids who are old enough to understand the facts of life. They don't need to see their mother hanging around with someone not much older than their oldest brother. When you leave here today remember what I've shown you and go screw every girl you meet, but don't show up on my doorstep ever again. Understand?'

Ed knew she was right "Ok, but you said we going to do it one more time?"

"That's right, I'm going to show you how to fuck a girl up the ass without hurting her. But first I gotta go make that phone call."

Joyce got out of bed and Ed watched her beautiful bare ass until it disappeared through the bedroom door. He thought to himself, "man I thought she was a hellva woman when I met her in the hospital, but I had no idea she was this good."

Joyce returned shortly her tits bouncing in time with each step. She noticed Ed looking at them and smiled. "They really fascinate you don't they? They're pretty flexible see." With that she twisted her shoulders and made her breasts flop from side to side and then moved her body up and down as she twisted her shoulders making the soft, flesh filled sacks rotate in a circle. Ed was bug eyed.

"Honey, I see and handle naked people every day. Some are old; some are young, male and female alike. Trust me, there is only one model for each sex. You've either got a crack or a cock and that's it. As you get older you lose the fascination for the naked body. Once you've seen one you've seen 'em all. Now let's get down to business."

Joyce sat on the bed next to Ed. "lay on your stomach and I'll show you what to do. I want you to experience what it feels like so you understand why I want to show you this. Because sooner or later in a fit of passion or for some other reason you're gonna fuck some girl up the ass. If you don't know what you're doing, especially if it's her first time, you could hurt her bad. Always lubricate your self and her with Vaseline, butter, or spit in your hand and rub the head of your dick with it. Don't ever try to go in dry; you'll rip her apart, especially as large as you are. I have this wooden simulator that I use on myself now and then; I carved it out of a piece of walnut. This will give you an idea of what dry is like." Joyce spread the cheeks of Ed's ass exposing his anis. She moved the device partially into the cavity and gave a little shove. Ed jumped from the sharp pain in his rectum.

"Ouch." He said; I don't want to do this. A man raped me when I was in Denver. This is not good."

"I am sorry to hear that, if you'll let me continue I'll show you how to do it with no pain. Don't forget you get to screw me." Ed thought a minute. He liked the idea of having sex with Joyce one more time. "Ok, but if it hurts we're done."

'Deal." Joyce said as she spread Vaseline on Ed's rectum. "What I want you to do is try to take a shit. I'm going to put my finger into your asshole up to the second joint. That's about two inches. You try to push it out just like you would when you crap. Sometimes it gets a little messy but don't worry about it." Joyce inserted her finger and Ed pushed. "I'm going to move my finger in and out. I want you to push as hard as you can so you open up and allow my finger access to your anal canal." Ed pushed and felt her finger slide into his lower intestine. It didn't hurt and was no more uncomfortable than having to take a large crap. Joyce showed him both of her hands. "See, that didn't hurt and you have six inches of wood buried in your ass." Ed looked over his backside and could see the end of a wooden dowel protruding from between his buttocks. "I'll be damned."

Joyce continued, "Now when you with draw be just as careful. Pull out slow and easy. We don't want the asshole to slam shut." She laughed at her own joke as she withdrew the wooden dowel from Ed's rectum. "Roll over, I'll give you a blowjob to get you nice and hard." Once she had Ed's penis stone hard she lay on her stomach and said "Your turn. Make it a good one, this is your last time in the saddle."

"I will. I won't pull out until I go completely soft."

"It's your nickel. Ride as long as you can."

Ed lubricated Joyce's rectum. Gently he inserted his finger and felt her push. When she opened up he spread the cheeks of her ass and inserted the head of his throbbing cock.

"Now in and out slowly going deeper with each stroke." Joyce prompted.

Ed noticed the difference between her asshole and her pussy. Joyce's pussy would grab and squeeze, her asshole didn't do anything, and it felt real loose. Ed finally buried his cock to the hairline. He knew if he didn't move around very much he could hold a hard on for a long time and he was determined to stay as long as he could. After about fifteen minutes of barely moving inside of Joyce he could feel her trying to make something happen.

"Did you want me to come and get out or can you take more?"

"Honey, I could go to sleep with your cock stuck up my ass. Suit yourself."

After another five minutes Ed felt her contracting and relaxing the vaginal muscles that tied to the thin membrane of the anal canal. Ed thought to himself, "I guess it's time to blow my wad and go." He started to pump. Moving slowly at first and then harder and faster. He'd been in Joyce long enough that it felt like he was getting a hard all over again. He blew his wad which was as large as his first one earlier in the morning and didn't lose the hard on. He kept on going, five minutes later he came again and two minutes of hard pumping after that he wilted and withdrew.

"Damn," Joyce said as she rolled over on her back. "I won't be able to sit right for a week. I've never had anyone hold a hard on inside me that long and come twice."

"You sure you don't want me to come back?"

"No way, I could get hooked on you. Get out of my life and stay out."

They cleaned up together; it was two thirty in the afternoon. Joyce fed him lunch and took him to the highway on her way to get her kids.

CHAPTER #13

LES SMILED TO himself as he drove Don's pickup down the highway leading to Laramie. He hadn't seen Alice since last fall before he left to go home to Pennsylvania. She was a little quiet on the phone when he called her this morning, but Les figured it was surprise and anxious anticipation. He remembered the good times they had last year and was anxious to renew the relationship. He pulled up to the curb, parked the truck, jumped out and took the stairs two at a time up to her apartment. She opened the door on the first knock. Stepping inside the door Les put his arm around her waist and kissed her hard on the lips. Alice didn't pull away but she didn't return the kiss.

Les finished and stepped back; "What's the matter aren't you happy to see me?"

Alice stammered, "Yes, I am happy to see you. How have you been?"

"Great, I started my first year of law school at Penn State. It wasn't quite what I expected, but I love it."

"You still want to be a lawyer?"

"Oh yeah, more than anything. I'll have to hire on with a firm for a couple of years, but I can't wait to get my own private practice."

"Well, come on in and I'll finish getting ready. Where do you want to go to eat?"

"The cattleman's club is real good. Maybe we can find a dance afterwards?"

"Sure that would be fun. I need to talk to you anyway."

Les felt his spirits soar; "Oh what about?"

"Later, let's eat and have fun."

"Sure, works for me." Les's level of anticipation for the upcoming nights implications were rising by the moment.

Alice came out of her bedroom, "I'm ready to go." Les opened the door for her and they stepped into the hallway just as the door to the apartment next to Alice's opened. An elderly man stepped into the hallway and closed the door as Alice and Les walked by.

"Hi Mr. Johnson." Alice said as the man looked up from locking the door.

"Hello sweetie. Going out for the night?"

"Dinner and dancing." Was her reply.

"Sounds like fun. Have a good time."

"We will, goodnight."

"Goodnight."

Going down the stairs Les tickled her waist and teased "Sweetie? You've been holding out on me. Harlot!!!"

Alice laughed and replied "Oh Les."

Dinner was good, the steaks were done just right and the atmosphere in the cattleman's club was dim and comfortable "What was it you wanted to tell me?" Les asked after they had ordered.

"Oh, nothing really, I just think we ought to talk about our relationship."

Les smiled at her across the table. "I agree. I want to see you a lot this summer. It should be a great year."

"I don't really feel comfortable discussing our personal life here in public. Let's wait until after we eat and get to the car."

"Ok." Les said with a confused look. The rest of the meal was engulfed in small talk about what each of them had been doing over the winter. Alice didn't talk about the time she spent at the ranch with Ed. After supper they headed for the pickup truck. Les tried to hold Alice's hand as they walked across the parking lot, but she wouldn't let him.

"What's wrong?" Les asked when she rejected him. They reached the pickup and climbed in. Les started the engine and said, "Let's go to Rock River, I like that dance hall."

"Ok." Alice sat quietly as Les drove out of town.

"So, you said you wanted to talk about us. Well, I do too. I really think I'm falling in love with you. I think you probably feel the same way about me. But I didn't think you would be as shy about it as you seem to be."

Alice sighed, "I'm not shy. I'm just having a hard time saying what I want to say."

"That's ok darling, I understand."

"No, that's the problem, you don't understand. There is no us. I can't see you like this anymore. I would like to remain friends but there is someone else."

"What the hell do you mean "someone else"? Who?" Les screamed as he jammed on the brakes and slid to a stop on the gravel shoulder of the paved highway. "You've been seeing someone else while I've been back east going to school? I thought after all the letters we wrote each other this winter you were interested in me. What the hell is going on?"

Alice looked across the cab at Les. He was angry and in a state of shock. "We've always been friends. I like you but I don't love you. You're nice and fun to be around but I don't think it's fair to you to let you think there ever could be anything serious between us."

"Bullshit," Les said with a sullen look on his face. "You met someone else. Who is he?"

Alice sat quietly trying to think of how to tell Les and make him understand. "You know him, its Ed Stoltz from the ranch."

"What!!!" Les screamed at Alice. "He's just a snot nosed kid."

"He's eighteen and I love him." Alice said defensively.

Les opened the pickup door and slammed it viciously after he got out. Alice could hear him talking to himself as he paced back and forth outside by the pickup door. Suddenly Alice was spattered with broken glass. Les withdrew his bleeding fist from the broken window and opened the door.

"I'm going to kick his ass when I see him."

"Les please don't, I'm sorry I upset you." Alice pleaded as she reached out and put her hand on Les's arm.

Les angrily shook her hand off his arm, "Get your hand off me. All this while I thought you and I were going somewhere. Now I find out you're robbing the cradle and leaving me high and dry."

Alice had her dander up over the way Les was reacting to the situation. "Now you listen to me." Alice yelled back at the frantic wanna be lover. "In the first place I'm only two years older than Ed, you and I are five years apart. Secondly, I wrote to you as a friend. I don't know how you read anything else into those letters, but if you did that's your problem. I figured you'd act like a gentleman when I told you I wanted you as a friend, but I guess I was wrong. You're acting like a spoiled brat that didn't get his way. I get the feeling I was going to be your toy for the summer."

"No, I really believe we could have fallen in love." Les said angrily.

"What do you mean, "could have"? Did you have doubts before we even went out?"

"Yeah, I did. I don't trust any woman. Most take and then after the good times are over their gone. I thought maybe it could be different with us."

"It could have been if there was something there in the first place." Alice snapped.

"I don't know what went on between you and Stoltz this winter, but I guarantee you when I get back to the ranch I'm going to stomp a mud hole in his ass."

"Do you think that will improve our relationship?"

"We don't have a relationship."

"So, what you're saying is if I won't become romantically involved with you, you're going to get revenge on the person I really do care for."

"I guess that's the way it is." Les said, as he looked Alice directly in the eye.

Alice opened the door of the pickup and got out into the dark night. "You're sick and spoiled. I feel sorry for you."

"Feel sorry for yourself, I'm going to make life really miserable for you and your pimple faced little boyfriend. By the time I get through with him he'll wish he were dead. Have a good walk back to Laramie." With that Les jammed the truck into gear and sprayed gravel on Alice and the roadside as he sped away into the night.

Les hurried back to the ranch expecting to find Ed at the bunkhouse. He was determined to thoroughly beat the crap out of him when he found him. Bursting into the dark bunkhouse, Les threw the door open and walked directly to Ed's bunk, which was cold and empty.

"Damn." Les muttered to himself. Walking to the open door he closed it and flipped the light switch. The building was empty. Everyone was still out drinking and chasing women. Les sat on a bunk and collected his thoughts. His temper cooled and he started to think rational once more. He knew if he had caught up with Ed at the ranch and confronted him it would have cost him his job. Emil was not joking last fall when he warned Les about his behavior concerning Ed. He knew if he was going to physically have it out with Ed it would have to be off ranch property. Les's mind started to churn in devious ways. He would show them. Nobody treated him like dirt and got away with it. By the time daylight came he had his revenge pretty well plotted out in his mind.

Alice turned her body and shielded her face with her arm while the truck showered her with sand and gravel as it sped away into the night. Brushing herself off, she started walking along the shoulder of the paved two-lane road toward the lights visible in the night sky over Laramie. Alice had only walked about a mile before she caught a ride that took her within two blocks of her apartment. Tomorrow morning she would call the ranch and talk to Ed, maybe he could come and see her for a while. After tonight's experience with Les, her emotions were a mess and she wanted to warn Ed to watch out for him.

Alice talked to Mrs. Schmidt on the phone while Emil went to the bunkhouse to get Ed. After a short period of time he returned and said Les was the only one in the bunkhouse. Alice asked Mrs. Schmidt to have him call as soon as he came in. She said she would and hung up.

Ed walked into the bunkhouse about five in the afternoon. Supper would be in an hour or so he kicked back and talked with Ron and the rest of the hands while he waited Ron, Mike, Buck and Don had arrived at the ranch an hour or so before Ed. They were battered and bruised, with missing teeth and black eyes. It looked like they had been pounded through a knothole backwards with the flat side of a shovel.

"Looks like you guys chased every women and fought every yahoo in town."

Mike looked like a half a raccoon. "But we sure had fun."

Ed shrugged and snickered, "I'll bet."

"What did you do this weekend, Ed?" Les said breaking into the conversation.

Ed looked over at him sitting on his bunk with a sneering grin on his face. "Not much. I closed out a bar, went to bed and headed back after I ate a good meal." Ed snickered to himself at his personal joke.

"What about you?" He asked Les, curious at his sudden interest in Ed's recreational time.

"Oh, I went out on a date, came back to the ranch and went to bed."

"Sounds boring to me," Don piped in.

Everyone laughed and started a new line of conversation.

After supper was over and the men started to leave Emil spoke up, "Ed, hang on a minute I want to talk to you before you leave."

Ed turned and walked back to stand in front of his boss while the rest of the men filed out.

"Your little girl from Laramie called this morning. She sounded worried and said you should call her as soon as you got in." Emil nodded toward the phone hanging on the kitchen wall. "Maybe you ought to call her before it gets any later."

Ed hesitated. She had stood him up to go out with Les and now he was supposed to call her? What did she take him for? Ed knew he was naive (not as much as he had been, after this weekend) but he wasn't a total idiot about what was right and wrong. Emil looked at Ed standing in front of him with a strained look on his face. Getting up he said, "I'm going in the living room and read the paper. When you're done, shut the light off on your way out."

Ed looked at the floor and mumbled an "Ok" as Emil left the room.

Realizing he would have to get this over with sooner or later he walked over to the phone and dialed Alice's number.

"Hello?" The feminine voice said on the other end of the line.

"Hello, Alice this is Ed."

Excitedly the voice replied; "Oh, thank you for calling. Where have you been? I've been trying to get hold of you all weekend."

"I'll bet. You evidently found it easier to make a date with Les than you did me." There was dead silence on the phone. Finally she came back in a shaky voice, "How did you know I saw Les?"

"You have gabby neighbors. I showed up on your doorstep shortly after you and Les had left to do whatever you two planned on doing. He even heard you mention his name as you were going down the stairs, so I know it was Les. Am I right?"

Ed could tell Alice was crying. "Yes," she said sobbing. "He called early in the day and I figured since you hadn't called that you had to work. It looked like a good time to let him know I wasn't interested. When you still hadn't called by late after noon, accepted his offer for dinner thinking I would tell him then. I chickened out until later when we were on our way to the Rock River dance hall. When I told him I didn't want to see him as anything other than a friend he threatened us and left me standing alongside the road."

Ed came to attention. "He what?"

"He had pulled over and was yelling at me. So I got out of the truck and was trying to calm him down through the open door. He told me he was going to beat you up and that he would make things really miserable on us if I didn't go out with him."

Ed was silent for a moment. He knew the Schmidt's could hear every word he said in the next room.

"How late are you going to be up?"

"Probably until ten or so. Why?"

"I'll call you back in an hour or so. Ok?"

"Sure, can't you talk now?"

"No, I'm at the ranch. I'll call you in a bit from Medicine Bow."

Alice understood. "Ok, I'll wait for your call."

Ed hung up and started for the door. He was just about to flip the light switch and leave when Emil appeared in the living room doorway. "You can take the pickup if you want."

"Thanks Emil."

Ed ran out the door jumped in the pickup truck and drove to the pay phone booth in front of the bar next to the Virginian Hotel. He got five dollars worth of change from the bar and dialed Alice. She answered the phone and excitedly said, "I love you." This was very upsetting for Ed. He wanted to reply but he didn't know what to say. "I love you" was not what he wanted to hear right now.

"Tell me what happened between you two. I couldn't talk at the Schmidt's house, but I'm in a phone booth in Medicine Bow now. Did Les hit you?"

"No, he never touched me. In any way." She added as an after thought. "He was extremely upset and threatened to "kick your ass" as he put it.

"You said you had to walk to Laramie?"

"No, I said he drove off and left me standing alongside the road in the dark. I started to walk but then I got a ride with a couple headed for Laramie. They dropped me off a couple of blocks from my apartment."

"Your ok then?"

"Yeah, I was very upset, but other than that I'm ok. I really need to see you. When can you come to town?"

"I don't know. We start haying tomorrow and there won't be anytime off until we're done. Besides I need to think about this for a while. I'll call you next Saturday probably after supper. We'll figure out where to go from there."

Alice knew Ed was done talking, so she responded with an "ok" and waited for Ed's response after she said, "I love you".

Ed didn't know what to say, so he said "thanks" and hung up.

When Ed walked into the bunkhouse the rest of the men were sitting around the table playing cards. They looked up and greeted him as he came in the door.

"Where have you been?" Les asked sardonically.

"None of your damn business." Ed said sourly as he crawled into his bed and turned his back on the card players.

Les laughed and turned back to the card game.

The men spent dawn to dusk working at putting the hay up. Each man had a specific job. Ed's was in the cage of the overshot stacker tromping down the hay. Les was driving one of the horse drawn sweeps. As he approached the stacker to push a load of hay on the waiting forks late in the afternoon, Ed saw him swinging what looked like a piece of rope over his head. He disappeared from view as he got close to move the hay pile onto the forks of the stacker. Suddenly the rope like object flew over the top of the stacker cage and landed on Ed's shoulder. The agitated three-foot grass snake wrapped around Ed's neck for an instant to catch itself and then straitened out and fell into the hay at his feet. Totally petrified Ed yelled, jumped back and fell into the soft hay. The snake disappeared in the opposite direction as Ed scaled the woven wire that made up the cage wall. Les was laughing himself sick as he pointed to Ed sitting on top of the narrow pipe high above the ground.

"Hey, look at the monkey. He's still scared of snakes."

Ed brooded the rest of the afternoon. In the bunkhouse while everyone else was washing up Ed confronted Les. "Why did you throw that snake on me?"

"Because I know you're scared of snakes and I thought it would be funny. You got a problem with that you little asshole."

Ed was not little. He was about three inches shorter than Les, build wise he was almost a carbon copy. But, unfortunately he didn't have the confidence in himself that Les did. He wasn't scared of Les, although the thought of picking a fight with him didn't appeal to Ed either. Les's participation in scholastic sports had taught him self-control and given him the confidence to confront another man. Ed on the other hand had been isolated much of his life. He had done farm chores instead of sports and dealt with animals instead of people. He knew what to do with an angry horse or cow, but had no clue when it came to people.

"Yeah, I want you to stop picking on me."

Les walked over and stood right in front of Ed. "What are you gonna do about it if I don't?"

Ed looked up and said, "I don't know."

Les laughed in his face. "You yellow bastard. You haven't got the guts to fight me, have you? I'll tell you what. I'm going to hand or toss you a snake every chance I get. Be careful, sooner or later one of 'em might be poisonous."

Ed turned and walked out of the bunkhouse and sat in the barn until he was sure everyone in the bunkhouse had long since gone to bed. Then he slunk into his own bunk as quietly as he could. The bunkhouse hands were extremely quiet that morning. Ed didn't know what if anything Les might have told the other ranch hands. He could tell by their silence that they knew something was going on between Les and Ed. All week Les tormented Ed with snakes and pieces of rope that appeared for a moment to be a snake. Ed was glad when Saturday evening came. He skipped supper and hitched hiked into Medicine Bow to call Alice like he'd promised her.

The fourth of July was the first day off the ranch hands got since the hay operation began. Ed and Alice spent the day in Cheyenne at her parent's house. Late in the afternoon they all went to the city park, had a picnic and watched the fireworks display after dark.

Ed liked Jim and Tracy Bernard. Even though Jim Bernard was an aeronautical engineer, financially secure, and very powerful in his company and the community, he was down to earth and genuine. He said what he thought and didn't put on airs. His wife Tracy wasn't as open and easy going as her husband but she was a gracious host. Physically she reminded Ed of Joyce the nurse. Blond hair and well built, but age was starting to show in her face and hands.

Jim Bernard graduated fourth in his class with a mechanical engineering degree from Notre Dame. In 1922 he landed a job with two partners by the names of Pratt and Whitney. Jim had become fascinated with aeronautics every since the Wright Bros. world famous flight at Kitty Hawk, North Carolina. He had been studying the theories and design aspects of aircraft ever since. That same year he married Tracy Enders, who waitressed a small café in South Bend that he frequented while attending the University of Notre Dame. Jim soon proved himself a valuable asset to the partnership, was made a third partner and set up an office in Cincinnati, Ohio in 1925. In 1928 he attended the University of Pennsylvania, and received a master's degree in aeronautical engineering in 1930. The Bernard's moved to Cheyenne, Wyoming from Cincinnati, Ohio in 1936 after the company that Jim Bernard worked for landed a large defense contract with the U.S. Government.

Alice told Ed everything Les said about both of them on the way to Cheyenne after she picked him up at the ranch in her car. They discussed it all the way to her parent's house and decided not to antagonize him by being together around him since he was only there for the summer. On the way back to the ranch Ed tried to think of a way to tell Alice about being harassed by Les without looking like a wimp. Finally, he gave up, disgusted with himself and fell silent the rest of the way home.

Les continued to harass Ed the rest of the summer. If he wasn't scaring him with snakes he contrived other ways of making life just plain miserable day in and day out. He never openly confronted Ed, but was constantly making him look bad in front of the other hands. Les found Ed and Alice in Laramie one weekend during the middle of August on their way out of a restaurant.

"Well, if it isn't the two love birds!" Les said as he stood in front of Alice and Ed on the sidewalk.

Ed's hackles went up. "Get lost Les, we're not looking for trouble."

Les stepped directly in front of Ed. "Maybe you're not, you little chicken shit, but I am. "With that Les hit Ed in the face and knocked him down on the sidewalk. Ed leaned on one elbow and wiped the blood from the corner of his mouth as Alice screamed at Les and punched him in the gut. He looked at her and laughed, "I will say one thing for you honey buns; you've got spunk. That's more than you can say for your yellow boyfriend here." Looking at Ed lying on the sidewalk leaning on one elbow. Ed rolled and jumped to his feet in one motion. Doubling a fist he threw a punch at Les. Les dodged the blow and gave one into Ed's solar plexus in return. Ed stumbled forward as Les stepped back and planted an uppercut on the end of Ed's nose. Blood splattered everywhere as Ed's head snapped back and he hit the pavement with his butt. Les reached down and grabbed Ed by the hair of his head, pulled him to his feet and hit him in the stomach again. This time Ed threw up on Les, the sidewalk and himself.

"You son-of-a-bitch. You puked on me." Les said as he held Ed at arms length by the hair of his head. Ed was gasping for air as he choked on the puke and the blood. Les looked at him and laughed. "I've got one more present for you" and kicked him in the crotch as hard as he could. Ed doubled up and fell forward on the sidewalk gagging and shuddering as the pain convulsed through his body. Les stepped over Ed's shaking body to look directly at Alice. "That ought to put a crimp in your love life for a while. If he ever was man enough to have one that is."

"You rotten, low down, miserable excuse for a man. Why did you do this? We weren't bothering you! You're lower than a snake's belly."

"My, my, does the little bitch have a temper? I told you I was going to make life miserable for the two of you. Next time you'll take him to the morgue instead of the hospital."

"I hope you rot in hell!" Alice said as she pushed past Les and bent over Ed. "Don't worry I'll get you to emergency." Alice said to the shuddering, moaning Ed on the sidewalk.

Les bent over Ed "Remember what happened here, because if you say one word to anyone back at the ranch, you and I are going to have another session just like this one, only longer and more graphic."

He straightened up, gave Ed a kick in the back and walked away. Alice took Ed to the hospital emergency room. They checked him over and admitted him for the night because of his bruised testicles and the possibility of blood in his urine. Ed was released the next afternoon, no permanent damage was done, but he couldn't believe how bad he hurt.

The confrontation had happened on Friday evening. Haying was done and Emil let everyone have a long weekend, so Ed still had Sunday to recover. He spent the day hanging around Alice's apartment.

"I guess I'm not much of a fighter." Ed said sheepishly as him and Alice discussed what happened. "I suppose I don't look very good to you right now."

"Don't be ridiculous, you didn't run. You stood up to him and tried. He's older and has a lot more experience fighting than you do."

"I feel bad. I couldn't even defend us, and that bothers me."

"Well, learn how to fight. I'm sure one of the hands at the ranch could teach you."

"You know, I think you're right. Mike has liked me from the get go and he's as rough and tumble as they come. I'll bet he'd be happy as a bee in honey to show me." The two of them spent the afternoon laughing and talking. After an early supper Alice curled up on the couch in Ed's arms and they talked until almost midnight. Finally Alice jumped up and announced that if she was going to get any sleep at all she had to take Ed to the ranch. Pulling up in front of the bunkhouse Alice turned to Ed and said, "Be careful."

Ed slid across the seat said "I will." And kissed her hard on the lips. Coming up for air he looked at her with glazed eyes and whispered, "I love you."

"Oh, Ed." Alice stared back through great big cow eyes and kissed him, slowly, softly and tenderly. As the two of them melted into each other's arms Ed knew his goose was cooked: and he loved it!!!

"We can't sit here like this all night, "Alice said as she pulled away. "I've got to go home and get some sleep before I go to work."

"Ok, one more kiss and then you go." Ed replied as he leaned toward her and puckered. Alice leaned forward to kiss him. Their lips met slowly and hungrily. Alice moved her hand on the car seat to brace herself, and inadvertently put it in Ed's crotch. His hardness surprised her and she pulled back. "Hold that thought, but it's time for me to go. Goodnight."

"Goodnight, Alice." Ed said as he slid out of the car and shut the door. Watching the car speed down the dirt lane toward the highway Ed mumbled to himself, "to be continued."

Breakfast the next morning was the usual chatter about things around the ranch. Everyone gathered at the corral afterwards to get their work assignments for the day.

"Load the flatbed with crib boards, and the fencing wagon with the tools. We'll start with the closest stacks and work our way out. You know what to do now let's get at it."

The men walked to the huge pile of boards that had been carefully stacked as the previous years haystacks were opened and used. Jake drove the truck into position and the men proceeded to load the sawmill slats on the truck. Ed was on the ground passing boards to the next man (who happened to be Les) in the human conveyor line that lead onto the bed of the truck.

"Did you and your girlfriend have fun in the car last night?" Les asked as he took a board Ed had passed him.

Ed gave him a disgusting look. "That's none of your damn business!"

Les laughed, "You sound frustrated, didn't you get any of that or did she just tease?"

Ed shoved the next board into Les's gut making him flinch. "Watch your mouth Les."

Les lost his smile, "Oh, touchy aren't we? If you want to tangle again, I'm ready. Only this time I won't be so generous."

Ed recalled the beating he had received from Les. "I will if I have to. What's your problem with Alice and me? Are you jealous? Does it bother you knowing when we're together? I can imagine what kind of thoughts are going through your sick mind." Ed ducked in the knick of time as the board Les swung at him swished inches above his head.

"Hey you two, knock it off and get back to work!" Jake yelled from the bed of the truck.

Les glared at Ed and passed the wanna be weapon onto Don. Ed returned the look and shoved the board Mike handed him at his brooding opponent. The two men went back to work but they both knew this wasn't over yet.

After supper and the men had left for the bunkhouse Jake brought up the incident to Emil.

"Damn it!" Emil said after Jake finished telling him of the confrontation between the two men. "I told Les last year when I paid him off I'd can his ass if he caused any more trouble." Emil slammed his coffee cup on the table.

"He hasn't really done anything yet. I need him in order to get the stacks cribbed before we start working cattle."

Emil grimaced. "If those two get in a fight their both gone. If Les can't stay out of Ed's way he's gone no matter what."

Jake knew Emil meant exactly what he said. "Ok, I'll go have a talk with 'em."

"Do what you have to but, they better cool their heels or they're down the road."

Jake nodded and left the room. He walked into the bunkhouse and simply said; "Les and Ed I want to talk to you two outside." Outside the trio walked out of earshot of the bunkhouse before Jake confronted them. "Look you two. If you have differences that's your business until it affects your work here on this ranch. Then it's my business. That little incident today was uncalled for. Les if you would've connected with that sawmill slat the three of us probably wouldn't be standing here talking about it." Les started to say something, but Jake gave him a stony look as he continued. "This is a one way conversation. I talk and you listen. The old man wanted to fire you on the spot. Unfortunately I need you're sorry ass until we get these cribs built, but don't let it go to your head. You give me any more trouble and I'll boot your ass out of here myself." Jake turned his wrath on Ed who up until now had been standing next to Les with a big grin on his face. "I understand Les has been giving you a hard time all summer. I can imagine why. Understand this, if you and Les get into a fight here at the ranch your both history. If you two need to knock heads do it off this property. I'd suggest you two get this settled. That's the long and the short of it. Do I make myself clear to both of you?"

Les spoke first. "Very!" He said as he spun and marched toward the bunkhouse.

"You got a minute?" Jake said as Ed turned and started to leave.

"Sure."

Jake walked over and stood next to the young man. "Don't let him get to you. If you have to fight do it in town or someplace where only the coyotes or cows will see it. Les won't be back next year I can guarantee it. He's been trying to get your goat all summer, hang in there a couple more months and you won't be bothered by him anymore. I wouldn't want to have to fire you over the likes of him."

"Thanks Jake, I understand." Ed stuck out his hand and the two men shook hands and went their own ways.

"You little son-of-a-bitch, you damn near got me fired. I guarantee you and I are going to tangle before I leave here and you can plan on going to the hospital." Les had Ed pinned up against the wall inside the barn as he delivered his message with a stiff punch to the gut. Ed's knees buckled and he gasped for air. Les released his grip on Ed's shirt and walked out of the barn laughing.

Something snapped inside of Ed. "I'm through taking your bullshit." Ed thought to himself as he got up off the dirt floor. Remembering why he was in the barn to begin with Ed gingerly walked to where the workhorse harness hung and pulled a set off the peg. He walked out of the barn and hung it on the corral as Les lead the workhorses over and tied them to the inside of the enclosure.

"Remember what I said you little pimple faced geek. I'm looking forward to really hurting you."

"Stick it up your ass, and your mother's too, if you got one." Ed turned to get the other set of harness from the barn as Les leapt the corral fence. He reached Ed in a couple of steps spun him around and hit him square on the jaw. Ed slid on his back a couple of feet and shook his head to clear the cobwebs.

"No one talks that way about my mother." Les said as he watched Ed get to his feet.

"I did and that punch probably cost us our jobs so we might just as well settle this right now."

Les gave a loud growl and charged Ed. Ed sidestepped him and punched him under the right eye as he did. Ed was mad but not out of control. Les was mad and out of control. "I didn't know you could growl Les! How about a bark? Is that something your mother taught you or did you learn that when you went to the pound to visit her?"

Les's face went absolutely livid with rage. "I'll kill you, you son-of-a-bitch." Looking around he reached in the wagon with the fencing tools and pulled out a corn knife that they used to cut brush out of the fence line with. "Your going to the hospital minus a few pieces asshole." Les said as he raised the blade and moved towards Ed.

"Whoa, wait a minute Les I'll take back what I said. Put down that knife. Let's go at this with our fists you know you can beat me." Ed was backing away from Les who was steadily approaching.

"When I get through with you your little whore girlfriend won't even recognize you. Then let's see if she's still interested in you." Ed hit the barn wall with his back. Les made a swing with the long handled blade and hit the wall next to Ed's head. Ed stumbled to the side and tripped over a four-foot piece of three-quarter inch galvanized water pipe that had been lying in the grass next to the barn. Grabbing the pipe he held it in front of his face just as Les swung again. The sparks flew as the blade made contact with the pipe. Ed was in a fight for his life, he stepped back and swung the pipe at Les's head like he was trying to hit a home run. When the pipe made contact Ed could hear a sound like eggshells cracking and then a kind of sickening squishy sound as the pipes momentum came to a sudden halt. Les's spun around, the corn knife flying out of his hands, and fell face first in the dirt. His hands opened and closed on the dirt beneath them and his legs moved spasmodically as his feet dug furrows in the soft ground. Blood was running from every orifice in his head, his mouth, nose, ears and eyes. The left eyeball was hanging by the optical cord across his face touching the dirt. He was making a low moaning sound and breathing extremely hard as he sucked the dirt and blood that was collecting in a pool around his face deep into his lungs.

Emil heard the commotion coming from the barn and looked out the kitchen window to see what was going on. Les was in the process of coming over the corral fence as Ed was walking away.

"Damn those two!" Emil said as he walked outside through the screened eating porch. Ed was just getting up off the ground when he stopped at the bottom of entrance stairs. "Might as well let 'em settle this and then I'll walk over and fire both of 'em." Emil thought to himself as Mrs. Schmidt joined her husband. "What's going on?" she asked as Ed hit Les with his fist.

"Those two roosters have finally decided to settle their argument." Les had stumbled and was looking around when he reached into the fencing wagon next to him and pulled out the corn knife.

Emil shouted but he knew the combatants didn't hear him. Running had never been his long suit and by the time he reached the scene Les was already down. Ed dropped the pipe just as Emil rushed past him and looked at Les.

"Shit! Marianne, call the ambulance and the sheriff. Hurry!!" Emil stooped over the moaning Les and scooped the blood soaked dirt away from his mouth. Mrs. Schmidt was halfway to the scene when Emil yelled for the ambulance and the sheriff. She immediately did a one eighty and raced to the house. Ed stood in a daze looking down at Emil trying to keep the blood and dirt away from Les's mouth.

It took approximately fifteen minutes for Doc Larson to come barreling down the lane off the highway from Medicine Bow. By this time Mrs. Schmidt had returned to the scene and was helping Emil keep the blood and dirt from collecting under Les's mouth. He had stopped convulsing and his moans were much quieter and shorter now. Ed was still standing in a state of shock watching the gorey drama unfolding before him. The Schmidt's gave way to Doc Larson as he bent over Les to assess the damage. After a minute or two he looked up and said, "Marianne, get a blanket or something we can put on him to keep him warm with." The rancher's wife ran toward the house and returned shortly with a brown wool army blanket like the men used in the bunkhouse. "All we can do is make him comfortable as possible until the ambulance gets here from Laramie." He said looking at Emil and Marianne Schmidt. "Emil, can I talk to you for a minute?" Doc Larson said to the ranch owner as he motioned with his head toward the barn. Once out of hearing Doc Larson turned to face Emil, "what happened Emil?"

Emil was still visibly shaken, but he was no stranger to the site of blood so he cleared his throat and explained what he saw happen. After he listened to Emil's short dissertation, Doc Larson gave him his medical opinion. "The young man has suffered severe head trauma.

From what I can see his skull is probably broke in more than one place, along with most of the major blood vessels on both sides of the bone. In other words he was a dead man when he hit the ground." Emil looked from the elderly physician's face to the ground and nodded. Doc Larson continued, "the moaning is just an instinctive reaction of the body because the heart and brain are still trying to function. I doubt if he'll be alive by the time the ambulance gets here."

"Damn it!" Emil shouted, "I knew last year when I paid him off there would be trouble if I let him come back."

Doc Larson put his hand on Emil's shoulder. "Hind sight is always better than fore sight. Emil, I've known you for a lot of years and as far as I'm concerned there isn't a kinder, more generous man in the county. Don't blame yourself for somebody else's actions. You had no control over what happened here. From what you told me these two would have gotten into it sooner or later anyway."

Emil looked at his friend, "Yeah, your right Doc. I just didn't think it would come down to this." The rancher said throwing his hands in the air to emphasize his point.

"It did get out of hand that's for sure. Do you think it was intentional on one or the other's part?"

"No, I think it was the heat of the moment type thing. Les was always the quiet type. Evidently he had a bad temper under it all."

Doc Larson nodded as the sound of sirens could be heard coming down the lane from the highway. "It's too soon for the ambulance it must be the sheriff. I suppose we'd better get out there and see if there is anything we can do for the living." Emil nodded and the two men walked out of the barn toward the scene of the tragic confrontation.

The sheriff and the State Police responded to Mrs. Schmidt's call. The two officer's surveyed the scene and walked over to confront Ed who was still standing in exactly the same spot that he was in when he dropped the pipe on the ground. Mrs. Schmidt was talking excitedly as Doc Larson and Emil walked up. Ed was staring straight ahead and not responding to the officer's questions.

"Son, you better snap out of it and say something. You're in a lot of trouble here and we need you to work with us." Sheriff John Stone was saying to the incoherent youth with the dazed look on his face.

"I don't think this is a good time to try and get any answers from the lad, John." Doc Larson said as he walked up with Emil. "He's in a state of shock. Put him in your car and I'll give him a sedative, you can question him later.

"Ok, Doc." The burley sheriff said as he took Ed by the arm and led him to his car. The doctor followed with his bag and after Ed was handcuffed inside the car he gave him the sedative.

"This will relax you. Stay calm and cooperate with the sheriff. He's an honest man and will do what he can to help you." Patting Ed on the shoulder the kindly doctor withdrew from the car and walked back to the scene with the officer. "Emil and Marianne witnessed the whole thing. You'll be able to get a statement from them."

"Good," the large man said. "That'll help him in court that's for sure. What about the victim?"

"He's a goner, I doubt if he'll make it until the ambulance gets here." The sheriff nodded matter-of-factly as they stopped in front of the Schmidt's already giving their statement to the State Police officer. It was One hour and thirty-five minutes from when Mrs. Schmidt had placed the call before the ambulance arrived. Les had stopped breathing and Doc Larson pronounced him legally dead before they loaded him in the ambulance. The two officers collected the information they needed for the present and followed the ambulance slowly up the dusty lane to the highway. The three participants in the sordid drama watched as the vehicles turned onto the pavement and headed in opposite directions.

By the time the sheriffs car with Ed in it arrived at the Carbon County jail in Rock Springs the sedative was working and he began to realize what happened. He was scared to death. Especially when he heard the sound of the iron door echo as it closed and the lock turn shut. Alone, he sat on the steel cot and cried for the first time since he'd come to this God forsaken place.

CHAPTER #14

THE PRELIMINARY HEARING for Ed's case was to be held two weeks after he was arrested. Emil arranged a meeting prior to the hearing with the presiding Judge to discuss Ed's situation. The Judge's name was the Honorable Thomas Penncha. He owned a large ranch near Garrett, Wyoming, north and east of Medicine Bow. He and Emil were old acquaintances; they traded herd bulls about every five years and were both active in the cattleman's association.

"Tom what's going to happen to the boy?" Emil asked as he sat in the Judge's chambers.

"Emil, I won't paint a rosy picture for you because a jury has to decide that. All I can tell you for sure is, we have to give him a preliminary hearing so he can legally enter his plea. Depending on how he pleads will determine how he's tried. If he pleads innocent we have to give him a jury trial. If he pleads guilty there won't be a trial and I'll sentence him."

"It was self defense. Marianne and I both witnessed it."

Judge Penncha held up his hand. "Has he got a lawyer?"

"No, he doesn't have two nickels to rub together."

"I will appoint a public defender for him then."

"Look Tom, I appreciate you being straight with me. Now, I need your advice as a friend. This boy doesn't have anybody to stand by him. I want to help him if I can, but I need you to tell me the best way to handle it."

The Judge looked at Emil and smiled. "I thought he was just a hand. What's he to you?"

Emil related everything that happened since Ed came to the ranch. "Marianne and I have taking a liking to him and I'd hate to see him take a bum rap for defending himself."

"Sounds to me like he's an accident waiting to happen. All right Emil, here's my advice to you, but this doesn't leave the room. Understood?"

The ranch owner nodded and leaned slightly forward to receive his friend's advice.

"Hire a lawyer for him; a good one. Any of them that are available for me to appoint are either wet behind the ears or to lazy to get a practice of their own. Get him a new set of duds. Don't overdress him with a suit and tie, but don't put him in Levis either. Give your lawyer something to work with and dress him like the all American boy. Make sure he's neat as a pin every time he is in court. Tell him to plead guilty to manslaughter by reason of self-defense. That's what the D.A. will be charging him with at the preliminary hearing. Understand there are no guarantees. A jury could find him guilty. If they do it's ten to twenty years with a chance for parole. Make sure you have your lawyer explain this to the boy and goes over all the options with him. Ultimately he's the one who has to make the final decision on how to plead. I'll give you the names of a couple of good criminal lawyers. They're not cheap but they are good."

Emil stood up as the Judge scribbled the names on a piece of paper. Once finished he stood and handed the paper to Emil.

"Thanks Tom, I really appreciate your help."

"Emil, we go back to far not to. I know you'd do the same for me if the opportunity arose." Tom Penncha walked around his desk and put his hand on the ranchers shoulder as he walked Emil to the door of his chambers. "Everything will work out for the best, you'll see."

"Thanks again Tom." Emil turned and walked through the opened door.

The lawyer Emil hired was from Casper, Wyoming. He was one of the two the judge had recommended and did a lot of legal work for the State Cattleman's Association. He owned a couple of ranches near Casper and one near Thermopolis, Wyoming.

When the day for Ed's preliminary hearing arrived he was brought to the courtroom in handcuffs and leg shackles. He had been transferred from the Carbon County jail in Rock Springs to the Albany County jail in Laramie the day before the hearing for the courts convenience. The Schmidt's were there along with the ranch hands and Alice. Every one of them had come to see Ed while he was in jail in Rock Springs.

Everyday somebody had shown up in a show of concern and support. Ed couldn't believe Emil had hired a lawyer to defend him. They showed up two days after Ed was incarcerated. The lawyer spent four hours listening to Ed and giving him advice. After advising Ed to plead guilty to manslaughter by reason of self defense, the lawyer gave him a couple of days to think about his options and the consequences before he came back to get Ed's decision.

"Just remember," the lawyer reminded Ed after he agreed to plead guilty. "The jury could find you guilty. If they do you will go to prison. I don't think that will happen because you have two reputable eyewitnesses but there are no guarantees."

"I understand," Ed said, picturing himself behind bars as a cold chill ran up and down his spine.

The bailiff announced the entrance of the judge and everyone stood up. He told everyone to be seated, gave the case number and announced the State of Wyoming verses the defendant Edward Spitzer of Medicine Bow, Wyoming. The judge asked the District attorney and the defendant to approach the bench. Looking at the papers on the desk in front of him laid them down and looked directly at Ed. "Young man, you are being charged with manslaughter. This carries a sentence of ten to twenty years and a fine of ten thousand dollar if you are convicted. You are also being charged with aggravated assault. This carries a maximum sentence of five years and a $1,000.00 fine. Has your attorney explained this and all of your options to you?"

"Yes your honor." Ed said as he looked at his lawyer standing next to him.

"Then how do you plead?"

Ed's lawyer spoke for the first time. "Your honor my client wishes to plead not guilty by reason of self defense to both charges."

"Very well. Do you want a jury trial or not?"

"Yes your honor we would like a jury trial and ask the court to set bail."

"If I set bail where will your client reside?"

"His employer Mr. Emil Schmidt has agreed to post bond if you will release my client to his custody."

Judge Penncha looked at Emil sitting in the front row of seats. "Mr. Schmidt, will you approach the bench please?" Emil stood and walked to the bench in front of the judge. "Do you realize the responsibility you'll be taking on if I grant your request?"

Emil looked directly at the judge. "Yes your honor I do." You realize if he runs you'll lose any bail money you post."

"Yes your honor."

The judge looked at the district attorney. "Does the state have any concerns before I make a decision?"

"The state would request that Mr. Spitzer be kept under constant supervision until his trial."

"Very well," The judge said looking at the calendar on the desk in front of him. "I am setting the court date for Thursday the thirtieth of September at ten o'clock in the morning. I will set bail at $10,000.00 dollars and release you to the custody of Mr. Schmidt. While in Mr. Schmidt's custody you are not to leave his property for any reason until the trial. If you do, you will be arrested, put in jail and Mr. Schmidt will forfeit the money he is putting up as a bond for you." Looking directly at Ed the judge waited for his answer.

"Yes sir." Ed's lawyer spoke up "Thank you for your compassionate ruling your honor."

The judge slammed his gavel on the desk. "Bailiff, remove the restraints from the defendant."

The bailiff took the handcuffs and shackles off Ed as the lawyers and Emil settled the bond. Alice came from the gallery to stand by Ed and wait until the restraints were removed. As the bailiff walked away she threw her arms around Ed hugging him tightly. "Oh thank God you're free."

"Alice, I'm not free yet. I could still go to jail. This was just a hearing to find out what I would plead. The trial will determine whether I'm guilty or not."

"Of course you're not guilty."

"We have to convince twelve people of that."

"We will, in the meantime I'll come out to the ranch every weekend to see you."

"Are you sure, I just killed someone. You sure you want to hang around with me?"

"You're not a murderer. You defended yourself. He would have killed you with that corn knife."

"Maybe."

"There's no maybe about it, from what Emil and Marianne told me he was trying to kill you."

Ed didn't say anymore. He still remembered Les saying he was going to send Ed to the "hospital minus a few pieces." Maybe that would have been better.

The ride to the ranch was a quiet one for most of the trip. Just outside Rock River, Wyoming Ed spoke up. "Emil, I hope you didn't waste your money on me."

"You aren't guilty of doing anything other than defending yourself. There isn't a jury in this state that would convict you after they hear the facts. The district attorney told me when I paid the bond that he was sending one of his colleagues to handle this case because he had bigger fish to fry. So, I think the State realizes they probably won't get a conviction here."

Why did you do all this for me? I mean the lawyer and the bail bond?"

"Look son, you don't have the where with all to defend your self. Understand justice in this country is not a given right. It's an affordable right. Did you ever stop and wonder about our symbol for justice?

A blindfolded woman holding a set of gold scales? This is the real world; you get what you pay for. A public defender may or may not do a good job for you, but privately paid lawyers will especially if he's a good one."

Ed thought about it for a minute. "So what your saying is; the more money you pay the better your chances of getting acquitted?"

"In a way, yes. You see it's no different than buying a good bull. You go on performance. If you are going to buy a proven sire you're going to pay for the fact that he has sired good stock in the past. With a lawyer or anyone who serves the public for hire you're going to pay according to how successful his track record is and when your future is on the line you want the best you can get. The world doesn't care what happens to you. Your family and friends do, understand that and you understand what life is all about."

Ed was humbled by Emil's analogy. "But, I'm just a hired hand why should you care about me?"

Mrs. Schmidt finally spoke up. "You're a decent young man with your whole future ahead of you. You have had some bad experiences since you went to work for us, your honest, and a hard worker. You haven't had the time to turn into a drunken bum like most of the hands we get. Emil and I see a lot of potential in you that you probably aren't even aware of yet. It would be a shame to let something like this ruin your life forever." Ed sat back in the seat and was quiet the rest of the way to the ranch. The rest of the hands all rode in Jake's car and followed Emil, it was a little past noon when they arrived at the ranch, Jake told them to get their clothes changed and go to work. "We need to get those cribs finished so we can start working cattle." He stated.

John Spitzer stopped the green Chevrolet he was driving next to the curb in front of the old Carbon County courthouse in downtown Rock Springs, Wyoming. The brick building had a run down, aged look to it. A sign indicated that the Sheriffs office and jail were located in the basement through a side entrance. John stood leaning on his car as he collected his thoughts and took in the scenery so different from his native Wisconsin. His adopted son was housed inside the barred building. Accused of killing another man with an iron pipe. John recalled the day he'd adopted young Edward. It was three months after John married Ed's mother. Mary and he talked about it almost as part of the wedding conditions. They both agreed that since the adoption must happen, it should take place sooner than later. Evan though the boy's father was killed in a farm accident when he was two years old, Ed knew and loved Carl Johnson enough to be hurt and confused when his father left and didn't come back. John courted Mary Johnson less than a year before they were married. He had known her and Carl for years through the Vernon County Grange. She was the secretary when he was president and Carl was vice president. When John and Mary were wed, they put a hired man in charge of the farm John owned, located on the other side of the county and started their new life together living on Mary's place.

Ed grew up surrounded by love and respect. The work was long and hard, but he was never asked to do more than his share. Ed lived for sixteen years on the Wisconsin dairy farm that Carl Johnson left to his widow. When he disappeared John and Mary were frantic. Their first thoughts were kidnapped, and then the slow realization that Ed premeditarily chose to leave ate at them like a cancer. Why? Where had they gone wrong? Where was he? Was he safe? Why didn't he write? How could he treat them like this? John remembered the bitterness he felt for a long time afterwards. Ed had hurt his mother deeply and John watched her go from the happy, lighthearted woman he married, to a quiet, bitter soul who no longer took an interest in anything. When Mr. Kilpatrick called them from Denver, it seemed to revitalize her. At least now they knew where he was and that he was all right. Ed's first letter came while he was in the hospital. It was a long letter apologizing for running away and the hurt he caused John and Mary to suffer. They corresponded regularly two or three times a month after that.

Mr. Schmidt had called him with the gory details after Ed was arrested and taken to jail. Now here he was standing in front of the building where his much loved adopted son waited to be tried for murder. Mary had a stroke the day after they received the news. John postponed the trip for two weeks just to make sure she was stable. He'd opted to drive his car because it was two days quicker than the train. With a sigh John stood up and walked to the entrance of the Sheriff's office and down the cold, dark cement stairs into the sinister room below.

"Can I help you?" the uniformed officer asked from the other side of the securely enclosed counter.

"Yes, My name is John Spitzer, I'm here to see my son who is being held here."

"Do you have any identification?"

John stepped up to the fenced window, "I have my drivers license."

"That'll do." The deputy took the drivers license scrutinized it, and wrote the number on a piece of paper attached to a clipboard. Shoving the clipboard through the opening in the wire enclosure, he looked at John and said, "Print and sign your name next to where I wrote your drivers license number."

John nodded and complied with the request.

The deputy took the clipboard John passed back to him compared the signatures and handed John his driver's license. "Your son was released on bond a week ago."

"Do you know where he is staying?"

"No, but a Mr. Emil Schmidt from Medicine Bow posted his bond. He might know."

"Ok, thank you." John walked outside to his car where he had Emil Schmidt's phone number written down.

John drove to Medicine Bow where Emil promised to meet him in front of the Virginian hotel. They met and John followed Emil to the ranch. The meeting between Ed and his Stepfather was heartwarming to say the least. They hugged and greeted each other on the porch where every one gathered to eat. Emil and Marianne sitting in their living room fighting back the lump in their throat as they overheard the emotional reunion. Marianne had put the coffee pot on and Ed and his stepfather spent most of the night talking and getting reacquainted. Ed was visibly shaken when he found out his mother had a stroke the day after the news about Ed reached John and Mary.

"It's my fault." Ed told his stepfather.

"Maybe, maybe not." John told the overwrought young man. "Your mom has been going downhill for quite a while now. I wouldn't blame myself if I were you."

"My running away probably started it. God, I wish I could take it all back."

"It doesn't work that way thank God. We're supposed to learn from our mistakes, some people must need to learn more than others though. It's when you do the same stupid thing more than once that it's no longer a mistake. You can't undo the past son, but you can control the future if you're man enough."

Ed thought about what John had just said as he sipped his coffee. "Thanks dad, you always seem to be there when I need you."

"That's what dad's are for, remember that when you get a family of your own."

"Dad, I am going to court on murder charges. I may not get a chance to have a family."

"Hogwash, there isn't a jury alive would convict you of murder for trying to defend your self from somebody swinging a knife at you."

"I know it's a long shot but it could happen."

"Like I said hogwash." The elderly gentleman got to his feet, "I don't know about you, but it's been a long day for me. I'm tired and going to bed. The Schmidt's were kind enough to put me up while I'm here, so I'll talk to you again tomorrow. Goodnight."

The two men hugged and went their separate ways. Over the next two weeks Ed and his father-in-law spent as much time as they could together getting reacquainted and talking about the recent past. John met Alice and loved her immediately. "I can understand you fighting over her, she's some gal." John told Ed after the first time he met her.

The time until the trial passed quickly. The hands gave Ed a lot of verbal support. Even Don who had been Les's good friend held no ill will towards Ed. "He got what he asked for," was the only comment he would make about the incident. Alice came to see Ed on her days off. She would pitch in and work right alongside the men when they didn't have the day off. Everyone at the ranch loved her to pieces. They all respected her relationship with Ed and she became a regular fixture around the ranch on the weekends. Finally the dreaded day arrived.

The courtroom was packed. Ed looked around at the crowd behind him. All the people he knew were there but he couldn't figure out why there were so many others. Leaning over to his lawyer Ed asked him what was going on.

"You're big news in these parts. People here haven't had a homicide in a long time." Ed shuddered at the morbid comment.

Judge Penncha entered with all the court formalities and the jury selection began. The process took a little over two hours. Once the jury was selected the court adjourned for a two-hour lunch. Back in session the prosecution presented its case and then the defense rebutted and then the court adjourned until the following morning at nine o'clock.

Back in session the following morning Ed was the first one called to the stand to testify. The prosecution was merciless. He forced Ed to recall why he ran away from home, and his experiences before the ranch and what lead up the confrontation with Les. Ed hated to bring Alice into the picture but there was no way for him to avoid it. By the time the defense lawyer got through with him he was exhausted. Since all the witnesses were excluded from the courtroom until it was their turn to testify Ed was surprised when the prosecution called Les's parents to the stand one at a time. He had no idea what they looked like or who they were.

Robert and Juliet Corbett both testified about Les's character and his academic achievements. They portrayed Les as the model son and student who came to the ranch to make a few dollars for his education and to expand his people skills. The Schmidt's, Alice, all the ranch hands, were all called to testify about Les and Ed. By the time the testimony was taken on both sides it was late in the afternoon and the court adjourned for the weekend to resume at nine o'clock Monday morning. On his way out of court Ed passed by the Corbett's talking to the prosecuting attorney. They both turned to glare at him and Mrs. Corbett hissed, "I hope you rot in hell, you damn murderer. We're going to make sure you go to jail for killing our son." Robert Corbett grabbed his wife's arm and said, "Julia, that's enough."

"What do you mean that's enough." She shouted. "This bastard kills our son and you say that's enough? What kind of a man are you?"

"This is not the time or the place."

"Bullshit." Julia said as she ripped her arm from Robert's grasp and stormed out of the room.

Ed's lawyer walked him out of the courthouse to the street. "Don't let the Corbett's upset you. They're just character witnesses."

"Can they do anything to me if I don't go to prison?"

"They could sue you civilly, but I doubt if they will. It's very costly and ultimately there would be no point. Do you have any questions about what's going to happen Monday?"

"No, the Carbon County sheriff John Stone, the Wyoming State policeman, Doc Larson and the ambulance attendants are the only ones left to take the stand. Right?"

"Correct, we ought to be able to get closing arguments before the end of the day. Judge Penncha will probably let the jury deliberate overnight and it should be over by noon Tuesday."

That weekend turned out to be one of the longest in Ed's life.

Ed was the first one called to the stand. Since this was his second time the judge reminded him he was still under oath.

"Mr. Spitzer." The prosecutor loudly announced as he stood facing the jury with his back to Ed. He paused a moment for effect and then turned on Ed. "At anytime during your confrontation outside the barn did you say anything that would have caused Mr. Corbett to attack you?" Ed sat mute as the thoughts raced through his mind. The prosecutor's loud voice echoed through the room. "Mr. Stoltz, we're waiting for your answer."

"Objection your honor." Ed's lawyer interrupted "The prosecution is badgering the witness."

"Sustained, give the witness time to answer the question."

"Yes your honor."

Ed knew what the prosecutor was driving at, no matter what he said it was going to incriminate him. "He threatened to put me in the hospital. He did in front of Alice and there at the barn. He said 'I'm really looking forward to hurting you', as I was hanging the harness on the corral. I told him to 'stick it up your ass.' That's when he jumped over the fence and attacked me." Ed intentionally left out the rest of the dialogue about Les's mother. He knew no one else heard their conversation and since Les couldn't testify there was no way anyone could testify against him about what was said between Les and him prior to or during the confrontation.

"Did you make any comments that would have caused him to become enraged enough to pick up a weapon and attack you?"

"After he hit me and knocked me down I told him 'that punch probably cost us our jobs, so we might as well settle this right now.' I got up and he came at me I hit him and he went to his knees. He caught himself on the fencing wagon that was sitting there. When he stood up he reached in the wagon and came up with the corn knife. I told him to put it down and let's settle this with our fists, but he came at me with it anyway."

"Mr. Spitzer, do you expect this jury of honest, intelligent men and women to believe that just because you threw a punch and hit a man who knew he had the ability to outfight you . . . . . .

"Objection, your honor, the prosecution is calling for conjecture and trying to lead the witness."

The prosecutor looked at the judge and held out his hands palms up. "Your honor through previous testimony we know of at least one confrontation between these two where Mr. Spitzer was physically overcome by the deceased. My only point is that, Les Corbett had no reason to become so concerned about the outcome of the confrontation at the barn that fateful day that he felt he had to pick up a weapon to insure it."

"Your objection is over ruled. Continue Mr. Prosecutor."

The prosecutor nodded gave a slight smile and turned back to Ed. "Mr. Spitzer are you sure you didn't say anything that was derogatory or inflammatory to make Mr. Corbett so enraged that he felt his only recourse was to pick up a weapon and try to eliminate you?"

"No sir, I did not."

The lawyer gave Ed a long disbelieving look for the jury's benefit and said "We'll see," as he turned, looked at the defense lawyer and said "Your witness sir."

Ed's lawyer walked over to the witness stand. "Ed, I want you to relate to the best of your knowledge everything that transpired either verbally or physically between you and Les Corbett from the first day you two were present on the ranch this year." Ed talked for almost twenty minutes. "The responses that led to violence. Were they designed to invoke anger?"

"No, I was the one that was mad."

"Did you ever consider saying something so Mr. Corbett would attack you?"

"Are you kidding? Les was a good fighter. I don't think I could have whipped him if I wanted to."

"Here's the question. Did you want to whip him prior to the fatal fight?"

"Yes, but I knew better than to try."

"Thank you." The lawyer turned and went to his seat at the defendant's table.

"Mr. prosecutor, do you have any further questions for this witness?"

"Not at this time your honor."

"Mr. Lyman, you may call your next witness."

"Thank you your honor." Ed's lawyer said as he rose from his seat. "I would like to call Mr. Donald Henry to the stand." There was a small wait as the court officers summoned Don, waiting in the hall outside the courtroom. Taking the witness stand, Don was reminded of his sworn oath by the Judge.

"Mr. Henry," Ed's lawyer started. "You were close friends with the deceased; were you not?"

Don nodded, "That's right."

"Did Mr. Corbett ever express his feelings about Mr. Spitzer to you?"

"Yeah, he told me a number of times he didn't like him."

"Really, did he say why?"

"Yeah, when they first met he thought Ed was a stupid snot nose kid who didn't know his left foot from his right. When Les met Alice a couple of years ago they hung out together when Les was out here working. Les told me that they wrote to each other while he was at school back East. When he came back this year Alice and Ed had become thick as flies and she wouldn't have anything to do with Les."

"Was Les mad? I mean did he make any threats of harm toward either of them in your presence?"

"Oh, he spouted off. But I don't think he meant anything by it. He was hurt and mad so he blew off some steam. I never took anything he said about them serious. Les was a good guy. See that scar? He saved my life a while back."

"Did Les ever lose his temper?"

"Sure, don't we all?"

"If you don't mind Mr. Henry, I'll ask the questions. Did Mr. Corbett ever do anything violent after losing his temper that you know of?"

"I've seen him in a couple of fights, you know at the bars and places."

"Did he ever lose control and pick up anything or pull a weapon during any of those fights?"

"Not that I know of."

"Thank you, Mr. Henry. Your honor I'm through with this witness."

"Mr. Prosecutor, your witness." The Judge announced as Ed's lawyer sat down beside him.

Ed leaned over to his lawyer. "What's going on? Why are we going through the witnesses again?"

"The Prosecution knows he can't make the manslaughter charge stick unless he can prove aggravated assault. So now he's going back through all the witnesses trying to show that you baited Les into coming after you."

"That's absurd. Les was always baiting me."

"I know and that's what we're going convince the jury to believe."

The day ended with the same number of people questioned as Friday. Tuesday came and went and still the lawyers were questioning witnesses. The prosecution summoned anyone in the vicinity who had ever met Les and had a good word to say about him. The defense cross examined everyone and called as many as he could in Ed's behalf. It was Friday morning before the summations began.

Ladies and gentlemen of the jury;" The prosecutor began, "the defense would have you believe that the violent and uncalled for death of Les Corbett was because of a bad temper on his part and the loss of a cheating girl who mislead Les in word and deed. Yes, Les Corbett lost his temper and did attack his assailant with a lethal weapon. The thing we have to ask ourselves here is; was he provoked prior to the fatal fight. We have shown that Mr. Spitzer time after time antagonized Les verbally and took away the affection that Alice Bernard felt for Mr. Corbett for two years. You've all heard from his loving, supportive and caring parents, Les was a good boy, a gentle, caring lad who worked at the y6 ranch to fund his schooling rather than expect welfare from his parents. Here was a young man, in the prime of life, putting himself through law school suddenly cut down by a vicious attack devised by a coolly calculated, predetermined plan. I ask you; was this not a cruel and intentional act to strike a blow to the head when it represents less than one sixth of his body mass. Ladies and Gentlemen it is my contention that Les was drawn into that ill fated fight so the defendant,,," the prosecutor turned suddenly and pointed directly at Ed, "could kill him in cold blood!!! Knowing that he would have reputable witnesses watching every moment out of earshot able to testify only what they saw. Why was that corn knife located where it was easily accessible? It seems improbable that a tool used so seldom would be on top of the rest of the tools used more frequently. Perhaps it was put there intentionally prior to the confrontation. Even though witnesses testified about the junk lying around the outside of the barn, it seems more than just a little convenient that Mr. Spitzer should come up with a four foot length of galvanized lead pipe at precisely the right time to defend himself. No, Ladies and Gentlemen everything is just a little to convenient to be an accident. Don't you agree? Think about it, and when you do you'll come back with a verdict of "GUILTY" to aggravated assault and manslaughter. Thank you." The prosecutor stalked to his chair red-faced and visibly upset by his performance.

The Judge looked at Ed's lawyer "Mr. Lyman?"

Ed's lawyer rose from his chair and walked slowly toward the jury box as if in deep thought. "Thank you your honor, and thank you Mr. Prosecutor for that overly dramatic and erroneous summation. Ladies and Gentlemen of the jury, the prosecutor has asked you all through this trial to think about what you heard. First of all, let's look at what the prosecutor does. He prosecutes!! It's his job to try and get a conviction for the State. This is a very demanding and honorable job, but he is bound to do all that is legally within his power to get a conviction on the accused. This is good because it forces all the evidence to be presented in order for you the jury to make an intelligent decision. As I am sure you already know there are two kinds of evidence: Hard evidence, which amounts to tangible items and direct witnesses who were present at the scene and either saw what happened, heard what happened or both. Then we have circumstantial evidence, which is based on what people think happened or what could have happened because there were no witnesses present or for some reason could not accurately or dependably relate what transpired at the time or place of the transgression. I would also ask you to think about what you heard and saw over the last two weeks. Did the defense prove through reliable witnesses that Les Corbett was the tormentor and the aggressor? Yes we did, and very certainly I might add. Did the defense show through the testimony of those closest to him that Mr. Corbett at times even bragged about what he was going to do to Ed Spitzer before he left the ranch?

Through the testimony of his own parents we learned that Mr. Corbett was an exceptional athlete, besides being seven years senior to his co-worker who he tormented mercilessly because of his insane jealousy and extremely bad temper. Not only did he intimidate Ed Spitzer physically but verbally as well. Les Corbett was training to be a lawyer, which gave him the tools to do this. This compares similarly to a trained fighter engaging someone off the street. There is no contest. Les Corbett's physical prowess in football gave him the confidence to engage another man in a rough and tumble manner. The sport of rowing; which he was deeply involved in at college gave him exceptional upper body strength. In short, Ed Spitzer was no match for Mr. Corbett. Knowing this, do you really believe that Ed Spitzer would intentionally create a situation to confront Mr. Corbett? Wouldn't it have been easier to avoid any confrontations until Mr. Corbett left to go back to school for the year?

How many of you have ever lost someone you thought loved you, or maybe you wanted to love you? Did you become obsessed with revenge, or did you get over it and get on with your life?

Does anyone here know what it costs to go to a graduate law school in a renowned institution like the University of Pennsylvania? More than the two hundred dollars a month that Les Corbett was earning, I can tell you for a fact. If his parents weren't subsidizing Mr. Corbett, then he had money coming from somewhere to pay his tuition and expenses. How about Mr. Corbett's round trip train fare? Did that come out of the money he worked for at the y6 ranch? Of course not, we all heard Mr. Corbett Sr. testify that he covered that expense for his son.

Now to the so called, 'vicious attack' that the prosecutor would like you to accept as gospel. What is so vicious about defending your self from someone attacking you with a knife that has a handle three feet long and a blade with a serrated edge measuring fourteen inches from tip to haft, that is heavy enough to easily severe a two inch branch from a tree in one stroke?" Ed's lawyer picked the vicious looking weapon from the evidence table and held it so the jurors could easily see it. "This is a lethal weapon capable of inflicting serious damage and death. An extremely agitated man superior in strength and maturity was swinging it at Ed Spitzer. Was Ed supposed to stand and meekly take the consequences? He couldn't go anywhere being boxed in by the barn, the corral and the wagon with his knife-wielding attacker blocking the only escape route.

I know some of you own ranches or farms yourselves. Is your property completely free of litter? Who amongst us doesn't lay thing that we intend to use somewhere else and figure on coming back to at a later date? Anyone knows that galvanized water pipe makes an excellent brace for corner posts or a great twist handle for tightening brace wire. That it was leaning against the barn would be the most logical place until it was needed for use. Can you believe that over the course of time it might have fallen into the grass next to the barn and been forgotten? There is nothing contrived about this unfortunate incident. It all boils down to an extremely jealous man unable to control his temper, trying to find a solution in a momentary fit of deadly rage. Ed Spitzer was merely defending himself from an older, stronger man who had bested him physically and verbally in the past.

Ed Spitzer feared for his life Ladies and Gentlemen, as any one of you would have under the same conditions. Yes, think about it. How would you respond if you were trapped and someone who had previously beaten you, came at you with a deadly weapon like this!!!" The lawyer snatched the cruel looking corn knife off the table behind him and swung it in a half swing stopping the jagged blade in front of the juror's. The front row sucked in air and leaned back as they instinctively reacted to the movement of the blade toward them. "Ladies and gentlemen, I apologize if I scared you. I did that to demonstrate a point. When did you become concerned for your safety? When the knife was displayed? When did you believe that bodily harm was going to happen? When the knife was descending on you? Put your self in Ed Spitzer's shoes at that moment. Do you remember in the testimony given by Emil Schmidt and his wife Marianne that Mr. Corbett swung that very same knife blade not once but twice at Ed Spitzer? Both times missing his head by inches. Here is the pipe that Ed used as a defense. Look again at the marks the corn knife made on it as Ed held it in front of his face to deflect the blow directed at his head by Les Corbett." The lawyer held the pipe and walked slowly in front of the jury deliberately showing them the deep gouge the corn knife's steel blade had made in the galvanized iron. "Does this look like Ed Spitzer was attacking or defending?

When you deliberate, consider the questions that have been presented to you. Consider the evidence carefully; if you do this you can only come back with a NOT GUILTY verdict on the charge of manslaughter and NOT GUILTY verdict on the charge of aggravated assault. Thank you for your time and attention." The lawyer turned, walked to his chair, seated him self and looked at the judge.

The Judge had been lounging in his chair listening to the summations, He sat up as he spoke, "Ladies and Gentlemen of the jury: You have patiently sat for almost two weeks listening to the testimony and reviewing the evidence. I commend you for your participation and your patience. Now you must decide unanimously whether or not the defendant Edward Spitzer is guilty of manslaughter and or aggravated assault. Manslaughter is defined as: 'the unlawful killing of a human being without express or implied malice.' The words express or implied malice are the key here and imply unintentional or intentional malice.

Aggravated assault is defined as: an assault that is more serious than a common assault or combined with the intent to commit a crime or any of the various assaults so defined by statue, in this case the death of Les Corbett with a lethal weapon at the hands of another human being. Here again the key words are 'more serious and intent'.

I charge you to go and deliberate until you can return unanimously with a decision to the charges of manslaughter and aggravated assault. This court will convene until the jury returns with their decision." The gavel fell and everyone stood while the jury was led to their room and the judge left through a separate doorway to go to his chambers.

It took the jury six hours to agree unanimously on the two charges leveled at Ed. The judge was notified and he ordered the jury to be sequestered until nine a.m. Saturday (the next day).

The courtroom was packed when Ed walked in and took his chair. As soon as he was seated the bailiff cried out "all rise, this court is now in session, the honorable Judge Thomas Penncha presiding." Everyone stood as Judge Penncha entered and took his seat behind the bench. The gavel fell as the bailiff made the formal announcement of the courts identification, location and legal position. The Judge looked at the jurors. "Ladies and gentlemen of the jury have you reached a decision?"

The jury foreman stood and stated, "We have your honor." Holding a piece of paper where he could read it he continued, "Regarding the charge of manslaughter; we find the defendant Edward Spitzer, 'NOT GUILTY'." A brief murmur filled the courtroom. "Regarding the charge of aggravated assault; we find the defendant Edward Spitzer "Guilty with no premeditated intent." The juror sat down.

When Ed heard those words his life flashed before his eyes, fear and panic gripped him. Ed looked pleadingly at his lawyer, turning the barrister whispered, "don't worry" as he held his finger across his lips for Ed to be silent while the Judge was talking.

The Judge was commending the jury for their diligence and patience on the verdicts rendered. "I thank you, you are now released from your duties as jurors. Will the defendant please rise? Edward Spitzer you will remain in the custody of the sheriff of Albany County in Laramie, Wyoming until Monday the fifteenth of September, when you will be brought before me and I will pronounce sentence on you according to the statutes of the State of Wyoming." The gavel fell as the judge announced to the prosecutor and the defense lawyer. "Gentlemen I want to see you in my chambers immediately. This court is adjourned." The gavel fell again and the two lawyers followed the judge out of the courtroom to his chambers as Ed was being handcuffed.

Judge Penncha was leaning back in the office chair behind his desk as he spoke to the two men standing in front of him. "The reason I called you in here is because I want to work out the boys sentence. Frankly I didn't think the jury would find him guilty on either charge. But they did, so now we have to figure out what to do with him. "Jim, what do you think?" The judge said as he nodded toward the prosecutor.

"It was clearly self defense, the jury evidently thought it was more serious than just plain assault, but not premeditated. Interesting."

Ed's lawyer spoke up. "What's the least he can get Tom?"

The judge looked at Ed's lawyer. This was an informal and relaxed atmosphere, so the formalities required under public scrutiny didn't apply here.

"I can put him on probation and use the time he's sat in jail to satisfy the law. What do you think we should do?"

"The kid is innocent. He got cornered, scared and struck out of instinct and fear. If he hadn't we'd be burying him and trying Les Corbett. I think it was a no win situation. One of them was going to die no matter what." The other two men nodded their agreement.

"Jim, would you have a problem if I put him on probation for a year in Emil Schmidt's custody? That is if Emil will go along with it."

"No not at all. I have to agree with Joe, I think the kid got cornered and did what he felt he had to, to stay alive. I know of the Schmidt's. Good, honest, hard working people out of pioneer stock. Emil's folks settled in this country shortly after the Indians were run off. I think that would satisfy everyone concerned."

"Joe, does that work for you?"

Ed's lawyer nodded. "If that's the best you can do then I'll go for it."

"With the attention this received from the press we have to do something with out ruining the boys life. This way his record will be wiped clean after a year and he can get on with his life." The other two men nodded and left the room.

The steel handcuffs felt cold and hard as they closed around Ed's wrists. They felt like they weighed a ton. Ed hung his head and shuddered as he watched the sheriff close them on his trembling wrists. Alice and John were standing by his side trying to console him. Ed was scared, and didn't understand what was happening or why.

John was excitedly saying; "I'll talk to the judge, we'll appeal this if we have to."

Alice franticly kissed him on the cheek and whispered; "I love you, and I'll always be here for you."

Both of them were talking, but it sounded distant and incoherent as the deputy led Ed away in chains.

Ed looked up from the worn steel cot with the chipped green paint he was sitting on as Joe Lyman waited to be let into the cell by the jailer. The six by eight foot enclosure was as worn and ragged as the steel cot. The walls were a faded lime green, with scribbling from past residents over the chipped and cracked surface. The steel bars at the front of the cubical had the same paint and texture as the rest of the rectangular box.

"Good morning Ed." The lawyer cheerfully said as he entered the depressing cell.

"What's good about it?" Ed said reflecting the doom and gloom his situation and his surroundings prompted.

"I'm sorry I couldn't see you sooner, but the news I have is good."

Ed's interest showed on his unshaven face. "How so?"

After the trial and Judge Penncha requested the prosecuting attorney and my self to his chambers, we talked about your sentence. None of us believed the jury would find you guilty of manslaughter; Judge Penncha and I didn't believe they would find you guilty of aggravated assault. But, they did. The good news is they found 'no premeditated intent'. Which means it is only aggravated because a weapon was used and someone died as a result of it. It does bring up the question of self-defense and the law says; the penalty can be as little as a fine, jail time, probation, or any combination of all three, to the maximum of ten years and a fifty thousand dollar fine. The presiding judge has certain guidelines he must follow according to State and federal statutes. By the same token, the presiding judge also has a certain amount of latitude with in those statutes to be able to use his own discretion in determining the severity of the sentence."

Ed stared at the lawyer with his mouth open as he sat on the stained canvas covered excuse for a mattress. "What are you trying to tell me?"

"As I said we discussed the alternatives available to your sentence. Judge Penncha informed us he was going to use the time you've spent in jail before sentencing and a years probation to satisfy the law."

Ed stood up tears running down his cheeks. Turning away he wiped them away with the sleeve of his shirt. "I'm sorry, I didn't mean to cry in front of you."

"Don't apologize, you've been through a very traumatic situation. I'm glad it turned out as well as it did."

"It wouldn't have without your help, thank you." Ed stuck out his hand and the two men shook hands.

"I was just doing what I was hired to do. Thank the Schmidt's, they laid out a lot of money to help you"

"I know. It bothers me because I don't know how I'm going to pay them back."

"I don't think they expect you to. As your lawyer I'm bound to defend your rights under the law. In all my years of practice I've seen and heard just about every kind of situation possible. Yours is not unique. But, your relationship with the Schmidt's is. They like and respect you, take some free advice and don't do anything to damage that relationship. They're good people and the kind you want on your side when things get rough." The lawyer called for the jailer to let him out. "I'll see you at the sentencing. Don't worry, this will all be over before you know it."

Ed shook the lawyer's hand, "Thanks again, for everything."

The jailer opened the cell door and the lawyer walked out. "My pleasure."

The sentencing hearing only took a half an hour, once Judge Penncha and everyone else in the courtroom were seated the Judge rapped his gavel and spoke.

"Edward Spitzer please rise. A jury of your peers has found you guilty of aggravated assault with no premeditated intent. The self-defense plea you entered was taken into consideration along with fact that you've not been in trouble or have a police record in your past. Therefore, I sentence you to one year's probation, with no fine and your jail time served to satisfy the law. Mr. and Mrs. Schmidt have agreed to give you housing and employment during this period of time. Once a month you will show up and report to the sheriff of Carbon County. You are confined to the boundaries of Carbon County during your probation period. You are not to leave these boundaries or break any conditions this court has established for any reason other than deemed acceptable by this court or the Carbon County Sheriff. If you do, you will be arrested and incarcerated at the State Prison at Rawlins, Wyoming for a maximum of five years. This court will hold your records, if you follow the courts instructions to the letter, the charge of aggravated assault will be dropped."

A loud scream filled the courtroom. "You're going to let him get away with killing my Son? You son-of-a-bitch! You're not fit to be a Judge. I hope the same thing happens to your children!" Juliet Corbett was standing in the aisle held by a court deputy as she screamed and shook her fists at Judge Penncha.

Judge Penncha pounded his gavel on the bench. "Order, order, bailiff remove that women from this courtroom." The deputy and the bailiff dragged the screaming and kicking Juliet Corbett through the doors and into the hallway with Robert Corbett following voluntarily. Judge Penncha looked at Ed, "Young man, I apologize for the disturbance. Do you want me to repeat the sentence I pronounced on you or do you understand what I said?"

Ed looked back at the Judge as his lawyer whispered in his ear to tell him he had. "Yes, your honor, I understand."

Ed's lawyer pleaded for the Judge to include Laramie and the subsequent highway in Albany County, so Alice and Ed could see each other, but it was denied.

'Mr. Lyman, if you have exhausted all of your concerns on behalf of your client, I will pronounce this hearing ended." The gavel fell and everyone rose as the Judge left the courtroom.

Winter on the ranch passed slowly even though Alice came to the ranch almost every weekend to see Ed. Over the course of the winter they openly fell in love. She would stay with the Schmidt's at night and spent the days with Ed. She became an excellent horsewoman and could outwork some men. The hands all returned in the spring like swallows coming back to Capistrano. Alice was a permanent fixture on the weekends and the hands accepted her with their famous brand of light-hearted good-natured humor. They loved to tease her and Ed, but whoa and behold to anyone else that would have tried it. They loved her so much; anyone of them would have jumped in front of a striking rattlesnake to protect her.

One day around the first of June Ed approached Emil and Mrs. Schmidt to find out if it would be all right to throw a small party in the bunkhouse to announce the engagement of Alice and Ed by giving her a ring.

"You'll do nothing of the sort," Marianne Schmidt informed Ed before her husband had time to answer. "You'll have it right hear on the back porch. I have some people I would like to invite if it's ok with you?"

"Sure, actually June twelfth is her birthday and I wanted to surprise her with a ring." Ed said surprised as Emil was at her sudden statement.

"Emil and I want to furnish the food and the booze." Emil looked at his wife with raised eyebrows, but knew better than to say anything. "I'll tell Alice we're throwing her a birthday party, which is exactly what it'll be, we just won't tell her it's also an engagement party!"

"Here's the ring I bought her. It isn't much, but I got a good deal on it at the pawn shop in Rock Springs when I went to see the sheriff." Ed held out the small gold band with a very small diamond set in it for Mrs. Schmidt to take and look at.

"Oh Ed, it's so pretty. She'll love it. Look Emil." Marianne said as she slid the ring past the fingernail of her index finger and held it out for him to look at. Emil grunted and leaned forward in a half-hearted attempt to placate his wife.

Mrs. Schmidt looked at Ed. "You invite the people you want and we'll do the same. Now let's see what day the twelfth of June is." Turning to the large Currier and Ives calendar hanging on the wall she put her finger on Friday June the twelfth. "Since she usually gets here about 7:30-8:00 o'clock any way lets have every one here at 7:00 and make it a surprise birthday party."

Ed nodded, "sounds great."

The party turned out to be larger than Ed thought it would be. All the ranch hands, Jake, Doc Larsen, High Sheriff John Stone, (Ed's parole officer) the Bernards from Cheyenne, and a few close neighbors that knew Ed made the gathering about twenty-five people. It was extremely unusual for a ranch owner to treat a hired hand like Ed was being treated. Midway through the party Emil clanged on a glass with a spoon for attention.

"Folks, I'd like to say a few words." He said as he put the glass and spoon aside. "All of you know Ed and most of you know Alice. Marianne and I threw this party for the express purpose of taking care of our own. Ed came here after making some bad choices and having some bad experiences. I'm sure we can all relate to that, as we all know that's what life is about, choices. As you also know it's not the choices you make, it's how you handle the consequences good or bad. You all know the tough times Ed here has been through since he came to this part of the country. I figured this would be a good way to welcome him into the community and let him know that he has friends that will stand by him."

Some of the neighboring ranchers looked at each other not quite understanding what was going on.

Emil continued, "Sorry if I got on my soap box. The reason we're here is to celebrate Alice's twentieth birthday. Marianne and I have come to know and love her almost like a daughter." Emil smiled and acknowledged the Bernards with a look in their direction. They returned it with a nod of approval. "But, enough of my ramblings. Now it's time for her to open her presents." Alice opened her mouth in awe as Marianne and Jake carried out a huge pile of wrapped presents and placed them on the table they had removed the food from as Emil was speaking.

Alice wiped a tear from her cheek and said a loud "Thank you everyone." When all were opened she looked at Ed with a questioning look because she hadn't received anything from him. Ed walked to where she was standing.

"Alice, you and everyone here has stood by me through tough times. I want to thank everyone here for believing in me, but I want you to marry me," he said holding out the open box containing the sparkling engagement ring, "will you?"

Alice's eyes and mouth popped open as she drew in a quick breath. Shakily she took the ring and put it on her finger, threw her arms around Ed and tearfully said "yes, oh yes, I will" to the applause of everyone present. Alice and Ed spent the rest of the evening receiving a lot of backslapping, hugging and congratulations. By the time the party broke up it was late. Alice and Ed drove in her car to a bluff that overlooked the ranch to be alone and enjoy each other's company. As soon as they parked the car they fell into each other's arms, gently kissing and whispering their vows to each other.

"Oh Ed, I love you," Alice softly said as she pressed into Ed's arms and kissed his neck. Ed buried his face into the soft, auburn hair that smelled like lilacs. "Sweetheart, I love you too." Ed's hands were exploring as were Alice's. This kindled the passion that was running through both of them like a forest fire. The kissing was slow and deliberate, the touching and stroking was easy and gentle. Ed unzipped the back of Alice's dress at the same time she undid his belt. Slowly his hands moved up her back to unfasten the bra strap. At the same time her fingers opened the buttons on his Levis. Ed could feel the tension in the bra relax as he unfastened it. They momentarily released their hold on each other to discard the cumbersome clothes. In the silvery glow of the moon each of them got their first look at the other. Alice had a soft glow about her that enhanced the creamy color of her skin. The gentle curve of her neck begged to be kissed and caressed. Her hair glowed in the moonlight as it fell over her soft straight shoulders and onto her chest. Her breasts hung invitingly, soft and supple, taking on a pointed pendulant shape now that they were free of the restrictive brassiere. The soft brown nipples appeared as brown rosettes, with a dark rose hip in the center. A round, indented belly button stood above the warm, flat stomach that led to the curly brown hair patch shaped like an arrowhead pointing to the dark recess between her hard, slim, and quivering thighs. Ed looked at her slowly and easily as she surveyed his strong well-muscled neck and shoulders. His skin was brown where it was exposed to the weather and white where it was constantly covered by clothing. Ed's upper body could have been a model for a weight lifting ad. His arms and chest were well muscled and a flat hard stomach was the background for a large, hard penis rising almost to his bellybutton, out of a brown curly mound of hair that produced two soft testicles about the size and shape of large eggs. His legs were like tree trunks, strong, sinewy and straight. Alice ran her fingertips gently down Ed's body from neck to crotch. When she came to his manhood she smiled and investigated every nook and cranny with those slow moving inquisitive fingertips.

Ed's hands were equally explorative. He gently moved his fingers over Alice's shoulders following the hair until it ended above her sweet expectant breasts. Slowly and softly he leaned over and nibbled on Alice's ear, remembering everything he'd learned in his encounter with Joyce. He could feel her quiver as his tongue played its way down her neck on the way to her shoulder as his fingertips gently stroked the underside of her breasts moving back and forth from her heavy breathing. All the while her hands were caressing and stroking Ed's ever growing genital area. As he moved from her shoulder down the side of her breast toward the nipple he could her feel wrap one hand above the other around his rock hard shaft. Reaching the nipple Ed used the tip of his tongue to play with the already swollen and hard jewel. Taking it between his teeth Alice shuddered and moaned as he gently closed his teeth on it and gave a small playful tug. He felt her hands tighten on his rigid shaft. Alice moaned as she slid herself into position on the seat. "Take me, Oh God, come into me. I need you, Please!!!"

She was sweating and undulating her pelvis. Ed could feel the warm wetness and smell the pleasant nutty Oder she was releasing as he prepared to insert himself in her. Softly laying the head of his large throbbing organ in the warm, moist slit he gently inserted the head of his penis into her throbbing opening. Alice gave a low moan as she raised her knees higher and spread her legs a little wider. Moving slowly Ed slid his eager staff in and out, going deeper with stroke. Alice was matching him thrust for thrust. Finally Ed was as deep as he could go. Alice was pumping hard, griping him with her heels in his back Ed started pumping hard, Alice kept screaming "More, more, harder, harder" Ed thrust as fast and hard as he could, Alice was screaming at the top of her lungs now. Ed couldn't hold it any longer and came with a long pent up flood of sperm. Alice gripped him harder with her legs and held him inside of her as she convulsed with spasms for almost ten minutes. The two of them lay quietly in each other's arms until the sweaty, hard breathing exhaustion wore off. Even though Ed's member was soft, part of it was still lodged inside of Alice. As he with drew the flood behind it was released and soaked the car seat.

"Looks like we're going to have something to remember this night with." Ed commented as he wiped up as much as he could with his t-shirt.

"Hopefully that's the only thing we'll have to remind us of this night!" Alice said through the big smile on her face.

Ed looked at his bride to be and laughed. "I guess we did get kind of carried away, if anything comes of it, so be it, it's not like we're already committed." leaning over he gently kissed her on the lips. "I know," she said as she kissed him, leading to extremely passionate kissing and sensitive foreplay. Ed kissed and worked his way to her willing breasts, Alice held them for Ed as he slowly licked and gently sucked on each one. Working his way down her belly she lay back and spread her legs as Ed's face entered the moist bush and descended into the soft pink slit it hid. Ed's tongue caressed the hot sensitive flesh inside the soft convulsing lips of her opening. Moaning Alice spread her legs as wide as she could in the confined area of the car, while Ed's probing tongue went deeper and deeper into its juicy folds. The tongue found the little lump and massaged it making it enlarge as it grew harder. Alice was sweating and groaning as she approached her orgasm. Finally it overtook her like an explosion, she screamed as she wrapped her legs around Ed's head, engulfing him as he continued to pleasure the spot with the tip of his tongue that was making her crazy, after the convolutions stopped and they regained some resemblance of composure. Alice pushed Ed backwards against the door and started kissing his belly. Working her way down to the pubic area she kissed and stroked his soft organ with the tip of her tongue until it rose to the occasion. Slowly she slid her lips onto the very tip of the enlarged head that was turning a dark red from the tightness being forced upon it. Gently she slid past the circumcision and then slowly with drew back to the tip where her tongue played with the opening. Slowly her lips wrapped around Ed's steel hard shaft as she sucked half of it into her wet, warm mouth. She held Ed in her mouth and sucked hard, Ed felt like she was inhaling his whole body. Relaxing her grip she dragged her juicy warm mouth back to the head of Ed's bulging penis, held it with her lips for a moment and then slid down as far as her throat would let her. When the head of his throbbing erection stopped at the back of her throat Ed couldn't hold it anymore and came hard. After about four or five ejaculations Alice choked, with drew and threw up on the floor of the car. Ed had come from himself and Alice's mouth all over his crotch. After she stopped spitting and gagging she looked sheepishly at Ed and said, "I'm sorry. That was the first time I ever did that and I didn't realize how it tasted. I felt like I was going to choke." Alice started to cry. Ed pulled her to him "It's ok, I appreciate what you did, but maybe it gets easier with time. If you're uncomfortable doing that, then you don't have to. Please don't feel bad, I love you and that's all that matters." Ed held her close and wiped away the tears.

It was almost time for everyone to roll out and start the day when Ed and Alice returned to the ranch. She was too embarrassed to go into the house at this hour in the morning so she dropped Ed off at the bunkhouse and drove back to Laramie.

"Tell the Schmidt's I'll be back this afternoon. I want to go home, clean up and do a few things."

Ed nodded and they kissed, "See you later, I love you." he got out of the car and quietly walked into the bunkhouse as the infamous alarm went off alerting everyone to the start of a new day.

Ed and Alice talked about their anticipated marriage from the time Alice got her ring until they finally decided to hold the wedding on the fifteenth of October, two weeks after Ed's parole ended. On the fourth of July Ed and Alice made their wedding announcement to the Bernard's. At first they were not thrilled, but by the end of the day they had accepted the inevitable. They made the same announcement to the Schmidt's after Alice returned Ed to the ranch and they were genuinely happy for the two lovebirds. Mrs. Schmidt fussed over them like a mother hen over new chicks. She wanted to hear their plans and the four of them spent the rest of the evening discussing the details of the wedding. The Bernard's insisted the wedding be held in Cheyenne because of the Catholic Church Alice grew up in and visiting friends and relatives. Ed agreed to give up the Lutheran religion and be baptized a Catholic, after the required religious instructions were completed so they could be married in the church. A wedding line with coffee and cake would be held in the church basement right after the wedding. The real reception was going to be held at the Schmidt's ranch the next day.

Emil and Marianne went all out. They reserved two floors of the Virginian hotel for Saturday and Sunday night of the wedding weekend. Arrangements were made with a bus service to transport anyone wanting to attend the reception to Medicine Bow and shuttle them back and forth to the ranch and finally back to Cheyenne late Sunday night. A side of beef would be roasted for two days over an open fire, a dance floor would be built and a band was hired besides the local musician's to entertain the quests. The better part of two counties, all the people from the wedding in Cheyenne and anyone else that dropped in were more than welcome. All the local women brought their favorite recipes and Mrs. Schmidt's kitchen would operate almost non-stop for a week prior to the event making the wedding cake and side dishes.

Alice found out in July that she was accepted into the school of nursing at the University of Wyoming starting with the fall semester. Because of their busy schedules Ed and Alice didn't see as much of each other the rest of the summer as they would have liked. Alice started nursing school at the end of August. Ed completed his religious instruction and baptism into the Catholic Church two weeks before the wedding. Ed and Alice rented a small house in Medicine Bow. Ed would work at the ranch and Alice would attend school in Laramie after they came back from their honeymoon.

The wedding day arrived and all the participants were decked out in the finest duds they had or could afford. Ed and the groomsmen (Ron, Mike, Jake, Buck and Don) were in tuxedos. Alice was stunning in her wedding dress as were the five bridesmaids who attended her. Ed was trying hard to restrain himself from laughing out loud at the ranch hands in their uncomfortable "city duds" as the hands called their clean, tailored, well pressed suits. They complained and tugged at the various places they thought ill fitting, until the bridesmaids showed up. Then they were transformed into the most pathetic, well-dressed, bunch of wanna be dapper Dans that ever walked the face of the earth. Watching these four grown men strut around in front of the ladies opposite them (Jake excluded, his wife was one of the bridesmaids) primping, pruning and generally looking ridiculous, was enough to make Ed, Jake, the Schmidt's and anyone who knew them break into fits of uncontrollable laughter. Even so, the wedding went off without a hitch. It turned out to be an hour and a half mass, because of the windy priest. When it was over the newly married couple walked out of the church into a hailstorm of rice and headed for the outside entrance door to the basement. Where the rest of the wedding party and parents were gathered inside to greet the guests. The Bernard's stood next to their daughter and the Schmidt's stood next to Ed. Due to the ill health of Ed's mother, his stepfather was unable to attend. Emil and Marianne were introducing Ed and Alice to the quests they knew like they would have a son or daughter of their own. After everyone had passed through the line Emil stepped forward.

"Ladies and gentleman, could I have your attention, Please!" the crowd fell silent and everyone turned to look in the direction of the speaker. "Maybe some of you missed the announcement in the wedding program, but my wife and I are throwing a reception party for the newlyweds at our ranch in Medicine Bow. All you can eat and drink. A live band, local entertainment and dancing until the last dog dies. We've arranged for the Sweetwater bus lines to transport free of charge anyone who wants to attend. A bus will arrive here in about two hours to transport anyone who wants to go to Medicine Bow tonight, and there'll be another one leaving from here tomorrow morning at eight o'clock. They'll return you to Cheyenne Sunday night and Monday morning. We've reserved two floors of the Virginian Hotel, so it won't cost anyone a dime. All you gotta do is show up!! The party starts as soon as we get back to the ranch. Bring friends if you want to, and don't worry about transportation from Medicine Bow to the ranch, the bus will take care of that too. That's all I got to say. Thank you!" A wild cheer went up from the crowd and the loud buzz of conversation returned to the room.

The reception party was the most elaborate thing in size and activity that Ed had ever seen. It took two large greyhound type busses to transport the people waiting at the church. That didn't account for the ones that drove their cars from Cheyenne. Ed guessed there must have been close to 250 people from Cheyenne alone. Then there were another 250 or so ranch people and residents of the general area from probably a hundred miles in any direction. It was not bad manners to attend a party without a personal invite in ranch country. Most of the time it was the only time you saw your neighbors or met new ones. Since parties involved a lot of dancing and drinking and were pretty far and few between, people would travel miles and bring the whole family even if they had to camp out. It was a rare opportunity to socialize in a land where your nearest neighbor might be ten or twenty miles away. It was quite a sight; rows of cars were parked in the pasture next to the house where the cattle had been fed. The men had removed about a thousand yards of fence so it would provide easy parking access. Tents were set up at one end of the parking area making the place look like a mining camp from years ago. The smell of beef being roasted on the open spit mixed with the sound of the music and people laughing and talking, created a mystifying atmosphere under a canopy of black velvet sky shot full of twinkling diamond like stars. People were everywhere; children were running and playing amongst the groups of adults. The wooden platform dance floor built between the barn and the house was crowded as long as there was music.

Ed and Alice got glimpses of each other now and then. Ed was trying real hard to stay sober. Every time he walked past someone they were shoving a bottle into his hand, so Ed would tip the bottle and pretend to take a swallow. Alice was always being dragged off into a group of women who would laugh and squeal like a bunch of teenage girls. Midway through the night the wedding dance was held. It took almost an hour for everyone to pay his or her dollar and dance with the newlyweds. Ed and Alice received almost two thousand dollars between the dance on Saturday night and Sunday afternoon. There was a mountain of presents, everything from home canned food to some real expensive furniture. Emil and Jim made the announcement of their present to the crowd on Saturday night. They took the floor as Alice opened her last gift.

Emil spoke first to get the crowds attention. "Ladies and gentlemen, can I have your attention please? Jim Bernard and I have an announcement to make. We are going together on a present for Ed and Alice. Since I've done most of the talking at this shindig, I'll let Jim tell you what it is." Emil looked at Jim Bernard standing next to him and stepped back. Jim cleared his throat, "Thank you Emil. We pooled our money because we thought we could do more with it. So we went ahead and bought a round trip cruise for two to Hawaii!!!"

Alice squealed loudly. Ed just stood looking at his father-in-law in shock. Finally he came to enough to walk over and shake the hands of his mentors thanking them as the crowd went wild.

CHAPTER #15

THE CRUISE LEFT San Francisco, California on October 30, 1950. The trip on the Union Pacific railroad took them through Salt Lake City, Utah to Promontory Point on the North end of the Great Salt Lake. This is where the Southern Pacific and the Northern Pacific railroads met to give the nation its first coast-to-coast rail service in 1869. In Salt Lake Ed and Alice had a four-hour layover so they decided to see a few of the sights. The Mormon temple towered above all the downtown buildings and was only four blocks away so they headed for it. A guided tour of the grounds and religious center was provided by some volunteers, after which they stopped at a restaurant on North Temple Street on their way back to the train station. The waitress was a friendly blonde who provided conversation as well as serving food. Her and Alice got into a lengthy discussion when she mentioned that she was working at the restaurant to pay her tuition while she attended St. Marks Catholic Nursing School in Salt Lake. Ed and Alice walked back to the depot and boarded the train to continue their trip.

The Sierra Nevada Mountains were spectacular with their snow-capped peaks surrounded by lofty vistas. The ride down the California side to Sacramento was the most scenic country the two of them had ever experienced. Arriving in Sacramento they were informed by the porter there was another layover, so Ed and Alice went sight seeing. Mid afternoon of the next day they pulled into the station in San Francisco, California. They still had three days to wait until the boat left for Hawaii, so they checked into a hotel overlooking the bay and spent the time looking around.

Hawaii was beautiful. Ed and Alice had never been in a tropical climate and this seemed like paradise on a stick, it was a perfect way to start their life together. They made love every night and played on the beach during the day. The time to leave this Garden of Eden came all to soon.

Back in Medicine Bow they settled into their small cottage and returned to their everyday lives. Ed went about the business of the ranch and Alice went back to her job at the hospital in Laramie and attended nursing school. They saw very little of each other except on weekends. The winter at the ranch was routine. Alice loved nursing school and it was the subject of most of her conversations. The hands returned for the spring work right on time. Ed was as glad to see them, as they were to see him. Evan Buck seemed to be more talkative now.

By now Alice was showing her mother hood quite well. The baby was due around the end of June. Alice had taken off work the beginning of April and completed her nursing school classes for the year in May. Mrs. Schmidt insisted Alice accompany Ed to the ranch every morning so she wouldn't be alone in case she needed help or the baby started to come. It also gave Ed more of a chance to see Alice during the long hours he spent at the ranch.

The baby came on July eleventh at about six pm. Alice started having labor pains the night before and Ed took her to the hospital in Laramie. Work on the ranch stopped for the day after the required chores were done and every last one of them showed up at the hospital along with Alice's parents and a couple of cousins visiting from Ohio. When the healthy baby girl was born that night the proud parents named her Olivia Benidt Spitzer. "We wanted to incorporate the Bernard's name, because they are the baby's natural grandparents, with the Schmidt's name, because they have been like family to me." Ed announced to the surprise and delight of Emil and Marianne.

Everyone fussed over mother and baby until the nurses asked the visitors to leave so the new family could rest. The nurses wheeled a folding bed into the room for Ed and the Schmidt's opened their house to the people from Cheyenne. Everyday the Schmidt's and the Bernard's showed up with flowers and baby gifts. On the weekend the ranch hands arrived bearing gifts. They had all pooled their money and bought one gift. It was a beautiful handmade oak wood crib, complete with bedding and blankets. They filed into the room like a bunch of packhorses. Each one loaded down with some part of the gift. Ron as usual was the spokesman for the group.

"The boys and I didn't know what to get ya, so we asked Mrs. Schmidt. Since we pooled our money she said you'd probably like something you couldn't afford right out of the gate. So we got you this crib for the baby, and we figured you'd probably need bedding and blankets to keep her warm with so we got them too.' Alice moved the baby to one side of her body.

She looked at these simple rough men and said "You set those packages down and get over here right now!" The men looked surprised but did what they were told. As each of the men approach her bed she reached up and pulled their head down so she could kiss them on the cheek and say "Thank you." When the men turned away their wasn't a dry eye amongst them as they picked up their packages and left the room.

Alice was in the hospital a week. Although she went home to the little cottage in medicine bow, Mrs. Schmidt would come every morning after breakfast and bring her and the baby to the ranch. Ed would take them home at night and they spent Sundays by themselves. The Schmidt's were named Godparents and treated the baby like one of their own. The ranch hands were fascinated by Olivia and watched over her and Alice like a bunch of mother hens. Anytime Alice and the baby appeared outside beyond the fenced yard of the ranch house one of the hands magically appeared and found important work to do in the near vicinity of mother and baby.

Alice still wanted to complete her nursing. Her goal was to become an LPN. She enrolled in the University of Wyoming at Laramie to take her second year of school. Mrs. Schmidt had agreed to watch Olivia on the days Alice had classes. The winter routine at the ranch was the same as it had been for years. Late in February Alice came home from her classes all excited with some news she had found out about concerning the graduate nursing program at the University of Utah in Salt Lake City.

'I could get a bachelor's degree and my nursing degree at the same time. Plus I could go for a Masters degree in hospital administration without having to leave the city." She said in an exhilarated voice as she talked to Ed about it.

"What would I do? I can't leave the ranch." Ed replied in an annoyed tone.

"Salt Lake is a big town. You could find a job there."

"What would I do? I don't know anything except ranching. We've got it good here. Why do you want to move?"

"It's called the future. Don't you want more than just a bunch of smelly old cows all your life? What about Olivia don't you think she deserves better than having a hired hand for a father. You'll never own this ranch or any other because we don't have the money or never will working here. Olivia needs to see the world, if not first hand, at least through the finer things that a city the size of Salt Lake can offer that Medicine Bow and Laramie can't. All I'm asking is that you think about it."

Although he knew this wouldn't be the end of it, Ed really wanted to get out of this conversation, so he mumbled, "Ok, I'll think about it."

Alice continued to bring the subject up and finally asked Ed if they could take a couple of days to go to Salt Lake and look around.

"I'll have to talk to Emil and see if I can get the time off before haying season starts." Ed told Alice in a move to pacify her. This happened on a day that Alice was in Laramie attending classes. Emil was out in the barn fixing some harness for the workhorses.

"Emil, I need to talk to you."

Emil looked up and nodded, "Sit down," as he motioned to wooden keg. "What's on your mind?"

"I've got a problem and I'm not sure what to do about it." Emil continued to work on the harness without looking up. "Alice wants to move to Salt Lake so she can finish her schooling. She loves you both but claims we don't have a future here and I don't know what to do or think." Ed sat quietly as Emil worked on the harness. Finally he looked up. "She's right you know. You stay here you'll be a hired hand all your life. How are you ever going to save enough money to have a place of your own on a hundred fifty a month and keep? Even with her earning an extra salary you would be an old man by the time you saved enough for a down payment on a place, and that's if the price of land doesn't go up, which it surely will. No, you need to think about your families future."

Ed nodded, "I guess your right. I really like it here, but maybe there is something better out there somewhere."

Emil put down the piece of harness he was working on, "look here Son, When you first came to this ranch I didn't figure you'd last more than a couple of weeks. You been through some pretty tough times since then. You proved yourself to be a man who could be trusted and is not a quitter. That says a lot in this part of the country. Now you're a man with responsibilities. You have a wonderful wife and daughter that depend on you. You need to put their best interest first and your own wants and needs second. If you don't they may not always be around. Do what you gotta do, and always remember your family is all you've got. When they plant you the only thing your taking with you is your name and the memories you leave behind with those who love you. Don't ever lose that."

Ed shook his head as he looked at Emil, "Thank you for the advice. I may need a couple of days off before hay season to go to Salt Lake and look around."

Emil nodded, "As soon as the hands show up take what time you need."

"Thanks Emil," Ed said as he rose to his feet, Emil nodded and went back to the harness he was working on.

The train ride to Salt Lake City was filled with mixed emotions for Ed. Alice was happy and excited but Ed was torn by wanting to stick to the things that were easy and familiar, versus stepping into the unknown and taking chances. After his talk with Emil he knew Alice was right about their future. It was hard to break the comfortable shell he'd built around himself, but now there were others to consider and he knew he had to try for something better. The hands had arrived at the ranch on the eighteenth of May. Alice and Ed boarded the train for Salt Lake City on the twenty fifth of May.

Salt Lake City, Utah was in Ed and Alice's eyes a large city. It had electrified busses, theaters, motion picture houses and a few barrooms. Not that much different from other cities, but there were two things that made it unique in comparison to other cities. One: The Mormons or LDS as they preferred to be called. Two: It was the only large, metropolitan cultural center for five hundred miles in any direction. As a result it had no competition for non-agricultural work, it was basically a closed society. Ed and Alice soon found out that LDS were hired before gentiles. Toward the end of their stay in the regimented community Ed, Alice and Olivia were riding a bus up the hill from downtown on their way to the University of Utah. Alice had an appointment with the Dean concerning her possible enrollment. Ed was talking to the bus driver, "I'm looking for a job but nobody seems to want to hire you if you aren't LDS."

"What religion are you?" The driver asked.

"I'm Catholic." Ed replied indifferently.

"We're always looking for people to drive bus. The hours are crumby but the pay is good and I don't think you being Catholic would bother them too much. The Catholics have a big Church here on South Temple just East of the LDS temple building. Besides Catholics were in this area long before the Mormons."

"No kidding?"

"Yea, you ought to go down and fill out an application."

"Where is the barn located?"

"It's called the 'City Lines' and it's located in Trolley Square, seventh east between fifth and sixth south. You can't miss it it's on the west side of seventh east and the brick bays for the trolley cars are what they're using to service the busses in."

"Maybe I'll check it out."

Ed and Olivia went into the dean's office with Alice. After the introductions and a few minutes of conversation Ed excused himself, took Olivia and went for a walk around the campus while Alice finished her business with the dean. Half an hour later Alice caught up with him and they sat and talked.

"The dean assured me I wouldn't have a problem getting accepted here."

"How much is it going to cost?"

"Since I would only have to do three years here, about fifteen hundred dollars."

"Five hundred a year, huh?"

"Yea, but we wouldn't have to pay it all up front. We could pay five hundred each year if we wanted to."

"What about your master's degree? How much is that going to cost?"

"The dean said not to worry about that now, it's at least three years down the road and things would probably be different by then."

"I'm sure," Ed said matter of factly. "On our way down the hill I want to get off at seventh east and go to a place called trolley square, the bus driver on the way up said they might be hiring bus drivers."

Alice's face lit up. "Good, here give me the baby, she needs to eat." Alice opened her blouse, attached Olivia to her breast and pulled a small blanket over the nursing infants head to block the early afternoon sun as they sat and talked.

Ed walked into the brick structure that housed the buses. It was a mixture of noise and diesel smoke.

"I want to apply for a job," a mechanic in dirt covered, greasy coveralls pointed Ed to an old, well used staircase standing against one of the dirt stained brick walls. "Up there," motioning with his hand as he spoke.

"Thanks," Ed turned and headed up to the offices that were closed off by a wood wall with huge glass windows from the smoky atmosphere created below. Walking into the room he was greeted by an older blonde woman with the bluest eyes he had ever seen.

"Can I help you?"

"Ah, yes. Are you hiring?"

"What are you looking for, administrative, driving or mechanic?"

"Whatever you have open."

"Do you have any office skills?"

"No ma'am, but I can drive or turn a wrench."

"We are always hiring drivers and mechanics. Here is an application. You can fill it out here or bring it back later."

Ed took the paper from the secretary and smiled. "I'll bring it back in the morning if that's alright."

"Sure, whatever works for you."

Ed turned to leave, "thanks I'll see you in the morning."

"Ok, have a nice day."

"I will," Ed replied as he bolted through the door.

Eight O'clock the next morning Ed walked into the transit office and presented the blonde secretary with his filled out application.

"Have a seat." As she pointed to a row of wooden folding chairs lined up against the wall. "I'll take this into Mr. Beasley right now."

Ed sat and looked out the big glass windows at the activity going on below. The wall did keep most of the noise and smell out but it was still detectable. After about forty-five minutes of waiting the phone rang on the secretary's desk. Hanging up the phone she looked at Ed, "Mr. Beasley will see you now, follow me."

They walked into a carpeted, room with matching wallpaper and a large mahogany desk. The man sitting behind it in the large leather swivel chair was about forty-five years old, balding, with a pasty complexion from to many years inside.

As they entered the room the man rose and extended his hand. The secretary introduced the men to each other as they shook hands and then she left the room.

"I've looked your application over and you've indicated you want to drive or work on the busses, is that correct?"

"Yes sir,"

"What brings you to Salt Lake all the way from,,, Medicine Bow, is it?"

Ed nodded, "Medicine Bow is about fifty miles west of Laramie on highway thirty. I work on a ranch there. My wife wants to go to the University of Utah and nursing school. I need a job to support her and my baby girl."

"Have you ever driven a bus before?"

"No sir, but I have driven the stock truck and a couple of thirty-five foot wagons that we use on the ranch."

"Do you have a drivers license?"

"I have a Wyoming drivers license."

"Let's see it."

Ed retrieved his billfold from his back pocket, took out the piece of paper and handed it to the man.

Looking at it briefly the manager handed it back and picked up the phone and spoke into it. "Jason, come up to my office. I've got someone here I want you to give a test ride." Hanging up he looked at Ed, "I'm going to have Jason give you a test ride. If you get past that we'll talk, if not maybe you'll need to look someplace else."

"If I don't pass the driving test is there a chance you would hire me as a mechanic?"

"We don't need any mechanics right now, but we could hold on to your application for six months or so."

Ed grimaced, "I see."

Jason knocked on the door and walked in. "Jason this is Ed. Familiarize him with a bus and then take him for a drive. I want to know how he does when you get back."

Jason nodded and looked at Ed. "You ready?"

Ed got out of his chair, "Yes sir."

"C'mon," the two men turned and left the managers office.

"So where ya from?" Jason asked as they walked down the stairs to the bus bays. Ed told him and explained why he was in Salt Lake City.

"These buses are pretty simple," Jason commented, "five speed transmission, hundred and eighty five horse engine, the only thing different from the stock truck your used to driving is the way you load your passengers. These walk in the front door and talk to you. On any given day that can be good or bad. If you don't like people you won't last long on this job."

Once inside the bus Jason explained the controls. "Just remember to keep your thumbs on top of the steering wheel. Otherwise you might get 'em broke if you hit a hole in the road. The steering is direct and the wheel will whip on you even though you've got hold of it. Those wheel spokes can really hurt."

They pulled out of the garage and went south on 700 east to 2100 south then west to State street north to 1300 south west to 1700 west (redwood rd.) north to north temple east to 300 west south to south temple east through the down town area to 700 east and south to the bus barn. Ed hadn't realized just how big Salt Lake actually was until now.

The two men walked upstairs and entered the managers office.

"Well, how'd he do?" The manager asked Jason.

"Fine, he can handle a bus ok, once he becomes familiar with the city he'll be alright."

"Thanks Jason," Jason nodded and left the room. The manager looked at Ed, "When can you go to work?"

"I have to go back to the ranch and settle some affairs. I would imagine I would be ready to go to work by the middle of August."

"I was hoping you could start sooner."

"Will it affect my getting hired?"

The manager looked at Ed for a minute while he rubbed his chin, I don't know. We're looking at about two months, you know. A lot can happen in that time. How do I know you'll still be interested in August?"

"Because my wife will be registered for classes at the University of Utah and we have to put $500.00 dollars up front in order to make that happen."

"Have you done that yet?"

"No, we didn't want to commit ourselves unless I had a job."

"Seems to me we have a bit of a quandary here. Somebody has to be the first one to go out on a limb."

Ed thought for a minute, "look I can't leave Mr. Schmidt short handed for haying season. I don't know what to tell you. I don't know what kind of a guarantee I could give you other than my word that I will be here the middle of August."

"I'm sorry but I'm a business man. We see a lot of people come and go here for whatever reason. Contact me the end of July and if I have an opening, you got it."

Ed felt his heart sink, "OK, I'll call you around the end of July." Getting up he turned to go as the manager stuck his hand out.

"Look, I hope there's no hard feelings. More than likely well have an opening, but I can't promise you anything that far down the road. It wouldn't be fair to you or me."

Ed pumped the man's hand and looked him in the eye. "I understand and thanks for your time and for being honest with me." Ed walked out of the bus terminal and went back to the hotel.

"That's what he told me," Ed said as told Alice what happened at the bus terminal.

"What do we do now?"

"I don't know. We've got enough money in the bank to pay your first years tuition, move here and rent a house for a couple of months. But not enough to keep going after that without a job."

"Do you think you can find a job before we run out of money?"

"I don't know. I think what we better do is put everything on hold until the end of July and then make our plans based on what we hear from the bus company. You don't have to pay your tuition until a couple of weeks after school starts and you are already enrolled in school in Wyoming."

Alice shook her head, 'why is this getting so difficult? I only want to go to school here because of the cultural advantages for Olivia and the fact that things are so much closer and convenient. We would get to see much more of each other and have so much more to do as a family."

"I'll tell you what," Ed said as he tenderly held her at arms length. "I'll call the bus place at the end of July. If they have something for me we'll move then. If they don't have anything for me, we'll come again next year and if I have to I'll spend all summer looking for a job. Can you live with that?"

Alice gave Ed a half-hearted smile, "I know your right, but I can't help but wish we could make it this year."

"We still might, you never know. But, if we don't, I just want you to know we'll do it for sure the next year."

"Thank you, sweetheart. I love you." Ed pulled Alice to close to him passionately; they embraced and fell on the bed.

The train pulled into the station at Medicine bow late in the afternoon on a warm rainy Saturday. Ed and Alice walked the five blocks to their house and collapsed on the sofa. They had used almost two weeks to go to Salt Lake City. Ed called the ranch to let them know they were back and talked to Emil about the trip for quite a while.

"Emil seems to think we did the right thing." Ed said to Alice after he hung up the phone.

"That's nice," patronizing him. Ed rolled his eyes and turned his attention to Olivia. Evidently Alice still had her own opinions about the excursion held inside her.

Time seemed to drag as Ed and Alice waited for the end of July to come. Finally on the 27th of July they couldn't stand it any longer and called the bus terminal in Salt Lake City at nine o'clock in the morning.

"Mr. Beasley please . . . yes, my name is Ed Spitzer. I talked to him about a job in June, he told me to call back the end of July and here I am. Sure, I'll wait."

After what seemed an eternity Ed's face lit up as the manager answered the phone. "Good day to you sir . . . We're fine . . . yes the weathers good here too. I was calling like you asked me to do about any job openings . . . You don't," Ed could hear Alice gasp as she turned away with her hands over her face. What about being a mechanic . . . Oh, I see . . . Don't you have anything? I'll sweep floors if I have too . . . Ok, well, thanks any way, I'll check back with you in the spring." Ed hung up the phone and went to find Alice. She was in the bedroom crying her eyes out. Ed sat on the bed and put his hand on her convulsing shoulder. "It'll be alright baby, we are snug and tight where we're at and in the spring we'll go back and I will find a job. It'll be alright, you'll see." Ed lay down next to her putting his arm over her to try and console her.

Five days later the phone rang at the ranch. Mrs. Schmidt gave Ed the message when he came in for supper that night.

"A Mr. Beasley from the Salt Lake City bus lines left a message that you should call him tonight." She handed Ed a slip of paper. "He said to call him anytime before ten p.m. here's the phone number he gave me."

Ed took the paper and excitedly glanced at the number. It wasn't the same one he had called earlier in the week, so he figured it must be the manager's home phone. It was eight o'clock; Ed gulped down his supper and raced home. With a surprised look on her face Alice jumped out of her chair as Ed burst through the door. Walking straight to the phone Ed jerked the piece of paper with the number on it out of his pocket and dialed the operator.

"Give me Salt Lake City, 262-5626, thank you." Putting his hand over the phone's mouthpiece Ed looked at Alice, "The bus company called the ranch. Mr. Beasley wants me to call him before ten tonight" Alice's face lit up as she covered her mouth with her hands.

"Hello Mr. Beasley, This is Ed Spitzer calling from Medicine Bow, Wyoming . . . Yes sir, I sure am . . . It'll take me about ten days to get my stuff together and two days to get there . . . Ok, I'll be there. Thank you so much . . . . I really appreciate you calling me . . . we'll see you then . . . goodbye." Ed put down the phone and turned to Alice. "I got the job," he shouted as Alice jumped into his arms and kissed him.

"What made him change his mind?" Alice asked as she put her feet back on the floor.

"He didn't change his mind. One of the drivers had a heart attack and I was next on the list to hire; besides I think he likes me. Anyway, we've got ten days to pack. What about the University of Utah and your nursing school, can you still get in?"

"I'll call them first thing in the morning and find out."

Breakfast at the ranch the next morning was a two edged sword. Ed was happy to break the news of his new direction in life, but sad at the thought of leaving the ranch and all it held dear for him. The Schmidt's had obviously guessed what was happening because of last nights phone call, but Jake and the rest of the hands were surprised when Ed made the announcement at the breakfast table.

"I have something I would like to say, while everybody is here." Ed spoke up as Mrs. Schmidt was serving the eggs. "Friday will be my last day here at the ranch." Everyone stopped what they were doing and looked at Ed. "I got a job in Salt Lake City, Utah, driving a city bus." Everyone was stone still and quiet, it was like the moment was frozen in time. Finally Ron broke the silence, "Well I'll be darned, our little buckaroo growed up." Then everybody chimed in with his or her comments and questions.

"Whoa, wait a minute," Ed said holding up his hands. "Alice and I made this decision for a couple of reasons. One: we wanted Olivia to have the educational opportunities that are available in Salt Lake. Alice has more opportunities to advance in her career, and I will be making $7.00 an hour plus benefits."

"What're you gonna do with all your money? Sounds like you're really gonna be rollin' in the dough." Don said sarcastically as he went back to eating.

Ed smiled as he acknowledged Don with a nod. "It'll be nice to have some extra money, that's for sure. But it's not going to replace what I've got here. Emil and I have talked about this a lot. I love all of you dearly and I don't want to leave, but I have more than myself to think about now. I'll never forget you or the things we've been through, but I guess it's time to move on."

"You better watch out for the Mormons, they'll have you growing horns and taking extra wives." Mike spouted off with a sad grin.

"What does Alice think about living amongst 'em and all their wives?" Ron said, trying to keep the momentum going.

"While we were in Salt Lake I didn't see anything like that," Ed said defensively.

Jake spoke up for the first time, "I don't know about extra wives and growing horns, but the Evans and a few other folks around here are Mormons and they don't seem so different. A little churchy maybe but they stick to themselves and don't bother nobody."

"I found them to be really clannish, while we were in Salt Lake." Ed interjected, "every time I applied for a job they asked me if I was LDS. That means Latter Day Saints, but they just say LDS. The minute I told them I was Catholic you could see 'em lose interest. The Mormon Church pretty much runs everything there. I don't know if we'll fit in or not."

Emil spoke up, "you'll do just fine. They're people just like anyone else. They have their own ways, but if you do your job and don't make fun of them you'll get along just fine."

"They do have a large Catholic Church there. Alice and I went to it while we were there. It's beautiful inside. I guess the Mormons helped to build it."

Mrs. Schmidt chimed in, "it sounds like the three of you will get along just fine. We will throw a going away party for you the day before you leave. I know you have a lot of packing and arrangements to take care of so I will watch Olivia any time you need me to."

Ed looked tenderly at the elderly woman, "thank you Mrs. Schmidt. Olivia is really going to miss you after we move."

"As we will her, but Salt Lake isn't that far. We'll see her from time to time."

The rest of breakfast was consumed with small talk about Ed and Alice's move. The week went fast, Ed and Alice found themselves packed and ready to go by the middle of the week just as they had planned. Emil loaned Ed the flat bed truck to haul the meager household items Ed and Alice had acquired. He was sending Mike to help unload and drive the truck back to the ranch. Ed had to check in on the following Friday so he could start work on Monday. The Schmidt's had thrown the going away party for Ed and his family on the Sunday before. It was every bit as elaborate as the wedding had been. The Bernard's and some relation came from Cheyenne and all the ranchers from miles around showed up with their families in tow to wish the departing youngsters well.

CHAPTER # 16

THE SMALL CONVOY arrived on the outskirts of Salt Lake a little before ten. Ed didn't know where a hotel was so the found a dark field and slept in the vehicles. Morning came clear and warm. After breakfast Ed drove to the bus barn and filled out the necessary paperwork, received his uniform and patches and found out what time to report to work Monday morning. The whole process took about four hours by one o'clock in the afternoon he was ready to start house hunting. Mr. Beasley had given Ed the name and phone number of his ward bishop. "Tell him I told you to call. He will help you find a house." Ed wasn't real sure he wanted to get involved with the Mormons right out of the gate, so they bought a copy of the Desert News and went house hunting. By six o'clock that night they still didn't have a house. The houses they had looked at were either in bad shape, to small, to expensive or refused to rent because Ed and Alice were not LDS. Ed had never run up against segregation directed at him before and he was starting to have a hard time dealing with it.

"I can't believe this place!" Ed raged at Alice and Mike. "These damn Mormons are a bunch of bigots. I can't believe this is happening, it's nineteen fifty-two and they're so damn prejudiced we can't even rent a house from them."

"I can't believe they're all that way, maybe you ought to try the man Mr. Beasley suggested," Alice replied as she winced under the black stare Ed directed toward her.

"My God, Alice, the man's a priest or bishop or something in the Mormon Church. Do you really think he'll help us?"

'Your boss seemed to think he would. Otherwise I don't think he would have recommended you to him." Alice's logic upset Ed immensely. He reached in his pocket and pulled out the piece of paper with the Mormon Bishops name and number on it. Thrusting it into her hand he snapped, "here then, if you have so much faith in these religious bastards you call him."

Alice opened the crumpled piece of paper and dialed the payphone. "Hello, Mr. Carlson, my name is Alice Spitzer. Mr. Cory Beasley the manager of the Salt Lake City Bus Lines on 700 East hired my husband Ed to drive for them. We are new to Salt Lake and he said you might be able to help us find a house to rent . . . . No, we're Catholic." Ed rolled his eyes and shook his head as he turned away. "We've tried the paper and couldn't find anything suitable. The ones that were the owners wouldn't rent to us because we weren't Mormon . . . . We are at a gas station on State Street and 2100 South . . . . Yes . . . Ok, I'll call you back in about an hour . . . No, we thought we would get a room somewhere . . . . Ok, I'll call back in about an hour, thank you." Alice hung up the phone and walked over to where Ed and Mike were standing. "Mr. Carlson said I should call back in an hour. He wants to call some people he knows that have houses for rent. "

Ed looked at Mike, "One thing we do have to do is find a place to stay tonight. I need a bath and a bed to sleep in. That truck doesn't appeal to me two nights in a row. I'm gonna go inside and see if they know someplace close that we can stay." Ed came out with a hangdog look. "There are three motels just up the street. If they're full we'll probably have to go downtown. Let's leave the big truck here with Alice and the baby and go see."

"Sounds good to me." Mike responded.

All three motels were full as were the hotels downtown because of a large convention being held at the Salt Palace on West Temple Street. It was after nine o'clock when Ed and Mike pulled the loaded pickup truck into the brightly lit entrance to the gas station they had started from. Alice was talking to a man dressed in a suit and tie. When she saw them she ran over to the pickup truck as Ed rolled down the window and pulled to a stop.

She was excited and bouncing up and down on the balls of her feet. "Oh Ed, we've got a place to stay!" The man in the suit walked up to the truck. "This is Mr. Carlson. He wants us to stay at his house for the night. He thinks he has found us a place to rent."

Ed stuck his hand out the window and shook the man's hand. "Mr. Carlson, I'm Ed Spitzer and this is Mike . . . Ed suddenly realized that he didn't know Mike's last name as the well dressed man shoved his hand past Ed from the open window. "Mike," Mr. Carlson responded as he pumped the big man's hand.

Returning his gaze to Ed, "Your wife said you didn't have a place to stay the night. My children have all grown and left our house to live their lives, so we have an empty basement full of rooms. My wife and I would like to put you up until you find a place. I have made some calls and I think we should be able to find you a place in the next day or so."

Ed looked the man over trying to figure out a motive for his kindness. "I don't get it. The minute a Mormon finds out we aren't one of them, they won't have anything to do with us and here you are wanting to put us up for the night, you claim you can help us find a house to rent and you don't even know us. Why are you doing this?"

"We're not all bad. Our religion tells us to be kind and help our neighbors. Some of us practice what we preach, some of us don't. Don't you have that in your religion also?"

Ed bit his lip, "Yeah, I guess you're right."

"Now, if you'll follow me, I have that black' 49 ford convertible over there."

It wasn't far to the Carlson house. They lived on 500 East and 1700 South the third house south of the intersection. It was a brown brick with green wood trim. An open field across the street sported its collection of grasses and weeds dried brown by the hot summer sun. It was a vivid contrast to the lush, green, irrigated lawns surrounding it. The houses up and down the block were all a neatly kept mixture of wood siding and brick. The street was lined with trees, planted between the curb and the sidewalk years ago.

Emily Carlson was a small, once blonde, silver haired woman. She had not aged gracefully. Whether it was bearing twelve children, age, or a combination of both it was hard to tell. What she lacked in looks she made up for in manners. Soft spoken, extremely efficient, gentle and gracious, it almost seemed like an act as she fussed over the three immigrants entering her home. "You folks give Gaylord your wraps and I'll show you your rooms." Ed and Mike took off their Levi Jackets and handed them to Mr. Carlson. Looking at her husband Mrs. Carlson said, "Sweetie, would you get some blankets from the closet and bring them downstairs?" Gaylord smiled at his wife and nodded, "be happy to my dear." The trio followed the lady of the house down a narrow wooden staircase. "Mr.?, "the ageing woman looked up at Mike questioningly.

"Mike, ma'am, everybody calls me Mike."

"Ok Mike, you can bunk in here," she said as she swung the door open exposing a small room with a carpet a double bed and a cherry wood dresser.

"Thank you ma'am." He said as he stepped through the doorway into the room.

"You're welcome Mike, the bathroom is at the end of the hall, breakfast is at seven. Have a good nights sleep."

"Yes ma'am, and he stepped back and shut the brown stained door.

Emily led Ed, Alice and Olivia down the hall to a larger room with a huge four-poster bed in it.

"One of my sons and his wife stayed here when they lived with us." She said wistfully. "It's big enough to hold all three of you," nodding at the bed and answering Ed's question before he could vocalize it. Stepping into the room with his family, Ed thanked the woman and shut the door.

Breathing a sigh of relief, Ed turned to the large bed and vaulted through the air bouncing as he landed. "Man this feels good!" All of a sudden Alice and Olivia followed, snuggling into the plush comforter alongside Ed.

Mike's knock on the door woke the three of them with a start. "Ed, it's six o'clock. I'm done in the bathroom it's all yours." Ed and Alice sat upright with a start. "Good God we must have passed out last night!" Ed said as he looked at the three of them still in yesterday's clothes. "Thanks Mike, we'll see you at breakfast in a little bit." Ed slapped Alice on the butt and bounced off the bed. "C'mon you lazy woman lets go get naked and shower." He ducked as she half-heartedly threw a shoe at him. "In your dreams. Be careful what you say in front of the baby. She's old enough to start understanding words you know."

Ed over exaggerated a devilish grin, "My darling I just wanted to run your milk laden breasts through my hot little fingers, surround your swollen nipples with my hot lips and enjoy the nectar of your body."

Alice took off her other shoe and heaved it at Ed with a vengeance. "Oh, you dirty old, no; young man. Wanting to take food from a baby. You can run your skinny cold fingers over the knot I'm gonna put on your head if you don't go take your shower. Preferably a cold one." She caught hold of his arm and playfully twisted it behind his back. "Go, before I have to hurt you," she said from behind him as she blew in his ear while she pushed him out through the open door into the hallway.

"Vixen, see how, you are? Lead a man on and then destroy him with only a word." Laughing as he let Alice push him gently into the hall.

"Oh, go clean up you poor deprived thing."

Ed put on his most painful look as Alice let him go and swept through the door. He could hear her cooing to the baby "Your father is a funny man, when he comes back he'll gitch ya, gitch ya, gitch ya."

Ed smiled as he heard Olivia give a loud shrieking laugh at having her belly tickled.

Breakfast was good and plentiful. "Emily and I would really appreciate it if you folks would accompany us to church this morning. It would give you a chance for the community to meet you. People that have homes for rent will be there and I can introduce you to them."

Ed thought about it for a minute, but only a minute. He knew exactly what the Carlson's were doing. "Sure we'd love to go." He gave Mike a stern look, as the man was about to speak. "But, we don't have a suit for Mike here."

The Carlson's gave the big man a perplexed look. "That's ok he can wear what he has."

After breakfast the three of them went downstairs. "I want you and Olivia to put on the best we got. I've got a hunch that old bird upstairs thinks he stands a good chance of converting us if he can get us around his Mormon buddies. Well, we'll let him believe anything he wants if it will get us a house. We'll play these Mormons for all they're worth. We aren't gonna join 'em, but we won't let them know that. We're gonna dress to the nines and put on our best front. Tell me what clothes you and Olivia want out of the truck."

The Church service was strange. There was none by Catholic standards. The only thing that was even vaguely familiar was the passing of the host and a little singing. Two and a half hours were used up talking and sending missionaries off to some god-forsaken places around the world. The other thing that was strange was the women sat separate from the men. After an hour or more in the pews the meeting broke for a few minutes while the children were sent off to various classes. Then it continued while one speaker after another droned on in monotonous dialog. It finally ended with great relief to the three non-Mormons. Almost everyone that came to shake their hand asked the same questions. What did you think of the service? Are you taking instructions? What ward do you live in? This is where the Carlson's standing at Ed and Alice's elbow would intervene with selected people and ask them about rentals they may or may not have available. After exhausting quite a few possibilities a man by the name of Levi Halgevson presented himself to the trio. In a heavy Swedish accent he introduced himself and greeted Gaylord Carlson. "Gut morning my name is Levi Halgevson and dis is my vife Lena." Ed, Alice and Mike acknowledged the couple. "Gut morning Gaylord, nice to see you, how is da misses?"

"She's just fine Levi, she should be along from her primary class shortly. Say Levi, don't you have a house over on ninth east?"

"Ya, it's a rental but it is empty now." Ed tensed and stared at the tall Swedish man.

Gaylord continued, "These people need a place to rent. They're staying at my place until they find something."

Levi turned to Ed, "Where you from?"

"Wyoming, I got a job with the city bus lines here in Salt Lake. My wife will be studying at the University of Utah and going to nursing school, we need a place to live."

"Is dis yust for you two and da baby?"

"Yeah, Mike here came along to help me move and drive the truck back to the ranch."

Levi smiled at Mike. "It's not far, if you vant ve can go look at it right now."

Ed nodded eagerly; "sure," he looked at Mr. Carlson.

"You go on, I have some things to do here. If you need me I'll either be here or at home. Either way let me know what happens."

"You got it." Ed turned his attention back to Mr. Halgevson, "Our pickup is around the corner. You can't miss it; it's the one with all the stuff on it. We'll follow you."

"I have a blue Pontiac station wagon. I vill drive around and find you."

Ed nodded and they all headed for their respective vehicles.

The house was located on nine hundred east and fourteen sixty-two south. It was an older brick with a nice fenced in backyard, an alley garage and flowerbeds in the front. There were three bedrooms, a finished basement, and bathrooms upstairs and down. The living room was wallpapered in floral velveteen with hardwood floors and a fireplace. The kitchen had oak counters, refrigerator, electric range, and porcelain sink. The house was old and well worn, but built good.

"How much do you want for rent?" Ed asked after they had seen everything.

"Oh, I been getting three hundred dollars a month. You pay da utilities."

"That's a little more than I had planned on. I'll have to talk to my wife and see if we can afford it."

"I tell you vhat, two seventy five if you take it now. It has been sitting empty for a couple of months. I need to rent it before vinter comes."

"Wait a minute." Ed said and took Alice outside. "I think we can do this honey. We have enough in the bank to pay the first two months rent and your tuition. What do you think?"

Alice was smiling "I like it. Will you make enough to pay the rent and the bills?"

"I am making seven ten an hour and Mr. Beasley assured me there would be overtime if I wanted it."

"Let's take it."

Ed walked into the house with Alice. "Mr. Halgevson, we'll take the house."

The tall man smiled, "I hoped you vould, and da name is Levi."

Ed stepped aside as Alice came up with the money. "Here is the first months rent."

"Tank you, you vill be able to go downtown and get da utilities turned on tomorrow."

"When can we move in?"

"Right now if you vant."

Ed started out the door, "Mike let's get this pickup unloaded." They worked until midnight unloading the pickup and the big truck into the house and garage. The Carlson's insisted that they spend the night at their house so Ed could get s shower and a goodnights sleep before going to work in the morning.

Ed's first day at work consisted of learning the schedules, doing paperwork and riding with a bus operator. The rest of the week was spent driving different operators routes while they rode along and coached him. The following week Ed received short "trippers" to run by himself. It turned out to be a good job and Ed spent his nights pouring over city maps while Alice did homework and tended the baby. Days ran together as the two of them put they're nose to the grindstone and started to build their future. One night while they were eating out in a popular little café called "Ted and Nilas" located near their house, Alice said; "I went to the campus clinic to day."

Ed gave her a concerned look, "are you ok?"

"Oh yes, I'm pregnant."

Ed's fork dropped out of his hand onto the table. "You're what?"

"I'm pregnant, silly. You remember how that works don't you? We make love, screw like bunnies and valla, Olivia pops out."

Ed looked at the people sitting around them. Hunching over the table he whispered, "Don't use that kind of language in front of the baby."

Alice rolled her eyes, "Oh give me a break. I've heard you swear like a sailor before."

"But not in front of Olivia or in public."

"Whatever, anyway the doctor said I was about six weeks along."

Ed reached across the table, "I love you sweetheart, and that's great news. We need to celebrate. How about we stop and get a bottle of wine on the way home?" After their meal was over and they paid the bill, Ed turned to the people seated eating their meal; "Hey everybody, my wife is going to have a baby!" Some laughed, some clapped as Ed, Alice and Olivia walked out the door into the night.

Ed and Alice's relationship with their landlords became warm and friendly. The Halgevson's loved Olivia and were always stopping to see her. They would come to the house for supper and spend hours playing with the baby and talking to Ed and Alice about the history of the area, religion, politics, anything that came up. The couples became good friends and saw each other often. Once Levi and Lena found out Alice was pregnant they fussed and doted on her like she was their own daughter. Alice's parents made reservations at the Little America Hotel in downtown Salt Lake to be with Ed and Alice over the Christmas holidays. Emil and Marianne showed up for Thanksgiving and took the five of them to a very large and swanky buffet at Little America in Salt Lake. They spent a week and went back to the ranch in Medicine Bow.

By the beginning of December, Ed was comfortable with his job and received his first raise. Alice was starting to show her condition. Olivia was walking and making talking noises. The Halgevson's baby-sat her whenever they were needed.

The holidays came and went. It was the best time of Ed's life. He had friends and family around him even his stepfather showed up for a couple of days between Christmas and New Years. Ed's world was better than he ever imagined in his wildest dreams. The only thing that would have made it better was if his bed ridden Mother could have made the trip also. That was one of the reasons his stepfather showed up. He informed Ed that his Mother probably wouldn't last much longer and she wanted to see Ed and his new family before she died. Ed agreed to make the trip in the spring. Sooner if need be.

The winter of 1953 was a typical Utah winter. The snow came shortly after the first of the year. It stayed cold enough to keep it from melting in the shady spots. The Wasatch Mountains and the okhirr mountains had been covered for a couple of months. The three and a half members of the Spitzer family spent a lot of time in front of the wood-burning fireplace when they were together. Ed and Alice often made love on a big soft quilt in front of its warm, soft glow, after Olivia had been put down for the night.

After a particularly passionate and tender session one evening in late January; Ed handed Alice a small covered box, as they lay naked, recovering from the intense bout of lovemaking.

"Sweetheart, I want you to have this."

Alice sat up legs crossed and took the little black box. "What is this?" she said naively.

"I couldn't afford to get you a real nice ring when we were married. Now I can. Open it and understand that I love you more than life itself."

Alice popped the ring box open and gasped. "Oh my God. What did you do?" The diamonds sparkled like stars in the dim firelight.

"I love you and you should have had something that nice on your wedding day."

Alice set the ring box on the floor and put her arms around Ed's neck. "You are something else. Thank you," as she kissed him and pushed him down on the blanket. After a lengthy and even more passionate session of lovemaking, they talked late into the night, renewing their vows and commitment to one another.

Ed couldn't understand why Alice was so late. It was six o'clock; normally she got home about four if she didn't have to pick up Olivia. Ed had worked an early shift so they agreed last night he would pick Olivia up when he got off work. "She's probably late because of the snow." Ed thought to himself. The snow started late last night and it was still coming down. Not as hard as earlier but a few flakes were still falling lazily from the sky onto the six inches of white powder already on the ground. Ed finished putting the left over stew from last night on the stove to heat and dressed Olivia in a snowsuit, wrapped her with a blanket then he carried her in a basket and set her on the porch. Ed wanted to build a snowman and surprise Alice when she came home. He was putting the round snowball for his head on top of the other two larger snowballs, when a Salt Lake County Sheriffs car pulled up next to the curb. Two uniformed officers got out and walked over to where Ed and Olivia were standing.

The older of the two men spoke as they stopped next to the uncompleted snowman. "Mr. Spitzer?"

Ed had a chill run up and down his spine as he answered. "Yes, I'm Ed Spitzer."

"Is your wife named Alice and does she go to the University of Utah?"

Ed replied anxiously, "Yes, is there something wrong?"

The older man looked up from the ground his face contorted, "I'm afraid there is. She was in a car accident up by the University."

Ed took a step forward, "is she ok?"

The man clenched his fists by his side as he said, "I'm sorry, but she was killed in the accident."

Ed went stone silent and turned as white as the snow around him. Everybody stood as if they were frozen in time. After what seemed like an eternity Ed fell to his knees and screamed, "OH GOD!!! NO PLEASE, NO!!! Ed was doubled over rocking back and forth on his knees screaming and yelling at the top of his lungs. Olivia started to cry, she was too young to understand what the man with the gun on his hip was saying. She was scared because of the way her father was acting. The younger sheriff walked over and picked her up, speaking to her in a soft soothing voice. The older sheriff was bent over Ed with his hand gently resting on Ed's back as he tried to comfort him. He finally got Ed to quite down and helped him to his feet. "Mr. Spitzer is there anyone we can call that can come and be with you?" It was a good hour before Ed collected his thoughts enough to tell them to call the Helgevson's. While they were waiting for them to arrive Ed asked what happened and where Alice's body was being kept.

The older man spoke up; "she was riding with another student. The approach to the intersection was a sheet of ice under the snow. They tried to stop and couldn't. They slid into the intersection and were hit by oncoming traffic. The car hit the right front door next to your wife. We're pretty sure she was killed instantly. She was pronounced dead on the scene when the ambulance arrived."

"What about the baby?"

"Your wife was pregnant?"

"Yeah, she was about six months along.'

"Damn," the man mumbled to himself under his breath. "I'm afraid there's no way the baby could have survived."

Ed could feel himself choking up again. The man leaned forward and put his hand on Ed's shoulder.

The Helgevson's arrived in a cloud of snow as Levi slid the car to a stop in front of the house. They barged in the door and Levi wrapped his long arms around Ed like a father would his son. Lena went immediately to Olivia who's cries had turned to sobs and took her from the willing deputies arms.

"My Got, Ed I am so sorry. Lena and I vill do vhat ever needs doing. Vhat needs to be done? Have you made any phone calls?" Ed shook his head no. "Ve vill help you vit dat later on."

The deputy looked at Ed, Mr. Spitzer, I know your having a hard time with this right now, but I really need you to accompany us to the morgue so you can make a positive identification of your wife. We'll take you in our car and bring you home afterwards."

Ed nodded. Levi spoke up, "I vill go vit you. You vill need someone to help you be strong, ya?"

Ed looked at the kind old mans concerned face, "thanks Levi, I would appreciate that."

Ed broke down when he saw how bad Alice's head was damaged. The coroner said the impact from the car that hit them caused her to hit the door with the side of her body hard enough to break bones. A rib bone had pierced the baby's skull killing the little boy instantly. Alice's head hit the glass window breaking all the bones on the right side of her face and splitting her skull open enough to make her brain visible. Ed looked at her battered, black and blue face, remembering how beautiful she had been and started to break down. He leaned over to kiss her one last time as the teardrops ran down his cheeks and fell onto her cold, lifeless lips. One soft kiss and a whispered "I love you, "was all Ed could manage as his composure buckled and he slumped sobbing against the cold metal drawer holding the remains of his child's mother.

Levi reached down and grabbed Ed's convulsing shoulders. "You must go now "as he gently helped Ed to his feet and turned him toward the door.

The coroner held the door open that separated his office from the morgue as Levi guided Ed through it. "I'm sorry to bother you at this time sir, but we have a paper you must sign, verifying that the body you viewed was your wife. I have it completed and on my desk. It will only take a minute on your way out."

The silence was deafening as they rode home in the sheriff's car. Lena had Olivia calmed down by the time they arrived at the house. Ed was numb and didn't want to talk. Levi made him produce the telephone numbers for work, Alice's parents, the Schmidt's, and Ed's parents in Wisconsin. It took Levi an hour to get all the calls made, but once it was done he went out to his car and brought back a bottle of whiskey. Pouring the fiery liquid into a glass he said, "You drink dis. It vill make you feel better by golly.' Ed looked at the glass containing the amber liquid. In one motion he snatched it and poured the whole thing down his throat in one swallow. Levi filled it again and Ed repeated the maneuver. By the fourth glass he started to get woozy and the flood gates of his emotions opened wide. It took three hours of crying and moaning before he finally passed out.

Ed could hear people talking far away. Everything was foggy and his head hurt like hell. The smell of food cooking was making him sick. Realization of the tragic events that recently transpired came as he groaned and rolled over on the couch. Awake but not wanting to be Ed swung his feet to the floor and sat up.

"You are avake?" Levi said as Ed sat on the couch shaking uncontrollably.

"Yeah, unfortunately." Ed replied.

"I know you are in pain now, and you should be. But you need to think about the baby? Olifia vill need you more than ever. Her mother is gone and she doesn't know vhy or vhere. You're crying and mopping is scaring her. You need to be strong for her. She is too young to understand death. So you must give her some of your strength."

Ed shook his head in agreement. "I understand Levi, but it's hard right now."

"Dat may be. Don't you think it's yust as hard on her for her mother to suddenly disappear for no goot reason?"

Ed hung his head knowing Levi was right.

"Vhat happened vas tragic, but don't sit around feeling sorry for yourself vhen der is someone who depends on you totally."

Ed looked up at the concerned Swede, "I know you're trying to help me Levi, but I am having a hard time pulling through this."

"Dat may be, but you have to for Olifia's sake."

Ed nodded, "I know, maybe if I get up and eat something it will help."

"Ya, you betcha."

Ed stood up and shuffled toward the kitchen while he fought back the urge to throw up. Olivia was sitting on a blanket that Lena had placed on the hardwood floor, playing with some wooden spoons and a bowl while Lena cooked food at the kitchen stove. Olivia looked up at him walking into the room and Ed almost broke into tears. Reaching down and scooping her into his arms helped him control his unpredictable emotions as he hugged her tightly to his chest. "I love you sweetheart," he whispered in a soft gravely voice.

The day got easier for Ed as it wore on. Levi and Lena stayed the night providing cooked food and gentle conversation. The following day the morgue called and inquired about funeral arrangements. Ed hadn't even though about that scenario, let alone make arrangements. With Levi's help he contacted a local mortuary and secured a burial plot in city cemetery over looking the valley. The funeral was scheduled for the following Tuesday. It was only Friday so Ed had time to pick out a casket, flowers and notify everyone concerned.

CHAPTER #17

THE FUNERAL WAS modest but tasteful. Ed didn't have a lot of money to spend, but there was enough to buy Alice a silk lined, cherry wood coffin with gold attachments. Levi, Emil, Jake, Alice's father Jim and two of Alice's college friends were the pallbearer's. The viewing lasted for three hours Monday night. Tuesday morning at eleven o'clock the eulogy took place followed by the graveside service. Jim and Tracy Bernard arrived Friday afternoon about four o'clock with half a dozen relatives in tow. The Schmidt's arrived with Jake, his wife and family a couple of hours later. Ed's boss and some of his co-workers attended, a good-sized group from the college, including her professors, her teachers and classmates from St. Marks School of nursing, members of the parish church, a few neighbors and people from Levi's Mormon church. Once the Priest consecrated the grave and coffin, the family and closest friends publicly said their goodbyes. Ed whispered a final goodbye and laid a yellow rose on the coffin as Olivia whimpered in her grandmother's arms.

The night after the funeral Ed and the Bernard's were engaged in a discussion about how Ed and Alice first met. Ed was commenting on what Alice had told him about her childhood memories of Cincinnati, Ohio.

"Alice used to talk a lot about your house and the landscape around it. It must have been really pretty."

"Oh, yes it was," Tracy Bernard, said wistfully, "there are times I wish I could go back there. It seems so far away and such a long time ago."

Jim spoke up, "I think at times we would all like to be able to go back to some time in our life that we have fond memories about."

Ed nodded, thinking about changes he would have made if he could have seen the future. "By the way, could you give me some specific information on Alice? I want to write down everything I can so when Olivia is old enough to understand I'll be able to tell her who her mother was and where she came from."

An ominous silence fell on the conversation as Jim and Tracy Bernard looked at each other horror stricken. It was as if their worst nightmare suddenly became a reality. Ashen-faced Jim looked at Ed, "what do you want to know?"

Ed could feel the tension in his voice and the little voice in the back of his mind said, "beware!!! All I wanted was the name of the hospital she was born at, maybe the time of day she was born, things like that."

Once again the Bernard's looked at each other in stony silence. Finally Jim kind of slumped at the shoulders and said to his wife, "I think we better tell him for Olivia's sake or before he finds out on his own."

Tracy Bernard looked at her husband, "are you sure?"

Jim replied, "Yes, he has a right to know."

By now Ed's curiosity was more than peaked. "What do you mean right to know? What's wrong?"

Jim held up his hand for silence as he started to speak. "Alice was adopted!"

"WHAT!!!"

Jim held up his hand again. "Sit down and we'll tell you the whole story." The Bernard's smiled as they joined hands and looked at each other with obvious relief. "Tracy and I were married in 1922 shortly after I landed a job with Pratt and Whitney. We tried for seven years to have children but it never happened. So, we decided to adopt. That was easier said than done." He shook his head and gave a wry little smile as if recalling something unpleasant that had mellowed with the passage of time. "We visited a lot of adoption agencies in two states that year. We saw a lot of babies that were possibilities, but we wanted to know the background of the parents. Most of the babies that interested us came from rape victims, alcoholics, criminals, and so forth. What we wanted was a baby from a good stable family. As you probably know, in 1929 the great depression hit. We stopped in a small town in southwestern Pennsylvania, Latrobe to be exact, on our way to an agency in Pittsburgh. Our car had a flat tire and we were getting it repaired at the local Texaco station. I was talking to the mechanic about how we were on our way to an adoption agency in Pittsburgh when a middle-aged man interrupted us. He apologized for eavesdropping, but stated that he knew where we might find a baby to adopt from a private family. He wouldn't give me anything other than his name, address and phone number at the time, but he did say to call him in three or four days. Needless to say we didn't find anything in Pittsburgh, so we called Mr. Corbett in Pennsylvania." Ed straightened up from his slouching position with a start. Jim gave him a quizzical look but continued on. "He said that his wife was about two months pregnant. They were caught in the depression and lost everything. He had just secured a job but after discussing it with his wife, he didn't feel they could take on a new baby and raise it properly. They had thought of adopting, but only to a well to do private family. We met with them a number of times. At first we wanted to get to know them, later it was to work out the terms of the adoption contract. After the contract was finalized and the child was born, the Corbett's kept her for almost two months so the mother could nurse the baby and give her a good start. We picked Alice up on the 1st of August and took her home to Cincinnati. The Corbett's agreed not to name her. Tracy and I decided on the name while we were waiting for her to be born. "Ed leaned forward from his sitting position on the couch and shook his head. "I know this came as a shock to you, but since you asked I think it was only fair that you knew."

"Your right it was a shock. I had no idea. Not that it would of made a difference, but Alice never said a word to me about it."

"That's because she never knew. It was part of the contract we made with the Corbett's that we never tell her she was adopted, or revel her first name to them."

This struck Ed as extremely odd. "You wouldn't happen to have a copy of that contract would you?"

"Yes, as a matter of fact we do. It was filed at the Westmoreland county court house in Pittsburgh, Pennsylvania two months before Alice was born.

"You said her real name was Corbett, what were her parents first names?"

"Robert and Juliet, but she preferred to be called Julia."

"Did she have any brothers or sisters?"

"There was an older brother, but I don't recall what his name was. Every time we showed he would disappear into the woods that surrounded the Corbett's farm."

"You don't have their address do you?"

"No according to the contract there was to be no communication between us, unless something happened that we couldn't keep Alice. The only place I know of that their address would be is on the contract we filed in Pittsburgh."

Ed was extremely curious to find out if Les was indeed the older brother, and how if he was, why he didn't recognize Alice as his sister when he tried to date her. Ed knew the Bernard's didn't know Les or they would have said so. Even though they didn't come to the trial they more than likely read about it in the paper. "Did Alice have any boyfriends that she was really serious about before me?"

"She had boy friends since she was ten years old. She was never one to get tied down to anyone of them, until she met you."

"Did she ever have any boyfriends that she didn't bring home?"

"I don't know, if she did she didn't say anything to us about them. What are you trying to get at?"

Now Ed knew for sure the Bernard's didn't know anything about Les. Ed figured that Alice never was interested in him. He was probably fun to do things with, but nobody she wanted to get serious about. "Oh, nothing, I was just curious to know how much she confided in you."

"Do you know something we don't?"

"No, I'm trying to figure what motivated her, that's all."

Jim gave Ed a doubtful look and grunted softly to himself.

"Well, let's talk about Olivia," Ed said in an effort to change the conversation. It worked! The three of them spent the rest of the night discussing Olivia's future.

"That's everything I know about her." Ed had related the conversation to Levi and Lena a couple of days later after all the relatives and company left. He asked Levi if he knew how Ed could find out about someone's past.

The elderly Swede replied eagerly, "you betcha, ve haff a genealogy library here in Salt Lake dat does noting but keep records on families history from all over da vorld. I vill check it out for you and let you know vhat I find."

"Where is it at? I can probably do it myself."

"No, it is part of the Mormon Church. You need recommendation from the ward bishop to get in. Let me look dis for you. If ve have to go back I vill talk to my bishop and see if you can go vit me. Now write down all the information you haff on paper. "Ed knew better than to fight the system, besides he knew Levi was good for his word and trusted him. It was almost two weeks before Levi came to Ed with the results of his search.

"I haff found out many tings." Levi said as he pulled a large number of papers from the manila envelope. "On April 18, 1930, a contract was notarized and filed in da Allegheny County courthouse in Pittsburgh, Pennsylvania, between Robert and Juliet Corbett of Rural Route #2, Latrobe, Pennsylvania and Jim and Tracy Bernard of 1256 Brockway Circle, Covedale, Ohio, outlining da terms for da adoption of da Corbett's unborn child.

On June 12 1930, 5:30 am, a doctor Francis Vhite delivered a healty 8 pound 6 ounce girl to Robert and Juliet Corbett, at home in Latrobe, Pennsylvania. Da contract specified dat da Corbett's vould keep da child until August 1st, 1930, so da natural mother could nurse da child. At dat time da Bernard's vere to pay da Corbett's $3,500.00 dollars in cash and accept da child as is."

"I'll be damned," Ed, vocalized his surprise.

Levi looked at Ed, "Something is vrong, ya?"

"No, it's just that the Bernard's never mentioned anything about paying money for Alice."

"Maybe day forget, ya?"

"Maybe. Do the Corbett's still live on the farm in Latrobe?"

"I don't know. I yust look for the information you give me."

Levi I'm going to tell you something that must remain between you and I. But only if you give me your solemn promise that you'll never tell another person, not even Lena." Levi was quite for a long time. "Look Levi, I need your help. You're the only one I can turn to right now. I need you to do some more research.

"Vell, if it is only research I quess it vould'nt hurt to keep a secret from Lena."

"I'll tell you what, after you do the research I'll let you decide whether or not to share it with Lena, ok?"

Levi thought some more, "ya, ok, I vill do it."

"Ok, a year and a half ago I killed a man in a fight."

Levi's eyes opened wide. "My Got." He muttered.

"The man attacked me with a corn knife and was trying to kill me. I picked up a piece of water pipe and swung it at him. It hit him in the head and killed him. I was arrested and put in jail. I was tried by a jury and found innocent by self-defense. The problem is the name of the man I killed was Lester Corbett." Levi put his hand to his mouth as his eyes opened wide once more. The Les Corbett that I killed was from State College, Pennsylvania. I remember from the trial that his father Robert was a Professor at Penn State University. I need to know if he was Alice's brother or not."

Levi was visibly shaken. "I vill find vhat I can," he said as he turned and walked out the front door.

It only took Levi a week to return with the information he gathered. When he sat down on Ed's couch he looked like he had aged ten years. "I am afraid you vere right." The man started in an abnormally weak voice. "Lester vas born to Robert and Juliet in 1925, at Latrobe. In 1930 a girl vas born and adopted out for money. She vas adopted by da Bernard's and vent to a small town on da outskirts of Cincinnati, Ohio. Two years later on April 18, 1932 a boy vas born to da Corbett's and adopted out for $4,000.00 dollars at age three weeks to Carl and Mary Yohnson in Hillsboro, Visconsin."

This peaked Ed's interest because he couldn't remember any neighbors by the name of Johnson in the area he lived in back in Wisconsin. "Oh well," he thought to himself, "It's an odd coincidence, but the rural postal district around Hillsboro covered a large area in four counties, I wouldn't know everyone in it."

"In 1940 the Corbett's moved to State College, Pennsylvania where Lester entered high school and Robert became a professor at Penn State University. Da summer of 1945 Les vent to vork for Emil Schmidt at Medicine Bow, Vyoming. On July 28, 1949 Les died from a blow to the head vith an iron pipe. Dat is all I could find on Les Corbett. Alice you already know about. Everything is yust as you know."

"Thanks Levi, I appreciate everything you've done for me. I always considered you a good friend, but now that you know about my past does that change anything between us?"

Levi looked at Ed as if he would cry. "No, you did vhat you had to do. Your past is between Got and you."

Tears came to Ed's eyes as he reached out and engulfed Levi in a bear hug. "Thank you for believing in me."

When the two men separated Levi's eyes were moist. "I must go now Lena vill haff supper on."

Things between Ed and the Halgevson's were strained at first but improved with time. They loved Olivia and couldn't stay away. The relationship turned out to be stronger than before.

CHAPTER #18

MARCH ENTERED THE Salt Lake valley like a lamb in 1953. Everything was showing signs of renewed life. Olivia was almost two years old and becoming a real chatterbox. She didn't know a lot of words yet but the ones she did know had a little bit of Swedish accent from being around Lena and Levi baby sitting her most of the time Ed was gone to work. She started to crawl in December, now was walking with the aid of any solid object she could grab onto. She was Ed's reason for existence, the two of them spent every moment they could together.

On the sixteenth of March Ed received a phone call from his father-in-law informing him that his mother was dying and wanted to see her son and her grand daughter before she passed away. They had talked about the trip back when John visited Ed and Alice at Christmas. They decided Ed and family would leave Salt Lake the end of March. John explained Ed's mother suddenly took a turn for the worse and the doctors predicted her demise within a month. John felt she was holding on only to hold her son and granddaughter in her arms before she died. Ed went to the manager at his work and explained the situation. Mr. Beasley didn't have a problem with it even when Ed asked him for some additional time to take care of other matters. "Take as much time as you need." were his exact words when Ed explained that he needed to go to Pennsylvania after he saw his mother. The train was the most economical and efficient way to go. Ed bought sleeper berth tickets to Wisconsin for him and Olivia on the next train out of Salt Lake.

Olivia loved the train. She was glued to the window watching the countryside pass by. She especially loved it when they passed herds of animals, domestic or wild. Ed identified what they were and by the time they arrived at their destination her vocabulary grew with words like; "horses, cows sheep.

Ed's stepfather met the train at the station in Lacrosse, Wisconsin and drove them fifty miles to the farm. By the time they arrived at the farm it was starting to get dark. Olivia was asleep, stretched out on the big, overstuffed back seat of John's brand new Hudson sedan. As they swung into the muddy driveway Ed felt a sudden pang of homesickness he hadn't felt in five years. The place looked the same as he remembered it. The big red dairy barn, with board fences surrounding the back end, the granaries, and the large machine shed that housed the power equipment during the harsh winters common to this part of the country. The big, white, two story farm house stood apart from the rest of the buildings, surrounded by a white picket fence on the front and woven wire fence on the remaining three sides. Pulling to a stop in front of the house, the familiar sight of the big screened front porch framed by two huge oak trees and the lights soft glow coming threw the curtained windows brought back memories of a time not so long past.

"I've got to check and see how the milking is going. Want to come along?"

Olivia woke when the car came to stop. Ed looked back at her rubbing her eyes, "hey sweetie, you want to see some real cows?" Olivia grabbed the back of the front seat as she stood up. "Uhuh," she mumbled sleepily. John and Ed got out of the car into the cold April air. Ed walked to the back door where Olivia was, opened it and picked her up. "C'mon baby, I'll carry you while we go see the cows." The cold air and the anticipation of seeing the cows had her wide awake by the time they reached the barn. She started repeating the words cows, horses, sheep, over and over again. Her chatter went silent as they entered the huge cow barn. The cows were all locked into steel neck stanchions. They were eating the corn silage that lay in a long continuous trough formed in the cement in front of them. There were thirty-five head on each side of the barn with a twelve-foot cement alley separating them the full length of the barn. Four milking machines were making a soft pulsating sound as they extracted the milk from the cows' udder while they hung by long adjustable belts placed over the animals back. Every now and then a cow would loll softly and the sound of their movement mixed with the sound of eating created a nice, serene atmosphere. It was warm and comfortable in the enclosed barn and the men worked in their shirtsleeves, and the smell of barn lime, animals, fermented corn and fresh milk was a little acidy but pleasant.

Olivia hugged her dad's neck and stared quietly with her mouth open at the unfamiliar scene. Two men moved back an forth between the animals changing the milking machines from one cow to another and carrying buckets of the white foamy liquid to a cooler located in a little room attached to the front of the barn called the milk house. There were half-dozen or more barn cats that hung around the milk pails and occasionally swiped a couple of fast licks, absolutely fascinated Olivia. Occasionally one of the men would pour a little milk into an old tin pan that sat near the door to the milk house. The cats would congregate around the pan and all you would see were various colored tails sticking straight in the air as the felines lapped their milk. This sent Olivia into squeals of laughter as she pointed and yelled "kitty". John introduced Ed and Olivia to the two men whose grip felt like a vise when they shook hands. "You boys stop up to the house when you get done and have a cup of coffee, I want to talk to you." The hired hands nodded and went back to the task at hand. The trio retired to the house, it was just as Ed remembered. Either John was an excellent housekeeper or he had someone doing it for him, everything was neat as a pin.

"The Strong's and the Simpson women take turns coming over and doing the house work." He volunteered when Ed asked him about it. "They even cook a meal and leave it for me now and then," he elaborated with a chuckle. "You guys have probably had a long day. Your old room is ready for you upstairs," looking at Ed. "I moved the day bed in so Olivia would have a place to sleep." Ed nodded, "Thanks John. She looks like she's ready for a bath and bed."

"After you get her down c'mon down have a cup of coffee and we'll talk."

"Thanks, but I'm tired myself. By the time I get her down I'll be ready for bed too."

"Suit yourself, have a good night. We'll go see your mother tomorrow morning."

Ed nodded, "sounds good, see you in the morning."

John reached over and gave Olivia a little peck on the cheek. "Good night sweetheart, sleep tight."

Ed turned and carried Olivia upstairs to his old bedroom.

Morning came with a shaft of bright sunlight shining into Ed's eyes as it started to rise above the horizon. Sitting up in bed he looked over at Olivia she was still sleeping soundly. The windup alarm clock ticked loudly and showed six am. Ed climbed out of the warm bed the room's chill and slid into a pair of pants and a shirt. When he put Olivia to bed last night she was almost asleep and not really aware of where she was. Ed didn't think it would be a good idea to let her wake up alone in a strange place. So he read a book while he waited for Olivia to wake.

After breakfast the three of them drove to the hospital in Reedsburg to see Ed's mother. On the way John tried to explain the critical state she was in. "Your mother has been in and out of the hospital constantly since she had her heart attack. We would bring her home, she'd be good for a month or two and then her health would start to fail again and we'd have to put her back in the hospital. At first she would only spend a couple of days. As time went on her stays became longer and longer and that's where we're at now."

Ed nodded "How is she doing right now?"

John turned into a parking space in front of the hospital, "she's dying, you can see it in her eyes. Like I said over the phone, she's hanging on to see you and Olivia one time before she lets go. I want to prepare you ahead of time; she is not the person you knew when you left.

Ed felt a twinge of apprehension surge through his belly. Something deep inside of him said this would be the last time he would see his mother alive. "Is she coherent?"

John turned the car's engine off and looked at Ed as he leaned back against the seat "She was yesterday just before I left to pick you up."

Ed sat silent, picturing the image that his mind conjured up of what his failing mother would look like. Opening the car door, he stepped out onto the hard concrete, and retrieved Olivia from the back seat. Ed could feel himself tense as they approached his mother's hospital room. His mother was lying on her back with the covers over her chest and under her arms. She was staring at the ceiling with unblinking eyes. Ed was afraid they were too late as he approached the bed with Olivia in her arms. It wasn't until he bent down and softly said "Mom", that her eyes moved and she looked at him. Her eyes were sunken and shallow as she looked at him with Olivia in his arms. For a brief moment he could see confusion, they recognition as she slowly raised her hand to touch his face. Ed grabbed the shaking, cold and bony appendage and placed it against his tear stained cheek. "Mom, I'm so sorry. Please forgive me. I would have come sooner if I had known."

In a whispery voice she replied, "There's nothing to apologize for, my condition would have happened anyway. The important thing is you're here now. Crank up the bed so I can see my granddaughter better."

Ed wiped away his tears as John cranked the head of the bed into a gentle upright position. A small amount of color came into her cheeks as the bed elevated her body.

"Set that baby on the bed where I can see her," Mrs. Spitzer demanded in a voice that sounded a little huskier than it did a few minutes before. Ed sat on the edge of the bed and stood Olivia next to her Grandmother. "Hello sweetheart." Olivia whimpered and tried to withdraw as Mary Spitzer stretched a pale, bony hand toward her. "Don't be afraid honey, grandma won't hurt you." The toddler turned and buried her face into Ed's chest.

"It's ok Olivia. This is daddy's mommy she wants to say hello to you." Olivia crept tighter into Ed's chest. "Ok, you snuggle where you think your safe while grandma and I talk." Turning his attention to the ailing woman, Ed reached out and held her hand. "Dad says you've been for a while." Ed said not really knowing what to say.

"I'm dying, that's the long and the short of it. I wanted to see you and your family. John told me about your wife. I'm sorry."

Ed hugged Olivia, "thank you but it was an unfortunate accident." Ed could feel the tears starting to make his eyes misty.

"God works in mysterious ways. Do you go to church?"

"Yes, I do."

"Good, make sure that little girl of yours is brought up in church. It will give her values and something to believe in. Remember you're the example. You can preach until the cows come home, but if you don't do what you preach she'll see you for the liar and hypocrite you are."

"Yes, ma'am."

"Enough of my prattle, let's hear about where you been and what you been doing for the last five years."

"Maybe I should come back later after you've rested for a while."

"Look son, I've never minced words with you before and I'm not about to do it now. I'm on my deathbed. My mind is clear and I'm in control of all my senses today, tomorrow I may not be. So, get comfortable and talk to me while you can, I don't have a lot of time left."

Ed smiled and turned Olivia to sit on the bed next to him. His mother had always been a very firm and direct woman. She was always soft spoken but when she talked to you she looked you directly in the eye and said what she had to say, once. She never talked down to you or played word games. She said it like it was because it was how she felt and what she was thinking. "Ok Mom, I'll tell you what. I'll fill in the last five years for you, but then I have some questions for you." Mary's face tensed and then relaxed as she lay listening to her Son describing his experiences when he left home. An hour later Ed finished his stormy history. Mary Spitzer lay with her unblinking eyes open staring at the ceiling. Ed looked at his father in law and motioned him toward the door with his head. Olivia had fallen asleep in John's arms. H e stood up without waking the child and they started for the door.

"I thought you had questions you wanted to ask me?" Mary Spitzer said in a soft, shaky voice. Ed stopped in mid stride and turned back to her bed.

"I thought you were asleep."

"I will be soon, so let's get all of our business done while we still can. What is it you wanted to know?"

Ed sat on the bed as John left the room with Olivia. Ed related the information Levi had gathered. "Les and Alice were brother and sister and neither of them knew it. Why?"

"I don't know sweetheart." Mary said as a tear ran down her cheek.

"Mom, did you know anyone by the name of Johnson?" Mary's face turned ash gray as the tears ran down both cheeks.

"I knew it would come to this. I should have told you a long time ago, maybe some of those terrible things wouldn't have happened to you."

Ed looked at his weeping mother and gave her a hug. "You can't change the past, you can only make the future. That's what you always used to tell me, remember?"

"Only too well, but there are things you should know." Ed sat back on the bed and listened. "Your name used to be Johnson. Your first stepfather and I adopted you from Robert and Juliet Corbett in Latrobe, Pennsylvania when you were one month old. We paid them $4,000.00 dollars and signed a contract agreeing not to reveal their identity or the adoption to you ever." Ed started to speak. "Please let me finish. Your first stepfather, Carl, and I agreed to raise you as our own son. He was a good man and loved you very much. Unfortunately he was killed when he got caught in the tractor's power take off. Do you remember him at all?"

"Yes, just barely. I remember his face and how he used to bounce me on his knee, but that's all."

Mary smiled as Ed wiped her cheeks with a tissue. "Time went by and John and I fell in love. We knew each other when Carl, John and I worked at the grange. When John and I married he agreed to adopt you. Your name was changed from Johnson to Spitzer. You were only three and we didn't think you would understand. You were born to the Corbett's but we raised you and loved you and didn't think you would ever find out that you were adopted."

By now Ed was shaking like a leaf. "Are you sure the people you adopted me from were named Robert and Juliet Corbett?"

"Yes, as sure as I know my own name. The contract is on file at the courthouse in Pittsburgh, Pennsylvania."

"Do you realize what that means?" Ed stood up, fists clenched, body shaking. "I killed my brother and married my sister!!!! Olivia is a product of my sister and me!!!! She might have suffered all kinds of physical or mental damage!!!! **WHY!!!!! WHY DID YOU DO THIS TO ME?????**"

"I'm sorry, we meant no harm. If we knew what would happen we would have done anything to prevent it."

Ed wiped the tears off his dying mother's face and bent down to kiss her forehead. "I know Mom, don't you fret, Olivia's perfectly healthy and what's done is done. I love you and I know you did what you thought was best for me. You need to get some rest now, I'll come back to see you later."

"Please don't leave." Ed's mother looked at him with pleading eyes and grabbed his hand in her weak grip.

"I have to Mom. I need to go and digest what you told me. I'm all mixed up right now and I need to think. Olivia and I will come back tomorrow to see you." Ed squeezed her hand gently and laid it on the bed. "I love you, get some rest now so we can talk more tomorrow." Ed kissed her forehead once more and left the room. In the hall way Ed lost the composure he had fought so hard to control in front of his Mother. He leaned against the wall and cried like a baby.

A gentle hand touched his arm, "Sir, are you alright?" Ed looked down at the concerned nurse trying to comfort him.

"Yeah, my Mother is dying and I'm upset that's all.

"I'm sorry, is there anything I can do to help?"

"You already have. You brought me back into the real world, thank you." The nurse gave Ed a doubtful look and continued her journey down the hall as Ed wiped the tears dry and blew his nose. Ed found his father in law and Olivia in a waiting room reading a magazine. They looked up as he walked in. "Are you ready?" Ed said with a quiver in his voice as he looked at Olivia.

The ride back to the farm was a silent one. Ed was pretty sure John knew that Mary Spitzer told Ed the story of his adoption. The realization that she wasn't his real mother was becoming a real issue. Things like; why did my real parents not want me, and why did they sell me like a piece of meat, where roaring threw his mind.

That evening after Olivia was in bed, John and Ed sat at the kitchen table with a cup of coffee and talked. "What happened, John?" Ed asked. John looked at Ed and sat quietly as he prepared his thoughts. Finally with a soft sigh he related the story of Ed's adolescent life.

'Your mother, and she is your mother. Even though she didn't give birth to you, she loved you more than life itself. All I know about the adoption was what she told me after Carl died. They couldn't have children so they decided to adopt. They went threw all the normal agencies and couldn't find what they wanted. The grange we belonged to sent a request to the University of Pennsylvania for an expert on soil conservation and contour plowing. He stayed a month and worked with the farmers in the area who were having problems losing what little topsoil was left after years of the conventional methods. During that time it was the custom for the host families to provide lodging and meals. He stayed with a family in Viroqua by the name of Peterson. Whatever family he was working with would feed him before he went back to the Peterson's for the night. His name was Robert Corbett and he was from Latrobe, Pennsylvania!!! Carl and your mother made arrangements to adopt the baby that his wife was pregnant with. They brought you home when you were only a month old. No one could have loved you more than Carl and Mary. As far as they were concerned the sun rose and set on you. After Carl died your mother and I started dating. We were married seven months later. Since we knew each other for years we didn't feel we needed a long courtship. One of the conditions of my marriage to your mother was your adoption by me and I promised her I would honor the contract that Carl and her signed when they adopted you. That wouldn't have mattered anyway; you've always been as much of a son to me as if I created you. We felt it would be less confusing and in your best interest to change your name from Johnson to Spitzer, which we did when I adopted you."

"When you came to my trail didn't you recognize the Corbett's."

"No, I never met them. I did recognize the name."

"Why didn't you say something?"

"I told you, I gave your mother my word that I would honor the contract between her and the Corbett's. Besides, think about it, what good would it have done? Nothing could be gained by reveling your past. It had no bearing on anything that happened."

Ed thought about it for a minute and finally had to agree with John's reasoning. "I'm concerned about Olivia and how much I should tell her. What do you think I should do?"

John thought for a minute, "I think you ought to find out everything you can about your real mother and father and get their side of it. They probably had their reasons for what they did. Remember there are only circumstances, not right and wrong. Until you've walked in somebody else's shoes don't judge them. We all do things we regret, that doesn't make us bad people, it just means that we don't always make the best decisions." Ed nodded his head in agreement, thinking back to some of his boners, like running away from home "If I were you, and had the time to do it I would go to Pennsylvania and find out what really happened. Sooner or later Olivia is going to want to know about her mother. When that day comes you better have your facts straight or she is going feel exactly what you feel right now."

Ed knew John was giving him good advice. "Olivia would need to know the truth someday." Ed thought quietly." At that moment he knew what he had to do.

Ed and Olivia spent most of their waking hours during the next two days with Ed's mother. On the second day she slipped into a coma. The doctors wouldn't say anymore than, "it didn't look good." Ed called his boss in Salt Lake City and explained his situation.

"Mr. Beasley, I know you told me to take as much time as I needed but things have not gone well here. I need to go to Pennsylvania for a week, with the travel time it'll probably take closer to ten days."

"Look Ed I'm sorry your mother is dying, and I know the last three months have been really tough for you. But I have a company to run, one with a high turnover of personal and a time schedule to boot. I can't afford to have you gone forever. If I have to hire extra people to cover your run I'll let you go and you'll have to wait until I hire again."

"Mr. Beasley please, I need my job. What is the longest you can hold it for me?"

The voice on the other end of the phone was quiet for a couple of minutes. "I'll hold your job until the tenth of April. If you aren't back by then I'll give your run to someone and hire you back the first time I open the applications."

"How long do you think that would be?"

"It could be the day you get back or it could be as long as two months after you get back."

Ed tried to think of a way he could get the manager to extend his leave. "My birthday is on the eighteenth is there anyway you could give me that?"

A loud snort came from the phone. "God your pushy. Let me see what I can do." The phone was quiet for about three minutes. "You still there?"

"Yeah."

"This is the best I'm going to do for you, and it's only because you're a good employee and you've had a bad time lately. The tenth is on a

Thursday you be here for your run the following Monday morning or your fired."

Ed was about to say something when the line went dead. "Damn, he hung up on me." Ed said out loud with a smile. Hanging up the phone he walked over to a calendar hanging on the wall. Ed ran his finger down the numbers. "Let's see, today is the twenty-fourth, ten days will be April third, four days back to Salt Lake from here, that gives me seven days to play with, six if I leave tomorrow." Ed walked back to the phone and called the train station in Hillsboro. He found out that all the main line trains went through Richland Center, Wisconsin, which was south and east of Hillsboro. The agent gave him the schedule and assured him it would be quicker and cheaper to catch it there. Ed discussed his plans with John that night and John agreed that he should go while he had the chance.

John waved goodbye to Ed and Olivia as the train pulled away from the station. Ed didn't know what to expect from Robert and Juliet Corbett, but he felt the best way to catch them was to show up on their doorstep with no notice. After the courtroom scene in Laramie, he knew they wouldn't welcome him with open arms, much less want to talk to him, but he had to try if for no other reason than Olivia. His ticket was to State College, Pennsylvania, via Pittsburgh. As the train followed the shining rails threw the green and verdant countryside, Ed's mind was free for the first time since his step mother broke the news to him at the hospital, to try and sort out the details of his childhood.

CHAPTER #19

PITTSBURGH, PENNSYLVANIA WAS dirty and smoky. Compared to Salt Lake, which had its share of haze during the winter it was a pigsty. Ed and Olivia checked into a clean, modest hotel and spent two days finding the contracts that had been placed on microfilm at the Allegheny County courthouse. Once Ed had the copies in hand they boarded the train for State College and the confrontation with Robert and Juliet Corbett.

State College was not a large town by any means, its population stood at about twenty thousand. This included the head count of the University of Pennsylvania that made up about seventy percent of its residents. The town received its name when the land the University sits on was given to the State by the federal government in the mid-eighteen hundreds under the agreement that it was to be used for a State College. It was an old fort that had been abandoned after the Indian threat had been eliminated East of the Mississippi River. The site was cleared and Pennsylvania State College was born. Around the turn of the century it was awarded University status and has been known as Penn State ever since. However the village that grew with the College retained the name of State College and became official after its incorporation.

It took most of the day after they arrived to find a place to stay for the week. The hotels were not located near the University and students had rented anything else available. By the end of the day Ed was getting ready to check into one of the two hotels. He made one more phone call to a boarding house about a mile from the University. A woman answered, Ed introduced himself and explained his situation to her. She had one room that had just vacated and it included two meals (breakfast and supper) and the downstairs sitting room until nine pm. Ed agreed to take it, he got directions and called a cab.

A gray haired woman named Mayble met them on the huge front porch that overlooked the street. It was a typical three story wooden structure built around the turn of the century from native wood. It was still elegant and in good repair. Whoever built it originally must have owned most of the land in the area and planned on raising their own work force. The house was huge and showed no additions. Inside it contained; ten bedrooms, the smallest were fifteen by eighteen feet. The parlor was about twenty feet square, the living or sitting room was big enough to hold three massive couches, two large overstuffed chairs and a fireplace on each side of the room. The dining room had a table in the middle of it eighteen feet long with hand carved legs and claw feet. The kitchen was equally as large and had an eight-foot by sixteen foot walk in pantry at one end.

Mayble talked constantly as she gave Ed and Olivia the grand tour of the great house. "It was built in eighteen and ninety two." The big boned, buxom woman said in a strong voice. My grandparents built it when my dad was a young man. I was born in this house, and I'm gonna die here. Everyone is buried out back in our private cemetery. This is your room here; you got a great view of the mountains out your window there. I'm gonna leave you two alone now. Supper's at six o'clock sharp." Ed put their bags on the floor and thanked the homespun landlord as she left the room.

Looking through the phone book, Ed found the Corbett's address and phone number. Juliet Corbett called him a "son of a bitch" and hung up the minute he identified himself. Thinking about it Ed laughed at his real mother's unknown insinuation. The question now was; "how am I going to be able to talk to these people? The phone is definitely not the answer. I need to meet them face to face in a place where they can't walk away or shut me out. If Mrs. Corbett won't talk to me maybe her husband will. He seemed pretty level headed at the trial." Ed looked up the Penn State administration office in the phone book. After being put on hold a couple of times he finally got the number of Professor Corbett's office.

"Botany department may I help you?"

"I'd like to speak to Professor Corbett please."

"Whom should I say is calling?"

"A friend."

"I'm sorry but I have to have a name."

Ed hesitated, "Ed Johnson," knowing he wouldn't talk to Ed Spitzer, Ed thought he might be able to spark some curiosity with a familiar name that Professor Corbett may or may not quite be able to remember.

After a short pause on hold the secretary came back. "I'm sorry Professor Corbett doesn't recognize the name. What is the nature of your call?"

Once again Ed was stymied for a minute. "I'm someone from his past that desperately needs to talk to him."

"What about?"

"It's really very personal. I only have a short time in town and I need him to clarify some things that happened years ago."

"Please hold I'll try him again."

"Thank you." Ed said into the quiet phone.

Finally the secretary came back. "Mr. Johnson?"

"Yes, I'm here."

"The Professor is extremely busy, but he will make an appointment for eight am tomorrow. Will that be alright?"

"Yes ma'am, if you'll give me directions I'll be there with bells on." The secretary told him where to go and hung up with a cheery goodbye.

At seven forty-five am Ed was standing in front of Professor Corbett's office with Olivia in his arms. He felt his stomach muscles tighten as he knocked on the door.

"Come in," a loud baritone voice called from the other side.

Ed opened the door and walked in with Olivia on his arm. "Professor Corbett I'm Ed Johnson and this is my daughter Olivia," extending his hand as he walked toward the elderly man sitting behind his desk.

Robert Corbett had not aged well since the last time Ed had seen him. His face was wrinkled, the hair was a dirty gray and rumpled. His suit needed a pressing badly, and the toupee didn't fit well at all. As Ed approached the desk Robert stood up. The weak smile was replaced by a sudden, disturbing recognition of who Ed really was. The pale, pasty skin color went to a shade of red. "How dare you come in here? What is the meaning of this?"

"I came to talk to you about my past."

"I don't know you other than the murderer of my son, now get out or I will call the authorities."

"I am your son too, you sold me and my sister when we were babies and I want to know why."

Professor Corbett's face lost its color and went ashen. "I have no idea what you're talking about. For the last time get out or I will call the police."

"I'll leave but before I go, I want you to take a good look at your granddaughter. She is the product of the two children you sold as babies. She will want to know about her grandpa and grandma someday. Here is something else you might have forgotten about." Ed threw the spare copies he made of the contracts on the desk in front of Robert Corbett. "I'm going to be in town four more days. I would like to know about my real mom and dad, if for no other reason than some day I'll be able to tell Olivia who her grandparents really are. I'll leave the number where I'm staying with your secretary on my way out. Goodbye and good day sir!!!" Ed turned on his heel and slammed the door behind him listening to the glass break as it hit the hardwood floor. The secretary and a couple of people waiting looked up in surprise as Ed walked over to the secretaries desk and made her write down the address and number where he was staying.

Two days passed before Ed heard from Professor Corbett. Ed was packing the suitcases after breakfast when the phone call came.

"Mr. Johnson or should I call you Mr. Spitzer?"

Ed smiled at the Professor's weak attempt at irony, "It doesn't matter. Whatever you feel comfortable with."

"Very well, Can we meet in my office this afternoon?"

"Sure, What time?"

"Let's say about three o'clock."

"Ok, I'll be there."

Ed hung up the phone and clenching his fists in front of him as he gave out with an emphatic "YES!!!" Olivia looked up from the living room floor where she was playing with some wooden spoons and other non-breakable kitchen utensils that Mayble furnished her with. "Wait here baby, I'll be right back." Ed said as he headed for the kitchen. He walked in to see Mayble wrist deep in bread dough.

"Mayble, can I ask a favor of you?"

"Sure, what do you need?" she said as she continued kneading the dough.

"I have an important meeting this afternoon and I wondered if you could watch Olivia for me."

"Not a problem. She's a little sweetheart, I'd love to."

"Thank you." If things got ugly between the professor and himself he didn't want Olivia in the middle of it.

Ed greeted the apprehensive secretary as he entered Professor Corbett's outer office with a smile. "I'm here to see Professor Corbett."

"I know," she replied as she picked up the phone. "Professor Corbett your three o'clock appointment is here. Yes sir." The woman got to her feet, "follow me," she said as she walked across the room and held the repaired door to the professor's office open for Ed to walk through.

"I promise I won't break it on my way out." Ed said, giving her a toothy smile as he walked past. The professor was behind his desk in the same position as the first time Ed saw him.

"Sit down." The wrinkled old man pointed at the chair across the desk from him. "What exactly do you want know?"

Ed didn't know where to start. "Are you my real father?"

"Hurmmph, real straight forward aren't you?"

"I try to be and I would like you to be also."

Robert settled back into his chair. "So you want the truth do you? Do you think you can handle it or do you just want the highlights?"

Ed sat on the edge of his chair and leaned forward. "I want to hear it no matter what it is!"

Robert hurmphed softly and allowed his gaze to drop to the hands folded in his lap. Opening a drawer in his desk he reached in a dragged the two contracts and tossed them across the desk to land in front of Ed. "Obviously you knew about those contracts. I'm still not sure who you are. Are you related to the Johnson in that contract? How do you fit into this mess?"

"I am the baby you sold to the Johnson's twenty-one years ago when you lived in Latrobe, Pennsylvania." Robert rested his elbow on the arm of his chair and cradled his chin in his hand. "The couple that adopted me and signed this contract was named Carl and Mary Johnson from Hillsboro, Wisconsin. When I was about two Carl was killed in a farm accident. My mother remarried a man by the name of John Spitzer who adopted me and promised my mo . . . . step-mother that he would honor that contract. I never knew the name Johnson until after my wife died. It was about the same time I found out my wife was also my sister and Les was my brother." Ed gulped in a big breath of air and was emotionally drained. Robert Corbett sat straight up in his chair.

"Good God," He reached across the table and grabbed the two contracts studying them intently. Looking up he shook his head in disbelief as the truth settled on him like an iron mantle. "O Lord what have I done? What have I done?"

"Didn't the name Bernard ring any bells when you and your wife were at the trial?" Ed asked as the mumbling old man got out of his chair.

Robert Corbett walked to the far end of the room and returned to his desk. "No," he said as he slumped into his chair. "Her parents weren't there and Julia and I never gave it a second thought." Robert reached into his desk again and came up with a bottle of scotch and two glasses. "This is not what I expected. I need a drink, will you join me?"

"Sure, Ed nodded.

Robert poured the amber liquid and handed Ed his glass. With one motion Robert tossed his down his throat and then poured himself another glass full. Leaning on the desk with his elbows Robert looked across at Ed sipping his whiskey. "My wife Juliet and I bought three hundred acres of prime farm land just south of Latrobe right after the first world war. We used all of our savings to pay down on it. Things went real good and we expanded according to our income. Les came along in twenty-five, he was a strong healthy boy. The farm was making money and we had it half paid off when the depression hit us. We couldn't sell our milk or anything else, we fell behind on our payments and finally the bank had no choice but to sell the place and everything on it at auction. It went for pennies on the dollar and still didn't cover what we owed, even though the land and buildings themselves were worth twice as much as we owed only six months earlier. They sold all the livestock, except for one cow I hid out in the woods so we could at least have milk. The only thing left was a couple of pieces of broken down machinery, a couple hogs and the poultry. I couldn't even work the land other than put in a vegetable garden. The bank let us live in the house until they could get it and the land sold. Like I said it went for pennies on the dollar. We didn't see any of the money, but at least we had plenty to eat. The people that bought it were fine furniture makers from Switzerland. They bought large tracts of forestland in the east for little or nothing right after the depression to harvest the timber. They bought twenty-five hundred acres east of Pittsburgh that included our three hundred. They found out I had a degree in agronomy and botany and made me an offer to manage the land they just purchased if I would get a degree in forestry at the local college. While I was in town one day I overheard a man inquiring about an adoption agency in Pittsburgh. Julia was pregnant at the time and we needed money for me to get the degree. I introduced myself, gave the man my card and told him to call me. He did a while later. In the meantime Julia and I talked about selling the baby she was carrying. She got extremely upset when I first approached her about it but thought better of the idea when a final price was agreed upon and my academic future started to become a reality with the acquisition of my bachelor's degree. The couple from Cinncinati, Ohio was eager for the deal and we formulated the contract you see in front of you." Robert sat back in his chair and continued. "I applied to various colleges in the east for a teaching position with possible tenure after I received my master's degree and pursued my PHD, two colleges responded and I chose Penn State. The only hitch was the finances to make the move from Latrobe to State College and fund the professorship. The Swiss couple left us money when we moved here but I needed funds to finish my masters and start my PHD before that. We decided to have one more baby and sell it. You were born in nineteen thirty-two and sold to the Johnson's who I met in Wisconsin on a field trip for the University of Pennsylvania. The farmer's in that area were having problems with the soil and requested professional help. I was sent to do the job and satisfy some of the work required for my PHD. I became tenured shortly after Les started going to the ranch each summer.

He was always a gifted child. Everything he did was easy for him. I was doing research at some of the potash plants in that area when I became acquainted with the Schmidt's. I knew ranch life and the people he would associate with would instill values he would never get in the east, so I encouraged him to take a summer job on the ranch. After the first summer he was hooked and couldn't wait for the scholastic part of his year to end. The year before his demise he talked a lot about a girl he had met from Cheyenne, Wyoming, by the name of Alice Bernard. Her father was an aeronautical engineer for Lockheed and worked with the military. That was all we knew about her or her parents. Julia and I discussed the similarity of her last name with the adopted parents name, but dismissed it for the time being as coincidence. When we appeared at the trial the last thing on our mind was the similarity of her last name. Since we didn't know your last name had been changed from Johnson to Spitzer and your address was the ranch at Medicine Bow, Wyoming, there wasn't any reason for us to suspect any kind of relational tie about you."

Ed sat mesmerized. What he heard just now was the truth and he knew it. Fate had played a very cruel joke on those left standing. "I called your house the first day I arrived here. Your wife hung up on me. I guess she's still pretty upset."

Professor Corbett smiled as he gently rocked his chair. "I imagine she is. Julia and I are divorced. It happened shortly after the trial. She always did feel bad about selling the babies and Les's death was the straw that broke the camels back for our marriage. She blamed me for us ending up with no children to give us grandkids. We divorced, she got the house and my retirement." Robert put his hands out palms up and sighed. "Now you know as much as I know."

Ed shook his head as if he were trying to clear his mind of the disturbing information he had just consumed. "I think I need another drink." He said as he reached across the desk and held out his empty glass.

Robert poured Ed's glass and then his own. "Good idea, I think I'll join you." Settleing back into his chair he held up his glass. "Cheers," and threw the contents down his throat. "What about, ..what did you say my granddaughters name is?"

"Olivia,"

"Olivia," The professor savored the sound of it like tasting a fine wine. "You didn't bring her with you?"

"I didn't know where this would go and I didn't want her in the middle if it got ugly."

Robert rubbed his chin with his hand. "Good thinking. Is there any chance of me seeing her before you leave?"

Ed thought about it for a moment. "You can come by the boarding house this evening if you want."

"I would rather see her the first time without strangers around gawking at us. Could you bring her here?"

Ed looked around at the sterile, institutional surroundings. "I suppose, our train leaves at two o'clock tomorrow, but we could make it for a while in the morning."

"I'll send a cab for the two of you at eight o'clock in the morning. We'll go to breakfast and maybe swing through the park and let her feed the pigeons. I will contact Julia and see if she wants to meet us there."

"Ok, sounds good to me," Ed said as he stood up and held out his hand.

Robert Corbett remained seated, "You'll have to forgive me but I refuse to shake the hand of the man who killed my son."

Ed's smile died on his face and he withdrew his hand. "I'm sorry." He said as he turned and headed for the door.

The professor said softly to himself, "so am I young man, so am I."

The cab arrived promptly at eight o'clock and loaded Ed and Olivia's bags in the trunk. Professor Corbett was in the back seat waiting for them. They drove to a nice restaurant located in one of the hotels and from there went to a large park so Olivia could sit on Robert's lap while he threw bread crumbs to the pigeons that flocked around their feet.

"Julia couldn't make it. She isn't able to get past the death of Les. She said she doesn't have any other children and wants to be left alone."

Ed smiled a Olivia as she dropped bread crumbs to the eager pigeons at her feet. "That's too bad, she could probably get over Les if she had Olivia in her life."

"That's not the way Julia thinks. Losing everything did something to her, she's never been the same since."

"What about you? It sounds like your divorce pretty well wiped you out?"

"It did, and at one point I even contemplated suicide. Life can be a cruel taskmaster, you do things that come back to haunt you. Then when you're at your lowest point a ray of sunshine breaks through and makes you want to live again." Robert looked at Olivia on his lap and smiled. After Olivia ran out of pigeon food she got restless so Robert decided to give them the grand tour of State College, Pennsylvania and the university before he dropped them off at the train station.

Ed looked out the passenger car window as the train wound its way through the mountain passes on its way to Salt Lake City. A lot had happened for Ed on this trip; he cleared up the question of his past, Olivia now had a real grandfather, (even though Robert wouldn't acknowledge a kinship to Ed, he accepted him for Olivia's sake), and Ed buried his mother who died the day before they returned to Hillsboro. The funeral was scheduled for Wednesday the ninth of April. It was going to be real close for Ed to get back on time to keep his job. The train was scheduled into Salt Lake at eleven thirty Sunday night. He called the Helgevson's and they agreed to meet him at the station and take Olivia home with them for the night.

The days following Ed's return to Salt Lake dragged into a living nightmare. Ed constantly thought about the events that brought him to this point in life. He started smoking, his drinking was becoming more frequent, and he wasn't as concerned for Olivia's welfare as he had been. He didn't neglect her needs, but he would sit for long hours staring into an emptiness he created. Church had become a thing of the past and his mother's dying words no longer filtered through his mind.

Levi and Lena Helgevson could see the deterioration in Ed's character and were growing more concerned on a daily basis. They babysat Olivia a lot and tried to spend time talking to Ed about his obvious physical and mental decline. Ed's moodiness became more evident as his personality started to do a reverse of what it had been when he first met the elderly couple. Levi approached him one day after a unwarranted verbal assault on Olivia who had accidentally dropped a glass of water. "What the hell is wrong with you?" He screamed at the crying child. "Can't you do anything right? You go to your room and don't come out until I tell you." Grabbing the three year olds arm he swatted her on the butt as he shoved her in the direction of her bedroom door. Levi looked up from the table he was setting for dinner. "Vhy do you yell at da child? She did nothing. Da glass can be replaced."

Ed's temper (which was growing stronger each day) flared. "God dammit Levi, don't try to tell me how to raise my kid."

Levi looked away to hide the hurt look on his face. "Lena, come on, ve go now, I have lost my appetite." Lena grabbed her bag and looked Ed directly in the eye. "You haff changed. You are no longer da nice person vhat moved in here. Vhat you are doing is not goot for Olifia. She is your child and ve cannot say how you treat her. But, Levi is my husband and no one talks to him da vay you yust did. I vant you to apologize to him, he lofes you and has alvaws trys to help you no matter vhat."

Levi walked over to the pair, "Lena, is alright Ed didn't mean it I know."

Lena stopped shaking her finger under Ed's nose. "You let me finish," as she snapping at her husband. Turning back to Ed with the menacing finger in motion she stared again, "You haff changed. You vere a good person until you vent back east. Now you smoke, you drink, you svear and you don't even go to church nomore. Don't you see vhat you're doing to dat little girl in her room crying her eyes out. She doesn't understand vhy you haff changed. If you keep acting the way you are you vill lose her too. Now, I vant you to apologize to my Levi before ve go. Lena removed the accusing finger and stared into Ed's eyes as she waited for his response.

Ed fidgeted; he had never seen Lena so upset and vocal as she was right now. He could tell she wasn't about to back down until she got what she wanted. "Levi, I'm sorry for what I said to you. I'm having a hard time dealing with my past. I'm sorry." Ed looked at the floor ashamed of himself.

Levi put his hand on Ed's shoulder and the couple left.

Ed went into Olivia's room. She was on her bed crying, large crocodile tears were running down her cheeks. She rolled over and buried her face in the pillow when Ed walked in. "I'm sorry baby." Ed said as she lay sobbing with her back to him. Ed tried to find the words to tell her how he felt, and how he loved her and that things would get better, but they wouldn't come. He turned and left her room before she could see him cry. The rest of the day was spent chain smoking and drinking. Ed knew way down deep he had to do something and soon. The thought of cleaning himself up and restarting his life was too hard to contemplate. Other thoughts and easier ways out ran threw his mind. Suicide and even murder were brought up from the dark recesses of his brain. Eventually he slipped into a drunken stupor where there were no thoughts and unconsciousness was a blessing.

"Daddy, Daddy, wake up" Ed felt his arm being shook. Olivia had a hold of his shirtsleeve and was tugging back and forth on it as hard as she could. Ed rolled his head to one side and looked at her tear stained face long since dried. "Daddy, get up I'm hungry." Ed looked at her again and then looked at his wristwatch. It was ten o'clock at night. Moving hurt; Ed's head felt like it would explode, and Olivia's constant shaking was an agony he knew wouldn't stop until he took care of her needs.

"Ok, baby, Ok. Help me up and I'll fix you something." Olivia went around to Ed's front and pulled on his arm as Ed pushed out of the big living room chair he had passed out in. Supper was cold and still on the stove where Lena had turned it off on her way out. Ed put some of the pot roast and potatoes in a pan and placed it in the oven to warm. Then he took Olivia into the bathroom to wash her and get her into pajamas for bed. Ed looked at the reflection of the two of them in the mirror. For just a second dark thoughts flashed threw his mind. He blinked and saw what was really looking back at him. An unkempt, unshaven, dirty man, holding a beautiful, little child, who loved her dad, even though she couldn't understand why he didn't like her anymore. Ed knew he had to do something and soon. When they finished in the bathroom they went to the kitchen. Ed watched while Olivia ate. Once she finished Ed picked her up and carried her to the bedroom. "Goodnight baby, I love you. I'm sorry I yelled at you today. Forgive me?"

Olivia wanted to believe the words, as she looked at her dad leaning over her waiting for a goodnight kiss. Reaching up from the bed with both arms she gave him a hug and a kiss on the cheek. "Goodnight sweetheart." Ed said, waiting for a response that didn't come. Olivia lay there looking at him with her mother's unblinking eyes.

Ed's boss called him in after his shift was over. "What's going on with you?" Cory Beasley asked looking at the filthy, unshaven, employee before him.

"Nothing." Ed replied.

"Nothing! Is that all you can say! Nothing??? You need a bath, a shave, your clothes look like you've been gardening in them and all you can say is; Nothing??? What the hell is wrong with you? In the last three months, ever since you got back from you're trip you act like you just don't care. We've had customer complaints about your rudeness and appearance, this cannot continue. Do you understand?"

Ed looked up at his boss pacing the floor in front of him. "I understand," he said in a downcast voice.

"You better because your job is on the line. If I get one more complaint about you you're history. Do I make myself clear?"

"Yeah, quite clear."

"Then get out of here and go clean up."

Ed got up and walked out of the manager's office thinking about how to end all the turmoil in his life when he got home. Since April his world had literally fallen apart. He was given to crying unexpectedly, and fits of prolonged depression hovered over him like a blanket. The weight was starting to become unbearable, even little things bothered him now. When he was in Mr. Beasley's office getting chewed out, all he wanted to do was get up and punch him in the mouth. Ed still hadn't lost control but he knew he was on the brink of it. Olivia was scared of him; he could see it in her eyes and body language. He didn't know what to do as the unnoticed paranoia set in and slowly began to take control.

By the time he pulled into the driveway of his house he had all the details worked out in his mind. As soon as the Helgevson's left, first Olivia and then him, it would be quick. Ed walked into the house to find more people than just the Helgevson's. Levi met him at the door. "Ve vant to talk vitt you. Dis is a good friend from our church Roger Benson." Levi motioned toward the short balding man in a brown suit who walked up and held out his hand. "He helps people when day are hafing trouble vit der lifes."

The company and the observation that things were not right in his life irritated Ed. "I don't think my life is any of your business Levi. I have things to do, so please leave."

Levi bit his lip, "I know you don't really mean dat. Please yust talk vit Roger for a litlle vhile. I know he can help you with some of your problems."

Ed could feel his anger intensifying as the door to the tiger's cage silently unlocked, "look you meddling old fool, I don't want or need your help and I certainly don't need any help from your short, fat, friend here. Now get out of my house, all of you."

The color in Levi's face went beet red and his lips started to quiver. "You listen to me and you listen vell. Dis is not your house, it is mine, I vill say who comes and goes here, by golly. You don't care about anyting anymore. You don't clean; my Lena comes over and picks up after you like you vere a little boy. Your poor baby runs around half dressed and dirty. Every time ve come ofer she tells us she is hungry and ve clean her up feed her. The only ting you keep in your refrigerator anymore is beer and salami. We bring food over for everyday and take her clothes home to wash. You don't seem to care anymore for her or anyone else, vhat is da matter vit you? You must change or you will end up in da gutter." The man in the brown suit stood quietly watching Ed as Levi verbally chastised him.

Ed was so angry that he was shaking visibly as he stood with clenched fists. "Levi, I am going to ask you for the last time. Get out of this house and take Lena and him with you."

"No, ve are not leaving until you agree to talk to Roger."

Ed knew Levi meant what he said. Ed screamed as the anger slowly started to swing the cage door open, "God damn it Levi, leave me alone." Ed picked up a vase sitting on an end table next to him and smashed it on the floor. The man in the brown suit stepped between Levi and Ed, as he put his hands on the Swede's shoulders he said; "Levi, we need to talk for a minute." He motioned to the next room with a nod of his head and turned to Ed, "let me talk to him for a minute and we'll do whatever it takes to settle this peacefully."

Ed looked down at the man, "you better, I've got things I want to do and you're in my way."

"Just give us a minute and everything will be all right."

"Ok, but make it fast or I'll throw you out myself if I have to."

The man nodded and pushed Levi through the doorway into the kitchen and closed the door. "Levi the man is extremely upset and emotionally unstable. He's a danger to himself and anyone around him. I deal with this kind of depression and withdrawal in my patient's everyday. If he doesn't get help immediately I'm afraid there might be some tragic consequences. He's already exhibited violent tendencies and I think that's just the tip of the iceberg."

Levi hung his head, "vhat do you tink ve should do?"

"I think we should call the police and have them here while we confront him about treatment. He's proven that he can be violent and all you've done is reminded him of his lack of responsibility. Since you are the landlord they would probably respond to you quicker than they would me."

"Vhat should I tell dem?"

"The truth, Ed threatened to physically throw you and your wife out of your own house. Tell them he is uncontrollably aggressive and there is a young child that your concerned about. If that doesn't work let me talk to them."

"I don't know, do you really tink ve need da police?"

"Look, Levi; he is bordering on schizophrenia with violent tendencies, he could be contemplating suicide or even worse. I know; this is what I do for a living. You saw something yourself or you wouldn't have contacted me about him. I know you love him and that's why you need to do this, if you don't sooner or later he's going to hurt himself or someone around him."

"You don't tink he would hurt Olifia do you?"

"That's a distinct possibility. In his condition he's capable of anything."

Levi's face showed real concern, "Alright, by golly I vill do it."

"Good, use the phone on the wall there. We don't want him to realize what's happening until the police arrive at the door. I'll wait until you get off the phone and then I'll go out and make some excuse to buy us the time we need." Levi shook his head and walked to the phone.

Two very large Salt Lake City police officers arrived ten minutes after Levi hung up the phone. Ed and Roger were in the living room talking while Levi and Lena were supposedly gathering their things to go. When the knock came on the door Ed was already agitated, "what the hell now?" He growled as he walked over and opened the door. The surprised look on his face faded into anger as the one of the officer's spoke up. "Mr. Edward Spitzer?"

Ed nodded, "Yes, that's me."

"We've had a domestic violence complaint on you and we need to step inside and talk to you about it."

Ed forced himself to keep his emotions in check. "There's been no violence here, I have a few friends over, but there's been no trouble. Who told you there was?"

"We don't know who filed the complaint. We received the call to check out a domestic violence situation at this address from the dispatcher, can we please step inside so we can talk to you?"

"What if I don't want you in my house?"

"Mr. Spitzer; we would prefer not to but we do have a warrant and can forcibly enter your house if we have to. Now, can we come in or do we have to do it the hard way?"

Ed knew this was a losing battle, "Ok, come on." He said and backed away from the door as the two officers's entered. They walked into the living room with Ed to where Roger Benson was standing. One them pulled out a pad of paper and started questioning Roger as the other one bent down to examine the broken shard's of glass on the floor. In the meantime Levi and Lena came out of Olivia's bedroom carrying the child. Ed leaned over and said to the officer examining the broken vase; "I accidentally knocked it off the table just before you came." The officer stood up and interrupted his partner, "I think we all should sit down until we get this sorted out." "Good idea," his partner responded. Why don't you folks have a seat on the couch? Mr.Spitzer you have a seat in that big chair there." Pointing with his pencil to the large easy chair Ed had passed out in the night before. When everyone was seated he continued. "Now, to make things go as fast and as smooth as possible, I would appreciate your cooperation. I'll ask the questions and I want the person and only the person to whom I am talking to respond. Just tell me what you know and don't lie, because if this should wind up in court I will have to testify based on what you tell me here and now." He looked at everyone except, Ed nod in agreement. "I will collect all of your names and addresses later, so let's see if we can figure out what the problem is. Mr. Spitzer; let's hear you're side of all this. The complaint we received, said you physically threatened bodily harm to Mr. Benson, Mr. and Mrs. Helgevson and were making threatening remarks. What's your side of it?"

Ed glared at Levi and Roger, "I rent this house from Mr. Helgevson and his wife Lena, they were babysitting my daughter Olivia while I was at work. I came home tired and wanted to rest. I found them and this stranger here. Levi insisted that I talk to someone I never met before about my personal life, which I refused to do. When he started to get insistent that I talk to this man I asked them to leave. Levi refused to leave until I spoke with this man. I yelled at them and told them if they didn't leave I would throw them out. That's about the long and short of it."

The room was silent while the officer finished writing down the rest of his notes. "Thank you. Mr Helgevson, what's your side of all this?"

Levi started from when he had first met Ed, Alice and Olivia. His broken English caused the officer to stop him occasionally while he wrote his notes. Levi finally brought the officer up to date. "Now dat you know all dat stuff look around at how he keeps da house. He never was dis vay before. I am concerned for da baby, he does not make regular meals for her, he does not wash her all da time. My vife Lena fixes meals and brings dem vit her every day vhen ve come to sit vit her. Ve take Olifia's dirty clothes home to vash because ve know he von't do it. Look at dis house my vife Lena vas cleaning everyday until she got mad at him. Now look at it, vould you vant to live here? When I talk to him about it he gets mad and tells me to leaf the house dat I own. I understand he feels bad about da tings dat happen to him lately, but he von't listen and gets mad. So I go to my friend Mr. Benson and I ask him vhat to do. He tells me he wants to meet Ed and I bring him here. When we try to talk to Ed he gets mad and throws the vase on the floor and tells us he will throw us out if we don't leave." The second officer looked at Ed, "you told me you knocked that vase over accidentally." The first officer looked at his partner and wrote on the note pad. Ed got a sullen look on his face but kept quiet as he slouched a little lower into the chair.

The first officer looked at Lena holding Olivia, "Mrs. Helgevson, do you have anything to add to your husband's statement?"

"You betcha, Ed used to be a good man, he took care of his family and deir affairs. Now he is a drunken bum dat neglects dis beautiful baby. I don't know vhat you can do but she needs someone to help her. Dat's all I half to say," as she shot Ed a daggered look.

The officer made some more notes. "Mr. Benson." The balding man looked directly at the officer, "How long have you been practicing psychology?"

"Almost ten years."

"How long have you know the Halgevson's?"

"About the same amount of time. When I returned home from school and set up my practice, the Helgevson's were one of the first people from our ward to pay my wife and I a social call and welcome us to the community, we've been close friends ever since."

"Give me your professional opinion of the Halgevson's character."

"They are as caring and sincere as anyone I have ever met. They are generous to a fault and truly concerned about their neighbors. I could give you any number of examples exemplifying this if you want."

"That won't be necessary. Why did Mr. Helgevson contact you about Mr. Spitzer?"

"Levi described Mr. Spitzer's situation to me in casual conversations at church about a month and a half ago. He was truly concerned about Mr. Spitzer's depression over the loss of his wife and some other personal concerns that I am not at liberty to talk about here. Levi expressed his concerns to me at that time about the deterioration of Mr. Spitzer's physical and mental condition according to his observations. The newly acquired smoking and drinking habits appeared to him to be affecting Mr. Spitzer's judgment and attention to committed responsibilities, namely the upkeep and welfare of his daughter."

Ed sat up on the edge of his chair. He was struggling to hold back the emotions that were about to consume him the cage door was opening farther and farther. "Levi, you son of a bitch! You been going behind my back to this lousy shrink and I thought we were friends."

The second officer gave Ed a hard look, "That be enough, let the man finish. Ed flopped back into his slouching position as Roger looked back at the officer and continued.

"I advised Levi as a friend only when he questioned me, as to how he should try to reason with Mr. Spitzer. Levi finally came to me last Sunday after church and asked me if I would talk to Mr. Spitzer, because things seemed to be getting worse and he didn't know what to say anymore. I agreed and that's why I was present when Mr. Spitzer arrived home from work this afternoon."

"How did Mr. Spitzer respond when you talked to him?"

"I didn't talk to him until just before you arrived. Up to that point Mr. Helgevson had all the conversation with him. It wasn't until after we came out of the kitchen that I conversed with him."

Ed came out of his chair and headed for the little psychiatrist, "so you're the son of a bitch that called the cops." As he reached for Roger's collar the two officers' grabbed his arms and put him back in the armchair.

"You sit there and don't move out of that chair at last, the door to the cage was completely open," the second officer said as he released Ed's arm. Ed looked at the man with a blind rage but didn't say anything. The officers returned to their seats but kept an eye on Ed.

"Sorry, go ahead and continue."

"As I was saying," Roger shot a look at Ed, "Levi and I came out of the kitchen. Levi went to the daughters' bedroom to comfort her and his wife, while I tried to calm Mr. Spitzer. You came shortly afterward."

The officer finished writing his notes, "now, does anybody have anything they want to say or add to what we already know?"

Ed stood up and said, "I want these people out of my house, now."

The first officer looked at Ed, "in a minute Mr. Spitzer. We have a few more things to do here and then we'll have everyone leave."

Ed nodded and stood glaring at Roger, and the Helgevson's.

Roger stood up and looked at the officer's, "I wonder if I might say something to Mr. Spitzer while you're here?"

The second officer looked at Roger, "sure, go ahead."

Roger took two steps to stand in front of Ed. "Mr. Spitzer I would like to give you a little bit of free professional advice You seem to me deeply troubled, get some psychiatric counseling, before you hurt yourself or your daughter, please get help."

Ed's eyes narrowed. Roger unknowingly touched a very sensitive spot in Ed's armor now the tiger was crouching. It was like shoving a sharp stick into an open wound. "Look you little weasel, don't you ever even suggest that I would hurt my daughter or I'll rip your head off and hand it to you on a platter."

The officer's stepped close, "Ok you two that's enough." But Roger continued.

"Your sick and you don't even realize it. You must treat it now before it's too late."

Ed hit Roger in the face with every bit of strength he had. Roger's feet actually left the floor before his body landed. Ed moved forward to finish the job and the second officer grabbed his arm. Spinning counter clock wise Ed did a three sixty and hit the man so hard he dropped straight to the floor on his butt. The first officer grabbed Ed and started wrestling with him while the second officer got to his feet and hit Ed with his night stick. Ed saw stars and went down. Before he had a chance to recover his hands were handcuffed behind his back. This was the final straw for Ed, he started thrashing around and screaming at the top of his lungs "You bastards let me go, I'll kill you, I'll kill you all. Don't do this to me. I'll get you. **Alice!! Alice!! Alice!! Help me, Alice I need you, please!!!!"** Finally he lay on the floor sobbing and blubbering incoherently. Roger got to his feet and pulled a handkerchief from his coat pocket. His nose was bleeding profusely and appeared to be broken. "I could see it coming but I didn't think he would lose it that bad." Roger said as he stuffed the linen handkerchief gingerly under his nose to stop the bleeding. The two officers got off Ed's back and stood up next to him. Levi came out of the bedroom where he had herded Lena and Olivia when the trouble started.

Levi looked down at the sobbing pile of flesh convulsing on the floor. "Vhat vill happen now?"

The first officer spoke up, "We'll take him downtown. He will have to see a judge after we figure out what to charge him with."

Levi looked at Roger, "Ve must help him. Vat can you do?"

Rogers voice was muffled as he spoke through the bloody handkerchief. "You still want to help him?"

"Ya, you betcha, he needs us more den ever now."

Roger winced as he moved the handkerchief to find a dry spot. "I'll see what I can do after they charge him tomorrow. Can he afford an attorney or will the court have to appoint one?"

Levi shook his head, "I don't know."

The first officer walked over to Levi. Mr. Helgevson, we have to do something with his daughter. Can she stay with you for a couple of days?"

Levi answered eagerly, "Of course, ve baby sit her all da time. She has stayed at our house many times."

"Good, I'll contact social services and have them send some one over to your house. They'll need to find a place for her to stay while her dad is incapacitated."

"Oh ve can keep her it von't be no trouble."

"That's for social services to decide. You talk it over with them."

"Ya I vill do dat."

"Ok, but for right now I want you to write your name, address and telephone number on this pad of paper while we load Mr. Spitzer in the car. Levi took the notepad and the officers picked Ed up by his arms and bodily dragged him out to the police car.

CHAPTER #20

ED SCREAMED AND cried for Alice and Olivia all night until his voice failed him. The jailor had moved him from the community cell to solitary because the other inmates were beating on him to shut him up. Roger came to see him the next day, and was appalled at Ed's physical condition. He had a black eye and multiple bruises on his face, plus he had urinated and defecated his pants. This didn't seem to concern him he just sat in it and stared into space. After a few futile moments of trying to communicate with him Roger gave up and left. He found out who the judge was that was going to hear his case and paid her a professional visit at her office.

"Ma'am, I have a psychiatrist by the name of Roger Benson in the waiting room. He claims he needs to see you before you hear this case." The bailiff said as he laid a manila folder in front of Judge Mary Backus.

"Thank you, hold my next appointment while I look this over."

"Yes ma'am." The bailiff left the room and closed the door.

Roger waited over an hour before the Judge told the bailiff to send him in. "I've looked over this file and I have a good idea why you're here. What do you know about this case?"

Roger related the recent events. "After comprehension testing, I strongly recommend confinement and treatment to a psychiatric facility."

"Thank you for your information and insight. I will take it into consideration at his hearing."

Roger thanked the Judge for her time and left.

At the hearing Ed looked and smelled a lot better than when Roger first saw him. He was cleaned up and dressed in orange coveralls with "Salt Lake County Jail" written on the back. His hands were shackled to his sides and he had leg irons and a six-foot chain with an officer holding the end of it. Ed sat numbly looking at the judge as she tried to get him to speak. When he remained mute she had him committed for psychiatric evaluation and set his next hearing to coincide with the findings. The findings recommended that he be confined for treatment of schizophrenia, paranoia, and severe depression, with evaluations every six months. The Judges gavel fell and Ed was on his way to the nut house.

The next six months started out as a foggy cloud for Ed. For the first couple of months his road to recovery was marked with chemical injections and occasionally an electrical shock treatment. Slowly his comprehension returned as he responded to the treatment. When he was able to feed and toilet himself the doctors started a program for recovering his short and long term memory. Ed's first bit of memory retrieval was the realization of where he was. It was as though he had gone to sleep after the confrontation at his house and woke up in the psychiatric ward. He had no recollection of anything happening in between. The stimulants had helped him back to reality. Now the doctors took over and were talking to him daily about his past. The first person they allowed him to see was his father in law John Spitzer.

"You gave us quite a scare," he said as he sat at the table with Ed and the two employees dressed in white. Ed didn't know what to say, so he remained silent.

"When the hospital called me, I thought it was a bad joke. They told me Olivia had been placed with her grandparents in Cheyenne and that you were in here for an indefinite period of time. They wouldn't let me see you until now." Ed still didn't know what to say, and remained silent. John talked about the farm and a few things that would have been familiar to Ed as a child. The doctors had coached him on what to say, their belief was that a familiar face talking about familiar things out of Ed's past would help to jog his long-term memory. John agreed to come once a month and do what he could. When the current session was over John shook Ed's hand. Ed let him squeeze his hand, pump his arm up and down, and replied "your welcome" when John said "Thank you for seeing me." The doctors thought the meeting was an absolute success and that progress had been made. John walked out of the hospital as depressed as he had ever been in his life. The hospital called the Schmidt's and they agreed to come once a month and visit Ed. The Helgevson's refused to have any contact with Ed what so ever and told the hospital not to even mention their name to him. They were told this would be impossible because of their involvement with Olivia after Ed was incarcerated. Social services had recommended the court allow them to keep Olivia, until the court decided what to do with Ed. By then the Bernard's had petitioned the courts for custody of Olivia, until such time as she could be reunited with Ed or adopted by them. The court granted their request and Olivia went to live with her grandparents in Cheyenne, Wyoming. The Bernard's agreed to visit, but showed up about every three months, and then only upon the doctor's request. By the time Ed's first evaluation came, Ed knew whom he was and what happened to get him where he was now. He could converse well enough, but not voluntarily. Needless to say the review board recommended continuing his treatment.

Over the next three months Ed's condition improved by leaps and bounds. His short-term memory returned completely and quite a bit of his long term. He was able to remember accurately everything that had happened to him over the last five years, but he was still having a slight problem with names and dates. Throughout all of his sessions with the doctors Ed was constantly asking about how to get his daughter back when he was released. The doctors told him he should concentrate on getting well and then that would happen in its own good time.

Ed's second evaluation by the review board showed immense progress, but did not recommend release. They felt he needed more time to demonstrate stability and long-term memory retention. Ed knew deep down in his heart they were right, but it still couldn't justify a certain amount of depression.

"I wouldn't worry about it Ed," Dr. Evans told him at the following session. "At the rate you're progressing I would predict your release in a year or less. Provided there are no setbacks, of course, and in your case I don't foresee that happening, but you never can tell about those things." Ed was encouraged and apprehensive both at the same time. "Now let's see if we can put some names and dates together." Dr. Evans looked at the clipboard on his lap containing papers with notes scratched on them. After about a half an hour of working on remembering names, dates and places. Dr. Evans decided to turn the session into an open discussion. "What would you like to talk about?"

Ed thought a minute, "the fastest way for me to get released."

Dr. Evans smiled and made notes on the paper in front of him. "Ok, I want you to think about it for a minute. What was the recommendation of the review board?"

It was difficult, but Ed pictured himself standing in front of the panel of five people as they informed him of their decision. Dr. Evans sat quietly with his hands folded on top of the clipboard and waited patiently for Ed to answer.

"I think they said I needed to prove my stability and improve my long term memory."

"Dr. Evans restrained himself from over reacting to Ed's major accomplishment. "That's right Ed, very good. You just demonstrated a major step in your recovery."

Ed smiled and said "really?'

"Oh yes," The doctor said as he scribbled more notes on his paper. "Now, back to your original question. What's the fastest way for you to get released? My recommendation would be to work on your long-term memory. That way you can alleviate their concerns the next time you appear before them by giving them a chronological history of your past. We will work on that daily, but I recommend you start with day one as far back as you can remember. Write it down and we will discuss your notes each day."

Ed Liked that idea, "how long do you think it'll take?"

"To what? Finish your notes to date or get you released?"

"Both."

"That will depend entirely on you."

Ed swallowed visibly, "Can I get started now?"

"Of course, I will give you an authorization to check out pencil and paper from the hospital library. You will have to do all of your writing there and turn the materials back into them before you can leave, including your written material. After we discuss some of your notes there's a very distinct possibility of moving you to a semi private room where you would be allowed to keep these things on hand and be able to write at your leisure."

The move happened after two months. Ed was ushered into another wing of the hospital that contained semi private rooms. His roommate was a black man named Henry Day. Henry was recovering from a traumatic blow to the head that had caused partial amnesia. The two of them got along great. Henry was a steel worker from Philadelphia; he came to Salt Lake on a construction project and was struck in the head by a steel beam. The only thing that saved his life was the steel helmet he was wearing at the time. Henry's memory would come and go depending how severe his headaches became. His wife and two daughters who were age three and six, visited him everyday. Ed had never been around black people, so he had no prejudices and they got along famously. Henry's three-year-old daughter took an instant liking to Ed. She would sit on his bed and talk to him while she played with the doll she always brought with her. One day Ed was telling her about Olivia and how much he missed her. "Why don't you write her a letter? That's what my daddy does for me." Ed thought about it for a minute. "Why not?" He thought to himself.

At the next session with Dr. Evans Ed told him what the little girl had said. Dr Evans thought about it a moment. "You know that might not be a bad idea." He said with an interested voice.

"What should I say?" Ed asked.

"I believe I would start at the beginning and relate the whole circumstance of events that brought her into your life. There will come the day that she will obviously want to know about her mother. I wouldn't spare the details and I would end it with your hopes and aspirations for the future."

Ed was excited, he began to see a lot of what he wanted to say in his head. After the session was over he went to the library and wrote until they closed. Each day he followed the same procedure. It turned into a daily quest for Ed as he searched for a way to open the document that would turn into almost four hundred pages. Finally the inspiration came to him:

"To my darling Daughter Olivia:

I am writing this letter to reassure you I have not forgotten you, and to rekindle hope in me and hopefully in you of our reunion in the future. Unforeseen events took place that you will never be aware of unless you hear it from me. I don't know when you will get a chance to read this, but hopefully I can read it to you myself someday.

I was born in Latrobe, Pennsylvania in 1932, I was adopted to a family by the name of Carl and Mary Johnson in Hillsboro, Wisconsin a month later,"--

--, the composition went on through the next evaluation, which was denied, but the evaluators expressed their agreement that the next evaluation would probably be favorable for parole if everything progressed as well as it had been. Two months before Ed's fourth evaluation he finished his dissertation to Olivia;--, "which brings us to what life may or may not hold for our future together. Only time will tell. I will close now with the thought of our eventual reunion and the hope that if it is not to be, you my darling daughter, and God will always love and forgive me in spite of any anguish I may have caused you.

My Love Always,
Your Father."